MASKS OF AUTHORITY

A VOLUME IN THE SERIES

MYTH AND POETICS

EDITED BY GREGORY NAGY

A full list of titles in the series appears at the end of the book.

MASKS OF AUTHORITY

*Fiction and Pragmatics in
Ancient Greek Poetics*

CLAUDE CALAME

Translated from the French by Peter M. Burk

Cornell University Press
Ithaca and London

First published 2005 by Cornell University Press

Printed in the United States of America

Library of Congress Cataloging-in-Publication Data

Calame, Claude.
  Masks of authority : fiction and pragmatics in ancient Greek poetics /
Claude Calame ; translated from the French by Peter M. Burk.
    p. cm.—(Myth and poetics)
  Includes bibliographical references (p.) and index.
  ISBN 0-8014-3892-6 (alk. paper)
  1. Greek poetry—History and criticism. 2. Narration (Rhetoric)—His-
tory—To 500. 3. Pragmatics—History—To 500. 4. Poetics—History—To
500. 5. Authority in literature. 6. Rhetoric, Ancient. I. Burk, Peter Michael,
1969– II. Title. III. Series.
  PA3092.C35 2004
  881'.0109—dc22   2004017457

Cornell University Press strives to use environmentally responsible sup-
pliers and materials to the fullest extent possible in the publishing of its
books. Such materials include vegetable-based, low-VOC inks and acid-
free papers that are recycled, totally chlorine-free, or partly composed of
nonwood fibers. For further information, visit our website at
www.cornellpress.cornell.edu.

Cloth printing   10 9 8 7 6 5 4 3 2 1

CONTENTS

FOREWORD

BY GREGORY NAGY

This book complements Claude Calame's earlier contribution to Cornell University Press's Myth and Poetics series, *The Craft of Poetic Speech in Ancient Greece* (1995). Both books rely on the methodology of semiotics, which has its own precise vocabulary. Calame applies this vocabulary consistently and with great care to a wide variety of forms under the general heading of ancient Greek poetics.

By "poetics" Calame means verbal art in general, including prose as well as poetry, song, and dance, in addition to verbal skill and creativity. An example of the relevant prose works is *On Airs, Waters, and Places,* a medical treatise stemming from the Hippocratic corpus and dating to the fifth century B.C. The anonymous author of this work may well have been the founder of the Hippocratic school himself, Hippocrates of Cos. Calame focuses on the authority of this ancient author, who says that his treatise is intended for physicians caring for patients not only in Cos but also in other Greek cities. Such authority, extending well beyond Cos, helps explain the vast scope of this relatively brief treatise, whose author presumes to sketch a typology of genetically transmitted physical differences between the populations of Europe and Asia. As Calame insists, such a typology may conceivably be described as "racial," but it is hardly "racist." It is not driven by Greek ethnocentrism, since the differentiating categories of "European" and "Asiatic" both involve Greeks. The term "Asiatic" in *On Airs, Waters, and Places* refers not to non-Greeks but to all Greeks who populated the cities of Asia Minor and the outlying islands, one of which happens to be Cos.

The ancient Greek poetics studied in *Masks of Authority* includes visual as well as verbal arts. For example, Calame shows how the occasions of songmaking at ancient Greek symposia were complemented by representations of songmaking painted on drinking cups used by the symposiasts. A red-figure cup painted by the artist Douris is the focus of attention in chapter 5. To drink from such a cup was not only to participate in a symposium: it was to become part of the songmaking, since the occasion of convivial drinking was integral to sympotic song.

Calame makes a comparable point about the use of masks in ancient Athenian theater. Taking a stand against the attempt made in Aristotle's *Poetics* to isolate the verbal from the visual in drama, Calame argues that the wearing of masks by actors was integral to their delivery of the words notionally spoken by the characters they represented. The mask helped distance the character from the actor, conferring authority. This insight leads to new interpretations of such masterpieces of classical drama as Sophocles' *Oedipus Tyrannus* and Aristophanes' *Acharnians*.

Other types of authority examined here involve poetic utterances spoken by authoritative figures in the first person. An example of such a speaker, which comes from the preclassical period, is Hesiod as self-represented in the prelude of the *Works and Days*. Another example, from the classical period, is the anonymous exegete of an Orphic theogony. This exegete's words, and the words of Orpheus as he quotes them, are preserved in the Derveni Papyrus, a partially burned document that survived the cremating fires of an ancient funeral pyre which has been excavated by archaeologists. The mystical text of the Orphic exegete, written down in the papyrus, had been destined to go up in flames along with the cremated body of the reader, but now, thanks to modern archaeology, it has achieved an unintended kind of afterlife, detached from the intended afterlife of its ancient reader. This new afterlife is precarious: the Derveni Papyrus now made available to readers is detached from the Orphic exegete, detached from Orpheus, detached from the mystical knowledge required of those who sought to become initiated into the mysteries of an Orphic afterlife.

For Calame, the authority of a speaker such as the Orphic exegete clearly precludes "fiction." Calame makes a similar point about Hesiod as speaker of the *Works and Days:* he too seems "real," not "fictional." The point is well taken, at least to the extent that speakers such as Hesiod were considered to be real, not fictional, in the preclassical and classical phases of poetic reception. In postclassical phases, on the other hand, as exemplified by the Hellenistic poetry of Callimachus and Theocritus, the term "fiction" is more apt: earlier poets such as Hesiod or Homer—or even Orpheus—had by that time become models for poetic imitation rather than poetic reenactment. Such authors as well as their works could then be viewed as fictional.

The fact remains, however, that the actual works attributed to ancient authors, whether the authors themselves are real or merely constructs of the real, are for us the ultimate reality. It is this reality that emerges from a close reading of Calame's work.

AUTHOR'S NOTE

While the essays collected in this book engage the same issue of poetic authority and adopt the same enunciative standpoint, elaborated within the domain of discursive analysis, they arose out of different extradiscursive occasions. Where applicable, I have indicated in a note in the relevant chapter my intellectual debts to those who organized and moderated the corresponding situation of enunciation. The chapters constituting this collection are thoroughly revised versions of the following publications:

"Variations énonciatives, relation avec les dieux et fonctions poétiques dans les *Hymnes homériques,*" *Museum Helveticum* 52 (1995): 2–19.

"Le proème des *Travaux* d'Hésiode, prélude à une poésie d'action," in *Le métier du mythe: Lectures d'Hésiode,* ed. F. Blaise, P. Judet de La Combe, and P. Rousseau (Lille, 1996), 169–89.

"Sappho et Hélène: Le mythe comme argumentation narrative et parabolique," in *Parole—figure—parabole: Recherches autour du discours parabolique,* ed. J. Delorme (Lyon, 1987), 209–29.

"Narration légendaire et programme poétique dans l'*Hymne à Apollon* de Callimaque," *Études de Lettres* 4 (1992): 41–66 (= "Legendary Narration and Poetic Procedure in Callimachus' *Hymn to Apollo,*" trans. M. A. Harder, in *Callimachus,* vol. 1 of *Hellenistica Groningana,* ed. M. A. Harder, R. F. Regtuit, and G. C. Wakker [Groningen, 1993], 37–65).

"Apprendre à boire, apprendre à chanter: L'inférence énonciative dans une image grecque," *La part de l'oeil* 5 (1989): 44–53.

"Vision, Blindness, and Mask: The Radicalisation of the Emotions in Sopho-
cles' *Oedipus Rex*," trans. M. S. Silk, in *Tragedy and the Tragic: Greek Theatre and
Beyond,* ed. M. S. Silk (Oxford, 1996), 17–37 (with the reply of R. Buxton,
"What Can You Rely on in *Oedipus Rex?* Response to Calame," ibid., 38–48).

"Démasquer par le masque: Effets énonciatifs dans la comédie ancienne,"
Revue de l'Histoire des Religions 206 (1989): 357–76.

"Nature humaine et environnement: Le racisme bien tempéré d'Hippocrate,"
in *Sciences et racisme* (Lausanne, 1986), 77–99.

"Figures of Sexuality and Initiatory Transition in the Derveni Theogony and
Its Commentary," trans. G. W. Most, in *Studies on the Derveni Papyrus,* ed. A. Laks
and G. W. Most (Oxford, 1997), 65–80.

"Espaces liminaux et voix discursives dans l'*Idylle* I de Théocrite: Une civil-
isation de poètes," *Études de Lettres* 2 (1992): 59–85.

I wish to emphasize my gratitude to Gregory Nagy, the indefatigable advo-
cate of this collection, which he so warmly agreed to welcome into his series
Myth and Poetics as an original publication.

Concerning the technical aspects of this work, I benefited from the valuable
assistance of Eric Le Berre during several phases of the preparation of the man-
uscript. I should add that the English translations of the Greek texts, when not
identified as those of a particular author, are by Peter Burk, whom I thank for
his competent and relevant collaboration. For chapters 4, 6, and 9 he relied on
earlier translations by A. Harder, M. S. Silk, and G. W. Most, respectively. The bib-
liography appearing at the end of this work includes only those books and arti-
cles that are cited on several occasions in more than one chapter. The complete
bibliography is thus to be found in the notes to each individual chapter. As far
as the Greek terms are concerned, only the accents have been transcribed, not
the long vowels.

The expenses for the translation into English have been covered by the Fon-
dation Irène Nada Andrée Chuard-Schmid and the Fondation du 450ᵉ Anniver-
saire, both at the University of Lausanne.

CLAUDE CALAME

Lausanne—Paris

MASKS OF
AUTHORITY

INTRODUCTION

Enunciative Games and Masks of Poetic Authority

> It is not right:
> the dirge does not belong in the house of the Muses.
> That would not be fitting for us.[1]

Who is speaking? Who sings these verses in Aeolic rhythm and Lesbian poetic dialect? The "poet's voice"? The "hidden author"?[2] To whom does the *us* refer who seems to be the speaker of these verses? The Platonic rhetorician from the imperial period who quotes these famous lines, for his part, does not hesitate to affirm that Sappho spoke these words to her daughter, just as Socrates, on his deathbed, would later admonish his wife, Xanthippe, for grieving. Far removed as we are from the historical performance situation of the poems published during the Alexandrian period under the name of Sappho, we perceive only the textual traces of a voice that once resonated out loud.

1. Enunciation: Between Fictional World and Historical Reference

Are these written traces, these graphic signs organized within the distinctive layout of a modern edition's printed page, still capable of offering us access to a poetic reality that escapes us almost entirely because of the historical and cultural distance separating us from it? To pose the question in these terms means facing the thorny problem of reference. Through the mediation of the complex processes by which meaning is produced from the articulation of words and sentences in a vocal flow transcribed by the graphic system of writing, texts "refer." Within this flow, a possible world is fabricated, a world that I call *fictional,* since it is constructed in and by the movement of "referentialization" within the text.[3] But syntactically articulated words also have the amazing capacity to evoke the external world, the empirical world, the world on which the constructed fictional world ultimately depends, and they do so through a movement of "referenciation" directed toward what is outside the text. As artificial and analytic as it may be, this distinction between intra- and extratextual, between intra- and extradiscursive (to include a notion that has yet to be introduced here), allows us to render operative the double aspect of reference.

Within this double movement of intra- and extradiscursive reference, pronouns clearly play a crucial role. Indeed, certain demonstratives make it possible to designate and refer both to the world constructed within the text and to what is outside it. As long ago as 1934, the German linguist Karl Bühler emphasized the role that pronouns play—in addition to anaphoric or cataphoric repetitions—in this phenomenon of double reference by distinguishing between the process called *demonstratio ad oculos* and the *Deixis am Phantasma* (in a curious mixture of terms borrowed from Latin, Greek, and German). This process of intra- and extradiscursive reference has since become an operative concept in literary criticism, especially concerning classical texts, to which it has been applied under the name of *deixis*.[4] The fictional character of Homeric epic poetry renders futile any attempt to attach the *demonstratio ad oculos* mode to poetry issuing from an oral tradition, while only the practice of writing would make a *Deixis am Phantasma* possible. Apart from the process of extradiscursive reference, however, one can find in every form of poetry an intradiscursive deixis that refers to the world erected within the text; it does so through the linguistic (and not the rhetorical) phenomena of anaphora and cataphora, which ensure the coherence of the meaning constructed in the discourse. This type of deixis, which is also present in narrative poems belonging to the oral tradition (such as Homeric poetry), calls upon the imagination. It must be distinguished from the process of inset internal deixis, which makes it possible for a story's "character" to refer within a dialogue passage—through speech that the author may attribute to him or her—to the world of the text.[5]

To take one example, after the prelude that opens Hesiod's *Works and Days* with an invocation to the Muses, and following a general discussion of the bard's position concerning the two kinds of Eris, the poem's speaker-*I* provides a few indications about his own situation of enunciation; he does so through an apostrophe to an addressee-*you* by the name of Perses, then by an allusion to the conflict between them over an inheritance. With a *we* that includes the addressee-*you* and the speaker-*I,* the poetic speech proposes settling the conflict through one of those straight judgments that only Zeus can guarantee. When the intention of removing the verdict from the authority of "gift gobbling" kings is expressed, the idea of passing judgment is referred to by the deictic demonstrative *hóde* (*ténde,* v. 39). On the one hand, this deictic no doubt points back—by anaphoric, intradiscursive reference—to the judgment just mentioned and now constructed within the text; on the other, it probably also points to the extradiscursive and historical arbitration into which the poetic speech itself intervenes.[6]

These deictic spatial indications are generally combined with temporal markers to define the intradiscursive frame of the (uttered) enunciation; this spatiotemporal frame itself refers, through linguistic and discursive mediation, to the extradiscursive context of the (historical) *hic et nunc* of the poetic performance. All of these spatiotemporal indications essentially converge toward the focal point of the enunciation. Related to each "instance of discourse" (understood by Émile Benveniste as the discrete and unique act by which "language is realized in speech by a speaker"), this point of origin of discursive production can be located in the textual manifestation by means of the different pronominal or verbal forms taken up by the *I*. The speaker-narrator's *I*, an element of an essentially linguistic order, refers only indirectly to a biographical and historical author, with the social and cultural parameters defining the author's functional profile.[7]

In other words, in its discursive (and, for us, textual) qualities and in its spatiotemporal extensions, what I will call the "instance of enunciation" (to avoid the psychological and philosophical misunderstandings raised by the notion of the "subject of enunciation") fully benefits from the play with semantic construction allowed by the fictional effects of any language.[a] I speak, once again, in terms of *fictional* effects, not effects *of fiction,* inasmuch as the world constructed through linguistic means maintains a relationship with *this* world, even in those texts that seem to us to be most "literary." In his famous discussion some years ago devoted to the notion of the "author," Michel Foucault embraced the position of linguists in readily accepting that the textual signs of an enunciative order refer not directly to the reality of an author but to an "alter ego whose distance from the writer can be greater or lesser and can vary in the course of the same work." Foucault avoided exploring the complex relationship between this textual figure and the "author-function" that he so brilliantly defined in the procedures of attribution and in its institutional profile. I wish to draw attention here to the fact that this textual figure of an enunciative and discursive order has many facets.[8]

Indeed, it is worth reiterating that, in the process of the "putting into discourse" (*mise en discours*), in the simple acts of predication and assertion, utterances constituting a description or narrative are generally taken under the speaker-narrator's responsibility (through various means). This is to say that, through the fictional world erected within and by the utterances of a linguistic manifestation, an equally fictional world is elaborated, the focal point of which is the "instance of enunciation." This latter, the "enunciative" (*énonciatif*) world,

a. Translator's note: the term "instance" in the phrase "instance of enunciation" (*instance d'énonciation*) corresponds to the second use of this term in Benveniste's definition of the first-person singular pronoun: "I is the individual who utters the present instance of discourse containing the linguistic instance *I*" (Benveniste [n. 7], 218 [= 252 of the French original]).

is inscribed within the texture of the former, the "enuncive" (*énoncif*) world. This process of fictional elaboration, inherent in the putting into discourse of manifestations that we deem literary or poetic, is obviously active, not only in its enuncive component but also in its enunciative dimension, and it is active in productions depending on an oral tradition as well as in texts that have been fixed by means of a system of graphic notation. Applied to the "utterance of the enunciation,"[b] the fictional potential of any linguistic construction provides the means for giving semantic substance and an enunciative profile to the instance of enunciation, making a verbal mask for the biographical author while also guaranteeing that author's discursive authority. Far from confining her or him within the text, the discursive and enunciative construction of the author situates this mask in relation to the real actors of the communication situation in their social interaction. Beyond the semantic, and thus fictional, capacities of every language, we must account for its pragmatic effects: thus the title of this collection of studies of Greek literature (*Masks of Authority*); whence also the attention devoted in each of its chapters to the enunciative and discursive strategies that make it possible to establish this authority of a discursive and pragmatic order in a given historical situation.

2. The "Lyric *I*": Speaker-Poet or Virtual Author?

If we want to address the issue of authorship in a few examples of Greek poetry, we should thus distinguish carefully between the enunciative authority constructed within the text and the authority of a biographical poet, in his "author-function," who is often recognized—if not invented and established—as the author after the fact (for instance, "Homer"). The relative autonomy of the enunciative and "authorial" apparatus appearing in any fictional text can be grasped in terms of a *simulacrum,* following the idea formulated by Algirdas J. Greimas and Joseph Courtès. On the one hand, the figure of the author fabricated within the discourse by linguistic means must be carefully distinguished from her or his biographical and historical reality, which is of an extradiscursive order; on the other, this enunciative figure differentiates itself, on an intradiscursive level, from the actors of the utterances themselves, who are generally of a narrative order. Borrowed from Roman Jakobson, the notions of "shifting in" and "shifting out" make it possible to distinguish between the enuncive level, that of the (descriptive or narrative) assertions, and the enunciative level, concerning the instance of enunciation's assumption of authority for the utterances. The source of the

b. Translator's note: the phrases "utterance of the enunciation" (*énoncé de l'énonciation*) and "uttered enunciation" (*énonciation énoncée*) designate the components of the utterance (*énoncé*) that point to its enunciation or performance.

enunciation, linked as it is to the utterance of the enunciation, is thus situated and constituted between the utterances themselves and the extradiscursive reality to which these utterances allude. Removed from any principle of immanence, the instance of enunciation, like the process of deixis, partakes of both the fictional capacity and the pragmatic dimension of language.[9]

It is in this context that one ought to read the distinction that we have attempted to draw not only between the real author or reader and the speaker-narrator with her or his "intradiagetic" (*intradiégétique*) addressee-narratee, but also between these last two entities, situated at the enunciative level, and the virtual (if not implicit) author or reader.[10] The virtual reader and author are considered to be "ideal," inasmuch as the former is seen as corresponding to the author's image of the reader and the latter to the reader's representation of an author whose reality is no longer any more than virtual. Based in part on the figures of the speaker-narrator and the addressee-narratee as they manifest themselves in the text, these representations are actually situated between the intra- and extradiscursive. This composite status has led to the multiplying of terms used to designate them (as implicit, abstract, virtual, ideal, model, etc. author/reader), along with (as a corollary) the epistemological fuzziness that the notion of implication inevitably entails because of its necessary appeal to subjectivity.[11]

These theoretical reflections concerning the instance of enunciation and its textual manifestation within the spatiotemporal frame of the uttered enunciation (or the utterance of the enunciation) may, perhaps, make it possible to project new light on the debated issue of the "lyric *I*." It has increasingly come to be recognized that there exists no exact correspondence between, on the one hand, the author's biographical and historical person and, on the other, the profile of the speaker-narrator who says *I* in the poetry that we call *lyric* (because of the very presence of an *I* that has traditionally been linked, without any intermediary, to the poet's person ...).[12] Thus, not only is it generally accepted that the speaker-narrator of the *Theogony* actively takes on the poetic identity whose name is "Hesiod" and that "Perses," the proper name of the *Works* addressee, refers, at least in part, to a "poetic persona," but also some critics now use the name "Sappho" to refer to the image that the Lesbian poetess gives of herself within her compositions and readily grant to "Boupalos," one of the preferred targets of Hipponax's iambic attacks, a ritual and poetic identity.[13] This is done in order to distinguish the profile and the intradiscursive and poetic functions of "Hesiod," "Perses," "Sappho," or "Boupalos," from the individuals who probably correspond to these names, but whose historical identity is vague, to say the least.

Nonetheless, the problem concerning the nature of the poetic identity of the melic (and, from now on, not lyric) *I* and the question of its enunciative authority become particularly complicated when we turn to choral poetry. The extradiscursive dissociation between the poem's composer and the choral group that sings and dances it can even cross the gender barrier: Alcman, a Lydian poet in the service of the city of Sparta, composes verses that are sung and danced on public and cult occasions by girls who collectively take up the speaker-*I* position, in the feminine gender and often in the plural. The use of a traditional poetic language facilitates the frequent co-presence of the poet's voice and that of the "performers" (boys or girls gathered in a choral group) in the manifestation of an instance of enunciation that refers to a complex extradiscursive reality.[14] It is from this perspective that it is possible to provide an answer to the much-debated question of whether the identity of the *I* endowed with the voice of authority that sings the compositions belonging to the different poetic genres practiced by Pindar, for example, is singular or collective, personal or choral.

Contrary to what one might have been led to believe by a recent controversy centered on the nature of the *I* appearing solely in the victory songs composed by Pindar, the melic *I* of the *Epinicians* allows the same strategies for delegating authority as that of the *Paeans* or the *Partheneia* composed by the same Theban poet. Thus, when describing in *Pythian* 5 the process of the legendary foundation of Cyrene (the colonial city of Libya), the speaker begins by referring to the family of Aigeidai, who—coming from Thebes and after a sojourn in Sparta—founded Thera and later instituted the Carneia (dedicated to Apollo) in Cyrenaica; if he calls the Aigeidai "my fathers" (*emoì patéres*) who represent "my glory" (*emòn kléos*), it is because the discursive and poetic *I* corresponds here to Pindar the Theban. A few verses later, however, in the course of the transition from the legendary past to the *hic et nunc* of the poem's performance, probably in the cult context of the Carnea, the speaker speaks in the plural (*sebízomen*) to refer to the present, collective celebration on the occasion of a banquet in the city of Cyrene. The speaker is no longer Pindar the poet, but the choral group that, now and in this place, sings of the colonial city's sovereign, whose chariot won the race at the Pythic Games, and of his ancestors, descendants of the founding hero from Thera.[15] Thus, it is as if, in the combination of pronominal forms and verbal actions on the discursive level, the poet had the power to delegate the authority of his voice first to the *choregos,* then to the choral group singing and dancing the verses he composed.

This play with authorial delegation through the means offered by poetic language is essential to a kind of poetry whose pragmatic dimension, often realized in a ritual manner, is constitutive of it. Furthermore, it is now generally recognized that fictional creation produces knowledge.[16] In this book, therefore, I devote special attention to enunciative strategies of authority through which some knowledge (generally figurative) can be asserted and made the object of argumentation, often within the frame of ritual poetic practices. Let us not forget that, over the span between the authorial fiction that is "Homer" and the tragedians of classical Athens, the Greek poet is simultaneously considered a creator of artifacts, in accordance with the original meaning of the term designating him (*poietés*), and a teacher of the art of the Muses (*khorodidáskalos*); the poet is as much an artisan of knowledge as a master of ceremonies.[17]

Organized and produced by means of being put into poetic discourse, these kinds of knowledge are illustrated and shaped not only by rhetorical figures, but also, above all, by the semantic means on which any traditional poetic language is founded. With regards to the approaches proposed in the chapters that follow, this process entails that the discursive organization of content, in its assertive, descriptive, or narrative actualization, calls for an analysis drawing on certain operative concepts elaborated within the context of semio-narrative reflection. Such is the case for the notion of "isotopy," used in the study of the prelude to Hesiod's *Works and Days* to determine the principal semantic lines or vectors extending across the whole poem; they guarantee its coherence with respect to the content, especially the semantic content. It is in this context that one can see the relevance of a distinction between the formal and syntactical nature of "actantial" positions that a semio-narrative grammar can determine ("Subject," "Predicate," etc., syntactic positions indicated by capital letters) and the semantic character of the elements of content that the discourse's development sets up in these positions. This distinction will prove to be essential, for example, in the reading of a poem of Sappho in which one of the actantial positions of the composition's narrative *mise-en-scène* happens to coincide with the poetic *I* of the speaker.[18] In addition to an enunciative identity that constructs itself as a discursive simulacrum through an argument of a narrative sort, we witness in these verses a "narrativization" of the uttered enunciation.[19] It is, then, an itinerary through different modes of this type of enunciative *mise-en-scène* of poetic authority that is proposed in the studies of Greek texts collected in this book.

3. Intellectual Games?

Since the excursion through Greek literature proposed here follows the semantic, enunciative, and pragmatic development of some major texts, one may rightly be astonished not to see any use made of the concept of "intertextuality."

3.1 Structural Intertextuality

Drawing on the notion of "dialogism" developed by Mikhail Bakhtin, Julia Kristeva, the creator of the concept of intertextuality, gave one often-quoted definition of it: "For the knowing subject, intertextuality is a notion that will indicate how a text reads and inserts itself into history. The concrete mode in which intertextuality is actualized within a specific text will provide the primary ('social,' 'esthetic') characteristic of a textual structure."[20] We can see that both the position of the "text" as grammatical subject (that "reads") and the use of quotation marks insert this definition into the strict structural paradigm of the 1960s, with its potential textualist excesses. From this perspective, a text can only refer to other texts or produce yet others, irrespective of all extradiscursive circumstances. Even if intertextuality inscribes a given text into a historical sequence or genealogy, it is ultimately a phenomenon to be understood on the basis of the principle of the immanence of the text; as such, it cannot be fully exploited within an approach focused on elucidating the enunciative and pragmatic dimension of a textual manifestation!

Owing to the same structural principle on which it is based, furthermore, the concept of intertextuality is a fuzzy notion. From a theoretical perspective, and in order to become operative, it required the elaboration of a veritable taxonomy of subordinate concepts: starting with the metamorphosis of intertextuality into "transtextuality," intertextuality in the strict sense includes explicit quotations, but also allusions, if not plagiarism; then "paratextuality," which includes allusions to another text that are present in any of what constitutes the "paratext" (title, preface, notes, etc.); "metatextuality," by which one text provides commentary on another; "hypertextuality," in which the "hypotext," underlying and earlier than the "hypertext," appears as a sort of palimpsest in the more recent text, following a transformation in the form of a parody; and finally, "architextuality," which defines one text's relationship to an entire group of texts, that is, to the genre to which that text belongs.[21] However complex its organization and however difficult its use as an interpretive framework, this nomenclature would require, at the very least, a distinction between explicit allusions (for example, indirect quotations in the form of paraphrase but attributed to a named author) and different kinds of "anonymous" allusions, which ought to be further sub-divided into conscious and implicit allusions. But who can gain access to the mind of the "author" in order to make such distinctions?

That is not all. It is most likely not by chance that the general concept of intertextuality has become more predominant, as an operative notion, in the analysis of Latin literature than in the study of Greek poetry.[22] By itself, the historical distance that makes it possible for the representatives of literary genres from ancient Rome to reformulate traditional literary practices provides these litterateurs—because of their multiple links of dependence to their Greek counterparts—with considerable latitude for maneuvering through different kinds of intertextual games. Despite the historical advantage of a poetic tradition with a particularly broad scope of development, however, the acknowledged forms and uses of the notion of intertextuality within the Roman literary sphere are, at the very least, divergent and unstable. Even in the case of an exhaustive study of the textual relationships between one particular poetic collection, such as Vergil's *Georgics,* and the work of a predecessor, such as Callimachus, focusing on obvious relationships of conscious and metapoetic transformation, the modes of intertextual reference are so complex that they can lead to a new taxonomy. Thus, we find successively "casual reference," "single reference," "self-reference," "correction," "apparent reference," and "multiple reference" or "conflation," the term *reference* being used to replace *allusion* in order to indicate clearly the system of conscious allusions that the author addresses to her or his reader in this literary kind of work. From behind the principle of an autonomously developing textuality, then, reappears the idea of an author's intentionality, if not that of a genetic relationship between one author or one work and another.[23]

From a perspective that is more structural than historical, however, it is rather memory that is to be seen as weaving intertextual relationships into a given broad literary movement. This singular memory of the poet is thus seen as reorganizing within the text different reminiscences from reading in a movement of *imitatio-aemulatio* through allusions, and it is seen as doing so as much from the standpoint of the use of vocabulary, expressions, or—beyond the level of the sentence—entire passages, as in the context of genre rules particular to the texts read by the author. Consequently, "proprio l'aver infatizzato il carattere funzionale della memoria poetica, il rivendicare insomma all'intertestualità uno statuto non diverso da quello che possiede la figura retorica, fornisce al filologo la possibilità fortunata di cogliere in atto il processo di produzione del testo letterario, e permette quasi di 'simulare' il meccanismo di formazione." ("Once the philologists have stressed the functional character of poetic memory and have allowed it equal status with the rhetorical figure, they can seize the literary process in action. It almost becomes possible to 'simulate' the mechanism of production of the text.")[24]

3.2. "Authorial" Diffractions

The difference in the degree of sensitivity to intellectual games manifested by Latinists, on the one hand, and Hellenists, on the other, is less a result of the historical depth of the traditions on which Latin poetry and Greek poetry respectively depend, or even of the huge gaps in our documentation concerning Greek poetic production, than a matter of fundamental differences in the poetic activity itself: on the Greek side, we have poems whose composition is closely associated with "performance" independent of any use of writing; on the Roman side, we have texts that are literary in the strict sense, being elaborated in a way that is directed toward a public of readers; and between the two, the complex manifestations of Hellenistic poetry occupy an intermediary position. This I say in brief while specifying that, with respect to the operative value of the notion of intertextuality for Greek poetry, what is determinant is not so much this poetry's links to an oral tradition dissolving the notion of author and the sequence of precise and "authorial" moments in a process of intertextual play; rather, what matters most from this perspective is that—from epic and Homeric poetry to the different manifestations of melic and didactic poetry to tragic representations—the constitutive pragmatic dimension of these composi- tions always assigns them a precise function within particular ritual and institu- tional circumstances. The extreme plasticity of Greek poetry in general is favored by the fact that every kind of poetic manifestation in Greece takes on the char- acter of a social practice; this plasticity often renders it pointless to assign poten- tial echoes repeated in the use of vocabulary, of expressions, or of entire segments to this or that kind of intertextual play, as defined in contemporary criticism. Greek poetic production generally depends too strongly on external social cir- cumstances and institutions to be subjected to a conceptual tool developed in the intellectual context of structuralism, then of poststructuralism, for a kind of late literature that seems to confirm the principle of the immanence of the text.

If we return to the example of the poetry of Sappho, scholars have long noticed in these fragmentary compositions the recurrence of vocabulary, for- mulas (noun plus epithet corresponding to a metrical unit), or entire phrases evoking Homeric poetry. When situating these analogies within a historical and genetic perspective, however, scholars have had to recognize that epic diction and material are completely reformulated in the famous narrative poem describing the wedding of Hector and Andromache.[25] This fact has not pre- cluded a contemporary work from presenting these lexical and formulaic echoes yet again as *Homerreminiszenzen*.[26] The hypothesis that there are more or less explicit Homeric references in such poetry has, furthermore, been revived in the context of gender and women's studies. By focusing less on lexical ref- erences and more on thematic analogies concerning "typical scenes," certain critics have thought it possible to demonstrate that Sappho consciously refor- mulated scenes from the *Iliad* in order to remove them from the masculine world of warfare and transpose them into the feminine domain of love.[27] From a linguistic point of view, however, a brief statistical analysis applied solely to the formulaic echoes in the extant fragments of Sappho's poetry shows that it actu- ally has many more points of contact with the *Homeric Hymns* than with the poems attributed to Homer or Hesiod. It is worth noting in this context not only that these hymnic compositions serving as proems for aedic and rhapsodic recitations were anonymous, but also that the first written, textual versions of them may be contemporary with or even later than the activity of Sappho of

Lesbos.[28] Rather than imagining the influence of epic poetry on Sappho, and instead of speaking of conscious borrowings from "Homer," it is preferable to think in terms of a poetic language and diction that are parallel to the language and diction on which the tradition of the epic narrative poem is based. The same is true of the rhythmic and metrical structures that give cadence to these poems composed and performed in early-sixth-century Lesbos.[29]

Concerning the incontestable thematic echoes that seem to link certain of Sappho's poems with the two long epics attributed to Homer, in place of the somewhat too symmetrical hypothesis according to which these echoes constitute the transformation of a written epic tradition originally addressed to a male audience into poems for oral "performance" by a female gathering, we ought at least to substitute the idea of a transposition of the Homeric tradition for a gathering of women who are no longer marginalized.[30] But there are objections even to this latter hypothesis: independent of the fact that Demodocus' audience in the *Odyssey*, just like the audience of rhapsodes in classical Athens, comprises both men and women, the divergences between, for example, the version of the rape of Helen presented by Sappho, the two versions of the legend given by Alcaeus, and (let us not forget) the reflexive version depicted in the *Iliad* lead rather to the hypothesis of poetic traditions that were parallel to each other even if they were in contact.

Many of those who apply analytical intertextuality to the field of ancient literature actually realize that their quest for more or less explicit allusions to earlier texts bears certain similarities to the philological practice of identifying *loci similes*.[31] Particularly useful for commentaries on texts whose general cultural context eludes us, and currently undergoing a revival thanks to the new cross-referencing that the inexhaustable resources of *Thesauri* on CD-ROM make possible, the search for "parallels" has often been oriented by the historical perspective concerning links of filiation to be sought between the target poem and its potential models. In other words, the locating of intertextual relationships between a certain text and neighboring ones is largely dependent on the interpreter's own literary sensibility and knowledge. In this respect, the system of poetic links that some have imagined between Sappho and Homer are largely based on the comparative choices and principles adopted in the modern reading on the basis of a corpus that is extremely limited in both cases and is very uncertain from a textual standpoint. The allusions that the Greek or Latin poet is supposed to have introduced more or less consciously into his or her composition, and to which the poet's contemporary reader is supposed to have been sensitive, may well be attributable only to the modern scholar's constructions and projections. Thus, in place of the textual intentions of "model authors" appearing more or less evidently on the enunciative level are substituted the literary sensibility and culture and the interpretive deftness of the philologist, wavering between "aleatory intertextuality" and "obligatory intertextuality."[32] While reflecting on the status of *cf.*, without recalling which of the studies I have been reading lately dealt with it, I find myself falling victim to the innumerable modalities of intertextual play.

3.3. Return to the "Instance of Enunciation"

Thus, we are referred back to the "model reader" that the "author" is supposed to have set up within his or her text by providing, through different discursive strategies, the keys for identifying his or her intertextual games. And if we are still actually inclined to insert ourselves into this intradiscursive figure of the implied reader, we are ultimately referred back to the articulation between the implicit author and the explicit speaker-narrator, and then to the articulation between this intradiscursive speaker, of an enunciative order, and the biographical author who is supposed to have organized this play with allusive reference.[33]

We thus find ourselves confronted once again with the question of the figure and the function of the instance of enunciation. Indeed, let us consider one of the scenarios presented by Greek poems still largely attached to an oral tradition, one involving a series of verses transmitted within a collection of anonymous banquet songs. Which biographical author are we to insert into the position of the speaker of these verses (who exhorts a "narratee," identified as a traveler, to prudence before a trip across the sea) before we see these lines on a papyrus integrated into a poem whose author could be Alcaeus, if not Sappho?[34] To remain in the sympotic context, which historical author is henceforth to be assigned to the groups of elegiac distichs taken up in turn and in echo of one another by guests at a banquet and recorded in the corpus of *Theognidea*— poetic sequences into which, furthermore, the ancients did not hesitate to insert (with variations) the verses of renowned elegiac poets such as Tyrtaeus, Mimnermus, or even Solon?[35] Or, while still reclining at the sympotic table, how are we—with our very limited knowledge of the burgeoning activity of sixth-century Greek poets—to judge the unilateral relationship that modern readers have wanted to see between the "lyric" scene in which, after a ball goes astray, Eros invites the poet to play with a girl who is paying no attention to him and the "epic" scene from the *Odyssey* in which Nausicaa's ball startles Odysseus, who has landed naked on a beach in Phaeacia? This putatively represents play with literary allusion, but the sort of allusion identified here depends on the interpreter: some see it as taking up a prototypical "model" coming out of epic poetry and supposedly known by Anacreon's audience, others as making an "intertextual" reference tinged with irony allowing the "lyric" *I* to identify himself with the Odysseus described by the "Homeric source text."[36] And what are we to say of the aulodes, like Sacadas of Argos, who put elegiac distichs to melody (*elegeía memelopoieména*), thereby attaching an author's name to brief poems that were probably anonymous? Or how are we to think in intertextual terms of the performance of rhapsodes who, according to the reverse scenario presented by Plato in the *Ion,* recited in the rhapsodic mode not only compositions by Homer and Hesiod but also those of Archilochus?[37]

Only the notion of the "instance of enunciation," actualized in the text through the different pronominal, verbal, and qualitative forms that the speaker-narrator takes up, can account for the various historical instances that may potentially occupy—whether simultaneously or in temporal succession—this discursive position. The detection of intertextual games, whatever their nature and infinite number of forms, cannot do without the enunciative distinction between intra- and extradiscursive, particularly in poetry where the notions of "author" and "authenticity" ultimately have no relevance and must be replaced by the notion of enunciative authority. Through the mediation of textual masks, the profile of this authority varies from one performance to another; it is subject to reformulations relative to a sung execution that must be considered each time as a ritual "reenactment" of discourse never made permanent as a text.[38] With texts henceforth detached from any definitive version—since they can always be reworked—and subject to the happenstance of "cut and paste" authorial identity, the diffusion of different forms of discourse on the World-Wide Web has probably put hypermodernity back into an analogous position.

4. Genres and Poetic Strategies of Authority

I would propose considering (poetic) genre as constituted by a series of both discursive and institutional rules that, while often implicit, are a part of the consensus and the tradition of a cultural community. Given this premise, one will grant that the composite nature of genres plays an essential role not only in the articulation between intra- and extradiscursive but also in the expansion of an "instance of enunciation," which itself lies at the meeting point between individual uses of a poetic language and uses that are institutionally and socially (if not psychologically and emotionally) determined, particularly through the "author-function". The issue of genre could thus offer a particularly fertile point of entry into the pragmatic aspects of poetic and "poietic" manifestations that, in ancient Greece in particular, take on highly specific ritual, cultural, and institutional functions. Nonetheless, there are so many misunderstandings perpetuated through the normative and evolutionist manner in which the issue of genre is traditionally approached in the field of Greek literature that there ought to be a monograph devoted to dissipating them. To see this, we need only recall the errors that the notion of "lyric poetry" has caused for Sappho or for epigraphic poetry. This modern notion shares practically no distinctive traits with the indigenous category corresponding to *mélos*. "Lyric poetry," though traditionally treated as a genre whose poetic manifestations are situated on a line of evolution between epic and dramatic poetry, is actually a category whose contours are so fuzzy that iambic and elegiac poems (these designations originally referring to little more than a metrical form) are readily included in it; it is a class comprising a whole series of specific, heterogeneous genres that, though practiced since the "archaic" period, were nonetheless deprived of a definition until the Alexandrian era, when they were given one for essentially editorial reasons.[39]

By contrast, and linked with a critique of the categories of genre that traditionally appear throughout our histories of Greek literature, what should emerge as a subtext to the semiotics of the enunciation approach proposed here—in passing from one concrete poetic manifestation to another—is the idea that we ought to remain at a distance from other broad modern concepts still in use. Such is the case for the use of notions such as that of "myth" for the religious dimension of most Greek poems, "archaic" for the periodization into which literary history inserts these poems, or "homosexuality" for their social range and function, not to mention idealizing and misleading holistic concepts such as "the Greeks" or "Greek thought."

From this perspective, taking a critical stance toward our own literary and anthropological categories, I propose here a series of incursions into the concrete manifestations of the art of *poieîn* by Greek practitioners of poetic speech: a series of readings that are sensitive to the enunciative, semantic, and pragmatic aspects of the texts that have come down to us. These readings tend to seize on that which is at first offered as a simple instance of enunciation in its enunciative complexity, in its qualitative density, and in its practical effects, while pointing to a polymorphous poetic authority with multiple discursive manifestations and with a wide range of social functions. It is thus a matter of catching in action some of the fundamental aspects of different types of Greek "authorial" poetics by focusing our attention more on the profile of the enunciative *I* itself than on the spatial or temporal location of this instance of enunciation.

A comparative analysis of the enunciative structure of the *Homeric Hymns* can show that, in the case of poems that introduce contests in rhapsodic recitation and are presented as an offering within a *do ut des* cult interaction, the pragmatic aspects of the discursive authority can make the song a performative cult act. Complementarily, the prelude of Hesiod's *Works and Days*, while pointing to the isotopies serving to guarantee the semantic coherence of the poem as a whole, provides a textbook case for the enunciative expansion not only of the figure of the speaker, but especially of that of the addressee as well. Through an enunciative *mise-en-scène* referring to a historical reality, the polymorphous character of these two masks or enunciative simulacra causes us to move from a personal conflict and legal dispute to a much broader social situation. In the case of the poem that Sappho devotes to Helen and her sojourn in Troy, the issue addressed concerns the practice of poetic authority through narrative argumentation: the episode that is chosen is exemplary relative to the underlying extradiscursive situation, in reaction to which the development of the "myth" is reoriented to constitute a new version, while the present situation acquires within the text (through subtle enunciative play) the fictional status of a paradigm. The Alexandrian hymn that Callimachus dedicates to Apollo stands in stark contrast to this, not only because the extradiscursive situation that is perceptible in Hesiod's *Works and Days* or in Sappho's poem is entirely reconstructed (through mimetic and fictional means) in the poetic discourse become text, but also because the cult form of the hymnic prayer is diverted in the Hellenistic period for the purposes of illustrating a scholarly poetics.

While the ancients always attributed the poems mentioned so far to an author (however ephemeral that author may be in the case of the *Homeric Hymns*), the verses that sometimes adorn the images on classical pottery are anonymous. This absence of "authorial" identification makes it possible to appreciate the educational role that is played by an art of the Muses widely practiced by citizens assembling at a symposium, where each guest is expected to turn himself into a poet, as reflected in the particular case examined here through a subtle enunciative interaction between the represented text and the depicted scene. But the authority of the poetic voice can also be put on stage; it is thus represented underneath enunciative masks of which the real masks worn by actors and chorus members in classical tragedy and comedy are the double. The plot of Sophocles' *Oedipus Tyrannus,* based on the dialectic between the ocular vision that one can deprive oneself of through blinding and the internal vision that may be inspired by divine light, casts doubt on the general dramatic identity that the mask confers on actors. The ritual masks and rags of comedy are used in Aristophanes' dramas to make possible the distancing of the civic identity of historical characters—politicians and poets—in order to put them on display and confront them with irony and derision before the audience of citizens gathered in the sanctuary-theater of Dionysus.

In the treatise on the environment attributed to Hippocrates, we have a representation of the inhabited world that is organized according to the principle of the influence that different qualities of water or wind and the orientation of various places have on the physiology of people living in those places. Instead of the assertive and objective enunciation that one attributes to "scientific" discourse and expects to find in a little treatise on human geography, discursive analysis reveals an enunciative orientation stemming from the doubleness of the authorial home, which in turn is due to the ambiguous geo-political position of Ionia, a Greek territory geographically attached to Asia. Alongside anthropological observation and theorization, commentary is also to be counted among the scholarly practices that were developed by poets of the classical period who would henceforth express themselves in prose. When the poetic text that is the object of exegesis is Orphic, the commentator's voice of authority is based on knowledge of a physical and philosophical order, so as to confer on this commentator's interpretive deciphering a didactic character that is, in turn, initiatory. And it is precisely into the field of erudition that Theocritus inserts the pastoral world of shepherd-poets, a world that he recreates in the bucolic mode through entirely discursive means. The poetic exchange staged by this new genre that is the idyll makes possible the "diffraction" of the poet's voice beneath the masks of authority of legendary figures, thereby transforming the "instance of enunciation" into a constellation of pastoral masters of an entirely constructed and fictional (if not fictive) world. This is the end of a trajectory and an opening toward new conditions of poetic enunciation, with the discursive staging of corresponding enunciative authorities.

PART 1

POEMS AS PERFORMATIVE
DISCOURSES IN ACTION

I

RELATIONSHIPS WITH THE GODS AND POETIC
FUNCTIONS IN THE *HOMERIC HYMNS*

I begin by singing of Demeter of the beautiful hair, the august goddess,
of her and of her daughter, the extremely beautiful Persephone.
Hail, goddess! Preserve our city, and guide our song!

(Homeric Hymn 13)

These three verses present in an autonomous poem the kernel of all of the
poems included in the famous collection of *Homeric Hymns.* Beginning with an
indirect address to Demeter and her daughter Kore, this hymnic composition
(the thirteenth in the corpus of hymns attributed to Homer) concisely indicates
the qualities of the two goddesses before addressing directly to the mother a
prayer; it calls for her benevolence toward both the city where the poet sings
and the execution of the song itself in exchange for the pleasure that the god-
dess may feel. In asking what poetic function, in terms of enunciative author-
ity and pragmatic effect, these compositions of vastly different lengths serve
through the descriptive and narrative construction of a fiction, we face the
question of the nature of the relationship that the speaker manages to establish
through poetic means with a divinity whose intervention he ends up request-
ing. In so doing, we are also faced with the task of formulating propositions
concerning the circumstances, probably ritual and cultic ones, of the sung per-
formance of such hymnic poems.

1. A Sketch of the Textual Tradition

It is well known that only conjecture and hypothetical reconstruction can allow
us to retrace the history of the *Homeric Hymns.* The poems transmitted under this
title are collected in around thirty manuscripts generally dating from the fifteenth

century and often including other texts, such as the *Hymns* of Callimachus, the *Orphic Argonautica,* or even Moschus' *Eros,* the *Iliad,* the *Odyssey,* and Hesiodic texts; this collection of thirty-three compositions of vastly varying lengths (from 3 to 580 verses) might have been assembled in the fifth century A.D. by Proclus, who apparently added to it his own *Hymns.* Beyond this *terminus ante quem,* a few extremely tenuous clues make it possible to work backwards, past the manifest editorial work of the Alexandrian era, to the classical period. These clues lead to the hypothesis that a "manual" published for the use of rhapsodes reciting Homeric poems was already in circulation in the fifth century B.C.[1]

Whatever the date of their collection, we may wonder what criterion was applied in collecting these compositions. Indeed, they have little more in common from a formal perspective than their language and their epic rhythm, and they hardly share more in their content than the final address to a god whose praises have just been sung. Despite the extreme disparity reflected in the corpus, might they not owe their assembly into a single collection to a shared function? This is in line with one of the fundamental traits of archaic Greek poetry, namely, the fact that up until the Alexandrian period at least, no literary manifestation was conceivable outside of precise ritual or cultic circumstances.[2]

From this point of view, nothing can be learned from the name itself by which these poems are designated. We know that at the time of their composition, the term *húmnos* covered such a vast semantic spectrum that it did not designate any particular genre or poetic form; this term's use can refer just as well to an epic song or Hesiod's *Theogony* as to a choral melic composition or an erotic elegy.[3] By contrast, Thucydides (who is the first source for us on this matter) has recourse to the term *prooímion* to designate the *Homeric Hymn to Apollo.* He cites this composition because it alludes to the festival that the Ionians held in the god's honor at Delos.[4] The supposed etymology of the term *prooímion* ("showing the path [*oîmos*]" or "preceding the song [*oíme*]," both of which had already been proposed by the ancients) and its usage, notably in Pindar's first *Pythian,* show that this word indicates a poetic prelude. This prelude seems to be able, according to the circumstances, to take the form not only of bardic or rhapsodic recitation but also of citharodic performance and even melic song.[5]

The vagueness that hovers around the designation of the *Homeric Hymns* as hymns or as proems also appears in the results of an analysis of their content. On the one hand, the *Hymns* are devoted to celebrating different gods: this is the one constant that Plato retains when, in a famous passage of the *Republic,* the philosopher excludes from the ideal city all poetic compositions except "hymns for gods and eulogies [*egkómia*] for good people." After looking over the corpus that has come down to us, we may add that these Homeric compositions are sometimes addressed to divinized heroes, such as the Dioscuri. On the other hand, the *Hymns* also present a request addressed to the divinity who is sung about in the poems; in this respect, these poems belong to the very broad category of prayer. This is another distinctive trait that Plato recognized in an equally often discussed passage from the *Laws:* among the traditional musical genres, prayers to gods, called *húmnoi,* are distinguished from the dirge, but also from the paean and the dithyramb dedicated to Dionysus. Furthermore, in answer to the question of what kind of poetry is to be preferred in the city imagined in the *Laws,* it is "the hymns for the gods and the eulogies [*egkómia*] associated with prayers."[6] Hymn, praise, and prayer thus come together to constitute a single genre of poetry, the poetry of praise addressed to gods or heroes.

From the point of view of a contemporary philologist, the primary distinctive feature characterizing the *Homeric Hymns* involves their forms of expression. Their hexametric rhythm, Homeric vocabulary, and epic diction immediately distinguish them from Sappho's *Hymn to Aphrodite* (in Sapphic strophes and Lesbian dialect) or from Pindar's *Paeans* or *Dithyrambs* (in Aeolic meter or dactylo-epitrites and with Doric vocabulary and dialectal features, just like the few fragments of his *Hymns* that have reached us). These characteristics also distinguish the *Homeric Hymns* from cult hymns like the famous Dictaean hymn to Kouros (in major Ionic meter and West Greek dialect), the hymn to Paean/Asclepius from Erythrae in northern Ionia (in dactylic rhythm and Doric dialect), or the "magic" hymn to Hermes (in prose and *koiné* Greek), not to mention the innumerable hymns that are obviously literary, such as those integrated into tragic texts.[7]

It would take a particularly inventive mind, however, to draw some clear distinction between these different hymnic compositions that is based on the forms their *content* takes. Analyses devoted to the structure of such poems have thus far highlighted instead the numerous similarities existing between hymns for gods, regardless of the poetic form they take, and cult prayers, for which Chryses' famous prayer to Apollo in the *Iliad* is often taken to be the prototype.[8]

> Hear me, god of the silver bow, you who protect Chryse
> and the divine Killa and who rule mightily over Tenedos!
> Oh Smintheus, if ever I have raised a temple for you that pleased you,
> if ever I have burned for you fatty thigh-bones
> of bulls and goats, accomplish my wish:
> may the Danaans pay for my tears through your arrows!
>
> (Homer, *Iliad* 1.37–42)

Indeed, it has been noticed that the tripartite structure, which was defined at the beginning of the last century through an analysis of the corpus of all of the addresses to gods in Greek literature and which has been considered characteristic of prayers, also appears in the poetic and cultic forms considered hymns, particularly in the *Homeric Hymns;* the Anglo-Saxon schema invocation—argument—petition is now preferred to the canonical triad *invocatio—epica* (or *media) pars—preces.*[9] For the purposes of defining the distinctive traits of the *Homeric Hymns,* modern studies focusing on content do not permit us to go much beyond Plato's reflections on poetry addressed to gods. Accordingly, close attention must be paid to the modes of address to the divinities in the *Hymns* and to the particular enunciative processes that they present. This approach should define the enunciative specificity of these hymnic poetic creations while at the same time giving some indications about their social and ritual function.

2. Questions of Structure: *Evocationes*

If we consider the *Homeric Hymns* in terms of the three constitutive parts that they have in common with other types of prayers, whether literary or cultic, we may note several striking differences. These differences concern above all the initial portion of the "invocation," which generally mentions the divinity concerned in the poem.

Unlike all of the texts classified in the general category of prayer, the *Hymns* do not begin with a direct address to the god. These *Hymns* open in one of three ways: (1) the speaker-narrator declares in the first person that he is going to sing about the divinity ("I begin to sing of Demeter . . . ," *Homeric Hymn* 13.1), (2) he asks the Muse to sing about the divinity ("Sing, melodious Muse, Castor and Pollux . . . ," *Homeric Hymn* 17.1), or (3) he presents himself as the addressee of the song requested from the Muse ("sing for me, melodious Muse, Meter . . . ," *Homeric Hymn* 14.1–2). In these different types of exordium, the divinity appears only in the third person as the subject treated in the announced song. This means that these three types of formulation correspond precisely to those that open the *Iliad* and the *Odyssey* or sections within them. In those passages, the speaker-narrator either affirms the authority of his own poetic voice or places this authority under the control of the Muses. Thus, we can compare these three types of exordium with, respectively, (1) the statement concluding the prelude to the "Catalogue of Ships" in the *Iliad* ("But I will tell of the commanders of the ships and the ships' total number"), (2) the very beginning of the *Iliad* ("Sing, Muse, the wrath of Achilles"), and (3) the beginning of the *Odyssey* ("It is the man of a thousand turns, Muse, that you must sing for me") or the first verse of the proem to the "Catalogue of Ships" ("And now tell me, Muses . . . , tell me who were the guides, the leaders of the Danaans").[10]

The presentation of the god in the third person facilitates the transition, after the enumeration of some qualifications and epithets, to the description of some particular good deed or the narration of an exploit from the deity's

biography. Such expansion upon the god's epithets through laudatory descrip-
tion or narrative is not absent from the other forms of prayer that have come
down to us, but this aretalogy opens the way to accounts of a Homeric sort
like those presented in the longest *Homeric Hymns.* The long narratives of the
hymns to Apollo, to Hermes, and to Aphrodite are introduced in each case by
the usual relative pronoun used predicatively, while an analogous opening for-
mula in the *Hymn to Demeter* is a little more complex because of the presence
of the goddess's daughter alongside the goddess herself. The use of this struc-
ture corresponds to a typically "hymnic" procedure of predication. "Muse, tell
me of the deeds of golden Aphrodite, Cypris *who* arouses sweet desire in gods
and who tames the races of mortal men . . ."; so begins, for example, the long
hymn singing of the love of Anchises and the daughter of Zeus, herself over-
come by the same erotic desire that she excites in others.[11] By contrast with
the shortest compositions, the medium-length hymns, such as those dedicated
to Aphrodite (6), Dionysus (7), Pan (19), or Artemis (27), give a good sense of
the possibilities for developing the narrative or the description.[12] These pos-
sibilities allowing the extension of praise of the god in several directions are
characteristic of a potential for expansion that is still largely dependent on an
oral tradition.

There are few exceptions to this hymnic presentation of the god. In four of
the collection's compositions, however, the speaker directly addresses the divin-
ity through forms of the imperative or vocative. In two of these, dedicated
respectively to Hestia (24) and to this goddess accompanied by Hermes (29),
the brief description introduced by the hymnic relative pronoun is carried out
in the second person, as in certain forms of prayer.

> Hestia, you who take care of the hallowed home of Apollo,
> the Lord Archer, in divine Pytho,
> flowing oil always drips from your braided locks.
> Enter this house, enter in agreement
> with prudent Zeus; also give your favors to my song.
>
> (*Homeric Hymn* 24)

Could this poem reflect an error of classification on the part of the collec-
tion's compiler? The allusion to song that concludes not only this *Hymn to Hes-
tia* (incomplete though it seems) but also the one in which the goddess is
evoked along with Hermes suggests otherwise. Indeed, the god's relationship
with the song determines, as we shall see, the orientation of most of the poems
in the collection.[13] The same is true of *Hymn* 21 devoted to Apollo. This
extremely brief composition presents an even more striking variation relative to
the three traditional forms of indirect invocation of the divinity:

Phoebus, it is you that the swan sonorously sings along with its wings,
when it heads toward the bank along the turbulent Peneus;
you are the one that the poet, holding his sonorous lyre,
always sings first and last with sweet words.
And so hail to you, Lord! Through this song, I am striving for your goodwill.

(*Homeric Hymn* 21)

The sung praise for the god is here entrusted not to the Muses but to the swan, that melodious-voiced bird protected by Apollo himself. It is perhaps because of this deft substitution that we have a reversal of the actantial positions marking the opening of this poem: Apollo takes the second person, the swan the third person.[14] There remains the problem posed by the *Hymn to Ares* (8), whose insertion into the collection of *Homeric Hymns* has been unanimously recognized as an error. Everything in this poem's structure, its vocabulary, and its accumulation of epithets points to its being a late philosophical prayer (probably inspired by Neoplatonism), or even an Orphic hymn.[15] This brings us to the limits entailed by any kind of classification within a category that was created *a posteriori*. In the specific case of the *Hymns,* the corresponding category was probably defined in accordance with the requirements of a published edition of compositions that, at the time of their creation and their execution, did not reflect any particular taxonomy whatsoever.

The unique kind of utterance constituted by the *Hymns'* introductory verses endows them with the form of an *evocatio* rather than an *invocatio*. Such an evocation tends to establish between the divinity and the speaker, whose expression is sometimes only implicit, a mediated relationship. This relationship is put in place through the act of singing itself.

3. Preces

This overview of the enunciative traces, wherein the authorial figures occupying the actantial positions organize the system of communication elaborated by the poem itself, takes us from the beginning of the various *Hymns* to their conclusion, from the *evocatio* to the *preces,* which are also called a "petition" or an "epilogue" by contemporary learned readers of the *Hymns.* From the perspective of enunciation, these concluding verses constitute a crucial shift. After having taken upon himself the role of conferring praise on the god through a description or narrative, or after having delegated the praise-song to the Muse, the speaker-narrator concludes by directly addressing the god whose merits have just been celebrated. These epilogues differ from one another somewhat in their formulation and their content; but, in addition to their shared use of a well-marked address to the god in the second person (indicated by the use of the imperative and the vocative and often underlined by the use of the pronoun *toi*, "to you"), they are generally constituted of a varying combination of recurrent elements. The most frequently occurring ones provide helpful indications concerning the function of the poems in the collection.

3.1. Explicit Requests

The concluding verses of a number of *Hymns* are just like texts of prayers inasmuch as they present an explicit petition to the gods: "grant us good fortune and happiness," the singer of *Hymn* 11 asks of Athena; "grant excellence and prosperity," the speaker asks of Heracles in *Hymn* 15, or of Hephaestus in *Hymn* 20. The request is sometimes limited simply to asking for the god's favor (*Hymn* 23, to Zeus); it can also concern the resources for life when addressed to the Sun, as in *Hymn* 31, which may be from a later period. Accordingly, it is not surprising to find a more specific petition, appropriate to the god's qualifications, at the end of the *Hymn to Ares* (8), which, as we saw, constitutes a prayer in the strict sense. But readers of the *Hymns* seeking clues about their poetic function have often pointed to the wish concluding *Hymn* 6, addressed to Aphrodite. The poem's "author"—as "instance of enunciation"—very specifically asks the goddess of amorous seduction to allow him to be victorious "in *this* contest" (*en agôni tôide*), a competition that has, of course, been identified with the rhapsodic contest for which this proem was presumably intended. *Hymn* 26, which is addressed to Dionysus as leader of a *thiasos* made up of boy-raising (*kourótrophoi*) Nymphs, may also present an allusion to an annual festival: the speaker in this poem petitions the god for the privilege of returning when the season comes around again.[16]

The prayer in the poem praising the seductiveness of Aphrodite dressed by the Hours (*Hymn* 6), as noted earlier, pertains to its enunciation circumstances. The same might also be said of *Hymn* 24. We have seen that this song began with an address to the second person: Hestia is entreated to come "into *this* house" (*tónd' anà oîkon*) to grant charm (*khárin*) to the speaker's song. The invocation of the goddess of the hearth in this *Hymn* is probably motivated by the fact that the song is for performance in a "private" house. In another *Hymn,* one dedicated to Aphrodite (10), the wish for a "lovely" (*himeróessan,* "which excites desire") song is explicitly linked to the desirable (*himertós*) quality of the love goddess's face and smile.[17] The relationship between the prayer, the god, and the song being performed can be so strong that, at the end of *Hymn* 6, the speaker asks for Aphrodite to sing his song, and not the Muse. Likewise, the speaker in *Hymn* 25, after praising the privileged relationship uniting the Muses and

Apollo with bards and lyre players, asks these children of Zeus to honor his own poem.[18] And *Hymn* 13 (cited in the epigraph to this chapter), while it does not make explicit the relationship between the divinity and the song, concludes with an invitation to Demeter to protect "*this* city" (*ténde pólin*) and to begin the song herself. This composition, comprising three verses in all, presents the minimal and canonical structure of the *Homeric Hymn: evocatio, epica laus* (through the qualities attributed to the two divinities), and *preces*.[19]

But studies concerning prayer in antiquity show that one never addresses a wish to a god without giving a motivation for it, or without reflecting a concern for reciprocity. A person is qualified to ask for something because he has given something, because he is in the process of giving something, because the god himself has given something in the past, or because it is up to the god to grant what is requested. This motivating of the request constitutes one of the foundations of the middle part of the prayer, which can thus develop into a long descriptive and/or narrative expression of praise.[20] In addition to the few cases I have noted where the request for a divinity's protection over the song is framed in terms of a quality corresponding to the god invoked, two texts are perfectly explicit in this regard. *Hymn* 30, addressed to Earth, makes a request to the goddess to bestow the resources of life that delight one's heart in exchange for the song (*ant' oidês*) that the speaker is performing. We find the same thing in the long hymn devoted to Demeter: the singer of the poem proposes to Demeter and to Persephone that they grant him "in exchange for the song" the fecund prosperity of agricultural civilization, for which the entire story told in the *Hymn* provides the etiological legend.[21]

3.2. Forms of Hailing

It is in this context that we ought to understand the "hail" to the god that opens, with the form *khaîre*, the final portion of most of the *Homeric Hymns* (in twenty-seven cases out of thirty-three). Though generally understood according to its secondary meaning as a send-off formula, this form of the imperative points rather to the literal meaning of the verb *khaírein*: "enjoy," "take pleasure in."[22] Indeed, the *khaîre* addressed to the god is often accompanied by the adverb *hoútos*, "in this way," which links the expression with what precedes (in eleven cases out of twenty-seven); the pleasure thus points back to the song of praise constituting the central part of the *Hymn*. The use of terms formed from the same root sometimes helps to render explicit the relationship between the request addressed to the god and the musical pleasure offered in exchange. Thus, the invitation to take pleasure in *Hymn* 18 is expressed twice so that it may be addressed to a Hermes who is himself generous in matters of pleasure (*kharidôta*).

Hymn 30 perhaps creates an echo between the *khaîre* addressed to Earth, who has been asked to provide the life resources that she has to offer, and the choral pleasures (*khoroîs . . . paízousai khaírousi*), of the young girls honored by the goddess. In *Hymn* 26, the pleasure of Dionysus is also that of the speaker (*hemâs khaírontas*) who wishes "to come back upon the season's return." But in addition to these apparent echoes pointing to the reciprocity of musical pleasure, the *Hymn to the Mother of the Gods* (14) and the *Hymn to Artemis* (9) provide *khaîre* with an unambiguous grammatical complement: the two goddesses are invited, along with their fellow goddesses, to take pleasure in the song (*aoidêi*). Similarly, during the famous self-referential scene closing the "Delian" portion of the *Hymn to Apollo*, the god is invited to delight in his heart (*epitérpeai êtor*, v. 146) as any mortal would do (*térpsaito thumón*, v. 153) at the spectacle of the Ionians, who themselves delight (*térpousin*, v. 150) in carrying out with "grace" (*khárin*, v. 153) dances and songs—songs which moreover celebrate (*mnesámenoi*, v. 150) the god himself in the festival (*agón*) held in his honor in Delos.[23]

> But your heart, Phoebus, finds the most charm in Delos,
> where the Ionians gather in trailing tunics
> with their children and modest wives.
> Through boxing, dancing and song, they
> mindfully please you, when they organize their games.
> One would say that the Ionians are immortal and forever exempt from aging,
> should he arrive when they are assembled:
> he would see the grace they all have, and his heart would delight
> in seeing the men, the women with beautiful belts
> and the swift ships and all their riches.
>
> (*Homeric Hymn* 3.146–55)

Musical pleasure is thus sure to bring pleasure to the god for whom it is meant; to sing of a divinity is to accord her or him an honor that can serve as payment for the favors the singer himself receives in return. Just as the god has the possibility of granting a lovely song (*Hymn* 10), so the poet, in moving from the intradiscursive to the extradiscursive, can cause the god to do him favors or thank the god for some through the offering constituted by his own song. In the *Hymns*, the *do ut des* reciprocity can be entirely fulfilled by the hymnic song itself.[24]

3.3. Contracts of Reciprocity

The fact that, in the concluding portion of most of the *Hymns*, the point is affirming the reciprocity of the services rendered, respectively, by the hailed god and the speaker-poet become a sayer of prayers is also indicated by the strong enunciative contrast between *you* and *I*. The appeal to the god in the imperative (*khaîre, dós,* etc., often rendered emphatically as *kaì sù mèn hoúto khaîre,* "you, too, for your part, take pleasure in this way") is generally answered with a highlighted affirmation of the *I*. As the conclusion of the whole composition, this enunciative formulation strongly asserts, once again, the speaker-narrator's function as singer, as bard.

Indeed, in twelve cases, the *I* is juxtaposed to the *you* through the formula *autàr egò kaì seîo kaì álles mnésom'aoidês,* "I, in turn, will sing both you and another song." The first thing to note is that the use here of the connector *autár* is particularly significant. Standing in opposition to the *mén* of the formula *kaì sù mèn hoúto khaîre* ("and you, too, for your part, take pleasure in this way") at the end of the *Hymn to Apollo* and the *Hymn to Hermes* (see also *Hymns* 19 and 29), *autár* renders the idea of succession that is close to its etymological meaning, since it is formed from *aûte* and *ár* ("in turn"). Furthermore, in the form *mnésomai* we can recognize one of those "performative" futures that we so often find in melic poetry; they indicate the ritual action that the speaker, and through him the (often choral) performer of the poem, is on the point of doing or intends to do.[25] The activity at issue, in the present case just as in many melic poems, is singing; it is designated by a verb referring to memory only to the extent that the function of recalling, incarnated in the figure of Mnemosyne, corresponds to the moment of the poem's creation and production in an essentially oral tradition. This verb referring to celebration attached to memory is used in the passage quoted from the *Hymn to Apollo* (v. 160: *mnesámenai . . . húmnon aeídousin*), but also in the introductory formula of *Hymn* 7, where it would be more usual to find the form *aeísomai,* or in the conclusion of the *Hymn to Dionysus,* where forgetting of the god brings with it, in the case of bards, "forgetting" of the song: "We bards sing you at the beginning and at the end of our song; it is not possible for him who forgets you to remember the sacred song." The occurrence of the verb *memnêsthai* in this context confirms the creative and productive significance of bardic "memory."[26]

The performance of the song, whose text corresponds to the *Hymn* itself, represents an offering; it represents the return-gift proposed to the god in exchange for the requested favor, a favor that often concerns the song itself. This is confirmed by three *Hymns* (16, 19, 21) in which the very means for the prayer (*lítomai*) or the propitiation (*hílamai*) is the song itself (*aoidêi*); conversely, in *Hymn* 25 (quoted earlier), the speaker asks Apollo and the Muses to ensure his own song's fame (*emèn timésat' aoidén,* "cover my song with honors"). Though anonymously, poetic authority henceforth receives divine consecration.

3.4. Transitional Formulas

More surprising is the allusion to another song that concludes, in addition to the compositions just mentioned, *Hymns* 6, 10, 25, 27, 28, 30, and 33: *álles mnésom'aioidês,* "I am about to remember another song." If the "hail" formula with *hoúto* actually points to the song of praise that has just been executed, the use of the performative future seems to confirm the reference, in this concluding expression, to a new song that is about to be begun and will also be sung in honor of the god. In any case, it is thus that we can make sense of the double *kaì* that associates the god with "another song" (*aoidê*) in this formulation.

Three often-cited *Hymns* present a formula that is much more explicit about the transition to another song. By concluding his brief poem with the expression *seû d'egò arxámenos metabésomai állon es húmnon* ("having begun with you, I am going to move on to another song"), the speaker of *Hymn* 9 to Artemis shows simultaneously that his song of praise for the divinity is now completed (use of the aorist), that this was only a prelude, and that he plans to follow it up immediately with the same type of song, also characterized as a *húmnos:*

Celebrate in song, Muse, the sister of the Archer, Artemis,
the virgin shooter of arrows who was raised alongside Apollo!
She waters her horses in the Meles, with its deep reeds,
and drives her all-golden chariot swiftly through Smyrna
to vine-covered Claros, where Apollo of the silver bow
sits waiting for her, the shooter of arrows who strikes from afar.
And so, in this way, take pleasure in my song, Artemis, you and all
    the other goddesses:
it is about you first and from you that I begin singing,
and, having begun with you, I will move on to another hymn.

(*Homeric Hymn 9*)

The prelude function served by these nine verses devoted to singing the joint merits of the goddess and of her brother Apollo at Claros is underscored by the verse preceding the concluding formula: it is by exalting Artemis and starting from this praise that the speaker begins singing (*autàr egó se prôta ek séthen árkhom'aeídein*), and he does so in follow-up to the request he himself addressed to the goddess and her fellow female divinities to take pleasure in hearing his song (*aoidêi*).[27] We find a shortened form of the same transition in the conclusion to *Hymn* 18, dedicated to Hermes, and in the closing of the *Hymn to Aphrodite*, following the long epic account of the love between the goddess of erotic desire and the young Anchises.[28]

It is in this context that one ought to read the typical *Hymn* 13, dedicated to Demeter and cited at the beginning of this chapter: after having declared that he was beginning by singing (*árkhom'aeìdein*) Demeter and her daughter Persephone, the speaker can, without any contradiction, pray to the goddess to start the song (*árkhe aoidês*). Responsibility for the prelude is assumed by the speaker, whereas the song that follows it benefits from the protection of the invoked goddess. *Hymn* 6, dedicated to Aphrodite, is organized around the same transition: after the speaker's declaration of his intention to sing the gold-crowned goddess (*áisomai*), and after his praise of her beauty, comes, in conclusion, the prayer to launch into the poet's song itself (*emèn éntunon aoidén*), presented in a second formula as "another song."

Naturally, we would like to know more about the form and subject of the song so introduced. Only two *Hymns* that are generally considered later are a little more informative about this issue. The speaker-narrator of the *Hymn to Helios* (31) declares, after the prelude put in the mouth of the Muse, that he wants to glorify (*kleíso*) the exploits of heroized mortals. Similarly, the poet of the *Hymn to the Moon* (32), after asking the Muses to celebrate Selene and after singing her praises, closes by telling of his intention—starting from the goddess (*séo d'arkhómenos*)—to sing (*áisomai*) the glory of demigods "whose exploits the bards, servants of the Muses, glorify (*kleíousin*)."[29] We have no need of an extended lexical analysis to show that the different terms used in the *Hymns* to describe the song introduced in the preludes refer to epic song, song of the Homeric type that takes the enunciative form of a rhythmic recitation and is accompanied by instrumental music without itself being melodic. Indeed, when it is not designated by the very general term *húmnos*, this song is called *aoidé*; the notion to which this term refers must be understood as an activity and as the product of this activity. Its "author" is either a bard or a rhapsode, if it is true that this second, much discussed term designates any singer who recites his poem without putting it to music.[30] Thus, the laudatory prayer to the gods in the *Hymns*, through its use of the procedures commonly employed in epic poetry and diction, simply serves to introduce the narrative celebration (of an *aedic* type) of Homeric heroes.[31]

4. *Epicae Laudes*

Framed by the speaker-narrator's poetic establishing of contact with the god and the prayer that the speaker-petitioner addresses to him, the descriptive and narrative part of the *Homeric Hymn* develops more specifically according to the modes of epic poetry, in particular in the longest compositions. By means of predication, through an accumulation of qualifying adjectives and *epikleseis*, through participial forms and/or a relative clause developing into narrative, this part of the hymn is specifically devoted to praising the god: thus it is the *epica laus* rather than the *epica pars*. According to a study of the content of the short *Hymns,* the praise of the divinity sung as a prelude to an epic recitation concerns either the efficacy of a specific deed carried out by the god among mortals, or his particular manifestation at the time of one of these deeds, or again an episode of his sacred biography.[32]

Whichever god is evoked, we may observe that music often occupies an important place in this "epic part." Although it is beyond the scope of the present discussion to examine all of the allusions to musical manifestations that are presented in the descriptive and narrative part of the *Hymns,* let us note a few significant cases. The evocations of music in the hymnic biographies of the gods can range from cries that the Earth bellows forth (*iákhese,* a verb perhaps used of song in *Hymn* 19.18) on the occasion of the birth of Athena in *Hymn* 28 to the beautiful chorus of the Muses and the Charites that Artemis leads to sing Leto when the goddess goes to Delphi to join her brother, Apollo, in *Hymn* 27. They range from the evocation of the sound of the rattles, kettledrums, and flutes cherished by Meter in the *Hymn* devoted to her (14) to the description of the seductive garments and jewelry donned by the Hours, along with Aphrodite, when they go to join the chorus of the gods (*Hymn* 6). But whether they be brief or long, the *Hymns* that have the most to say about musical manifestations are, of course, those consecrated to gods whose domain of activity includes music. The narrative part of *Hymn* 19 to Pan elaborates at some length on the dances of the Nymphs guided by the melodies that the goatish god plays on his syrinx; the narrator manages to put into the mouth of these young dancers the story of the love of Hermes and the daughter of Dryops that leads to the birth of the monstrous god. And need we be reminded of the long narrative about the invention of the lyre and the giving of it to Apollo which takes up a large part of the *Hymn to Hermes?*

But it is obviously Apollo himself who holds the privilege of musical expression in all of its forms. In the strange *Hymn* 21, where the task of conferring epic praise (*aeídei*) on the god is entrusted to the swan, the descriptive part (unusually pronounced in the second person) establishes a relationship between the god and the sweet-voiced bard who sings him while holding the melodious phorminx.[33] This privileged relationship is made still more specific in *Hymn* 25, dedicated to the Muses, Apollo, and Zeus. While the last takes kings under his protection, the entire earthly lives of bards—as we have seen—depends on the Muses and Apollo. This brief evocation of the attributions of the gods that are sung culminates in a *makarismós:* happiness is defined there as constituting a privileged relationship with the Muses; through their agency, the voice (*audê*) flows out sweetly from the mouth. Moreover, in the long, bipartite *Hymn* dedicated to Apollo—that god so often sung (*eúumnon*) that the speaker does not know and ask how to celebrate him (*pos . . . s'humnéso,* vv. 19–20)—both the Delian development and the Delphic narrative lead to the description of musical representations. Thus, *Hymn* 3 both evokes the singing and dancing of the great Ionian festival in honor of the god of the lyre at Delos, devoting particular attention to the song performed by the chorus of Deliades (vv. 146–73), and describes the paradigmatic procession of Cretans who, accompanied by the sounds of the god's own phorminx and singing the Paean inspired by the Muse, head to Delphi to occupy the oracular sanctuary there (vv. 513–23).[34]

When the praise is directed to the god of music, the descriptive and narrative part of the *Homeric Hymn* takes on a strikingly reflexive character in relation to the role played by the composition as a whole. The song of the Deliades takes up the content and function of the *Hymn to Apollo,* since these young girls, after having celebrated (*humnésosin,* v. 158) Apollo, then Leto and Artemis, sing a "hymn" in praise of the heroes (*mnesámenai . . . húmnon aeídousi,* vv. 160–64) to charm the tribes of mortals. What is more, in the verses that are presented as a veritable hymn within the hymn through the direct address to the Deliades (*khaírete,* v. 166), the speaker introduces a *sphragís;* while conferring on him the quality of being the sweetest of bards (*hédistos aoidôn*), this signature identifies the author and singer of the present poem with "the blind man from Chios" (vv. 165–76). In the Deliades' hymnic praise, the prelude (*prôton humnésosin,* v. 158) that they address to the god of Delos and that introduces a song of an epic kind is performed by a chorus of girls. Does this mean that the *Homeric Hymns,* whose introductory function should no longer be doubted, were sung by a chorus, or, if not by a group of chorus members, by a bard accompanied by a chorus, according to the citharodic mode illustrated by numerous descriptions of epic performances in the *Iliad* and the *Odyssey?* In comparison to the citharodic compositions of Stesichorus, for example, the vocabulary, diction and rhythm of the *Hymns* bring the proems of the collection closer—as has already been indicated—to bardic or rhapsodic recitation.[35]

However that may be, the *Homeric Hymns* are, in their structure and their content, centered essentially on song, through a transition from the intra- to the extradiscursive: the enunciative formulation of the *evocatio* directs the listener's attention to the discursive competence of the speaker-narrator[36] and to his poetic authority, or the forms of the *preces* focus the *do ut des* reciprocity on the song, or again the *laus epica* purposefully records the musical qualities of the divinity whose epiphany is often called for at the end of the hymnic composition. Could there be a better way to introduce the singing of an epic tale while placing the authority of the one who is going to sing under the protection of a god?

5. Beyond the *Hymns*

As much by their enunciative form as by the semantic relationship of their content with the song, the *Homeric Hymns* affirm their specificity. A study contrasting them with contemporary poetic forms of an analogous function would only confirm this specificity. By way of a conclusion, I can provide only a brief survey here.

If we set aside simple appeals to the Muse that make of the poem concerned the divinity's own expression, as in the *Iliad* or the *Odyssey,* some elegiac poems present an exordium that, like the *Homeric Hymns,* seems to propose the terms of an exchange; the relative enunciative autonomy of these introductory verses (with the presence of *I* and *you* forms) seems to make them brief proems. This is particularly true for two groups of two elegiac distichs that open the corpus of poems attributed to Theognis. Their editorial location at the head of the corpus is probably itself significant with regards to their status as preludes. In the first of these two groups of verses (1–4), the speaker assures Apollo that he will sing the god at the beginning, middle, and end of his poem; in exchange, he requests from him all sorts of boons:

> O lord, son of Leto, offspring of Zeus,
> never will I forget you when beginning or concluding;
> rather, I will sing you first and last and in the middle, always.
> As for you, hear me and give me good things.

> (Theognis 1–4)

In the second group of verses (11–14), Artemis is invoked to turn the powers of death away from the speaker, but the request is not explicitly accompanied by a term indicating reciprocity.[37]

> Artemis the beast slayer, daughter of Zeus, whom Agamemnon
> honored with a temple when he was setting sail for Troy in swift ships,
> hear my prayer and ward off the evil spirits of death:
> for you, goddess, this is a small thing, but for me it is a great one.

> (Theognis 11–14)

While this second address introduces, through the hymnic relative pronoun, a very brief *epica laus* that could state the terms of the exchange, the first one does without it. But, from a comparative and contrastive perspective, the reader is above all struck by the fact that such requests are attached to the final portion of the composition in the *Homeric Hymns.* The forms *dós* or *dídou* ("grant") bring to a close *Hymn* 11 addressed to Athena, for example, or *Hymn* 15 for Heracles, but the invitation is accompanied by the form *khaíre* ("enjoy").[38] Furthermore, the two compositions attributed to Theognis are characterized by a direct address to the divinity. This is also the case in the three introductory distichs of Solon's first *Elegy*. These verses addressed to the Muses, who are invoked in the second person, formulate—without a proposition of reciprocity—a general request for happiness (*ólbon dóte*, "grant prosperity"); then they express the wish that men may acquire a reputation (*dóxa*) related to the poet's function and, consequently, to the didactic poem that follows.[39] These few initial direct addresses to the divinity are very much like the final part of the *Homeric Hymns* (*preces*) from a formal point of view, but they also do not introduce a different song. Despite their enunciative and semantic autonomy, they are an integral part of the poems that they open; accordingly, they cannot be presented as themselves constituting the compensation for the favor requested from the god. They do not constitute "proems" in the original sense of the term.

In this respect, the differences between the prelude to Hesiod's *Theogony* and the introductory verses of the *Works and Days* are quite revealing. As several scholars have noted, the prologue of the *Theogony* (vv. 1–104) is presented as a veritable hymn to the Muses; more precisely, it assumes the enunciative and structural forms of a *Homeric Hymn* addressed to the daughters of Zeus. In the formula of introduction and in the echo of it at verse 36, the Muses appear in the third person as the object of the song that the speaker—with an inclusive *we*—proposes to begin singing. From this point on, they are the protagonists—continually in the third person—of the narrative that follows this double enunciative intervention. This narrative part is introduced by the usual hymnic relative pronoun (vv. 2 and 36; see also the echoes at vv. 22, 53, 68, etc.). The *evocatio* and the long *epica laus*, which develop into narratives within the narrative for over one hundred verses, lead to a final brief prayer (v. 104). Its formulation takes up the same terms as the prayer in *Hymn* 25, addressed to the Muses and Apollo: in exchange for the pleasure provided to the Muses (*khaírete*), the speaker asks of them a song that is, in turn, charged with erotic charm (*dóte himeróessan aoidén*). As for the theogonic narrative itself, it is launched at verse 105 through an invitation to the Muses to celebrate "the race of immortals who . . ."; its formulation recalls the beginning of an epic poem such as the *Iliad*.[40]

As we shall see in the next chapter, the brief prelude that opens the *Works and Days* starts like a *Homeric Hymn* addressed to Zeus. The speaker speaks to the Muses and asks them to sing Zeus, whose great deeds are introduced by the traditional relative pronoun of hymnic predication. But when the speaker turns to speak directly to Zeus at the end of the ten-verse prelude, as in a *Homeric Hymn*, it is not to ask him to favor his own song. What is asked of Zeus is to redress judgments, and it is the *I* who, as in Solon's *Elegy to the Muses*, takes upon himself the poetic discourse that follows, which is presented to a specific, named addressee. As in Solon's poem, the mode of didactic poetry has taken the place of the epic mode of narration.[41]

By contrast with the proem of the *Theogony*, the second proem of Theognis, the prelude to the elegy of Solon, and the prelude to Hesiod's *Works* are no longer presented as an homage to the divinity.[42] These essential enunciative modifications find their explanation less in the rhythmic form of the poems concerned than in their purpose and their enunciation situation: they are poems addressed not to a god but to a man (even if Perses or Cyrnus can correspond to generic figures), in the context of a banquet and not a large cult occasion, with a pragmatic function of paraenesis unheard of in the *Homeric Hymns* and in the epic poems they introduce. The pragmatic force of the *Hymns*, as prelude songs, is, on the contrary, centered on the relationship between the divinity and the activity of the poet, through the intermediary of an "instance of enunciation" that is endowed with the poetic authority granted by the god who is sung and, consequently, by the song itself.

II

PRELUDE TO A POETRY OF ACTION

The Proem of Hesiod's Works and Days

Since scholars began believing that it represents a decisive stage in the development of Greek poetry, the prologue of the *Theogony* has led its numerous readers to vie with one another in philological prowess and interpretive cunning to provide a reading of it that treats Hesiod as a veritable Heideggerian metaphysician. Owing to the role that the inspiring instance plays in it, this hymn to the Muses of a Homeric type has become the battleground for different modern conceptions of Greek poetic truth.[1] In the race to outdo rival interpretations, commentators have often forgotten the introductory verses of the *Works and Days*. It is probable that Alexandrian philologists had already questioned the authenticity of its first ten verses, but they expressed the same skepticism concerning the long prelude to the *Theogony*.[2] What are we to draw from these doubts if not proof, from the point of view of ancient readings of these texts, of the relative autonomy of these poetic exordia? This provides one more reason for likening them to the *prooímia* constituted by the *Homeric Hymns,* most of which were composed (as we saw in the previous chapter) to introduce epic recitations.[3]

But the *prooímion* is essentially an introduction to a subsequent poem. As such, the proem of the *Works*—like the prelude to the *Theogony,* the introductory verses to the *Iliad,* or those of the *Odyssey*—resonates with the rest of the opus. Though not truly anticipating it, the prelude to the *Works* orients the whole poem with regard to both its thematic content and its modes of enunciation. It is this relationship between the prelude and the rest of the poem that I would like to demonstrate here, on the basis of the distinction between the historical enunciation circumstances and the (textual) "utterance of the enunciation" and through an analysis that is sensitive both to the enunciative markers of speech in action and to the isotopies that develop from the central themes of the poem.[4] Since it is not possible to discuss the whole poetic composition here, this analysis will be limited to noting the occurrences of enunciative positions and the general lines of semantic development defined in the prologue concerning the story of Pandora. This discussion consists of three stages: through an enunciative and comparative analysis of the structure of the prelude and of the profile ascribed to the "instance of enunciation," I (1) determine the isotopies that span the first part of the poem, via the intermediary of enunciative positions, following which I (2) examine the echoes of these within the account of Pandora's creation, in the aim of (3) defining its function.

1. Hymnic Proem or Affirmation of Authority?

Muses from Pieria, who glorify through songs,
come and tell in hymn of Zeus, your father,
on account of whom mortal men are unheard of or famous,
mentioned or unmentioned, according to the will of great Zeus.
Indeed, easily he gives strength and easily he crushes the strong;
easily he diminishes the preeminent and raises the little-known;
easily he straightens out the crooked and withers the haughty,
Zeus who thunders on high and dwells in a lofty palace.
Hearken as you see and hear, and you make judgements straight
    with righteousness,
while I, for my part, would like to tell Perses items of truth.

(Hesiod, *Works and Days* 1–10)

Like its counterpart in the *Theogony*, the prelude of the *Works* presents numerous distinctive structural traits properly belonging to the *Homeric Hymns*. We have seen that, regardless of their length, ten of these compositions offer an appeal to the Muse or Muses analogous to that which opens the *Works;* likewise, in the first three verses of this poem, the Muses are invited to sing in a glorifying voice—perhaps for the narrator (*moi*)—the divinity that is at the center of the hymnic celebration (*evocatio*). In the *Homeric Hymns* as in the Hesiodic poem, the attributes and actions of this divine being are introduced by the "hymnic" relative pronoun that opens the descriptive or narrative part of the proem (*epica laus*). Finally, the description or third-person account concludes, in verse 9 of the *Works* as in the *Homeric Hymns,* with a second-person address no longer to the Muses but to the celebrated god (*preces*). As here, at the end of the Hesiodic prelude, the hymnic narrator often intervenes after this final formula of direct address to the divinity. In the *Homeric Hymns,* to be considered as *prooimia,* the narrator indicates that, for his part, he—in the first person (*egón*)— is going to remember or sing another song.[5]

But comparative analysis is fruitful only when it can become contrastive, as it can in the case of the Hesiodic text. Let us, then, reverse the terms of the comparison and take the structure that the various *Homeric Hymns* have in common as our point of reference in order to contrast it with the structure of the prelude to the *Works.*

1.1. First Isotopies

The qualification of the Muses, which is general in the *Hymns,* is precise in a way that is doubly meaningful in the *Works* (v. 1). Whether or not it constitutes an echo of the prelude to the *Theogony,* the mention of Pieria, the Muses' place of origin, evokes their father, Zeus, through his union with Mnemosyne. Furthermore, the attribution to the Muses of the function of celebrating through song announces the role attributed to Zeus himself in verse 3.[6] For those who are familiar with the *Theogony,* it is not surprising to hear the Muses sing and praise their own father (v. 2).[7] Nonetheless, at verse 3, Zeus himself becomes the foremost holder of this capacity of conferring renown, if not glory.

Despite the practically redundant and quasi-reflexive repetition, however, we witness semantic slippage in the prelude to the *Works.* On the one hand, to the positive celebration of the Muses is opposed the contrasting action of Zeus, which is both positive and negative, as is repeated five times in the verses that follow (3–7). On the other hand, if *phatós* means one "benefiting from *phéme,*" this term has the ethical connotation attached to *phéme* in the *Works*: by following Hesiod's precepts, men can avoid the contrary of *phéme,* a bad reputation. Promoted by the opinion of others, Pheme acquires the permanence that makes it a goddess. While *phéme* depends on respect for the rules of conduct in society, it is sustained through speech—speech that, according to the polarity evoked in the prelude to the *Works,* can be blame or praise, criticism or celebration.[8]

Some scholars have observed the high density of rhetorical figures marking the six verses (3–8) devoted to the enumeration of Zeus' functions: instances of chiasmus (*áphatoi . . . árretoi,* vv. 3–4; *ithúnei . . . kárphei,* v. 7), an etymological figure (*día . . . Diós,* vv. 3–4), assonance (-*toi,* vv. 3–4), phonetic play (*minúthei . . . ithúnei,* vv. 6–7), and rhymes (-*ei,* vv. 5–8). These are signs of the refined elaboration of the Hesiodic composition, which is also marked by the anaphora at the beginning of each of verses 5–7.[9]

If we shift from phenomena marking the forms of expression to the organization of the content, we may notice that, despite the fact that their structure is also polar, verses 5–7 are far from constituting a simple repetition of verses 3–4. At the heart of this ternary group is the verse that is closest to the idea that Zeus intervenes in the function of celebration and criticism, the central verse 6. By according prosperity or, on the contrary, by inflicting failure, Zeus in his omnipotence not only has supreme control over a man's reputation but also can strike down one who benefits from his reputation, since the adjective *arízelos* actually refers to renown, to the fact of being "conspicuous." It is Zeus' lightning that sends forth brilliant (*arízeloi*) fire in the *Iliad*, when the god means to show mortals a sign (*sêma*); but, in the same Homeric poem, this brightness can also be that of Achilles' bronze voice.[10] Through syntactic variation of two forms of the verb *briáo* and through what is perhaps an etymologizing allusion to Briareos, however, the preceding verse of the *Works* (v. 5) emphasizes only the strength granted or, on the contrary, diminished by Zeus. It is animal strength, as attested to by Hesiod's other use of the verb to indicate the joint action of Hecate and Hermes, who are capable of increasing (*aéxein*) the number of cattle by fortifying (*briáei*) or diminishing the amount of livestock; it is also the kind of physical strength that Briareos, along with his hundred-armed brothers, puts in Zeus' service in his struggle against the other Titans so as to achieve brilliant renown through this combat.[11] As for verse 7, it introduces, perhaps through the intermediary of the phonetic "straightening out" of *minúthei* into *ithúnei,* a new semantic value: from the idea of strength, then of the reputation that prosperity confers, we shift to the concept of setting things straight, in the literal and figurative sense—in English as in Greek. Indeed, while the first part of the verse shows Zeus literally straightening out the person or thing that is crooked, the second inflects the god's action toward the figurative meaning: the god withers the one who is arrogant (*agénor*), as old age wrinkles the skin.[12]

Such an action evokes that "archaic" conception of justice which, through the intermediary of the image of the straight[a] line or the level surface, envisions justice as being in balanced conformity with an order guaranteed by the divinity. Whoever transgresses the balance of law and the limits assigned to men infringes on the order established by Zeus, whose elevated position is reaffirmed in verse 8. This reference to Zeus closes upon itself the hymnic development entered into at verse 2. The figurative uses of both the verb *ithúno* and the adjective *skoliós* (v. 7) introduce us at the outset to that very representation of justice. In the *Works*, crooked speeches (*mûthoi skolioí*) fall, as we shall see, in the domain

a. Translator's note: The same French word, *droit,* is rendered both as (the nouns) "justice" and "law" and as (the adjective) "straight" (cp. English "right").

of oath-breaking and *húbris,* which are means that the *kakós* has at his disposal
to impose his excessiveness by force.[13] A little later, in Solon, it is no longer Zeus
but Eunomia who succeeds in straightening out crooked cases (*díkai skoliaí*)
while laying low acts of arrogance. According to Solon, providing a written ver-
sion of rules and laws (*thesmoí*) means reconciling violence and justice; it means
organizing and adapting the judicial imperative in order to make it "direct" for
everyone (*eutheîan eis hékaston harmósas díken*), whether *kakós* or *agathós,* "bad"
or "good."[14]

But verse 9 leaves no room for doubt about this issue: the straightening out
(*íthune*) of the rules of justice by the prescribed norm, by "balance," is in Zeus'
power. In semantic terms, it emerges that the isotopy of celebration and criti-
cism centered on vocal power, which was first evoked through the invocation
to the Muses at the beginning of the prelude, is also realized in the first part of
the description of Zeus' functions. A new isotopy is defined, however, in the
accumulation of contrasting statements in verses 5–7, namely that of the
restoration of justice. This latter isotopy is implicated in the legal sphere in verse
9, through the use of the terms *díke* and *thémistes* (we shift from the rectification
of individual cases to the prescription of the norm allowing good administra-
tion of customary law), but also through the enunciative procedure of the direct
address to Zeus. As Émile Benveniste's etymological and comparative analyses
have shown, *díke* can correspond to the notion of a norm that is prescribed and
shown (from the root *★deik-*) through the intermediary of speech. As for *thémis,*
the root *★dhe* (underlying *títhemi*) refers this concept to the idea of institutional
foundation and legal disposition; *thémistes,* as prescriptions concerning what is
licit, designate legal decisions.[15] In the text of Hesiod, the isotopy of the admin-
istration of justice is thus developed on the basis of the theme of legality.

1.2. Enunciative Interventions

The structure of the proem as it appears in the *Homeric Hymns* generates the
expectation of seeing a transition at the end of the composition from descrip-
tive and narrative utterances in the third person praising the qualities of the cel-
ebrated divinity to a direct address expressed in the second person. But in the
Works, the general formula (*khaîre*) that usually concludes the proem by invit-
ing the god to take pleasure in the song is replaced by the *klûthi* demanding the
god's direct and immediate intervention: the hymn-proem is transformed into
a cletic hymn, if not a cult hymn, through a progression that is accentuated by
the presence of the forms *Zeús, klûthi,* and *túne* at the beginning of each of verses
8–10.[16] It is thus Zeus, in this introductory prayer, who has supreme control
over the kind of justice (*díkê*) that can be pronounced in the correct manner

(*ithúntata*) when a dispute (*neîkos;* what Louis Gernet would call a "trial") arises between two men in the middle of the assembly over the settling of a debt; Zeus controls the verdicts capable of restoring (*itheîa*) justice (*dikázein*) in a contention over the prizes awarded following a chariot race; he keeps an eye on the crooked judgments (*skoliaì thémistes*) that men can formulate with violence (*bíei*) while gathered in the agora, casting aside the established norm and justice (*díke*) without regard for the control exercised by the gods, in which case Zeus intervenes in order to ruin (*minúthei*) men's works (*érga*). In these three passages of the *Iliad,* the straight or crooked line imposed on the juridical decision depends on man and his speech; if Zeus intervenes at all, it is only to warrant the authority of this speech. The prescribed law—in other words, that which is licit (*thémis*)—is, for Hesiod, attached to speech, to the verdicts pronounced in each particular case; it does not yet reside in a written law code, which would be an intermediary between Zeus and what is said by men, a straight authority to which everyone can refer.[17]

But the isotopy of rebalancing justice, which appears throughout Hesiod's poem, does not entirely take the place of the isotopy of celebration (and blame). Through the contrastive juxtaposition of the forms *túne* and *egó,* the speaker-narrator takes responsibility for this isotopy in the song: to you, Zeus, belongs the function of straightening out verdicts in the service of justice; to me, the speaker, belongs (in an attenuated form) the speech initially attributed to the Muses. And there appears a new addressee or narratee: it is no longer the Muses, as at the beginning of the poem, but Perses, to whom the poetic speech is addressed in the second person starting from verse 27. In speaking to Perses, the speaker-narrator takes over from the Muses the function of the proclaiming poetic voice, though with an authority that is still cautiously affirmed (*ke muthesaímen,* v. 10, in the optative). The prelude thus concludes the way it began, with a transition from an enunciative mode characteristic of the *Homeric Hymns* to a mode properly belonging to so-called "lyric" poetry (which I prefer to call *melic*). At the beginning of the prelude, the adverb *deûte* referred simply to the *here* of the enunciation; at its close, the address first to the Muses, then to Zeus, gives way, in the *nunc* (the near future) of the enunciation's utterance, to the address to a narratee who is named and discursively situated opposite the *I* of the narrator-speaker; like Polycrates for Ibycus, Atthis in the poems of Sappho, and above all Cyrnus in Theognis' sympotic verses, Perses as addressee is a "poetic persona" before possibly corresponding to a "real person."[18]

What to say of the poet's concluding promise to provide true speech, given the innumerable attempts that have been made to provide an exegesis of the analogous promise made by the Muses themselves within the prologue of the *Theogony?* Is the substitution of *etétuma* ("reality") for the *alethéa* ("truth") from the Homeric formula *alethéa muthésasthai* used (as a *varia lectio*) in the *Theogony* significant? On the basis of this, should we contrast the content of the *Theogony* with the object of the *Works?* Does the *Works* aim at complementarity with the past and future that the poet, inspired by the Muses, speaks of in the *Theogony* (in terms of eternal existence), by focusing on the missing term, *tà eónta,* that which exists, the *hic et nunc?* Only the development over the course of the composition of the isotopies and the enunciative positions defined in the prelude will allow us to sketch out a prudent response concerning the authority attributed to a poetic "instance of enunciation" claiming to draw on the juridical authority of Zeus.[19]

2. Work, Law, and Speech

After the prelude, the introduction proper to the *Works* breaks down into two parts of practically equal length.

> So, there is not one kind of Strife on earth;
> there are two. Seeing the first, one would praise her,
> but the second is blameworthy. Their souls are opposed.
> Indeed, one fosters evil war and battle, the wretch!
> No mortal likes that one, but, under compulsion
> by the will of the gods, men pay homage to the Strife that is onerous.
> The other is the one that somber night gave birth to first
> and that the high-seated son of Cronos, who dwells in the firmament,
> set in the earth's roots, a much better thing for men.
> She stirs even the indolent to work,
> for, when a man lacking work looks upon another man,
> a rich one who hastens to plow and plant
> and put his house in good order, neighbor envies neighbor
> as he hastens after wealth. This Strife is good for mortals.
> Potter holds a grudge against potter and craftsman against craftsman,
> beggar is jealous of beggar and bard of bard.
>
> (vv. 11–26)

As for you, Perses, set these things in your heart,
and do not let the trouble-loving Strife keep your heart from work
while you watch the disputes of the agora as a bystander,
for disputes and agoras are of little concern
for a man who does not have laid away in store plentiful food,
the ripe harvest that the earth bears, Demeter's grain.
Wait until you have plenty of that before raising disputes and combat

over another man's property. You will never get a second opportunity
to act like this; rather, let us settle our dispute on the spot
with straight judgments, the kind that, coming from Zeus, are best.
Indeed, we divided up our inheritance, and you kept snatching and carrying
off
much extra, paying great tribute to kings,
gift gobblers who were willing to render this kind of judgment.
Fools! They do not know how much more the half is worth than the whole,
nor how much wealth there is in mallow and asphodel.

(vv. 27–41)

The first, gnomic part of this poetic introduction presents a general truth in a mode of assertion; that truth is then applied to the specific case disclosed in the second part.[20] This truthful assertion concerns the earth inhabited by mortal men; it introduces a third isotopy: no longer the administration of justice, but agricultural production centered on work that brings prosperity. Nonetheless, there are many semantic links with the lines of development traced in the prelude.

2.1. The Two Erides: Praise and Blame

Limiting ourselves to the phenomena of the enunciation, we could begin by advancing the hypothesis that the general truth in the introductory section quoted here corresponds to the *etétuma* that the speaker-narrator announces he will communicate in verse 10. We could find in this correspondence confirmation of the meaning "factual reality" attributed to the term *etétuma,* though we must also recognize that the genealogy of the good Eris (vv. 17–19) causes the gnomic assertion to slide toward narration. Does this serve to announce the great "myths" narrated from verse 42 on? The brief genealogical account makes it possible, at any rate, to reaffirm the instituting power of Zeus within the sharp contrast between the world above and that of mortals. If there is in fact a relationship with the end of the prelude, the narrator would be asserting as his own the distinction between bad Eris and good Eris, between Dispute and Emulation. This stands in contrast to the *Theogony,* which is sung by the Muses and knows only of the Eris that is at the heart of violence, Eris the hateful.[21]

There might be an echo of this taking up of the discourse by the speaker-narrator in the inclusion, at the end of the first part of the poem, of the bard's activity in the productive emulation that spurs artisans. The play with assonance in the two concluding verses of this passage (25–26), through a dual process of phonic differentiation and semantic dynamization, furthermore highlights somewhat the poet's activity among the enumerated crafts.[22]

However that may be, let us return to the beginning of the first part of the introduction. The assertion concerning the existence of two Erides is immediately linked to the two opposing modes of poetic discourse in ancient Greece. If one of the Erides can be praised, the other must be blamed (vv. 12–13). The introduction of the *épainos–mômos* (praise–blame) polarity as a way of speaking of Eris echoes the function of Zeus in relation to the *phéme* of mortals. This discursive process thus picks up on the isotopy of celebration and criticism but combines it with the isotopy introduced by the double figure of Eris: the "economic" production of prosperity and its negative pole, destructive warfare. This isotopy focused on the theme of speech thus qualifies the assertion about emulation and dissension by basing it on one of the foundations of "archaic" poetics. Good emulation and its corollary, productive work, are henceforth dependent on poetic speech: a celebratory voice that can also shift to criticism and blame, a voice marked by the presence of the speaker-narrator who strongly affirms his function before the Muses and Zeus.[23]

In the conclusion to the passage concerning the Erides, the use of the deictic *héde* may well refer to the extradiscursive context of the enunciation: beyond the semio-narrative and intradiscursive position of the speaker-narrator, the enunciator-poet expresses support for the good Eris, for the Eris that is favorable to mortals (v. 24). This deictic form pointing to the present situation heralds, in any case, the direct address to Perses and the transition from gnomic assertion to exhortation concerning a particular case.

2.2. The Poem as Judgment

The various isotopies and enunciative indicators noted thus far come together in the second part of the introductory passage devoted to the Erides.

First, the isotopy of the administration of law is given new specificity. Here it is through straight judgments (*itheíeisi díkeis,* v. 36) inspired by Zeus that an arrangement, a settlement (*diakrinómetha,* v. 35) for a dispute (*neîkos*) is found. Through the opposition represented in the doubling of Eris, however, there are good and bad conflicts; alongside positive Emulation arise the juridical disputes of the *agora* which, fomented by the Eris that relishes calamity, distract men from productive work and the prosperity protected by Demeter. The isotopy of the administration of *díke* and that of agricultural production (at v. 28, *érgon*) are thus combined: in wanting to gain more to another's detriment, one wastes time in litigation that would be better devoted to one's own *bíos,* to the production of one's own resources. It is in this sense that "the half is worth more than the whole" (v. 40). The evocation of productive work presupposes equitable administration of justice. Since these two complementary activities also have a negative aspect, the dividing up of disputed property and the straightening out of judgments are ultimately based on speech, within the poetic dialectic between *épainos* and *mômos,* praise and blame.

It is for this reason that, in the new apostrophe to Perses that follows the narrative of the long "myths," *díke* can be opposed to *húbris,* in the sense of a violent overstepping of the limits (vv. 213–24), and crooked judgments (*skoliaì díkai,* vv. 219 and 221) can be associated with men who are "gift gobblers." By contrast, upon straight verdicts (*díkai ítheiai,* vv. 225–26) depend the prosperity and flourishing of a whole civic community, free from the repressive interventions of Zeus.[24] This argumentative development concerning "justice" closes upon itself, since, at its conclusion, justice and prosperity appear as corollaries (vv. 279–85) in speech: to the one who pronounces just judgments, Zeus grants *ólbos*—both to him and to his progeny—while the god lets languish the descendants of the man who manifests scorn for what is right through deceitful declarations. The three isotopies running through the poem's introduction come together here, as they are narratively subordinated to the polar function attributed to Zeus in the prelude itself.[25]

With regard to the enunciative markers spread throughout the second part of this double poetic introduction, they cause the isotopies that have been mentioned to shift from a general and prudent gnomic assertion (*ken epainéseie,* with an implied *tis,* v. 12: "one could praise") to the urgent appeal called for by the specific case; the markers of the second-person address multiply starting at verse 27 (*you* forms and the imperative; *I* and the optative mood expressing a wish at v. 28; second person and the potential optative at v. 33; *soi* at v. 34; second-person form at v. 38): we see a shift from the expression of a *one*-validity to an *I*-truth, from *épainos* (praise) to paraenesis.[26] The particular case introduced in these verses corresponds to a *neîkos,* a dispute (vv. 29, 30, 33, and 35). In this conflict, the *we* forms used at verses 35 and 37 embrace the narrator and the narratee, while at the same time giving content to the dispute: the case that needs to be settled through straight judgments inspired by Zeus (vv. 35–36) concerns the dividing up of an estate. The authority of the speaker-narrator, at first expressed in the potential optative, progressively affirms itself as the extradiscursive reference is specified. The matter that needs to be resolved is now "this" actual and particular case (*ténde díken,* v. 39), which it is imperative that "we resolve, you and I (*diakrinómetha,* v. 35), here (*aûthi,* where we are for some time)"; "and you will not have a second opportunity to act like this (*hôde*)." The deictic *ténde,* supported by the use of the subjunctive and *aûthi,* undoubtedly refers to the enunciation situation. Or, more subtly, this operator for directly showing may just as well refer intradiscursively to the situation expressed in the discourse (through a process of "referentialization") as to the external, extradiscursive circumstances of its communication (through a process of "referenciation").[27]

We observe an analogous oscillation between a particular concrete case and a general fictional situation in the passage that concludes the section about justice, which is once again generalizing. From the starting point of the poor administration of justice that the poem describes (*táde, ténde díken* at vv. 268–69; see also v. 249; internal referentialization), the strong enunciative intervention of the *I* into the present of the poem's enunciation (*nûn dè egó*, v. 270), then the addressing of Perses (vv. 274–75) causes us to shift from the intradiscursive to the extradiscursive: we shift to "this" order, "this" mode of life (*tónde nómon*, v. 276), which is granted by Zeus and distinguishes us—through the gift of law—from animals. This is the present order, celebrated in the poem but existing outside of it.

> But, now, may I no longer be just among men, myself
> and my son, too, since it is bad to be a just man
> if the less just man will get the *better* judgement.
> But cunning Zeus, I reckon will not yet bring *that* to pass.
> As for you, Perses, lodge these things in your heart,
> and heed justice, leaving off altogether from thinking about violence.
> Indeed, this is the law that the son of Zeus has prescribed for men:
> it is for fish and beasts and winged birds
> to devour one another, since there is no justice among them,
> but to mortals he gave justice, which is the best of things
> by far; for, if someone knows what is just and is willing
> to utter it, perspicacious Zeus grants him wealth.

(vv. 270–81)

Insofar as the two-part introductory section of the *Works* presents a strong relationship between the intra- and extradiscursive levels, the *aûthi* in the second half of this introduction (v. 35) might well be picking up on the *deûte* opening the prelude to the poem. Henceforth, the appeal to Perses to resolve here and now the conflict between him and the narrator is substituted in place of the appeal to the Muses, then to Zeus. Could the straight judgment capable of resolving the dispute be so different from the poem itself, this poem that comprises judgments that the narrator's *I* takes up as his own and pronounces, this true poem that stands as a substitute for the customary law set straight by Zeus (v. 9) in order to settle (*diakrinómetha*) the particular case? The contrast that I noted at the end of the prelude between *toi* (Zeus) and *moi* (the poet) is actually only one of complementarity. The poetic speech of the speaker-narrator has become, through the use of deictics and the transition from the intra- to the extradiscursive, that of the enunciator, that of the poet opposing his brother, Perses.

The poet's authoritative speech is all the better metamorphosed into a conciliatory judgment for the fact that it must explicitly take the place of the verdict desired by the "gift-gobbling" kings (v. 39; see also vv. 221 and 264), these kings to whom the poetic speech is also addressed (vv. 202, 248 and 236), who warp judgments (*parklínosi díkas*) by pronouncing crooked words (*skoliôs enépontes,* v. 262), who are entreated to forget their crooked verdicts (*skoliaì díkai,* v. 264) and straighten out their speeches (*ithúnete múthous,* v. 263).[28] This metamorphosis is made that much easier by the fact that, from Menelaus in the *Iliad* to Andocides in early-fourth-century Athens, it is the injured party that directly and orally takes up his own defense in ancient Greece. In Hesiod's poem, it is true at least until verse 285, where the isotopy of the administration of the law practically disappears to allow that of productive work (once the conflict has been settled?) to be developed, that the poem is a straight judgment.[29] Poetic speech, in its celebratory function, is able to transform the particular case into a general one and to make of it a paradigm whose sphere of application can extend beyond the limits of the *polis*. From the enunciative point of view, the progressive disappearance of Perses from the narratee position to open the way for a general *you* highlights this shift from external to internal reference, from the real communication situation to generic circumstances constructed within the poem itself. Through the shift from the extra- to the intradiscursive, this process of fictionalization makes it possible for the poem, which is placed under the authority of Zeus through the intermediary of the poet's voice, to address a public that ultimately encompasses not just kings but the whole civic community.

It is worth remembering that, in the *Theogony,* it is thanks to his fostering by the Muses, his inspiration from Calliope, the Muse of the Beautiful Voice, and his descent from Zeus that the king decides through sweet speech what is authorized, what is legal, in straight judgments (*diakrínonta thémistas itheíeisi díkeisi*). Assuming functions analogous to those of the poet, the inspired king thus calms the conflicts (*neíkos*) within the *polis*.[30]

3. Incomplete and Performative Narratives

Three narratives included in the "judiciary" section of the *Works* follow the long introductory part: the creation of Pandora, the "myth of races," and the fable of the nightingale and the hawk. They are integrated into the line of argument through strong enunciative markers and interventions: the double *gár* in the story of Pandora (vv. 42–43), the intervention of the *I* with an appeal directed to the narratee in the *lógos* about the different ages (vv. 106–8),[31] the decision of the *I* to address the *aînos* of the hawk and the nightingale to the kings now (*nûn,* v. 202). This discursive gesture is repeated, at the end of the three successive stories, through the addressing of judgments concerning justice and its violation directly to Perses (*su ákoue*, v. 213). These stories should be considered arguments in the long harangue pronounced by Hesiod: explanatory in character, all three of them become *aînoi* of sorts; they serve the paraenesis that is henceforth linked with an extradiscursive situation.[32] Accordingly, they are "myths" only insofar as we understand this notion according to the ancient meaning of the term *mûthos*, discourse that sometimes takes a narrative form and always has a strongly argumentative and pragmatic dimension.

3.1. The Reinterpretation of the Pandora Story

I shall limit myself here to providing the outlines of a demonstration about the narrative as argument based solely on the story of the creation of Pandora, since the extension of the pragmatic study to include the three narratives would require a whole separate chapter. By comparing and contrasting the Pandora story in the *Works* to the treatment of it in the *Theogony*, we shall see that certain irreducible differences exist between the two Hesiodic versions of the episode.[33] In the absence of a study taking into consideration the values traditionally attributed to the figure of Pandora outside of Hesiod's texts and allowing a broader comparative analysis, the divergences in the discursive line adopted in each of the two versions will make it possible to determine the distinct orientation that the story takes in the *Works*. The differences between the two Hesiodic treatments are, in brief, as follows:

• As noted, the story of the giving of Pandora to mankind opens with a double *gár* (vv. 42–43). The first *gár* links the situation of conflict mentioned in the preceding verses to the observation that the gods keep life resources (*bíos*) hidden from men,[34] while the second *gár* helps to account for the current attitude on the part of the gods (indicated by *ékhousi*, followed by the participle) by evoking the situation that would exist without this dissimulation (vv. 43–46, with corresponding verbs in the potential optative); in this latter situation, there would be no need for work to produce food (the term *érgon* appears four times in these four verses). The narrative proper does not begin until verse 47, where the verb *krúpto* ("hide") is repeated in the aorist indicative, the tense of narration; now the verbal action has a subject: Zeus.

For the gods keep hidden the food that is for men.
Indeed, otherwise you would easily work for one day to produce
enough to feed yourself for a year without having to work.
Straightaway, you would put the rudder away over the smoke,
and gone would be the work of oxen and mules!

But Zeus, seething with rage in his heart, hid it
because Prometheus of the crooked cunning deceived him.
So, because of that, Zeus plotted dreadful sorrows for men:
he hid fire. But the noble son of Iapetus stole it
back for men from cunning Zeus
by hiding it in the hollow of a fennel-stalk from Zeus who delights in thunder.

(vv. 42–52)

While establishing a strong relationship between the activity of the gods (v. 42) and that of Zeus, the verb *krúpto* and the act of concealment that it expresses are left without an object in verse 47. That object is not provided until verse 50, where *krúpse* is repeated: it is no longer *bíos,* as at the beginning of the story, but fire. Why this shift? To introduce as the proper explanation for the initial and present attitude of the gods the story of Prometheus in his dealings with Zeus, and not the story we expect, that concerning the hiding of *bíos.* The beginning of the story is actually quite allusive, and the elements provided barely allow us to follow the logic of the action: Prometheus deceives Zeus, Zeus gets angry and hides fire from men, Prometheus steals it for men, Zeus promises to give a baneful gift to Prometheus and mankind in compensation for the fire (vv. 48–58), that gift being Pandora (vv. 59–105). It is obviously not primordial "sacrifice" that is at issue here. In actuality, in contrast to the narrative of the *Theogony,* the story told in the *Works* turns out to revolve entirely around the creation of Pandora. Conversely, the account in the theogonic poem addresses the fate of Prometheus, with which it furthermore concludes; although the *Theogony* refers to the crafty gift of the girl, this version of the story does not name her Pandora![35] The anaphoric repetition of *krúpsantes* (v. 42) twice through *(é)krupse* (vv. 47 and 50) in the *Works* substitutes a situation of production without work akin to the Golden Age in place of the primal state of conviviality between men and gods found in the *Theogony;* but, through the surreptitious transition from *bíos* to fire and the brief (to say the least) mention of Prometheus, it also contributes to focusing the version of the narrative in the *Works* on the figure of Pandora.[36]

• The summary of the Prometheus story is present only in order to evoke the imbalance (the Titan's double ruse) that can introduce the narrative of the creation of Pandora. From a semantic point of view, the existence of Pandora is directly linked, in the *Works,* to the gods' hiding of *bíos,* which corresponds here to a primary abundance independent of any kind of productive labor.[37]

• Before even being named, Pandora is defined in all her duplicity as an inside and outside: an evil that charms and is embraced (vv. 57–58), a *méga pêma* (v. 56), like Helen in the *Iliad,* with her appearance of a wife having a lovely form (*eueidés*).[38] As for the outside, Pandora is adorned with all of the enticements of Aphrodite; decked out in finery inspiring erotic desire, she changes from a girl (*parthénos*, vv. 63 and 71) to a woman (*guné*, v. 80; cf. v. 94). On the inside, she harbors a human voice; it is on this verbal ability that Pandora's predisposition toward perfidy and dissimulation (vv. 67 and 78) depends.[39] The opposition between divine appearance and mortal reality is thus focused on the deceiving voice.

• The transformation of Pandora from a young girl into an adult woman is carried out not by her going through the stage of being a young bride, as in the *Theogony*, but by Hermes' naming of her (vv. 80–82). Through morphological-semantic play, but perhaps also by the use of the deictic indicating proximity, *ténde*, this etymologizing naming refers doubly to the story's introduction: the gift of Pandora compensates the hiding of *bíos* that the gods have taken upon themselves, and the isotopy of work to produce food is picked back up by the way in which men are qualified (v. 82), as "grain eaters."[40] The ring structure, which is created on both the syntactic and semantic levels, highlights the instrumental character of the Prometheus story in the *Works*.

• The brief episode about the transmission of Pandora to man through the two intermediaries, Hermes and Epimetheus (vv. 83–89), is centered on both the negative quality of the gift of Zeus—a *kakón*—and the reaction of Epimetheus, who is likened to a mortal and who, like a mortal, allows himself to be deceived despite the warning expressed by his brother Prometheus. According to the etymology of his name, accented by the chiasmus of verses 85–86, *Epimetheùs ephrásato—éeipe Prometheús*, the brother of the Forethoughtful One does not understand (*enóese*) until the damage has already been done. As the son of Iapetus, Epimetheus is, admittedly, mentioned in the *Theogony*, where the etymology of his name is rendered explicit in order to be contrasted with that of Prometheus, and where he is presented as "a bane for men, who eat grain"; but he has no involvement whatsoever in the theft of fire and the fabrication of Pandora.[41]

• The final episode of the Pandora story (vv. 90–105) is not at all necessary from the perspective of narrative logic. It is simply an explanation of the *kakón* that holds sway among mortals since the giving of Pandora, which was provoked by Prometheus' ruse and Zeus' rage. Moreover, in narrative terms, this final act is connected not to the Prometheus story but to the primal state without work that reigned before the gods' hiding of *bíos*. Verses 90–93 or 94 pick up on the idea expressed in verses 43–46, but evoke its negative side: any reference to work also entails *pónos* and hardships. This passage further elucidates that idea by linking illness and mortality with toil and misfortune.[42] The repetition of analogous terms in verses 113–14, in the middle of the description of the golden "race," shows (as at the beginning of the narrative) that the mortal condition is the antithesis of the Golden Age.

• The brief account of the opening of the jar (vv. 94–105) simply provides the narrative and genetic reason for this sentencing of men to work and reorients it toward the notion of mortality. At the end of this passage, in ring position, we find illnesses and death. They have taken over the quality of spontaneity (*autómatoi*, v. 103), otherwise ascribed to food production close to the Golden Age, and, being deprived of voice by Zeus, they cannot lie like Pandora.[43] This is probably an allusion to the fact that they are ineluctable; in any case, the gnomic utterance concluding the story points in this direction: "thus, there is absolutely no way to escape the mind of Zeus" (v. 105). Whereas, in the *Theogony*, the impossibility of eluding Zeus' will is the moral explicitly drawn from Prometheus' fate (v. 613), the lesson of the story in the *Works* is the omnipresence of afflictions. This reorientation of the gnomic affirmation driving the narrative is homologous to the reorientation of the Prometheus story at its beginning.

3.2. Death and Voice

The etiological character of the Pandora story, in its relationship to the introduction to the *Works,* is no longer contested.[44] But does the narrative develop the isotopy of the administration of law, or that of productive work, or even that of glorifying speech, in an explanatory manner?

We have seen that the account, through its dynamism, and at the cost of some shifts in its narrative logic, takes up the isotopy centered on the theme of *érgon* in order to reorient it toward mortality through a deceptive being endowed with *phoné*. To this extent, the version of the story in the *Works* stands in contrast with the parallel story in the *Theogony,* which, through the transformation of Pandora into a wife, is focused on marriage in its reproductive function and, consequently, its function of guaranteeing a permanence beyond the mortal condition.[45] At the risk of being schematic, to say the least, we may say that the *kakón* of the *Theogony* (despite all) leads to life, while that of the *Works,* in a paradoxical and almost chiastic way in relation to the theme of the *Theogony,* results in death.

And yet ... From a narrative perspective, the Pandora story, which opens with the anger of Zeus and its two effects, the concealment of *bíos* and the hiding of fire, could well conclude with two punishments: the giving of the "beautiful evil" that is Pandora and the diffusion of the inescapable afflictions, which ultimately derive from the will of Zeus. But that would mean leaving aside the survival of Elpis: inside (*éndon*, v. 97) the jar presented as an unbreakable dwelling, she occupies the same spatial position as the lying voice inside the body of the virgin, gift of the gods. But, when she is surrounded by the ills that escaped from the inside of the *píthos*, she assumes within this the inverse semantic position of an evil adorned with the graces of Aphrodite: she is a good surrounded by evils. Using the polar language dear to structuralists, we could say that Elpis represents, as it were, the positive reverse of Pandora. This optimistic attribution of a positive value to Elpis, which is confirmed by the representation of Hope in archaic Greek thought, confers on the story an openness and impetus that extend beyond it and find an echo in the remainder of the poem. Whether we interpret it figuratively as the store of bread allowing man to survive or, more subtly, as man's companion and the ambivalent symbol of the human condition, between beasts and gods, Hope subsists as the only stable point of reference among the afflictions affecting man's destiny at all times and in all places so as to drive him toward death.[46]

The appearance of Elpis at the end of the story prolongs it beyond its narrative sanction. The logical conclusion for the narrative as a whole is actually provided by the poem itself, first in its "judiciary" section (vv. 213–85), then in the complex section with advice about work (starting at v. 286). Indeed, by opposition with mendacious and deceitful speech, not only do straight judgments (vv. 225–26, 230, 263, 280, etc.) ensure the triumph of *díke* over *húbris*, but also, above all, they lead the human community (*pólis*, v. 227) to a prosperity and (agricultural) abundance that evoke those of the Golden Age.[47] Work, however, also ensures the abundance whose corollaries are merit (*aretê*) and repute (*kûdos*, vv. 312–19). While, starting from the theme of speech, the isotopy of celebration is combined in the paraenesis with the isotopy of justice, the isotopy of productive work subsumes the issue of reputation raised in the prelude in connection with the same theme. As for blame, the negative counterpart of the praise isotopy, a figurative and narrative echo of crooked judgments (vv. 219, 221, 250, 258, 262, 264; cf. 194) is found in the lying voice of Pandora. Only illnesses are without voice. Thus, following the etiological story about Pandora, man proves to be fundamentally mortal, and, if a single bad man (*kakós*) plots overbearing acts (*atásthala*), Zeus intervenes by sending famine and epidemics—the first corresponding to the impossibility of working, the second to the negation of law. The consequence: death, a *méga pêma* (v. 242) that can take various forms (sterility, ruin of the house or the city, warfare on land or sea) but no longer adopts the anthropomorphic figure of Pandora.

Ultimately, with Elpis as the only fixed reference among the deadly afflictions prowling about without any voice, the straight judgment has the possibility, within the limits assigned to mortal man, of rectifying the negative effects of Pandora's deceptive voice. The straight judgment points to the speech of the narrator, and probably to that of the poet. Although it is not necessary from the perspective of narrative logic, the Epimetheus episode nonetheless shows what happens when one does not comprehend (*oud' ephrásato*, v. 86) advice that has been transmitted by word (*éeipe*) and only recognizes its meaning (*enóese,* v. 89) once the harm has already been done. Beginning with the desire expressed in the prelude to tell Perses true things (*etétuma,* v. 10), all of the apostrophes to the poem's narratee are precisely accompanied by an appeal to his attention and intelligence (vv. 27, 107, 213, 274, etc.); the same is true when the kings take the brother's place in this narratee position (vv. 202 and 248).[48] Through straight speech, only the poet's song can—within the limits of the order prescribed by Zeus—effect the reinstatement of a truth guaranteed by the divinity in opposition to the lying voice introduced through Pandora.

4. Sanction in the Paraenesis

By way of its narrative opening onto the present situation, the "mythic" story guarantees the performative aspect of the poem itself; it is poetic speech that sanctions the *mûthos,* which is also a *lógos* (v. 106), and ensures its completion. It would be possible to carry out the same demonstration for the story about the "ages," explaining in this way the projection of the iron *génos* into a prophesied catastrophic future and so getting around the tour de force of the ternary structural interpretation. It is worth noting here that, with the approach of the iron generation, the narrative is interrupted by a strong enunciative intervention (*egó,* at v. 174), which establishes as concurrent the time of the story and that of the enunciation (*nûn,* v. 176) before projecting it into a potential future.[49] Introduced as confirmation of the Pandora story, the succession of "races" leads to a state of raw violence dominated by crooked speeches (v. 194): if Honor and Reproof abandon the human world, there will no longer be any space for reputation, there will no longer be any place for the narrator, there will no longer be any defense against evil (*kakoû alké,* v. 201) and, consequently, against death. The only hope for avoiding this potential state of affairs is the poet's speech.

It is likewise impossible to grasp the lesson of the fable of the hawk and the nightingale if one does not understand that its narrative logic leads up to the maxims that constitute a follow-up to it.

Now I will tell a fable to kings who themselves have understanding.
A hawk spoke these words to a nightingale with dappled neck
while carrying her off high up in the clouds having snatched her with his
  talons—
she, pierced by his hooked talons, cried
pitifully, but he spoke to her sternly:
"Gracious, why this outcry? One much stronger now holds you.
You will be borne wherever *I* carry you, singer though you be;

I will make a meal of you, if I please, or let you go.
Whoever wants to withstand one who is stronger is out of his mind:
he is deprived of victory and suffers pains in addition to humiliation."
So said the swiftly flying hawk, the broad-winged bird.
But you, Perses, listen to what is right and do not favor violence,
since violence is bad for a lowly man.

(vv. 202–14)

Prisoner of the powerful talons of the hawk-king, the nightingale-bard (v. 208) is able to free no more than its voice, which it regains at verse 213.[50] The discourse, which is marked by a strong enunciative intervention, leaves off from the mode of narration to turn to that of gnomic exposition. In this new address to Perses, the warnings about the administration of justice are expressed in the register of the gnomic truth to broaden it to include men in general (v. 220) and the civic community (v. 222): a gnomic sanction for the three incomplete stories, which introduce the sequence of moral maxims through paradigmatic figures from legend and give color to this sequence through the intervention of anthropomorphic figures such as Oath, Law, Peace, and, above all, Zeus.

Hope is ultimately to be found, perhaps, in the narrator's voice and Hesiod's poem, in the effort to rectify acts that run counter to the order desired and imposed by Zeus. The narration of the *Theogony* leads to the deployment of a permanent and transcendent order; the didactic paraenesis of the *Works,* through the effects of a poetic authority with a direct relationship to Zeus, the master of justice, aims at better managing the condition of mortal man in its finitude.

III

FICTION AS NARRATIVE ARGUMENTATION

Sappho and Helen

I.   Some claim that it is a group of horsemen, others an army of foot
       soldiers,
    still others a fleet of ships that is the most beautiful thing
    on the black earth, but I say
    it is whatever one loves.

II. 5   It is perfectly easy to make this apparent
    to everyone. Indeed, Helen, who far surpassed
    humans in beauty, left
    the best of husbands

III.   behind and embarked on a ship for Troy
  10 without any regard whatsoever for her daughter,
    or her dear parents. But it is [Aphrodite]
    who led her astray . . .

IV.   . . . .
  15 [Helen] just evoked the memory of Anactoria,
    though absent.

V.   I would rather see her charming step
    and the luminous gleam of her face
    than Lydian chariots and foot soldiers
  20 under arms.

(Sappho fr. 16 Voigt)

In Mytilene during the sixth century B.C., singing a poetic form and using arguments to make a demonstration can apparently be combined in perfect accord. But, without justifying the countless interpretations of these strophes, the development of the argument in this lacunose poem is perhaps not as clear as the narrator-*I* seems to want to have his or her narratee believe at the beginning of the second strophe. This speaker-narrator, in the position and role of "instance of enunciation," has generally been identified as Sappho, the uncontested empirical author of these endearing verses. Yet (to leave aside the uncertainties caused by the lacunae in a restored text from a fragmentary papyrus), Sappho adopts an unusual approach here: she combines several of the forms that "archaic" Greek argumentation and reasoning can take in order to conduct her demonstration.

1. Whatever One Loves

The first strophe associates the two means that the "archaic" poet chooses to employ when wishing to formulate a personal view while diverging from received or previously expressed opinions. From a purely formal standpoint, it begins with the use of contrastive parataxis that the philological tradition designates with the German form, *Priamel,* of the medieval term *preambulum:* an enumeration, often in negative form, of a series of elements wherein the speaker-narrator positively affirms the last by contrast with the others, which are henceforth left aside. The closest parallel to Sappho's "priamel" is from Bacchylides.[1] The poet from Ceos proceeds, however, in an inverse manner to Sappho: Bacchylides first evokes the particular situation that is subsequently justified through a universal argument, while Sappho (as we shall see) begins by establishing the general framework, then inserts a specific situation into it. Bacchylides makes an argument in order to set up the warning addressed by Apollo to Admetus about the ephemeral condition of mortal mankind:

> What I say is comprehensible for one with wits.
> The deep firmament is incorruptible,
> the water of the sea does not rot, and gold is a delight;
> but it is not permitted for a man to doff graying
> old age and get back blossoming youth.

> (Bacchylides 3.85–90)

In the first strophe of the poem by Sappho, the affirmation through contrast made possible by the *preambulum* form is put to the service of a second topos from "archaic" Greek poetics: literary play with definitions, particularly to designate what corresponds to the highest value. Identifying what is most precious, most fortunate, or most beautiful constitutes a recurrent line of intellectual and poetic inquiry. This kind of play with definitions is often performed in the context of the symposium. It is one of the manifestations of the agonistic and playful aspect of that type of occasion. We find echoes of this kind of query in literature about legendary biographies, particularly that concerning the Seven Sages. One may recall the question that Solon poses to Croesus in the *lógos* reported by Herodotus. Contrary to the Lydian king's expectations, the happiest man (*olbió-tatos*) is not the one who is the richest. Henceforth eliminated from the competition, Croesus must yield the status that he thought he held by virtue of his prosperity to Tellus, a simple citizen. This Athenian got as his lot children endowed with the highest qualities before meeting the most beautiful death for which a man could wish: falling on the battlefield in the service of the city and, consequently, earning national honors. After Tellus, Solon mentions Cleobis and Biton, who died while replacing the oxen that were to draw the cart of their mother, the priestess, to the Temple of Hera.[2] In the anecdote reported by Herodotus, legendary examples serve directly as predicates for the concept to be defined—predicates that (as we shall see) correspond to an instrumental semio-narrative notion.

Although it starts with the same topos of defining a superlative value, the poem of Sappho only partially adopts the model used in the exemplary anecdote reported by Herodotus. Initially, the predicate of that which is to be defined is also expressed in an assertion. The poetess does not immediately mention, however, the example that is able to give the concept under question its content. *Tò kálliston,* the most beautiful thing, is first defined in an assertion formulated in general terms: "it is whatever one loves." These terms are doubly undetermined. The grammatical subject of the verb "love" corresponds to the indefinite pronoun *tis,* "one"; its object is introduced by the indefinite relative pronoun in the neuter. As in two other fragments of Sappho, this relative pronoun can only have the general meaning of "that which, whatever it be."[3] The refusal to give specific valences to the verb *ératai* focuses all attention on the state this term denotes: loving; a loving relationship between the most beautiful thing, whatever its nature may be, and a grammatical subject, whatever its identity may be.

To take up one of the models of formal expression from semio-narrative grammar, according to which the narrative proposition is conceived as a predicative relationship (P) between a semio-narrative Subject (S_1) and an Antisubject (S_2), the definition proposed by the speaker-narrator would make the *kálliston* a state of love (*ératai*) that creates a relationship between S_2 (*hóti*) and S_1 (*tis*).[4]

Through the intermediary of the rhetorical forms, that of the *preambulum* followed by that of the definition, the semio-narrative Antisubject (S_2) in which beauty is incarnated is thus firmly attached to the feeling designated by the verb *eráo,* "love" (P). This discursive "subject" can only be the "object" of the feeling of love. Accordingly, whatever the semio–narrative Subject (S_1), this love, as a Predicate, cannot apply to a troop of horsemen, nor an army of foot soldiers, nor a fleet of warships: the argumentative figure of preterition takes on its full force here.[5] The procedures and words used by the enunciative instance, which technical prudence requires us (without disrespect to Sappho) to call the speaker-narrator, could not be more transparent: for the woman or man who takes responsibility for the enunciation of the poem, the most beautiful thing is that which arouses in the anthropomorphic subject, whoever it be, the feeling of love.

We should not expect to find in such a definition the subtleties of a relativist argument (seeing in it sophism before its time); the definition is harmoniously integrated into what is now widely recognized as the Greek conception of love as an external force that emanates from the love object toward the lover, who is subjugated by it.[6]

2. Helen, the Most Beautiful of Mortals

Any such definition in abstract terms requires an illustration. In "archaic" Greek poetry, furthermore, the use of examples is among the very procedures for building an argument. Neither Paris nor Cassander nor any of the other sons of Priam, nor even the Achaian heroes of the Trojan War—whether it be swift-footed Achilles or Ajax, Telamon's valiant son—could exemplify the beauty of Polycrates as only Troilus, the most attractive, can; it is in these terms that Ibycus, a slightly younger poet than Sappho, speaks to the young tyrant of Samos, directly combining the *preambulum* form with the heroic or epic example that we consider "mythic."[7]

Sappho is much more explicit. After the preamble, which provides general content for the definition of beauty, the example taken from the heroic past is announced in terms of its very function: that of making the result of the most abstract part of the argument understandable. Once again, the procedure is not unparalleled in Greek lyric poetry; as scholars have noted concerning the cited poem, Bacchylides uses the same terms that Sappho does to effect the (inverse) transition from the exemplary, "mythic" model to the maxim with universal validity.

2.1. Helen Possessed by Love

It is the figure of Helen that is evoked in the second and third strophes of the poem to make it "perfectly easy to grasp" (*pálgchu d'eúmares súneton*) the beauty that the narrator attaches to the rousing of Eros' power in the person who perceives it. Only two elements of the myth of Helen are singled out for use here. The first consists of the (semio-narrative) attribution of a Predicate. Accordingly, it falls within the province of definition: Helen surpasses all other human beings in beauty. The other element belongs to narrative: Helen abandoned her husband to go to Troy, being struck with amnesia about both her daughter and her parents and being led astray by love, or the goddess who incarnates it (there is an unfortunate lacuna in the text here). Exceptional beauty, flight to Troy, abandonment of her husband, forgetting of family ties, under the impulse of a force that is probably animated by Aphrodite: such are the Predicates and the narrative actions attributed to the Subject of the legendary story line told by the author of the demonstration concerning the definition of the most beautiful thing.

A first observation: Sappho gives a remarkable version (to say the least) of the legend about the abduction of Helen by Paris, the direct cause of the Trojan War. To see this, we need only compare Sappho's version to that told by her contemporary and fellow Lesbian, Alcaeus, who speaks of Helen, the source of bitter ills for Priam and his children; Helen who, driven crazy by desire for Paris, follows the handsome Trojan across the sea, abandoning at home her daughter and her husband's bed; Helen, struck with love by Aphrodite, to the detriment of the heroes and warriors of Troy.[8] Like Sappho's heroine, the Helen of Alcaeus is subjugated by the power of Eros wielded by Aphrodite. And, as in Sappho's poem, she abandons the conjugal and familial abode. But, instead of contenting herself with simply incarnating beauty, the Lacedaemonian is taken away by Paris; she will bring about the death of his brothers and the ruin of their city.

For Homeric poetry, the first written transcriptions of which seem to have been before Alcaeus' time, saying that Helen constitutes the cause of the downfall of many Argives and Trojans is a topos belonging to a formulaic kind of expression. Even if the story of Paris' seduction and abduction of Menelaus' wife was actually narrated in the poem called the *Cypria*, the "responsibility" of Helen for starting the Trojan War is a leitmotiv in the *Iliad*, if not the *Odyssey*.[9] This situation, in which the most beautiful of heroines is the origin of the Trojan disaster, is likewise mentioned by several representatives of "archaic" melic poetry. In the poem by Ibycus cited earlier, for example, Paris is depicted as betraying the hospitality that he enjoys in Sparta. Furthermore, did not a famous biographical legend, mentioned by Socrates in Plato's *Phaedrus*, affirm that the citharodic poet Stesichorus was struck blind for having spoken ill of Helen? Whence the poem titled *Palinodia*. The composition of this second poem, by showing that only Helen's simulacrum participated in the Trojan War, supposedly allowed the Sicilian melic poet, Sappho's contemporary, to get back his eyesight. The rhetorician and sophist Gorgias was not able to remain insensitive to the question of the Trojan heroine's guilt; his eulogy of Helen turns into a defense of the young woman who was seduced by the erotic powers of speech or by Eros himself.[10]

The stories concerning Greece's heroic past, which we call "myths," are characterized by a remarkable degree of flexibility and polymorphism. Sappho did not pass up the opportunity of making good use of their "plasticity."

From the historical and genetic standpoint that they hold dear, classical philologists have not, of course, failed to raise the question of what the—obviously epic—source is of the version presented by Sappho. Going even further with this historic filiation approach, they have wished to see in Alcaeus' "accusations" of Helen a conscious reaction to the "provocation" purportedly represented by Sappho's positive valuation of the Spartan heroine, in the same period at the same place.[11] Given the still largely oral character of the tradition to which melic poetry and "mythic" narration in general belong before the fifth century, such speculations about origins and poetic filiation are doomed to aporia; they are all the more futile for the fact that every city in ancient Greece had its own legendary tradition. Comparison of a single story to other versions can, however, decisively contribute to an understanding of Sappho's particular use, within the framework of her demonstration, of the "mythic material," whether it derives from the epic tradition or not.

2.2. Narrative Reasoning

In the story of the flight of Helen from Sparta to Troy, the poem attributed to Sappho erases the role played by Paris. It also rubs out the consequences brought on by the abduction of the young woman; there is not a word about the destruction of Troy. Helen faces Aphrodite alone, abandoning husband, daughter, and parents under the influence of the power that the divinity incarnates.

Is it only at this cost that the "mythic" story manages to become a piece of linear argumentation in the poem? Nothing is less certain, since (as we shall see) the story can divert and partially reorient this narrative argumentation. The legendary example initially seems to pick up on the two constitutive elements of the definition proposed by the narrator: (1) superlative beauty, which is incarnated in the figure of Helen, and (2) love, which is made concrete by the flight of Helen to Troy and by her amnesia, probably under the influence of Aphrodite.[12] Thus, in the context of the "myth," the *kálliston* is not defined by a Predicate in the form of a clause but is equated with a name: the most beautiful thing is Helen. At first, the heroine is simply equated with *hóti*, the object of the love inspired by the *kálliston*.[13]

But the clause that served as the semio-narrative Predicate of *kálliston* in the general definition of the first strophe ("[the *kálliston*] is whatever one loves") is not forgotten: while she possesses the quality that the equation with the *kálliston* just conferred on her, Helen also becomes the Subject of a micro-narrative that picks up on precisely this clause, further developing it. To form a story, the action expressed in the original proposition is "manipulated" by what, in semio-narrative terms, is called a "Sender"; as a result, the corresponding proposition is inscribed in a causal chain. Furthermore, it becomes double in order to stage a change in state and thereby fulfill one of the minimal conditions for narrativity.[14]

From this point on, while she represents an incarnation of beauty capable both of arousing love and of being its object, Helen also finds herself occupying the actantial position of Subject in the micro-narrative: she is the one who loves by Aphrodite's will.[15] Even as she replaces the Predicate of the *kálliston*, the heroine also takes the place of the *tis*, the impersonal "one," which is the grammatical subject (in the clause expressing the initial definition) of the verb *ératai*, "(she/he) loves." The conversion into narrative discourse that this simple assertion undergoes through the "mythic" story is carried out by two different means: through the designation of a Sender defining Helen's competence in love and through the changing of actors in the position of the beloved and love-inspiring object; the latter is no longer the Lacedaemonian husband but (by Aphrodite's will) Troy. The city of Troy thus becomes a sort of euphemism, by synecdoche, for designating Paris. This change of state of the Subject in its relationship to others indicates that there is narrative here, even if it is in embryonic form. Through this conversion into narrative discourse, Troy appears less as the emblem of the war, with its destructive consequences, than as the site of divinely inspired love.

The two qualities, eros and beauty, that the definition of the first strophe presents as equivalent, while placing them in what are naturally different actantial positions, are thus combined in Sappho's Helen. Taking the place of the *tis* as the Subject (S_1) feeling love, Helen is affected by its manifestations: the straying willed by Aphrodite, the abandonment of the familial household, the flight to a foreign land. To the extent that Helen is "manipulated" by Aphrodite, her competence in love, as the legend defines it, gives additional specificity, in turn, to the meaning attributed to the verb *ératai*: the love (P) in relation to which one may be the semio-narrative Subject is willed by Cypris. As the incarnation of the *kálliston*, however, the heroine also eminently represents the quality that is capable, from the position of S_2 (the indefinite pronoun *ótto*)—that is, the position of Antisubject or "object"—of provoking the manifestations of feelings and passion that define the Subject S_1.

This is, no doubt, a paradoxical conclusion. The fact is that the demonstration carried out by the singer of the poem does not conclude with the legendary example. It continues beyond the poem's third strophe in a development that suddenly takes a very personal turn.

3. Helen, Anactoria, and the Narrator

From the beginning of the fourth strophe, which has come down to us in tatters, we have at least an explanatory *gár* with which to work. This connector situates the clause of which it is a part in the same logical perspective as what was just expressed. This clause refers, through a complete shifting-in, to the situation in which the narrator-*I* finds herself at the moment of the enunciation of the poem: the evocation of Helen ends up recalling the figure of Anactoria, to whom the poem speaks. Anactoria, for her part, is not alongside the speaker-narrator at the present moment, designated by *nûn*. Through recollection, the verbal tense, spatial framework, and actualization of the *I* make the story of the "myth" coincide with the *hic et nunc* of the sung recitation of the poem.[16]

3.1. Anactoria's Gleam

The use of *gár*, which seems to present the situation in which the speaker-narrator claims to find herself as a motivation, a justification for the evocation of Helen, is paradoxical (from now on, I will assume that this *I* of the speaker-narrator corresponds to "Sappho" as a poetic persona, and not to Sappho as a historical author). From the standpoint of the semantic development linking the fourth strophe to the third, however, the shift to personal reminiscence on the part of the *I* is presented as the result of the description of the Spartan heroine's beauty. But this does not take into account, at least at first, the striking significance of the connector *gár*, which can refer the clause in which it appears to an emotional expression of approval on the part of the narrator without strictly respecting the logical link between cause and effect.[17] At this stage of the discursive analysis, this "indeed" would seem simply to underline the transition to the description of the feeling caused (in the *hic et nunc* of the recitation of the poem) by the brief account of the beautiful Helen's being led astray by love.

It is the absent figure of Anactoria that the story of Helen evokes in the memory of the singer of the poem. The allure of the young woman, who evokes eros, and the gleam of her countenance (or her look) are, through a projection into the future carried out through the use of the potential optative, the object of the wishes of the singer of the poem (fifth strophe). The spectacle of this manner and glow is preferable to that of Lydian chariots or foot soldiers decked out in full armor. Even if we are far from certain that the poem ends with the fifth strophe, the line of reasoning begun in the *preambulum* in the first strophe finds a first conclusion here. The annular structure that closes this reasoning in upon itself has not escaped anyone.[18]

The evocation of the situation of the speaker-narrator at the moment of the poem's enunciation is thus an integral part of the demonstration. This situation can be compared term for term to the definition given in the first part of the poem. Just as the most beautiful thing on earth is not a squad of horsemen or an army of foot soldiers but that which one loves, so, in the present, what occupies the narrator's mind, what she would like to look lovingly upon, is not Lydian soldiers (who cannot be the object of the verb "love") but Anactoria's demeanor and face. This woman thus becomes the source of the feeling of love implicitly felt by the *I*. The indefinite *tis* is now the *I*. The feeling of love henceforth manifests itself in the form of desire (for an allure and a face or a look that answers the lover's). The object of this desire (the most beautiful thing, whatever it may be) corresponds to the person set apart by this demeanor and this face (or this look), even if she is currently absent: it is Anactoria, whose allure and face equate her to the *kálliston*.[19] What remains, framed between the initial definition and its illustration through the situation in which the speaker-narrator is currently the protagonist, is the legendary story, which has been turned in a different direction from its usual narrative course.

3.2. The Narrative Status of Helen

The "mythic" narrative, even while turned from its habitual narrative course, does not exactly conform to the gnomic proposition that it is supposed to illustrate, nor to the particular personal situation that it seems to evoke. The fact is that Helen, who is (as we have seen) both the incarnation of beauty capable of arousing love and the subject of this same love, participates in two different relationships. The person who occupies the position of "instance of enunciation" also finds herself in two different relationships to Anactoria: one, now in the past, in which she feels love for the girl and which she would like to relive; the other, in the present, wherein Anactoria stands spatially separated from the narrator.

To begin with the latter relationship, which is of a narrative order, Helen, the incarnation of the woman who loves (probably by the will of Aphrodite), abandons her husband and familial household to sail off to Troy (where, implicitly, she joins Paris). Following an analogous course that is referred to the historical situation of the enunciation, Anactoria would appear to have left Sappho and her group of girls to return to Lydia, where she now lives as an adult woman in the company of her young husband. This metaphorical assimilation has already been revealed several times; we shall see that it is analogous to the kind of thing we find in parable. It tends to place "Sappho," in her relationship to Anactoria, in the position of Menelaus with respect to Helen.[20] Yet, just as Helen is also the mythic incarnation of the *kálliston*, so is Anactoria the earthly representative of this beauty because of the charm of her carriage and the gleam of her face. This beauty has a Platonic flavor, even if the path down which Sappho's poem leads us is exactly the inverse of that which Diotima lays out for us in the *Symposium*: one leading not from beautiful bodies to the form corresponding to the Beautiful, but from the most beautiful thing to the woman who incarnates it. Thus, just as Helen was capable of arousing through her beauty the love of Menelaus and especially Paris, so Anactoria, from a historical perspective, would seem to have stirred "Sappho's" passion (before giving rise to that of her husband). The proposition about the relationship of equivalence between the most beautiful thing and the love that Anactoria provokes in the singer of the poem thus belongs, with regard to its content, to a past close in time to the present of the enunciation.

The strange status of Helen as occupying in the "mythic" narrative the two actantial positions of the proposition that constitutes the initial definition—Helen is the one who loves and the one whom one loves—is thus explained by the two situations in which Anactoria finds herself with respect to the speaker-narrator: Anactoria, who is the subject of the verb "love," is now absent (since she is with her husband), but was once able to provoke through her glow the love felt by the one who says *I*. The link between these two situations, in the present and the past respectively, lies in the memory of the narrator who establishes it, conferring (as is often the case in the poems of Sappho) an idealizing tinge to a past that, though close in time to the present, verges on a legendary and fictional reality.[21]

Because it is told before the disclosure of the double enunciative situation in which the narrator stands with respect to Anactoria, the story about Helen makes it possible to distinguish the two moments that constitute this situation and to establish a narrative relationship between them. Consequently, the primary effect of the legendary narrative is to place under Aphrodite's influence the love that the *I* felt and still feels for Anactoria (the girl who was able to arouse this desire through her beauty). Subsequently, however, and through a shift from the intra- to the extradiscursive, we infer from the micro-narrative that the most beautiful of girls followed the same course as Helen, leaving the narrator (henceforth identified as Sappho) to go to Lydia, where she now lives, probably with her husband. This narrative shift from the heroic past to the present of the enunciation situation, which is now linked to the implicit intervention of Aphrodite, can be expressed in three distinct semio-narrative propositions: the Sender (Aphrodite) provokes the desire that S_1 (*I*) feels for S_2 (Anactoria); then, through Helen's example, the Sender makes S_1 (now Anactoria) take her love away from S_2 (the *I*) and give it instead, in a third proposition, to a new S_2 (the Lydian husband).[22]

While it subordinates to Aphrodite's will the actions and love relationships from which the poem's enunciation situation results, the heroic and epic example of Helen makes it possible to reverse the roles of the actors involved in this situation. Initially, Anactoria is the object (S_2) of the feeling of love (P) that her beauty incited in the narrator (S_1) and thus fits with the definition of the *kálliston* given in the first strophe; at a second stage, Anactoria, like the Spartan heroine, assumes the actantial position of the Subject S_1, loving in her turn and thereby causing the *I* to shift to the position of S_2.

Helen thus also becomes, alongside Aphrodite, the Sender of the empirical action carried out by Anactoria, who left the narrator to join the man she loves (effecting a substitution of the person standing in the position S_2). But all in all, this second moment in the micro-narrative no longer interests the narrator: evoked through a euphemism in the legendary story, it is erased from the narration of the circumstances leading up to the enunciation situation. The *I* is less concerned with her position as Antisubject or patient S_2 than with the situation in which she occupied the position of Subject S_1 (loving). What continues to attract the attention of the *I* despite the absence of Anactoria is the girl's beauty, along with the love it arouses; Anactoria has, perhaps, become all the more lovable for the fact that she is now in love herself. It is memory that makes it possible to evoke the original situation. This situation corresponds to the general definition formulated in the first strophe; thanks to the poem, it is possible to relive it.

If it is true that the narrator's *I* corresponds to a woman (if not to "Sappho" herself), the heterosexual relationship staged through the myth becomes—in the described enunciative reality—a relationship of homoerotic love, which will not surprise anyone in the context of a poem attributed to Sappho. In this context, the shift of Anactoria from object of love to loving subject corresponds to a transition from the status of *erómenos* to that of *erastés*. The transitory character of the relationship that existed between the *I* and Anactoria in the past fits perfectly with the initiatory character of "homosexual" love in Greece. It also corresponds to its function: making perfect lovers of young people who are loved, at the moment when they make the transition to adulthood. Because of the asymmetrical relationship it creates between an adolescent and an adult, Greek homophilia is only one specific manifestation, with an initiatory character, of that which we call "homosexuality"; as a (ritual) practice, it is conceived solely as a transitional stage on the way to heterosexuality.[23]

Consequently, both in the "homosexual" past evoked and poetically relived by the *I* and in the heterosexual present in which Anactoria is involved, it is indeed what one loves that is the most beautiful thing on earth, and this thanks to the action of Cypris, probably evoked in her function of inspirer of love through the legendary example of Helen. The demonstration concludes with the expression of the *I*, who is capable—through the mythic narrative, then through memory—of making her love for the most beautiful of young women coincide with that which led Helen astray as well as with that which no doubt strikes Anactoria herself now. The double intervention of the *I,* at the end of the *Priamel* and in the exposition of the enunciation situation, definitively eliminates martial pleasures from the definition of the *kálliston*—and in so doing eliminates the masculine sphere. The only *pólemos,* the sole combat that merits being waged, is that which the goddess of love provokes.[24]

4. The "Mythic" Narrative as Argument

When we are confronted with a legendary narrative that is so well subordinated to a very specific situation, can we still speak of it as a myth? It is here that the category of the parable can contribute to our comprehension of the line of argumentation that Sappho's poem develops.

4.1. The Use of Helen in Parable

It is precisely in the context of a discussion about the means of persuasion used in all genres of oratory that Aristotle offers his considerations about the parable (or illustration) in the *Rhetoric.* Among these forms of argumentation, the informal syllogism that is the enthymeme is distinguished from the example. Within the category of the example, which is considered as a means of induction, Aristotle draws a new distinction between examples referring to facts from the past and examples issuing from the orator's imagination. Finally, among these invented examples, the fable is differentiated from the parable. The invented story, then, is opposed to the exemplary historical account, which is narrated in the past tense, and from which it is possible to derive a rule (such as the way in which a Darius or a Xerxes can be seen to have acted). If we pass over the fables told by Aesop, imaginary examples are given their own paradigm: the analogies elaborated by Socrates to illustrate a specific situation. These illustrative (or "parabolic") examples are characterized by the drawing of a relationship, through a Predicate, between two generic Subjects, one of which corresponds to a *one* (*tis*), the other to a social group: "Choosing magistrates by lot is the same thing as though one were to choose athletes by lot (*hósper àn eí tis toùs athletàs kleroíe*)."[25]

From the standpoint of its syntactic and semantic articulation, the proposition corresponding to what Aristotle designates as a parable provides a striking analogy for that which is used in Sappho's poem to define the *kálliston.* Sappho's proposition, however, which is used in the service of the demonstration culminating in the complex situation in which the speaker-narrator is implicated, is invested with meanings that are too abstract, too indefinite to become exemplary. It is not enough to follow the Aristotelian model and establish a relationship of semantic analogy between each of the terms constituting the situation to be illustrated and those of the illustrative proposition that represents that situation. From the semantic perspective, it is still necessary to secure the transition from the figurative to the thematic, the transition from the feeling provoked by the contemplation of Anactoria's face and bearing to the love for the most beautiful thing: whence Helen as "parable."[26] Furthermore, from the syntactic standpoint and according to the perspective developed in the poem attributed to Sappho, it is necessary to find the illustrative equivalent of a "narrativized" situation. Indeed, this situation is confronted with a state experienced earlier than the one that coincides with the moment of enunciation in the poem.

This twofold use of parable to mark an analogical relationship on both the semantic level and that of syntactic "narrativization" is achieved through the part of Helen's story evoked by Sappho. But Sappho's recourse to legend can accomplish this only through the narrative distortions and silences that have been mentioned. The "mythic" narrative in Sappho's poem is thus given a particular status, one that lies between legendary narrative and parable. When taken separately, neither the narrative nor the parable is capable of mirroring the complex situation that the narrator attempts to describe and justify through subtle use of the role of memory. The memory of the *I*, which contrasts with Helen's amnesia, renders it possible to make the past coincide with the present while at the same time inscribing it in the idealized reality of legend.

4.2. Parable and Figurative Argumentation

If we measure it against the Aristotelian definition of the parable, the use of parable in the evangelical *lógoi* of Christ is rather similar to Sappho's poetic practice. As in the case of the Lesbian poetess's illustrative micro-narrative, the biblical parable cannot be reduced to a unique proposition wherein the actantial positions would be occupied by more or less "generic" actors who correspond to social roles.[27]

Compared with the Evangelists' use of parable, Sappho simply goes a little further, in that she separates the abstract (thematic) moment of the parable, which becomes the proposition-predicate of the definition of the *kálliston,* and its narrative (and figurative) moment, which corresponds to the myth of Helen. As is often the case in biblical parables, however, Sappho does not offer the key for "decoding" the narrative until its conclusion: her disclosure of the enunciation situation in the fourth and fifth strophes of the poem renders explicit the argumentation structuring the preceding strophes while also closing out that argumentative structure. The apparent contradictions that have been noted in the way the parable narrative is conducted are organized into a coherent whole only through the situation in which the narrator presents herself as the protagonist. Within this framework, the emotional *gár* linking the two final strophes of the poem to those that precede them takes on its full explanatory significance: it is on the level of pragmatic argumentation that the enunciation situation becomes a justification supporting the parable.

I shall make just two observations. First, the categories defined in Aristotle's *Rhetoric* overlap only very partially with what are supposed to be the use of such categories in literary texts, whether they be melic or biblical. The parable cannot have the argumentative significance that is attributed to it without developing into a narrative, however brief that narrative may be. It is only on this condition that the parable can play the role of "figurative model of the line of reasoning" that is attributed to it.[28] In light of this, we should not be surprised that it takes the form of a version of a legend in Sappho. Second, use of the parable is always linked, through analogy, to an enunciation situation that evokes its pragmatic impact and within which its persuasive function may be deployed. This takes us back, despite everything, to Aristotle's definition, whose reference to Socrates' words and their demonstrative impact is often forgotten: we are aware of the propaedeutic, if not initiatory, significance of Plato's staging of Socrates in dialogues. The parable is indeed an instrument for creating belief.

4.3. Argumentation, Enunciation, and Poetic Authority

In conclusion, we must remember the definition given to argumentation in natural logic; this argumentation is differentiated from a formal line of reasoning inasmuch as it combines knowledge about the objects that are spoken of with information concerning the subjects who speak about them.[29] In the poem attributed to Sappho, the narrative considered as mythic does not refer to the timeless and paradigmatic situation of a primordial, sacred reality providing a foundation for daily life in its profane aspect, as has been affirmed ad nauseam following Mircea Eliade.[30] On the contrary, we have seen that it is the concrete situation itself, as it is narrated in the poem, that determines the reorientation of the mythic narrative and the ambiguous role attributed to its primary protagonist. The legendary story is thus present to give narrative form to the proposition of the definition expressed at the beginning of the poem; above all, it is present in order to prepare the way, in the mode of parable, for linking this general definition with the situation mentioned in the fourth and fifth strophes. The link between the legendary narrative and the situation wherein the narrator is the protagonist makes the former an indispensable segment in the development of the argument. Moreover, it is solely in the poetic composition's (provisional) conclusion that the contradictions observed in the way the "mythic" narrative is conducted come to be organized into a coherent whole: only the account of the situation set forth by the *I* can complete the argument as it is conducted through what is probably a shift from the intradiscursive to the extradiscursive.

When we speak of argumentation, we are also speaking of persuasion. It is, indeed, in "make-believe" that the *I* attached to the enunciation of the poem and its content is engaged. While, on the one hand, the legendary narrative depicts Helen's amnesia, in the narrative in which the *I* is involved, on the other hand, it is memory that secures the link between the past and present situations; and this play with memory can be carried out only through the actual recitation of these verses, through play with the enunciative authority of the poetic voice. Anactoria's beauty at the moment when it struck the speaker-narrator, even when it is inserted into the idealizing framework traced out by the myth of Helen, exists only insofar as the poem is sung; it exists only to the extent that this poem is perceived by an audience that is witness, within the reality of the enunciation, to the truth of the actual situation. The very "performance" of the sung and danced poem thus tends, through the play with memory, to confer permanence on the love relationship, which is transitory by definition. If the poem was indeed addressed to the aristocratic girls who came to the Lesbian poetess to acquire the qualities of grace and courtesy that were to make adult women of them, then it is actually the situation described by the speaker-*I* that takes on the paradigmatic and illustrative character that is usually attributed to the "myth." The "make-believe" entailed in the act of reciting the poem is ultimately aimed at making the situation in which the girls find themselves coincide with that of Anactoria, who—like Helen—is lovable and lover all at the same time. Transitory though it may be, only love that has been lived, then evoked in music, is capable of convincing. Through the authority of the poetically reworked parable, it is this empirical love that ultimately takes over the function of a parable.

I V

LEGENDARY NARRATION AND POETIC PROCEDURE
IN CALLIMACHUS' *HYMN TO APOLLO*

There is no reason to doubt that the Greeks, throughout their history, sincerely believed in their myths. Nevertheless, can we really say as much about the Hellenistic poets, in particular Callimachus? His position as librarian in the House of the Muses created by Ptolemy I and his work collecting and collating literary manuscripts gave him the opportunity to compare and refute different versions of the same legend. In at least one of his own compositions, however, the learned poet achieved the opposite result in his comparative work. In his *Hymn to Apollo,* Callimachus combines different versions of the legend of Cyrene in order to restore chronological coherence to the reconstructed "mythic" story. Perhaps the form of the Homeric hymn, with its epic rhythm and language, was felt to be the most fitting to treat the story in terms of linear development, writing it into narrative and historiographic order. But was this kind of formal and chronological normalization of the story of the founding of Cyrene a simple question of "rationalization"? Is it merely the product of patient philological work focused on scholarly coherence? Was the choice of the Homeric prooemium simply a literary-critical decision? Does not the striking enunciative turn of this hymnic composition reflect truly poetic work both on the traditional narrative and on the hymnic form, such that the speaker-narrator figure appears not only as a *kritikós* but also as a *poietés* (in the etymological sense of the term)?

These questions take on extra edge when we acknowledge that in Greece, at least, there is no such thing as an essence of a myth; that myth is a category created by modern anthropology and has real substance only in certain well-defined narrative forms; that myth exists solely in forms of literary expression as diverse as an epic poem, an epinician, an epigram, or a tragedy. Which is to say that, linked as they are to precise types of enunciative circumstances, each of these forms confers a particular function on the chosen story; and this function defines itself in relation to the text within which the story is inserted and in relation to its performance context, which is often of a cultic order.[1] With this in mind, it would be fruitful to look at the strange story reconstructed by Callimachus in his *Hymn to Apollo* from three different angles: (1) that of its poetic construction and how it has been put into discourse, (2) that of its enunciation (to the extent that it is explicit), and (3) that of its internal "contextualization" relative to the text of the *Hymn* and the poetic form this composition takes. This tripartite essay thus examines first the way in which the story is constructed from a semantic rather than a syntactic perspective (by comparison with earlier versions of the legend); it then looks at the enunciative markers lying within the story itself and at the "instance of enunciation" underlying the narration; and finally, it deals with the insertion of the story into the enunciative structure of the poetic authority embracing the poem as a whole. This threefold analysis leads to a few reflections raised by the function and target audience of the poem—if not by the circumstances of its performance—in connection with the ritual character of the Homeric hymn, whose form (as defined in chapter 1) Callimachus' composition takes up and deeply transforms.

1. Versions of the Legend of the Founding of Cyrene

We know that, in the first half of the fifth century, Pindar gave three parallel versions of the founding of Cyrene in three different epinicians. In the first version, the eponymous Nymph, hunter and guardian of her father's flocks in Thessaly, founds the Greek colony in Libya after her abduction by Apollo and their marriage there. The second version uses the legendary expedition of the Argonauts to excite interest in this particularly fertile territory: Medea predicts the Greek colonization seventeen generations after the sojourn there of Jason's companions-in-arms. The third version recounts the act of founding the city by the daring Battus of Thera; it portrays him as the venerated founding father of the cult dedicated to him, but also situates his action within the double perspective of the Trojan Antenoridai's passage through Cyrene and of the Spartan ancestry of the Therean founders. Herodotus then made his contribution by working up this third version in order to present the two perspectives, Theran and Cyrenean, of the story. Through genealogies, the founder Battus is presented as descending either from the Argonauts, whose descendants had emigrated from Lemnos to Sparta and then to Thera, or from a royal Cretan family.[2] Time of the gods, time of the heroes, and time of (heroicized) men could be a useful paraphrase of this series of narrative versions, but that would be overly schematic. Even when organized into a single chronology, as they are in part by Herodotus, these three stories remain quite disparate as concerns their respective actors and temporality.

1.1. An Etiological Plot Line

Rewriting the story of the founding of Cyrene in the form of a hymn to Apollo allows Callimachus to combine the "divine" (Apollo and the Nymph Cyrene) and "human" (Battus) versions to make them coincide.

> Phoebus also told Battus about my city with its fertile soil; as a raven, he conducted the people while they made their way into Libya, keeping to the founder's right; and he promised that he would give city walls to our kings. Apollo is always true to his word. O Apollo! Many call you Boë-dromius, (70) many Clarius; everywhere you are called by many a name. But I call you Carneius; that is the tradition of my forefathers. Sparta, Carneius, was your first abode, the second was Thera, the third the city of Cyrene. From Sparta, a sixth-generation descendant of Oedipus (75) took you to the colony of Thera; and from Thera, mighty Aristoteles deposited you near the land of the Asbystae. He built you a very beautiful shrine, and established in the city annual rites, wherein many bulls, Lord, fall on their side for the last time. (80) *Hië, Hië,* Carneius of the many prayers! In the springtime, your altars bear all the multicolored flowers that the Hours bring forth when the Zephyrus breathes dew; in the winter, they are adorned with sweet crocus. Your fire is ever undying, and never do yesterday's ashes smother the coals. (85) Greatly, indeed, did Phoebus rejoice while the belt-wearing men of Enyo danced in chorus with the tawny-haired Libyan women, when came the season of the Carnean festival. But the Dorians were not yet able to approach the springs of Cyre, but dwelt in Azilis of the lush vales. (90) The Lord himself saw them and showed them to his bride while he stood on horned Myrtoussa, where the daughter of Hypseus killed the lion that ravaged the cattle of Erypylus. Apollo has seen no other chorus more divine than that one, nor has he accorded as many blessings to any city as he has to Cyrene, (95) remembering his earlier abduction. Nor have the sons of Battus themselves honored any other god more than Phoebus.
>
> (*Hymn to Apollo* 65–96)

Instead of the oracle at Delphi, which plays such a crucial role in Pindar's versions and in Herodotus, it is Apollo himself who takes control of the colonizing operations in Callimachus' hymn.[3] This he does by transforming himself into a crow and by leading Battus directly to the Libyan coast, with the promise to build the walls of a city (65–68). From this first anticipatory move, the narrative recounts the different stages of colonization in linear fashion: the descendants of Oedipus, having left Thebes in the sixth generation, as in Pindar, find Apollo Carneius in Sparta and take him to Thera; then, from Thera, with Battus as intermediary, the cult of the god is transported to the territory of a population of natives in Libya, the Asbystae (72–76). It is here at this first Libyan settlement, at Azilis, that the Doric Greeks manage to move Apollo with their dances; the god, accompanied by his young wife, contemplates them from the future site of Cyrene (77–90). The clever ring structure closing the narrative in on itself allows Callimachus both to use allusion to lead the Greek colonists near the site of the city of Cyrene under Apollo's protective gaze and, with a discreet reference to the archegetic function of the god, to evoke his union with the eponymous Nymph; on this occasion, the struggle between the young girl and the sheep-killing lion is moved from Thessaly to Libya (91–92). In addition to the ring structure so often used in the poetry of the "archaic" period, we also find the etiological explanation so dear to the Alexandrian poets: the protection provided to the colony of Cyrene by the god is to perpetuate the memory of the abduction of the girl of the same name.[4] A literary device and an *aítion* are combined to bring together the "divine" and "human" versions of the legend into a single narrative.

This first combination of a reflexive device making the narrative close in on itself with an etiological explanation, both of which cause a backward temporal movement to the "time of origins," is matched by a second synthesis of the same type. The reflexive aspect of the ring structure can be located not only in the fact that Apollo is invoked as Carneius at both the beginning and the end of the colonial itinerary (72 and 80), but also in a quite unexpected narrative procedure that immediately brings us into contact with the enunciative strategies of the narrative: while, at the beginning of the narrative, Apollo (in the form of a raven) leads the colonial expedition headed by Battus toward Libya (65–68), the sudden invocation of the god as Carneius, starting at verse 69, causes Apollo to shift from the third-person grammatical and narrative position to the second-person enunciative position. Even as he occupies the role of protagonist of the narrative, the god also becomes the "narratee" or "addressee," the story teller's (or "narrator's") interlocutor. From this point on, when the poem returns to the colonists' itinerary from Sparta to Libya by way of Thera, Apollo—the strange protagonist of the story who is henceforth evoked in the second person—goes from leading to being led by the city founder, Battus

(74–77). Divided between narration and enunciative address to the god, this development not only introduces a second invocation of the god Carneius (80) but also enables the god to be represented as participating in the establishment of the festival in his honor (80–96).[5] Within this enunciative game, the desire for etiological explanation is so strong that narrative time and enunciative time (as expressed in the text) come to coincide in this description of the first celebration of the Carneia; aorist forms (77, 78, 86, 87, etc.) are mingled with present forms (79, 81, 82, 84, etc.), preparing for the final affirmation: there was never a god as honored at Cyrene, in all the generations descending from the heroic founder, as Apollo himself.

The new plot line conceived by the author of the hymn thus manages to make of the standardized narrative of the colonization of Cyrene both an invocation addressed to the tutelary god of the Greek city in Libya and an etiology of the festival imported from Sparta and celebrated annually by the Cyreneans in his honor. But this rewritten plot line is itself inserted into a much larger narrative structure. Indeed, Callimachus' hymnic composition, adopting the tripartite structure of the Homeric hymn (as described in chapter 1), offers an unusual *evocatio* (1–8, followed by a transitional part at 9–16, or 31) and very brief *preces* (113, introduced by the end of the narrative at 105–12); between them, there is a long *epica laus* divided into two distinct sections, the first of which is descriptive, the second narrative (with a transition at 47).

1.2. New Semantic Directions

The strictly narrative part of the hymn (the second section of the *epica laus*) is introduced by two preliminary episodes. These episodes, along with the long narrative about Cyrene, make up a whole that is coherent less on the syntactic level of the plot than from the semantic standpoint of the isotopies that are developed there (that is, on the level of the construction through the text of constant semantic strata).

First, we find an isotopy of a spatial kind centered on the theme of construction: through the episode recounting Apollo's love for the young Admetus near the river Amphryssos in the Thessalian mountains (47–54), the god reveals his qualities as guardian and protector of flocks in their fecundity. The space circumscribed by the power of the shepherd god is pastureland, which remains open and free because still attached to pastoral activity. This activity corresponds to the classical Greek representation of the pre-civilized nomadic life.[6]

From this first yet-to-be-built space the narrative takes us to Delos, where Apollo puts his skills as surveyor and founder of cities into practice (55–64). More precisely, he is represented, in a veiled etiological and reflexive perspective, as the god who delights in tracing out new cities (55–57), as the "weaver" of foundations (*themeília*, at 57, 58, and 64). It is Apollo who, as a very young child on Delos, sets an example by assembling the building materials for his own altar. That altar is presented, in a second *aítion* that implicitly explains its traditional name of "Altar of Horns" (*Keráton*), as being made not out of blocks of stone but of a structure of horns (the word *kérata* is repeated three times in ll. 62–63). The horns used are the spoils of Artemis' hunt in pursuit of goats grazing on the wild hills of Mount Cynthos; Apollo's architectural weaving (*huphaínei*, 57; *éplek,'* 61) thus imposes the first civilized structure on virgin territory.[7] A new ring structure, which is simultaneously linguistic and thematic, closes this brief etiological narration in upon itself: such were the first foundations built by Apollo (64).

It is only after these preliminaries concerning the delimiting of spaces that the narrative of the founding of Cyrene begins: Cyrene is presented as a city worthy of the name (65) and having walls (67). By taking us from Sparta to Thera, then from Thera to Libya, however, the narrative does not allow us to be present at the planning and construction of the city itself, but rather has us stop (as I have already pointed out) at the land of the Asbystae, in the native settlement of Azilis "of the lush vales" (76 and 89). It is here that Battus, the founder, raised the first temple to celebrate Apollo Carneius and to institute his cult (77). The site of the future city of Cyrene is still marked only by a rocky hill, Mount Myrtoussa, where the Nymph carried out her exploit of hunting down the sheep-killing lion; it is, in other words, a space still bearing the signs of its extreme savagery. It is, indeed, the very description of this mountainous landscape, perfect for hunting wild animals and pasturing livestock, that leads to the recollection—in the ring structure that encircles the narrative—of the abduction of the young Cyrene (95), a scene written into literary tradition, notably by Pindar's ninth *Pythian,* which describes the hunting expeditions of the daughter of Hypseus (see v. 92) to protect her father's flocks in the "shady mountains" of Thessaly.[8]

The narrative's semantic development adds a second isotopy to the spatial one centered on the construction theme, this time concentrating on intimate social relations. The first episode shows Apollo in a love relationship with the young Admetus, the (future?) king of Pherai in Thessaly, without exactly making clear what the role of the god is, that of *erastés* or that of *erómenos:* the desire he feels for the young man, who is still "untamed" (*á-dmetos*), and his traditional function as teacher imply the former, while his own youth and the service rendered to a hero suggest the latter. The sort of asymmetrical homoerotic (or, better, homophilic) relationship practiced and institutionalized in the archaic and classical cities, with its educational function, has certainly been redefined here, as is often the case in Hellenistic poetry; it has deliberately been inserted into a bucolic world of fiction in order to be idealized.[9]

The second episode, which moves from the mountains of Thessaly to the island of Delos, is dominated by the sibling relationship between Apollo and his sister, Artemis the huntress: it establishes the cooperation between the god and goddess in the first civilized construction. The third and principal section of the narrative has to be concluded and the transfer of the narrative action to the plains of Libya completed before we see Apollo at work alongside Cyrene. The qualification of *númphe* that is assigned to her establishes her legendary and heroic status as Nymph, but also refers to her social position as young wife. The union and marriage between the god and young heroine are alluded to very discreetly with this term, just as the settlement on the very site of Cyrene by the Doric Greeks (protagonists of the colonial relationship initiated by Apollo) is only indirectly evoked. The narrative is silent about the essential function of the matrimonial relationship in Greece: procreation. By contrast, the Pindaric version of the marriage of the god and the girl is not so chary about the expected consequences of the conjugal union, since it goes on at length about the birth of Aristaeus.[10]

Callimachus' narrative moves from a pastoral setting within a mountainous landscape to an insular space reserved for the building of a shrine, then to a continental space suitable for the construction of a city and cultic celebration, but it also stages successively a relationship of homoerotic love, sibling cooperation, and conjugal union. Through this double movement, the spatial isotopy and the social isotopy combine to trace out the same trajectory. Through these three episodes, the narrative takes us from a pre-civilized state to the civilization of the *pólis;* it takes us from a transient relationship with an immature young man in a relatively wild context to a permanent union with a woman on stable ground, marked as such by a city and temple. But within these two lines of semantic development, the narrative does not quite achieve its objective: the colonial movement does not end with the founding of Cyrene itself, nor with agricultural activity, and the marriage does not lead to procreation.[11] Therefore, it seems, no production and no reproduction.

The fact is that the story is not quite "pure" in narrative terms. Before concluding, in a complementary manner, with a brief fourth episode, the narrative is marked at its center by strong enunciative interventions on the part of the narrative voice, one example of which I have just cited; these interventions are a constant factor in directing and orienting the narrative development.

2. Enunciative Interventions in the Narrative

Just as the narrative section of Callimachus' poem and its *epica laus* are introduced by a list of Apollo's functions (42–46), about which I shall have more to say directly, so also is the transition between each of the three episodes constituting

the poem underlined by the mention of a specific *epíklesis* of the god: Apollo
Nomius, the shepherd who guards Admetus' flocks in the Thessalian episode
(47); Apollo Phoebus, the shining Purifier who constructs the Altar of Horns in
the Delian episode (56); Apollo Carneius, native of the Doric country for the
narrative of the founding of Cyrene (70). This last *epíklesis* of Phoebus can be
related to his more general function as the god who "shows" (*éphrase*, 65), but
it also stands as distinct from the *epíkleseis* Boedromius and Clarius (69–70) that
the god assumes at Athens and Claros, in Attic and Ionian territory: a subtle way
of calling to mind the fact that Cyrene was founded by Dorians (89).[12] Yet the
reintroduction at this point in the narrative of the enunciative forms of *I* and
you places the protagonist of the narrative, Apollo, in a strange relationship with
the speaker-narrator.

2.1. The Narrator's Positions

From the very first line of the third episode, the colony to be founded is pre-
sented as the speaker's hometown (*emèn pólin*, 65). From this point of view, the
entire Callimachean narrative of the founding of Cyrene is situated within the
perspective of the privileged relationship between the speaker and Apollo; this
relationship is founded on the benevolence demonstrated (throughout the nar-
rative) by the god toward the colonists and the honors rendered by the colonists
to Phoebus Carneius. The city designated by Apollo thus becomes "my city"
(65); the sovereigns who, after Battus, will control the city are "our kings" (68);
and, with the narrator's use of the *epíklesis* Carneius, Apollo becomes the god of
"my forefathers" (71). From that point on, as I have pointed out, the divine
protagonist of the foundation story is also the interlocutor and addressee of the
speaker-narrator, who constantly refers to him in the second person (74, 75,
77, 79). These repeated references lead up to the ritual invocation of verse 80
(*hiè hiè Karneîe polúllite*). This hymnic appeal, at the heart of the narrative's third
episode, tends to make the poem that announces this cry a part of the very rite
that it describes. By this means, the narrator-*I* places his poem within the con-
text of the first colonists' carrying out of the Carneian ritual in honor of the
founder god. This insertion is all the easier because the description of the cult
concentrates on its choral and musical elements (86 and 93): there is a kind of
coincidence (in the strong sense of that term) created between the present
poem's enunciative form, a hymn, and the content of what is uttered—the
description of a ritual musical performance. I shall return later to this mimetic
aspect of the song suggested by the poet.

But, parallel to the fact that the narrative does not lead the colonial expedition
to its completion on the actual site of the future Cyrene, the speaker-narrator also

strangely disengages himself from this final part of the foundation story. Starting from verse 85, Apollo regains his place as protagonist of the narrative in the third person, alongside which the *I*-forms mysteriously disappear until verse 96.

Whatever the reasons for this suspension of enunciative markers, the "authorial" interventions appearing throughout the first part of the foundation narrative help to establish the narrator's claim to descent from Battus; they reach back beyond the royal dynasty that really reigned over Cyrene during the classical period to link this royal family with the founder. And the protection that Battus receives from Apollo establishes a privileged relationship linking the city of Cyrene, the first-person narrator, and the god.[13] Insofar as the biographical tradition makes Callimachus a Cyrenean, while also attributing the name of Battus to his father, the narrator's textual figure refers us directly to the historical person of the "enunciator," the poet. It would nevertheless be prudent to ask whether the Cyrenean origin that the biographers claim for Callimachus was not itself drawn from the figures deployed in the work.[14] It might be possible to avoid this vicious hermeneutic circle by proposing the hypothesis that Callimachus exploited, in his own interest, the fact of his father's name and his Cyrenean origin to construct within the legendary narrative his descent from Battus and, what is more, a direct relationship with Apollo. That line of descent is all the more vague and fictive for the fact that, in the utterance alluding to the present moment of the poem's performance in verse 27, "our kings" becomes "my king," a king whom the scholiast (because commenting on an Alexandrian poet) identifies with Ptolemy III, venerated as a god.[15] But why all this apparent mythological and literary fiction?

2.2. Philological Explanations

It ought to be stressed again that the narrative section of the hymn does not end at verse 96 with the founding of Cyrene; after the repetition of the ritual appeal to Apollo at verse 97 and the introduction of a new *epíklesis* (*Paiéon*), the narrative continues with a short concluding episode, which constitutes a sudden new development. Once again the hymn goes into an etiological mode. What we need is an adequate explanation for the origin of the name *Paiéon;* it coincides with the refrain of the song addressed to Apollo, a paean, but also in part with the appeal addressed to Carneius in the story of the founding of Cyrene (80). Through this ritual song, *both* the god Paean *and* the song addressed to him are skillfully evoked.

As for the *aítion,* it subtly combines narration and etymology. By taking us from Cyrene to Delphi, another key locality which (like Delos) is under

Apollo's control, the narrative recalls the death of the snake that gave its name to the site after being killed by the god's arrows; and it is to the etymology that the poet attributes the relationship between the shooting of the fatal arrow at Python (*híei bélos*, "shoot a shaft") and the ritual cry it provokes (*hiè hiè paiêon*, "*Hië, Hië*, Paean," heard as *hiè hiè paí ión*, "shoot, shoot the arrow, boy!"). The etymological wordplay is itself placed in the mouth of the people of Delphi, the first to "invent" the refrain (99). At the same time, the Delphian populace acts as a kind of collective spokesman for the second *aítion* by glossing the *epíklesis*, *Paiéon*, in their exclamation that the healer god—who takes his *epíklesis* from the name of the Homeric doctor to the gods—is a "helpful" god (103–4).[16] The main isotopies deployed throughout the first three episodes of the narrative section of the composition reach completion in this final episode: while the space of Delphi is civilized by the elimination of the monster and attached to the Paean *epíklesis*, a new social relationship between the god and the chorus that sings him is established through an *aítion*.

This subtle interlacing of scholarly reflections is marked by the return of the *I*, or rather the *we* (*akoúomen*, 97): upon leaving Cyrene, the enunciative and poetic authority expands to encompass a more general personality. But it also restores Apollo to his role as interlocutor (addressed in the second person at vv. 99 and 102). Moreover, the "people" of Delphi are involved in the same kind of dialogic relationship with the god as that formulated by the narrator in the third episode, since they are represented in action, directly addressing Apollo, and since they refer through their etymological explanation (quoted in direct speech) to the wording of the paean refrain. This narrative relationship is the primary and original basis for the enunciative one. It constitutes the legendary and etiological paradigm for the relationship between the speaker-narrator and his narratee, the god: like this latter relationship, it is established entirely within the song (98 and 104). The interaction here between the chorus members, who sing Apollo (within the narrative), and the figure of the speaker-narrator, who addresses his hymnal song to the god, is analogous to the correspondence noted earlier (§ 2.1) between the description of the colonists' choral celebration of the Carneia and the form of the speaker-narrator's poetic speech itself. In fact, this interplay is constitutive of the enunciative structure of the composition as a whole, wherein the authority of the poetic voice oscillates between the poet's *I* and the chorus (whose refrain, as we shall see, is supposed to punctuate the poem). In the play with verbal tenses and enunciative stances, this interaction between speaker-narrator and chorus tends to efface the limits between the time of legend or "myth" and the time of the poem's execution (the time of the "rite"); a continuity is woven between these two temporal dimensions that aims at superimposing them.

3. Structures and Functions of the Poem

It is now time, before we move on to the poem's conclusion and consider its overall function, to focus on the deliberate inclusion of the long narrative section within the general development of the composition; I shall do so (briefly) from the standpoint of both the enunciative stances that are elaborated within this section and the isotopies guaranteeing its semantic coherence.

3.1. Enunciative and Mimetic Effects

The mysterious *we* that describes itself as listening to the Apollonian refrain being glossed at Delphi is, in fact, nothing more than the product of an enunciative synthesis that emerges from the very beginning of the poem:

> How Apollo's laurel sprig quivers!
> How the whole shrine quakes! Away, away whoever is immoral!
> Yea, Phoebus surely knocks on the door with his beautiful foot.
> Do you not see? The Delian palm nods pleasantly
> all of a sudden, and the swan sings beautifully in the air.
> Push yourselves back from the gates, you bars;
> slide yourselves back, bolts! Indeed, the god is no longer far away.
> Ready yourselves, young men, for the song and the choral dance.
> Not to everyone does Apollo show himself, but to the good.
> Great is the man who has seen him, a poor man the one who has not.
> We shall behold you, Far-shooter, and we shall never be poor.
> Let the boys keep neither the lyre silent nor their step soundless
> when Apollo is present,
> if they plan to get married and continue cutting their hair when it is gray,
> and if the wall is to stay standing on its old foundations.
> I am delighted with the boys, since the lyre's shell is no longer idle!
>
> (vv. 1–16)

If we compare the overall structure of Callimachus' composition with the tripartite structure of the *Homeric Hymns* (as defined in chapter 1), we can note meaningful enunciative differences. The prelude of Callimachus' poem (1–8), which corresponds to the initial part of the *evocatio* of a Homeric proem, also presents the god as sung in the third person. Rather than launching into the descriptive-narrative part constituting the expected *epica laus*, however, this first part describes the signs announcing the god's epiphany on the isle of Delos. And it does so through a sophisticated shift from the past (marked by aorist forms) to the present, which corresponds to the very moment of the poem's utterance and probable performance. Scattered across these introductory verses are second-person apostrophes. First, the speaker-narrator addresses the supposed receiver of the poem through a rhetorical question formulated in the generalizing second person (*oukh' horáais,* "do you not see [the signs of the god's approach as announced by the swan's song]?" v. 4), an apostrophe that evokes Alcman's "first" *Partheneia*. Following this, it is the bolts of the temple doors that are addressed (6). Finally, the speaker-narrator invites the young people to strike up a danced song (*enthúnesthe,* 8) to accompany the god's epiphany.

Instead of the expected hymnic relative, the *epica laus* itself is introduced by Apollo's name (9), taken up directly from the standpoint of its relationship to the god's devotees. This relationship is very quickly personalized: following this brief evocation of his epiphany in the third person, the god is invoked in the vocative as archer (*ô Hekáerge,* 11), while the group of his servants is included in a generalizing *we* (*opsómetha,* "we will see," 11) that picks up both on the general *you* in the rhetorical question at the beginning ("do you not see," 4) and on the speaker's *I*. We also find this first-person plural reappearing at the end of the poem. In this shift from the immediate future to the present, we move—between the beginning and end of the poem—from seeing to hearing. Henceforth, the direct apostrophes to Apollo punctuate the two sections (one descriptive, the other narrative) of the *epica laus*. This is the case until the final verse of the poem, which—in the guise of *preces*—addresses Apollo by bidding him to "take delight" (*khaîre,* 113), as is obligatory at the close of a *Homeric Hymn*.

Paradoxically, however, in this first part of the transition from *evocatio* to *epica laus,* which sets out the characteristics and functions of the young god, Apollo is most often replaced, in the position of receiver of the poem (as defined by the vocative and second-person forms), by another addressee, another interlocutor: a chorus of young men addressed from verse 8 on with a form of the imperative in the second-person plural.[17] Through the repetition of the same kind of forms at verses 17 and 25, the *choreutaí* are, it seems, even being invited to sing (probably at Delos) the poem composed by the one who says *I*. In an even subtler manner, the young chorus members are called upon to take inspiration from the song sung by Apollo himself. They are invited to listen to his music with the same respectful silence due when *aoidoí* praise Apollo's lyre or bow (18–19), just as Thetis stops her song of complaint when she hears the refrain of the paean (20–21) and Niobe's rock ceases to lament for the same reason (22–24). These legendary examples make the reflexive dimension of Apollo's song so explicit that the *choreutaí* themselves—despite the silence they have just been urged to respect—are asked to sing out the refrain (25). Essential to the poem's ring structure, the refrain is itself the object of the learned explanation referred to earlier (97–104). The explanation places Apollo's role as *aoidós* and his skill as archer into an etiological relationship with each other, for they are enigmatically juxtaposed not only at the beginning of the poem (11 and 19) but also through the allusion to Niobe's fate as parallel to that of Thetis, the list of the god's golden attributes (33), and the parenthesis in verse 44: "to Phoebus are entrusted both the bow and the song." The mysterious combination of Apollo's duties as archer and bard is not explained until the epilogue of the poem.

In raising the issues of both silent listening and musical voice, the reflexive component of Apollo's song no doubt inaugurates the metamorphosis of the *you* addressed to the young *choreutaí* by the speaker-narrator (8) into the *we* that includes both the chorus and the speaker-narrator (11). Both the adolescents and the *I* (as well as his audience?) are called upon to attend to Apollo's epiphany: the young chorus members are inspired to play the lyre and dance (12–3); the speaker approves their song (16). But who really *is* the singer of the poem that we are reading? Is it the chorus that Callimachus represents in action at Delos? Or is it Callimachus himself? And for whom is it sung?

The echo effect in the narrative section of the poem between the enunciative authority and the legendary, paradigmatic chorus members of Cyrene and Delphi is transferred onto the enunciative relationship set up between the narrator and his double narratee: the god and the *choreutaí*. The mirroring quality conferred on Apollo's song further accentuates these enunciative ambiguities: Apollo's musical epiphany both interrupts and inspires the song sung by the young *choreutaí*. And these young singers are also encouraged by the narrator, who joins them in praising the god. It is true that the use of first-person plural future forms in verse 11 calls to mind the "performative" future used by the *choreutaí* of archaic melic poetry when describing in the first person the action that they are in the process of performing.[18] Nevertheless, the constant interplay among persons occupying in succession enunciative stances that are usually kept distinct gives the strong impression that this "mimetic" effect is operating on the level of literary fiction. Insofar as this enunciative interplay provokes the many convergences I have outlined, wherein Apollo's song, the song of the chorus, and the poem sung by the *I* of the speaker-narrator coincide with one another, the "mimesis" is in fact hermetic: its construction is such that it is probably self-referential and intradiscursive and does not refer to any action outside the poem itself (unlike what we find in archaic melic poetry, where singers refer to the external ritual actions in which they are involved).[19] From this point of view, it is particularly significant that the poet has so much more to say on the (fabricated) performance context of his poem than the *Homeric Hymns* or the archaic melic poets do. Thus, it comes as no surprise when we see, at the end of Apollo's song, the *we* open up, by way of a rhetorical question with *tís*, into a generalizing *who* (31). If Apollo is so worthy of being sung (*eúumnos*), that is because it is so easy for every man to sing him.[20]

When the speaker-narrator, in this highly complex enunciative development, comes out on his own as *I,* it is in relation to "my king" (26–27), much as he later manifests himself in relation to "my city" and "our kings" in the narrative about the foundation of Cyrene (65 and 68). In the ambivalent way I have shown, this shift draws the genealogical line (constructed by the narrative) linking the narrator-*I* with the founder of Cyrene and, through him, with Apollo. In contrast with the choral aspect of its context, this strong enunciative intervention on the part of the *I* is immediately presented as having a relationship with the supposed homeland of the poet and his tutelary god.[21] Such are the forms successively assumed by the "instance of enunciation" in what is quite a scholarly prelude.

3.2. Semantic Constructions

The first part of the poem (the *evocatio,* which is transformed into an appeal to observe the god's epiphany, and the descriptive section of the *epica laus*) is essentially devoted to listing and portraying Apollo's characteristics and modes of action. This whole first part of the poem focuses on the activities of the cult, on the rites, as seen from the point of view of the god's partners. This first "ritual" section prepares us for the second narrative section, in particular with the transitional verses listing the types of practitioners of specialized skills under the god's aegis (archer, bard, diviner, and doctor, 42–46);[22] and it does so not only from an enunciative standpoint but also on the semantic level, in the isotopies that it draws.

First (to be brief), there is the spatial isotopy centered on the construction theme: Apollo's epiphany is immediately signaled by the quaking of his temple and the kicking at the doors (2–3). He alone is capable of shaking the foundations (*thémethla*) of the walls that he otherwise protects (15); and, in the end, it is the entire city, and more specifically the soil, that benefits from the curative virtues of the balm dripping from the locks of the god of eternal beauty (38–41). There is also the social isotopy focused on intimate relations: this is present especially in the ritual and cultic relationship between the chorus of young men (*néoi,* 8) and the eternally young god (*aeì néos,* 36); but unlike Apollo, who will never see his cheeks covered with "peach-fuzz" because of his divine nature (36–37), the *choreutaí* can still hope to reach the stage of maturity that is sanctioned by a conjugal bond, through the god's benevolent influence (14). Furthermore, in imitation of the intimate relationship established between Phoebus and the young chorus members who sing the god, an affinity is suggested

between "my king" (the speaker-narrator's sovereign) and the divinity protect-
ing him (26–27). In this reciprocal movement between men and god, and its
discreet and ambiguous allusion to the city to be founded, Cyrene (or Alexan-
dria?) is situated between the two geographic and religious poles of the cult of
Apollo: Delos, where the god's epiphany seems to take place (1–8), and Delphi,
where his civic function is achieved (32–41). These two religious centers are
also the two poles of Greek civilization, according to the model offered through
the two sections of the *Homeric Hymn to Apollo*.[23]

But the essence of these spatial and social isotopies, and the essence also of
the intimate ritual relationship woven between chorus members and god in
places of unshakable foundations, is achieved through musical activity. Intro-
duced by the swan's song signaling the appearance of Apollo at the beginning
of the poem (5),[24] this musical isotopy centered on ritual song runs through the
whole poem in such an obvious way that it would be overly fastidious to list all
of its occurrences. Suffice it to say that the musical shows of homage rendered
to Apollo by the choral group of Dorians and the blond Libyan women cele-
brating the Carneia (85–95) are but the narrative and legendary counterparts to
the ritual gestures that the narrator recommends to the chorus of young men
to perform when they seem to be performing his own song.

3.3. The *Hymn* as Poetic Program

In the best tradition of Alexandrian poetry and, especially, epigram, this strange
insertion of Cyrene between Delos and Delphi, but also the breaking off of the
story in the narrative section and the focusing of the poem as a whole on the
activity of singing, find their justification in the concluding lines of the poem:

> Envy said surreptitiously into Apollo's ear,
> "I am not pleased with the bard who does not sing of things as great in
>   number as the sea."
> Apollo pushed Envy away with his foot and said,
> "The Assyrian river's current is great, but it carries much
> filth from the earth and much debris in its water.
> The Melissae do not carry water from every source to Deo,
> but only the tiny trickle that seeps up pure and unpolluted
> from the holy spring, the very finest to be found."
> Rejoice, Lord! As for Blame, let him go the way of Envy.
>
> (vv. 105–13)

It is unnecessary to point out that this final development, the confrontation
between Apollo and Envy (105–12) concluding the *epica laus,* emphasizes the

musical isotopy focused on the song theme. There is a linguistic echo worth noting, however, which relates this last scene to the etiological narrative preceding it (the fourth episode of the narrative section): the singing rejected by Envy (*aeídei*, 106) echoes both the singing punctuated by the refrain for which the *aítion* is given in the confrontation between the god of Delphi and the serpent Python (*aeídei*, 104) and the singing of the swan evoked at the beginning of the poem (*aeídei*, 5). In each of these passages, the verb *aeídei* occupies the same metrical position. The famous programmatic scene, where Apollo, kicking aside Phthonos, contrasts the river song with the poetic drops of water from a pure source, thus echoes the killing of the monster plaguing the site of the future sanctuary of Delphi. The connection between the two passages is reinforced by the civilizing aspect of both of Apollo's actions: the god eliminates a wild animal (100–101) that is associated through legend with putrefaction, then rebuffs a river carrying the filth of the earth (108–9).[25] The expression *exéti keíthen* ("from that place and that time onward") in verse 104 establishes an etiological relationship between the last narrative action taking place at Delphi and the final episode, which stands outside of time and space.

Discussion of the purifying and civilizing effect of Apollo's interventions raises the question of how the poem's conclusion relates to the composition as a whole. The semantic coherence of the entire poem, too, is guaranteed by the presence of the obvious musical isotopy running throughout it. In follow-up to the echo discussed earlier, it would be worthwhile to focus on a single repetition that is at once phonic, metrical, and linguistic. Just as the end of the poem's narrative section is linked to the conclusion of the composition as a whole through the repetition of *aeídei* (in the subjunctive and indicative, respectively) in the same metrical position (104 and 106), so the same term is used to introduce the musical isotopy at the very beginning of the piece, in the comparison with the swan (5); and the same word occurs, in different forms, at the end of verses 17, 18, 28, 30, 31, 43 and 44.

There are at least two particular ways in which the speaker-narrator's allegorical exposition of his poetic program is very closely related to the unusual version of the story of the founding of Cyrene given in the poem.[26] These two aspects ensure that the story finds its fulfillment—and therefore its narrative sanction—in the programmatic close of the poem. One commentator on the *Hymn to Apollo*, who summarizes the contradictory interpretations of his predecessors and draws on a series of ancient texts, has been able to show that the opposition between the "river of Assyria," which rushes along with its muddy water, and the bees, which carry the drops of pure water from a "sacred spring" to Demeter, is operating on three different semantic levels. First, in Aristotle's zoological work, bees are represented as avoiding putrid matter to feed on the sweet juices and dew with which they make honey. Second, from a cultic point of view, the priestesses of Demeter are frequently associated with bees. Finally, and above all, the poet himself, insofar as he produces a honey-sweet song, is often compared to a bee, from the time of Pindar and Bacchylides on.[27]

To these three literal and figurative levels of expression, we must add the bee as metaphor for the happily married woman, incarnation of the civilization brought about by Demeter's efforts, of the grain cultivation promoted by the goddess. Furthermore, since the etiological legend concerning the services rendered to Demeter by the bee-women represents the creation of the loom and the gift to men of their first clothes, the bee reference might also be related to the common metaphor of the "weaving" of the poem. An echo of this can be found in Apollo's "weaving" of the foundation of the Altar of Horns (61): Apollo's architectural construction parallels the construction of poetic "making."[28] The bee dedicated to Demeter, in producing honey and protecting the weaving trade, fulfills the civilizing work undertaken by Apollo and the Nymph Cyrene—a young couple who are married but have yet to become progenitors, on a site freed from wild beasts but yet to be transformed for agriculture (90–92).

From the spatial point of view, the spring producing pure water drunk by the bees recalls the source Cyre, which the Doric colonists celebrating Apollo Carneius had not yet been able to reach (88–89).[29] If it is true that, according to the programmatic reading of the concluding verses, the bee that slakes its thirst at the sacred spring beneath the benevolent eye of Apollo is none other than the poet himself, the poet by inference must occupy a privileged position with regard to the Cyre spring. The true colonizer of Cyrene, then, is the poet who conforms to the poetic program proposed by Apollo.

By virtue of his invitation to the divine lord to rejoice in verse 113 (*ékhaire*, echoing the god's joy at Cyrene as expressed by *ekháre* at v. 85), the speaker-narrator implicitly affixes his signature to this allegorical poetics while bringing the poem to a close. By opposition to the recommendation to the chorus to praise Apollo (especially 25–31), the speaker-narrator (who is henceforth a founder) expresses in the closing verse his wish that Blame should go the same way as Envy, whom the god shuns. In this way, the speaker bases his literary program on one of the fundamental features of Greek poetics from the archaic period on: the opposition between "praise" and "blame."

In this context, the criticisms embodied in *Mômos* and provoked by *Phthónos* cannot be made to fit with the biographical interpretations suggested by modern readers of these lines.[30] It is true that, through the enunciative games I have described, the narrator-*I* who identifies himself with the poet-colonist is more than likely to correspond, in turn, to Callimachus, the Cyrenean who changed the nature of the entire legend of the founding of his homeland to make it into a kind of narrative prop for a poetics designed to outlive its occasion.[31] But this does not alter the fact that the biographical allusions are above all a means for the poet to claim, through royal ancestry and legendary narration, to draw on the authority of the god of song himself. The final prayer to the god, which is accompanied by a personal wish, underlines the privileged relationship between poet and divinity. The epiphany of the god of the lyre serves the poetics advocated by Callimachus' authoritative voice, which takes on the depth of a chorus through the enunciative and mimetic play I have described. Acting both as poet and as master of ceremonies, Callimachus provokes the divine apparition through his poem.

On the one hand, through various narrative procedures, Callimachus redirects the "myth" to fit it into the situation of the Hellenistic poet that he aims to defend through this poem. In so doing, he restores to the legendary narrative the practical function that it always had in ancient Greece; but here that function is not to serve any specific cult celebration but to defend a poetic program. On the other hand, he reactivates the very function of the *Homeric Hymns*. He does so by beginning with an evocation of the god, then calling upon Apollo as the poem's addressee in a choral mode—in the poetic construction of an "instance of enunciation"—in order to list his divine attributes before launching into the story of the god's career. Even as he modifies the hymnic form's enunciative character, Callimachus presents a variation on the general structure typical of the genre. Moreover, in constructing a complex poetic "instance of enunciation," he presents to us a choral song in the form of a hymn. Read as such, the *Hymn to Apollo*, like the *Homeric Hymns*, is nothing more than the prelude to other songs; transformed into a poetic program, it becomes the "source" of those songs.[32] The rearticulation of the epic prooemium therefore underlines the programmatic character of Callimachus' composition. Far from being designed for ritual performance within the context of a festival for Apollo, the poem is entirely devoted to the cult of learned poetry, reserved for a privileged circle of literati.

The pragmatic function of a Homeric hymn and the practical function of legendary narration have been brought under the sway of a poetic program consecrated to Apollo. But, through the privileged relationship that Callimachus establishes with Apollo by means of his hymnic composition, and through the fervor of repeated apostrophes to the god made under a choral mask, the labor of learned poetry is transformed into a religious act.[33] This act is worthy of a poet who, in the Mouseion and the "thiasos of the Muses," has put himself in the service of the divinities of poetic inspiration.

PART 2

GAZES OF AUTHORITY

V

LEARNING TO DRINK, LEARNING TO SING

Poetic and Iconic Speech in the Symposium

"In the same way, I suppose, we will say that [like the painter] the poetic imitator also paints colored pictures of each of the crafts by means of words and phrases, even though he professes knowledge of nothing other than imitating." From the critical standpoint adopted by Plato in the *Republic,* as is well known, painting and poetry cannot be anything more than imitative types of knowledge. What is more, the imitation involved is at two removes, being the *mímesis* of objects that are themselves artifacts and, thus, the products of technical knowledge. Beyond the strikingly "productivist" ideology that runs throughout Plato's civic utopia, what I wish to focus on here is the equivalence established between the productive activity of the poet and that of the painter: linguistic creation and iconographic production work toward the same kind of symbolic effect. If we go back one century earlier, it is not only in Simonides' famous definition of poetry as "painting that speaks" that we find the painter set alongside the poet. Indeed, as early as the beginning of the sixth century, Solon included in the same list of itinerant trades maritime commerce, agriculture, sculpture, poetry, prophecy, and medicine. In his manual practice, the sculptor is assured the technical assistance of Athena and Hephaestus; in his intellectual activity, the poet has at his disposal a certain quantity of knowledge or, more precisely, know-how, object of the Muses' instruction.[1]

Of course, at the juncture between what the modern tradition calls the "archaic" and "classical" periods, the technical activity of writing began to play a certain role, perhaps less in the composition than in the learning of poetry. In a "song culture" such as Greek civilization was in its first phases of expression, poetry was not only part and parcel of musical practice (understood as a whole including rhythmic speech, instrumental melody, and choreographic movements) but also the cornerstone of the traditional educational system.[2] The poetic creations attributed to Homer, Hesiod, and Sappho that have been considered thus far belong to this tradition of civic instruction through music. This tradition reflects the educational dimension of the poet's authority as it is expressed in her or his verse. Early-fifth-century iconography does not just provide illustrations for this education through poetry; it even occasionally incorporates inscriptions putting it into practice. It thereby illustrates one of the procedures of poetic activity taken as a craft.

The Muses have long been seen as the source of the poet's inspiration, and there are good reasons for this. But, while it is true that the formulas used to invoke these goddesses suggest that they express themselves directly through the bard's mouth, poetic inspiration, in its archaic Greek conception, does not exclusively constitute possession. As early as Homer, poetry represents a practice that is the object of instruction received within a privileged relationship with the Muses and their mother, Memory. If Demodocus is particularly honored by Odysseus, it is because "the race of *aoidoí*" enjoys the love of the Muse, if not Apollo, who taught (*edídaxe*) them the ways of song. While appearing to the poet in a famous inspirational vision, the Muses perform this same didactic function for Hesiod. Knowing how to articulate discourse (*artiépeiai*), they both taught (*edídaxan*) the poet his *Theogony* and breathed it into him (*enépneusan*).[3]

Poetry, a craft like painting or sculpture, always carried special respect and honor in Greece. Near the end of what is conceived as the "archaic" period, poets were becoming increasingly aware that what they produced depended on their *sophía,* their technical skill. Thus, Pindar proudly and peremptorily affirmed at the beginning of one of his praise poems for a winner at the Panhellenic Nemean games:

I am not a sculptor, so as to fashion stationary statues that stand on their same
  base.
Rather, on board every ship and in every boat, sweet song,
go forth from Aegina and spread the news
that Lampon's mighty son Pytheas
has won the crown for the pancratium in Nemea's games ...

(*Nemean* 5.1–5, trans. by W. H. Race)

What distinguishes the poetic object from the iconic object is its mobility.[4] Both of them, however, enjoy the same autonomy as products of an inspired artisan's activity.

1. Iconic Enunciations

Whatever the outcome of this rivalry, this confrontation between linguistic art and figurative art, whatever their respective merits, whatever the degree of awareness poets and visual artists had of their respective arts, the products of these two technical crafts share at least one common trait: they both address a public. In other words, while they cannot be reduced to simple vectors for a message, they are involved in a process of fabrication and communication. Moreover, in their linguistic or figurative manifestations they bear the traces of this act of authority before an audience that is to be influenced, if not made to participate in the poetic performance. Following others (as has already been noted), Benveniste forcefully showed that every enunciation, every putting of words into discourse, results in the uttered object—the "text" produced by the "putting into discourse" (*mise en discours*)—bearing the marks of its process of production. The inscription of the utterance of the enunciation on an authoritative artifact does not belong exclusively to linguistic manifestations or purely textual products. Whether through language, writing, flat images, or three-dimensional figures, enunciative manifestations can use widely varying semiotic means in their "putting into discourse."

In ancient Greece, the development of the utterance bearing traces of the enunciation (i.e. of the performance) as we observe it in poetry follows a course that is contemporary with and parallel to such development in the images on ceramics. Paradoxically, perhaps, the progressive growth in the use of alphabetic writing, in both literary creation and image production, seems to have opened a wide array of new technical possibilities, particularly in the materialization of traces left by the enunciation and of the "instance" on which they depend. Indeed, even in the "archaic" period, writing is not used in iconic representation solely to dispel ambiguity concerning the scenes depicted by appending brief legends to them in the form of proper names; it is not the sole function of writing to provide (often redundant) commentary or *diegesis* concerning the story. At the very same time when the first "signatures" are appearing in poetic works, painters, too, are refering to themselves in their work. And, like the poets, they do so in the third person: "These are the verses of Theognis of Megara," the poet has his elegy say; "Sophilos drew me," says a vase painted by this Athenian craftsman at about the same time. Like the poet, the painter has his product bear his signature; the work is henceforth supposed to proclaim his proper name. The signature affixed to the craft, which is underscored in ceramics by the attribution of the first person to the vase, might confer on the object (outside of any animist incarnation) a function analogous to that which the *sphragís* (the Theognidean "seal") bestows upon the elegiac poem: making it into a *mnêma,* a memorial on display before a community of citizens.[5]

Parallel to this indirect expression of the iconic object's speaker, we often also witness the evocation of its enunciatee in the form of an erotic declaration (e.g., "Leagros is beautiful") or an address to the user of the receptacle (e.g., "Be well and drink").[6] In this case, it is no longer the maker of the vase but probably its buyer and owner who speaks to the addressee in an utterance that makes a brief allusion to the circumstances of communication conditioning the use of the object and its images. As we shall see in the case of erotic plaudits, however, the performance situation thus evoked is more complex than the simplicity of the utterance pointing to it suggests.

It also happens that the Greek figurative artist makes himself into a comic-strip writer and contrives to put brief utterances, which are given poetic form, into the mouths of the protagonists in the depicted scenes.[7] These iconographic protagonists, whether they are reclining at the banquet or executing a dance step, sometimes break into song. But insofar as they are integrated into the represented scene, these utterances are of a narrative order; they belong to the story. For these enuncive and narrative markers to take on enunciative significance with respect to the communication and performance process, the scene depicted must correspond to the enunciation situation and the function of the object, as is the case in the symposium.[8]

Writing is not the only means that the figurative artist has at his disposal to give utterance to the enunciation, that is, to the act of performing in the different modes I have evoked. Indeed, the *grámma,* the letter, the graphic sign of writing, belongs to the same practice as *gráphein,* incising, which in Greece designates the whole process of iconic representation. Confirmation of this lies in those garlands of *grámmata* that do not constitute any coherent phonetic sequence but serve the same decorative function as meanders or palmettes. If writing is painting, then the utterance of the enunciation can manifest itself by other means than the graphic materialization of language. For example, given that the general practice in Greek figurative representation is to depict the human figure, and especially the face, in profile, the exceptional frontal view often has specific enunciative significance. Furthermore, play with the visual interrelationships linking the various figures of a single scene through the direction of their gaze can end up constituting an appeal to the spectator of the representation.[9]

2. Schoolmasters and Students

We can illustrate these general remarks through a reading of a single iconic object that is both apposite and very unusual.

Between 490 and 480, at a time when the utterance of the enunciation was being given particularly subtle forms by Pindar, an Athenian potter and painter

named Douris decorated and signed a drinking cup.[10] Inside this *kýlix* we see—
in what is, alas, a fragmentary image—a young athlete grooming himself. The
signature inscribed within the circular area of the scene appears in a regular,
expected form: *doris egraphsen,* "Douris drew." On the outside of the cup, we
find two scenes symmetrically related to each other in which pedagogical exer-
cises are depicted; these scenes surely resonate with the palaestra scene on the
inside of the cup.

These two scenes (B and A, analyzed in that order) are given rhythm by the
symmetrical and homologous positioning of five figures. On the left in scene B
appears a seated ephebe playing the flute, a seated adult holding a lyre in scene

Red-figure cup of Douris, F2285 (*ARV,* 2nd ed., 439.48), interior. Photo, Ingrid
Geske-Heiden. Antikensammlung, Staatliche Museen zu Berlin. Photo credit:
Bildarchiv Preussischer Kulturbesitz/Art Resource, NY.

Red-figure cup of Douris, F2285 (*ARV,* 2nd ed., 439.48), scene A. Photo, Johannes Laurentius. Antikensammlung, Staatliche Museen zu Berlin. Photo credit: Bildarchiv Preussischer Kulturbesitz/Art Resource, NY.

Red-figure cup of Douris, F2285 (*ARV,* 2nd ed., 439.48), scene B. Photo, Ingrid Geske-Heiden. Antikensammlung, Staatliche Museen zu Berlin. Photo credit: Bildarchiv Preussischer Kulturbesitz/Art Resource, NY.

A; on the right in both scenes there is a seated adult whose staff signals that he is a pedagogue. Facing the flutist in scene B and the lyre player in scene A is a child whose stature indicates that he is a *país* on the threshold of adolescence. At the center of scene B is a seated ephebe about to practice his writing, as indicated by the stylus and the *déltion tríptukhon,* the triple-paneled wax-covered tablet used for school exercises; the youth's gaze is directed at these two objects. At the center of scene A is a seated adult holding an open papyrus roll on which a few words are written. Facing the central figure in each scene is another *país,* whose eyes are turned toward the schoolmaster. The symmetrical organization of the two images, which is broken by the sequence of two couples plus one isolated figure (the pedagogue), is cleverly restored by the alternation ephebe/adult—child—ephebe/adult—child—adult, and by the focusing of the pedagogue's gaze toward the center.

Objects in the background (hanging from the wall?) indicate to us that the scenes are set in a closed interior space. In scene A, two drinking cups and two lyres symmetrically surround a flute case and the kind of basket that is usually used for gathering fruit or the like, perhaps used here for holding the papyrus rolls. The symmetrical positioning of these objects suggests that an analogous organization is to be reconstructed for scene B, the edge of which is missing. In any case, from right to left we can discern a papyrus roll, two writing tablets, a lyre, a cross shape, which probably represents an instrument for tuning the lyre, and an unidentifiable fragment of an object.[11] Each of these scenes is bordered with the same erotic inscription: *hipodamas kalos,* "Hippodamas is a beautiful (young man)." In both cases, the letters of the inscription run evenly along the edge of the cup, such that they touch the lips of the drinker who uses it.

In scene B, we see a writing lesson—or is it a grammar and dancing lesson? In scene A, what is represented is no doubt a poetry lesson.[12] That this is the high point of these few hours of class is indicated not only by the central position of the bearded man but also by his position seated on a chair with a backrest, a *klísmos* (by contrast with the stools, *díphroi,* on which all the other protagonists are seated), and, above all, by his papyrus roll, the only element facing the spectator and addressee of these charming scenes.

3. Philological Kaleidoscope

The double "breaking" of the general rule calling for representation in profile in the depiction of the papyrus roll clearly points to the enunciative function here. As a result of the first ninety-degree rotation performed in the depth of the field, such that the flat surface of the papyrus is presented to the spectator of the painted scene, the papyrus is made impossible for the schoolmaster to read. Furthermore, as a result of an analogous turn, this time performed on the surface plane, the written lines, which should have been traced vertically, are presented to be read horizontally by the same recipient of the cup. In the jargon of semiotic linguistics, we would call this a double enunciative "shifting out" with respect to the depicted scene's narrative.

But what is the meaning of these four lines, which are extracted from the "story" narrated by the pedagogical scene so as to become an utterance pertaining to the level of the enunciation? It is actually quite a strange inscription: it draws its interpreter into a labyrinth—of a kind that the classical philologist frequently encounters—of syntactical, semantic, morphological, graphic, dialectal, and metrical arguments that confront one another without ever converging toward a common solution. Let us look first at the syntax and semantics. This utterance comprises an assemblage of three "formulaic" expressions marking it as poetic:

a. *moisa moi* . . . . : "Muse, (tell) me . . . ," as the Homeric narrator requests when beginning his recitation of the *Odyssey,* the *Little Iliad,* or the *Hymn to Aphrodite;*[13]
b. *aphi skamandron euron:* "about the wide-flowing Scamander," following Homeric usage for the qualification of the Scamander and using a construction with *amphí* that we find precisely in the first verse of various *Homeric Hymns* (poetic preludes);[14]
c. *arkhomai aeindein:* "I begin to sing," a veritable formula that is widely used by the authors of the *Homeric Hymns* at the conclusion of the periodic opening of these bardic compositions.[15]

The *Homeric Hymns* also contain examples of the combination of these formulas in pairs, either a + b or b + c. The narrator of the *Hymn to Pan,* for example, asks his inspirer, "Muse, tell me about the dear son of Hermes"; and the narrator of the brief *Hymn to Poseidon* affirms, "I begin to sing about the great god, Poseidon."[16]

From a linguistic standpoint, this comparison can fully work only if we morphologically normalize the terms of the utterance written on the papyrus roll. The philologist is thus faced with accomplishing the kind of work that the Alexandrian editors carried out on literary texts. The verses presented to the reader of the vase were inscribed in the early fifth century, a time when Greeks did not show the same respect for the form of the written word that the scholar-critics at the Alexandrian library would later manifest. These verses present the kind of graphic inconsistencies that we find in other contemporary inscriptions:

- Concerning *aphi* for *amphí*, we may note that a nasal preceding a labial is often not written.[17]

- In *euron*, the painter-scribe did not transcribe the dieresis or the double rho marking the metrical pronunciation of this term in its poetic use; we find the uncontracted form *eúrroos* in Homeric poetry.[18]

- In all of the Homeric formulas just quoted, *árkhomai* is elided (*árkhom'*) before *aeídein*. The *scriptio plena* does frequently appear, however, in Attic poetic inscriptions of all periods.[19]

- Finally, the form *aeíndein* can be explained as comprising a "parasitic" addition (which is occasionally attested) of a nasal before a consonant.[20]

This morphological normalization allows us to recognize in the utterance what is almost a regular dactylic hexameter. The verse, though epic in metrical structure and theme, is nonetheless often classified as a melic fragment.[21] One reason for this is its dialectal coloring. Far from being written in the *Kunstsprache* rooted in the Ionic dialect that is used in the Homeric poems, this verse comprises forms from Aeolic poetry and melic poetry in general. First, the form *Moîsa,* instead of the *Moûsa* that we find in epic poetry, could be considered an Aeolic trait, since we find it in Sappho, but it is especially well attested in the "Doric" melic poetry of a Pindar or a Bacchylides. The same is true of the contraction of -oo- into -õ- in *euron,* marked by the very exceptional use—in the fifth-century Attic context—of an Ionic omega; this letter was not officially introduced into the Athenian alphabet until the end of that century. From a dialectal standpoint, this is an Aeolic trait that we find in the poetry of Alcaeus and Sappho, used here in place of the contraction into -ou- that we expect in Attic. Finally, infinitives ending in -*en* (or -*ên* when the *eta* came into use) are attested in practically all dialects except Ionic, and thus, except the Epic language.[22]

To temper our surprise at this mixture of melic linguistic forms and epic meter, we need only think of the similar fragmentary image on a red-figure shard contemporary with the Douris cup. On this shard, a young man sits between a flute player and a scribe; the young man holds a papyrus roll open in the same "enunciative" position as the schoolmaster painted by Douris. The utterance written on the papyrus in boustrophedon (as frequently in inscriptions of this period) presents Aeolic dialectal forms and meter that is probably dactylic. This utterance on display before the spectator, in speaking of *stesíkhoron húmnon ágoisai,* "guiding the hymn that initiates the choral dance," also takes up a formula from a poetic prelude.[23]

There remains, however, one unavoidable and insurmountable difficulty: even after being normalized morphologically, dialectically, and rhythmically, Douris' utterance does not make sense. From the standpoint of syntax, the dative *moi* is absolutely incompatible with the first-person nominative conveyed through the middle verb *árkhomai*.[24] Corrections and conjectures (the last recourse in philological normalization) only displace the problem. Is there a way out of the interpretive impasse to which philological reasoning leads us?

4. Craft Writing

Attention has, it seems, never been devoted to an utterance transcribed in letters that Greeks comprehended in sequence, as a phonetic chain.[25] When seen in light of the visual impression that Greeks attributed to inscriptions, the way in which the hexameter I have been discussing is written manifests striking irregularity of "rhythm." The letters themselves are uneven, almost cursive in shape; the rules for fitting these shapes into squares along two axes are hardly respected: their unequal spacing strongly contrasts with the calligraphy of the cup's other inscriptions.[26] Might not the awkwardness here point to a school exercise, even if such an exercise would (in reality) more likely be written out on a wax-covered tablet like the one figured in scene B than on a papyrus roll?

This hypothesis would at least account for the irresolvable syntactical incoherence of the inscription's content. Both form and content would, in this case, refer to the depicted scene, to the "story." In any event, the two poetic incipits awkwardly articulated around the announcement of the poem's (epic) subject emphasize the pedagogical character of the scene. Furthermore, the lack of savoir-faire manifested through this amalgam of three formulaic expressions is emphasized by the inconsistency of the metrical structure of the verse, which has only two secondary caesuras.[27] We are indeed dealing with a scene depicting instruction in music, in the Greek sense of that term: the art of poetry to be recited or sung while dancing to a rhythm or a melody. The writing—or "grammatical"—activity serves only as an aid for memorizing in this context. Although our sources (which are full of gaps) do not list writing among the various mnemonic techniques (perhaps based on iconographic analogies) that Simonides reputedly developed in the same era, a good century later Plato was to make his famous critique of writing through the "myth" of the Egyptian god Thoth, the technician-inventor who devised *grámmata:* for a learner, writing is a *phármakon,* a "remedy" for memory, but, in resorting to this technical means, the student entrusts his knowledge to external, foreign marks (*allótrioi túpoi*) and deprives himself of the ability to memorize it internally; this only produces *doxósophoi,* "pseudo-sages." For Aeschylus, writing (as Prometheus' invention) was already nothing but a *sóphisma,* a *mechánema,* a mere tool for memory.[28]

As a matter of fact, are not the writing implements in both scenes A and B solely in the hands of the schoolmaster? The student learns not only how to

write but also, above all, how to enunciate—how to recite, if not how to sing.
Once again it is Aeschylus who, in the famous tirade in which Prometheus lists
all of the technical inventions he has passed along to mankind in order to
enlighten and civilize them, sees in the combining of letters "the artisan who is
mother to the Muses."[29] Within a conception of poetry as a craft, writing is thus
actually capable of making its technical contribution to Muse-inspired creation.
The inscription integrated into the scene painted by Douris plays on this very
paradox: it fixes in writing a (clumsy) request to the Muse to inspire the begin-
ning of an oral song. Furthermore, this awkwardly written verse presents, in the
"errors" just discussed, all the marks of a phonetic transcription.

Thus, we have confirmation of the relationship between the physical form of
the writing and the scene as a whole, the story encompassing that writing. On
top of this internal reference, however (wherein the inscription relates directly to
the figuratively represented scenario into which it is inserted), there is also an
external, extradiscursive reference to the "performance" (wherein the inscrip-
tion relates to the enunciation situation). The relationship between the "story"
depicted and the context for "performance" and use of the vase is established
through the "shifting out" produced by the double rotation (of the papyrus and
of the text written on it, respectively) which I have described.[30] What the image
presents is no longer just narrative (a story) but also discourse (directed at an audi-
ence): while the poetic inscription emphasizes, through both its form and con-
tent, that the figuratively represented story is about musical instruction and the
various technical tools used for it, it is also offered for reading by the cup's user.

5. *Potor in fabula*

But who is the user of this cup and in what context? In scene A, two markers
with enunciative significance can point us to the answer. First, as noted earlier,
the musical instruments suspended in the background are framed by two cups
replicating the precise form of the object made by Douris. They are drinking
cups for use at the symposium. In such a context, the circulation and consump-
tion of wine was accompanied by the recitation of *skólia,* melic songs intended
for this kind of occasion. We have every reason to believe that one of paramount
aims of musical instruction was to enable adolescents to participate fully in the
banquets of citizens for which Douris' cup was conceived. In fact, Douris him-
self painted a scene depicting an adult singing a *skólion* while an adolescent
accompanies him on the flute.[31]

In addition to the twin images of cups, which may be markers pointing to the
performance context of Douris' *kýlix,* we also find matching erotic inscriptions
crowning both scenes A and B. There is no room for doubt: reference is being

made here to the user of the cup, or at least to the context in which it is to be passed from one pair of lips to another; the reference here is clearly extradiscursive. It should be remembered that the homoerotic relationship between an adult and an adolescent, between an *erastés* and an *erómenos,* is a social bond that is regularly evoked as being formed in the symposium. Accordingly, we have grounds for making a connection (of external reference) between, on the one hand, the story of Greek musical instruction, wherein the homophilic relationship between schoolmaster and student has an important function, and, on the other, a sympotic context, wherein such relationships are actualized. Even if scenes A and B do not seem to be marked by the presence of Eros (apart from the erotic praise inscriptions, of course), the pedagogical relationships depicted in them display the asymmetry that is also characteristic of the love bond between an ephebic or adult *erastés* and his *país erómenos.*[32] For a fifth-century Athenian reader, it is probable that the juxtaposition of an older man and a very young adolescent boy necessarily evoked a masculine homophilic erotic relationship, but such a reading of the image depends on an inference concerning cultural tendencies.[33] In connection with this, the erotic praise of the *kalós* inscriptions may well evoke Hippodamas as an ideal enunciatee; though this is probably a reference to a real young man who was famous for his beauty, Hippodamas would probably have been perceived by the speaker of the words in which he is praised as paradigmatic. The inscription would thus call forth the image of an exemplary "pederastic" relationship, one serving as a model for the kind hoped for by the different users of the cup as they participate in the banquet. However that may be, it is certain that this declaration of love introduces into the iconic utterance of the enunciation a secondary process of communication: between the recipient(s) of the object and his (or their) beloved.

The story, the iconic markers pointing to enunciation, the inscriptions integrated into the story or crowning it are all oriented toward the recipient of these finely contoured images. The utterance pointing to enunciation does not so much concern the enunciator (i.e., the speaker in the performance situation) but rather is oriented more toward inviting—through very different processes—the (extradiscursive) enunciatee and addressee to determine himself relative to the "narrative."[34] These two scenes painted by Douris thus evoke the circumstances of the reception and "fruition" of the painted object rather than the conditions of its production; the scenes incite par excellence what Umberto Eco would call the reader's "interpretive cooperation." They bring to their recipient, as he dines and drinks, confirmation and enrichment of his own universe of reference; they serve as the emblems of the ideological configuration of the community of belief to which the symposiast belongs.[35] To raise Douris' cup to one's lips during convivial wine consumption is to remember the process of learning song and receive an invitation to create and sing poetry in what amounts to a subtle transfer of poetic authority.[36]

VI

VISION, BLINDNESS, AND MASK

Enunciation and Emotion in Sophocles' Oedipus Tyrannus

Considered from the standpoint of the authority and linguistic expression of the poet's voice, classical tragedy clearly presents a specific problem. Indeed, given that it is simply a "script" for the dramatic staging of a narrative action, the tragic text is characterized by the disappearance of enunciative markers, in the strict sense: there is no speaker-narrator and, consequently, no biographical author present behind it. The same is true (as we shall see in the next chapter) in that other dramatic genre, comedy, but also in certain forms of dithyramb, such as Bacchylides' famous poem 18. Plato himself, in the *Republic* passage devoted to traditional poetry, remarks that pure narrative (which he calls *diégesis*) can assume mimetic form: the statements attributed to the various protagonists involved in the narrative action are formulated in direct discourse; in this form of dialogue, it is as if the narrator—whose enunciative figure points to the author of the narrative—delegated his voice to the actors. In a narrative form that remained mixed, Homer would provide the example for a process of mimetic dramatization that was to be systematized in the fifth century to become tragedy, comedy, and, in some cases, dithyramb.[1]

We shall see, however, that Greek tragedy as a poetic genre does not directly present an action to its spectators' vision and affectivity, as if that action were played and incarnated by living actors; rather, the action is mediated through the

This is a revised version of "Vision, Blindness, and Mask: The Radicalisation of the Emotions in Sophocles' *Oedipus Rex,*" trans. M. S. Silk, in *Tragedy and the Tragic: Greek Theatre and Beyond,* ed. M. S. Silk (Oxford, 1996), 17–37.

discursive processes of narrative, the responsibility for which redounds to its "author." The enunciative distance engendered by third-person and past-tense narrative is partially reconstituted in the dramatic forms of classical Athens by the masks, costumes, and ritual gestures of the actors and chorus members. These participants of the drama act on stage not as "characters" but—owing to the worship that they (along with the spectators) devote to Dionysus—as heroines and heroes from another time and, in many cases, another place. This means that the voices of the actors and chorus members only very indirectly represent the voice of a speaker-narrator who might be identified as the author, but it also means that the narrative voices—in the dramatized, mimetic form that the tragic genre entails—are diffracted into a complex polyphony pointing to a polymorphous "instance of enunciation."[2]

Furthermore, concerning the rules of the genre, particularly from an enunciative standpoint, the plethora of attempts to define Attic tragedy and the notion of the tragic in Greece have left only one avenue open to the interpreter working at the dawn of the twenty-first century: the return to indigenous theory and categories. If we wish to avoid the pitfalls of the caricatural image of contemporary tragedy found in Old Comedy, however, we must confront the profusion of readings that Aristotle's *Poetics* has elicited. And if we find our way through this forest of interpretations, we are still faced with the difficulties and paradoxes involved in a text written from class notes, which appears to be interpreting tragic performances only from a certain remove, from the point of view of a philosophical culture henceforth devoted to the written word.

This, in any case, is one way of explaining a strange omission that we find in the *Poetics*. Let us look briefly at the beginning and end of the text in question.[3] We can see that, in Aristotelian terms, the specific nature of tragedy is determined by six hierarchically presented elements: plot, character, thought, diction (or delivery), song, and, finally, the element Aristotle calls *ópsis,* which covers everything having to do with vision and sight, and which is generally translated into English as "spectacle." Although visual expression complements diction and song, it is definitively excluded from Aristotle's definition of the poetic art; it is removed from the sphere of the poet and relegated to that of the costume designer. The consequences for Aristotle are clear: tragedy can create its effects outside the context of theatrical competition, even without actors. Ridding tragedy of all elements of *ópsis* means reducing tragedy to a text, removed from its public performance context of the cult of Dionysus. It makes of tragedy a modern literary text that is cut off from its enunciative context.

This exclusion of *ópsis* becomes a paradox when Aristotle nevertheless takes up the problem of vision in his discussion—no longer in the descriptive but now in the normative mode—about the emotions that tragedy is meant to engender. The essence of the poet's art is to arouse fear and pity in the audience, not by means of spectacle, which is ultimately only a problem of staging (*khoregía*), but rather through plot. Aristotle sees in the story of Oedipus, as told by Sophocles, the model for a plot capable of arousing properly tragic emotions—for an audience that Aristotle imagines as listeners, not as readers.[4] It is thus paradoxical that the tragedy Aristotle chooses as a model (oral) text should be the *Oedipus Tyrannus,* the whole of which, as many readers have pointed out, is concerned with the problem of vision.

1. Aristotle and Tragic Spectacle

We must start by returning to Aristotle's text, where we find that the hierarchy of six elements distinctive to tragedy is part of a larger semiotic division at the heart of his reflections on the poetic art. At the beginning of his treatise, the critic posits that every poetic expression can be defined as a product of representation (*mímesis*). The mimetic procedure is then divided into three aspects: the means employed (*en hoîs*), the object represented (*há*), and the mode of realization (*hós*).[5] In the case of tragedy, diction and song belong to the category of means employed, plot, character, and thought to the object represented, and spectacle to its mode of realization. Aristotle goes on to conclude that, as a mode of tragic representation, the visual aspect encompasses all five other elements. Thus, if spectacle is not part of poetics, this is simply because—in the Aristotelian perspective—it is a technique of a different order. From Aristotle's essentialist point of view, the tragic text itself appears distinguishable from its relation with the theater, that is, from its ritual and dramatic execution.[6]

While the conclusion of this chapter devoted to defining the specificity of tragedy thus excludes the visual aspect of tragic representation from the poetic art, the visual is nonetheless that mode which best "seduces the spirit" (*psukha-gogikón*). Aristotle's whole attempt to define tragedy through its distinctive elements is guided by the themes of *mímesis* and *kátharsis.* On *kátharsis,* which is deemed central to the essence of tragedy, I note here only what Aristotle himself says: by evoking fear and pity, tragedy purges these emotions in the audience. This proposition (which has frequently been discussed on account of its synthetic character) is obviously taken up and developed when the time comes to define the aim of tragedy and the means by which it achieves its effects. While emphasizing the role of plot—and, in particular, plots in which great men such as Oedipus fall from happiness to misery because of a tragic fault—Aristotle cannot deny that fear and pity arise as much from the spectacle itself as from the organization of the dramatic action. At the same time, however, Aristotle excludes the visual from the poetic art and, as I have mentioned, imagines a rendition of the story of Oedipus that would cause shivers of pity and fear merely upon being heard (if not read).[7] Vision makes a surreptitious reappearance, however, in the last chapter of the long discussion devoted to the role of plot. Aristotle asserts there that the aim of a correct organization of the story line is, ultimately, to "place before the eyes" by means of linguistic enunciation, that is, to transform the listener into a spectator. Thus, the images called into being by words should coincide with the representation on stage and, more specifically, with the emotions evoked by the gestures and performance of the actors.[8] Given the vividness (*enargéstata*) assigned to the art of poetry, it is clearly impossible to overlook sight.

2. A Visual Inquiry

From Aristotle's reflections on the paradigmatic nature of the *Oedipus Tyrannus* as tragedy, we turn now to the text itself of this drama. Let us begin (as others have before) with the observation that the entire prologue of the tragedy plays on the theme of sight. The priest opens by inviting King Oedipus to observe with his own eyes the miserable state in which an epidemic has left the city of Thebes (15 and 22). The priest addresses Oedipus as a god from whom divine intervention is required, as indeed Oedipus has intervened in the past to help the city (47–48 and 52–53). In this passage he evokes the knowledge of the current king of Thebes, knowledge that depends on "the voice of the god" or the "experience of a man" (40–45), "knowledge" (*oîstha*) that can be etymologically traced to the root designating sight, *wid-,* and that, by analogous etymological means, Sophocles' text links to the name "Oedipus" (*oidi-pous,* 8, during the king's introduction).[9]

In the tension between past and present—between Oedipus' past acts of salvation upon arriving at Thebes and the city's current state of desperation—the theme of vision undergoes two simultaneous narrative transformations operating at the level of the plot as Sophocles has reformulated it for the Athenian stage.

2.1. From Linguistic Knowledge to Visual Knowledge

In the past and present of the drama, Oedipus is faced with the task of solving a riddle; that is, he is asked to interpret equivocal language. In Proppian terms, the ordeal that has made him "first among men" (33 and 46; cf. 507–11) and the ordeal that should confirm his reign for "raising up the city" (46–51) both depend on the decoding of enigmatic speech. But these oracular pronouncements are of very different origins.

It is not because we rank you with the gods that I and these children are seated at your hearth, but because we judge you to be the first of men, both in the incidents of life and in dealing with higher powers. For it was you who came to the city of Cadmus and released us from the tribute we were paying, the tribute of the cruel singer; and that with no special knowledge or instruction from us; no, it is by the extra strength given by a god that you are said and believed to have set right our life.

But now, Oedipus, mightiest man in the sight of all, all we suppliants implore you to find some protection for us, whether your knowledge comes from hearing a message from a god or from a man, perhaps; for I see that the setting together of counsels is most effective for those who have experience. Come, best of living men, raise up the city!

(vv. 31–46, translated by H. Lloyd-Jones)

The first enigmatic pronouncement was made by the Sphinx, a singer, even a poetess, but also a "harsh bard" (*sklerâs aoidoû,* translated in this passage as "cruel singer," 36), a woman "of crafty song" (130), a "rhapsode bitch" (391), a young "prophetess with hooked talons" (1199). Independently from the iconography of the day, which represented the Sphinx as a monster with the wings of a bird and the body of a lioness, the text itself pushes the Sphinx toward the animal sphere: while her voice (like that of all bards) can deceive, it does so not through its sweetness or charm but by its hoarse, beast-like barking. Nonetheless, in contrast to the literary tradition, which represented the Sphinx as a beast that devours raw flesh and abducts men, Sophocles brings more ambiguous qualities to her poetic voice.[10] It is a voice that contents itself with posing enigmatic questions, a feminine voice that usurps the predominantly masculine role of bard or rhapsode, in short, a voice that takes on the deadly qualities of the songs of Homer's Sirens.

By contrast with the bestial voice of Oedipus' first trial, the second ordeal involves a divine voice, that of Apollo, the god who reveals (77), whose arrival strikes the sight (81), who gives clear orders (*saphôs,* 106). Unlike the voice of the Sphinx, the voice of the god asks no questions; instead, it answers one. Furthermore, contrary to its own custom, this voice—which is no longer poetic but oracular—points directly to knowledge based on visual observation. Without employing his usual enigmatic language, Phoebus the Brilliant orders "in broad daylight" (*emphanôs*) that the land be rid of the evil that is sullying Thebes (96–8). Creon, questioned by an Oedipus "eager to know" (*eisómestha,* 84), has no trouble identifying this evil as the murderer of the city's previous king, Laius.

Oedipus, of course, is in a most peculiar position with regard to the experiential knowledge referred to so clearly by the god of Delphi. A newcomer to Thebes, he knows of his predecessor only through hearsay; he has never actually seen him (*éxoid' akoúon; ou gàr eiseîdón gé po,* 105). Without going into all the details of the investigation that Oedipus conducts on Apollo's orders, what is important to notice at this point is that Oedipus' entire search, the (transparent) oracle about his own fate, and the (equally transparent) oracle given to Laius (711–14) all elaborate on the theme of visual knowledge.[11] We find Jocasta stating that the contradictions she has discovered in Apollo's pronouncement might prevent her henceforth from "seeing" the oracular statements (851–58; cf. 720–25). Furthermore, the revelations of Oedipus' origins by the Corinthian shepherd are understood by the king as signs revealed "in broad daylight" (1050 and 1058–59). Later on, the Theban shepherd, from whom Oedipus demands an answer, looks him straight in the eye (1121) and draws on knowledge that the king recognizes as superior to his own because it is based on sight (1115–16). As Creon has already stated in verse 119, he is the only one capable of "showing what he has seen" (*eidòs phrásai*). It is thus doubly ironic when Oedipus himself concedes that "no one sees the one who has seen" (293). Finally, we may recall Oedipus' conclusion upon hearing what he has been seeking from the shepherd, sole eyewitness to the fateful events:

Alas, alas, everything becomes clear (*saphê*)! O light, may I look upon (*prosblépsaimi*) you for the last time now, since I am revealed (*péphasmai*) to be the son of those whose son I ought not to have been, the companion of those whom I ought not to have frequented, the killer of those whom I ought not to have killed.

(vv. 1182–85)

Here we see a narrative reversal expressed on two levels: first, in place of human knowledge, which is directed by the questions of a creature simultaneously divine, bestial, and feminine, is substituted divine knowledge, which becomes the object of humans' questions; second, knowledge based on words is replaced by knowledge founded on sight. Not only does Creon claim that the deceptive songs of the Sphinx have prevented the Thebans from looking "at their feet," that is, at what was clearly before them, tempting them instead toward the invisible (*tà aphanê*, 130–31), but also Oedipus himself declares that the solution to the riddle posed by the Sphinx was merely a matter of language (*dieipeîn*, 394). This rejection of the riddle (which Sophocles declines to cite in its well-known formulation) as mere language is perhaps underscored by Oedipus' pun on his own name here: *ho medèn eidòs Oidípous,* "Oedipus who knows/has seen nothing" (397). However we are to interpret this pun, it is clear that the episode of the Sphinx, though unnecessary to the narrative logic of the plot, serves to emphasize through contrast the nature of true knowledge.[12]

2.2. On Vision and Blindness

It is precisely this narrative reversal between linguistic knowledge (required by
the riddle) and visual knowledge (divine in origin) that brings us to the second
narrative transformation on which the drama of the *Oedipus Tyrannus* is based.

Let us reexamine here the famous confrontation between King Oedipus and
Tiresias, the soothsayer. While recognizing the necessity of what has been made
manifest (*exéphenen*, 243) in the oracle, and while protesting against Tiresias'
prior refusal to reveal anything (*xuneidòs ou phráseis*, 330), Oedipus himself
refuses to see upon being confronted with the truth as the soothsayer finally for-
mulates it. No sooner has Tiresias made his revelation (*ekphéno*, 329; cf. 343),
however, than we are taken from the realm of the visual back to the linguistic:
the coincidence between "polluter" and "Oedipus" is merely a matter of words
(*rhêma*, 355; *lógos*, 359); it is nothing more than a riddle (439). Tiresias is also
hiding behind words (358, 360, 362, 364, etc.). Oedipus does not simply take
the soothsayer's blindness at face value; in his anger, he proceeds to accuse the
old man of deafness: it is in fact Tiresias' sanity that is put in question (*noûs*,
370–71). This echoes the reference to *phroneîn* that Tiresias had claimed for him-
self in his first pronouncements at verses 316–18 and 326–29, as well as in the
last words he utters at verse 462 (forming a ring structure). The soothsayer has
no further reason to withhold the truth. It is not he, a spokesman for Apollo,
who is blind but his questioner, who "sees without seeing" (*kaì dédorkas kou
blépeis*, 413) the house in which he lives and the people with whom he lives,
who does not know (*oîstha*, 415) who his parents are. Note that Tiresias' claim
is symmetrical with the statement by Oedipus at verses 1182–85, which effects
the play's first narrative transformation. It follows that the voice of the sooth-
sayer announces the outcome of the second narrative transformation structur-
ing the plot of the *Oedipus Tyrannus:* he who now can see the light of day will
see only darkness (419); the man of sight will become blind (*tuphlòs ek dedorkó-
tos*, 454).[13] It is at this point that Oedipus is revealed (*phanésetai*, 453 and 457)
to be of genuine Theban origin and not a "metic foreigner," as formerly sup-
posed (*lógoi*, 452)—brother and father of his own children, son and husband to
his wife, incestuous rival and murderer of his own father.[14]

Thus, the transition from linguistic knowledge to visual knowledge orches-
trated by the plot causes, in a kind of figurative chiasmus, the material transition
from vision to blindness. The vision of mortal men who think they can see
through words is replaced by the belief of the blind, whose mutilation puts them
in contact with real visual knowledge, that of the gods. It is necessary, therefore,
that Oedipus become a new Tiresias so that his literal blindness may be trans-
formed into metaphorical vision, and so that the text may move from the
domain of supposition and opinion (*gnóme*, 398) to that of (revealed) truth

(*alétheia*, 356 and 369). To rephrase this transformation in the words of the chorus marking the end of the scene, Oedipus' simple skill (*sophía*) for solving the Sphinx's riddle becomes true knowledge about the affairs of men, comparable to that possessed by Zeus and Apollo (*eidótes*, 497–511).

2.3. The Elimination of Sensory Powers

The moment he possesses true knowledge, Oedipus blinds himself in one destructive motion. The text, through parallel use of the term "ankles" (*árthra*), seems to suggest a relationship between the feet pierced at the moment the child was exposed (1032–36; cf. 718) and the adult eyes pierced by two golden hooks (1270). In such a context, Oedipus' blinding of himself can be interpreted as the annihilation of an identity, or rather as a change of identity. In blinding himself, Oedipus renounces an identity associating him, through his name, with knowledge and vision (*eidós*, 397), and takes up instead the identity of a child "of Fortune," Oedipus of the pierced feet, Oedipus the Swollen-Footed (1036 and 1080).[15] Readers have, of course, attempted to go further. Thus, this self-mutilation can be seen as expiatory self-destruction, which, in parallel with Jocasta's suicide, was provoked by the unspeakable act of incest. Others have associated Oedipus' blinding of himself with his desire to go into exile (1436 and 1452) on Cithaeron, which, in turn, has been interpreted in an overly simplistic way as the expulsion of a scapegoat. And, if we abandon the text altogether in favor of the symbols to which psychoanalytic criticism holds the secret, feet and eyes become signs for the penis, and Oedipus' act signifies self-castration, that is, a means of inflicting upon himself the punishment that follows from parricide and incest.[16]

Nevertheless, prudence requires that we set aside theories of expiatory suicide, *pharmakós* expulsion, and symbolic castration and get back to the text itself. From a simple narrative point of view, Oedipus' self-blinding provokes an ironic reversal of the initial situation. This king, who insists from the outset of the tragedy on his desire to know (*tách'eisómestha*, 84), who wants to conduct his inquiry face to face (1118–20), and who finally submits to the obvious (1182; see the passage quoted earlier), can, upon his return to the stage, be heard only as a voice emerging from the shadows (1313–15), a voice which sounds strangely like that of Tiresias (1323). Oedipus' voice is also accompanied by heightened auditory perception (1325–26). Like the soothsayer on his first appearance (324–33), however, the dethroned king, reduced to a simple voice, refuses all face-to-face encounters from this point on. Revealed now in his polluted state, he can no longer look into the eyes of his own parents, whom he expects to join in Hades soon (1371–72), nor can he bear to see his own children (1375–76), the city, or the statues of the gods (1377–79 and 1384–85, in a ring structure). After this rejection of vision (in language bristling with terms denoting sight), the king then expresses his wish to deprive himself of the sense of hearing as well (1386–89). Oedipus the Blind and Deaf, in his desire to be hidden, rejected, even killed, calls down upon himself a misery far greater than the punishment inflicted on Tiresias: from this point on, he insists that he be seen and heard by no living person (1436–37). This demand confirms his refusal of all light at the moment of self-recognition (1183–85).

Deprived of sight, refusing to hear, Oedipus now has only a tactile link with the outside world (1413); it is touch that takes the place of sight when, in the final scene, he tries to communicate one last time with his daughters (1464–70, where the verb for touch appears three times): "Si je les touche, je les verrai" (if I touch them, I shall see them), in the French translation of André Bonnard. It is also by touching the hand of Creon that Oedipus solicits his protection for Antigone and Ismene (1510). In this way, the blind man, still speaking, accomplishes his last act on stage.[17]

We thus see a progressive self-deprivation of all sensory capacities, ending with the sense of touch. Accompanying this deprivation is an emotional responsiveness clearly activated as soon as Oedipus realizes the truth of his fate. This emotion is apparent not just in the exclamations punctuating his speech (*ioù ioú*, 1183; *aiaî aiaî*, 1307; *ió*, 1313 and 1321; *oímoi oímoi*, 1316; *pheû pheû*, 1324); it is also felt in the use of melic rhythms in the second *kommós* and, more particularly, in the melic anapaests (1307–11) and dochmiacs (1314–15 and 1322–23) in some of Oedipus' responses.

> Alas, alas, miserable am I! Where am I being carried in my sorrow? Where is my voice borne on the wings of the air? Ah, god, how far have you leaped?
>
> (vv. 1307–11, trans. H. Lloyd-Jones)

Oedipus can no longer speak of his fate except as an accumulation of "ills" and "afflictions" (*kaká, páthea*, 1330) expressed in melic rhythms.[18] Nothing is left to Oedipus, beyond perception by touch, but to cry over his lot. This is what he twice declares (1467 and 1486; cf. 1515), at the moment when he becomes aware, through touch, of the presence of his two daughters, also in tears (1473). After lamenting his own fate, Oedipus expresses fear about that of his daughters, and Creon is called upon twice to take pity on their tragic lot. Therein lies the lesson drawn by the chorus—whether or not the verses in question are authentic—when the *choreutaí* sententiously conclude that no mortal can "see" (*ideîn*) himself happy unless he is capable of "seeing to it" (*episkopoûnta*, 1529) that his life comes to its final days free from suffering (*pathón*, 1530). This is also the final word of the play. When the hero of the tragedy has deprived himself of his means of perception and communication with the outside world, a residue remains: the "pathemic."[19]

3. Spectacle and the Purging of the Emotions

The *páthos* imposed on the hero as the plot unfolds is not without effect on those interacting with him in the tragic fiction constructed on stage. From this point of view, Antigone and Ismene are not the only ones to mirror the tears of their father with their own. In the *stásimon* immediately following the visual revelation of Oedipus' identity, and again at the beginning of the *kommós* after the news of his blinding, the chorus of old men from Thebes clearly anticipate the reactions of the hero himself. In the last strophe of their last ode, the *choreutaí* point to the role played in Oedipus' self-recognition by time, time "which sees everything" (1213); later, by contrast, they voice their desire, analogous to the hero's own, to "close their eyes" (1220–21).[20] Most notably, when confronted with the spectacle of Oedipus blinded—"a spectacle the sight of which causes pity" (*théama eisópsei . . . epoiktísai*, 1295–96), as the messenger says—the first reaction of the chorus is to cry out in pain at "a dreadful fate for men to look upon" (*ô deinòn ideîn páthos anthrópois*, 1297):

> O grief terrible for men to see, o grief most terrible of any I have yet encountered! What madness has come upon you, unhappy one? Who is the god that with a leap longer than the longest has sprung upon your miserable fate? Ah, ah, unhappy one, I cannot even bear to look on you, though I wish to ask you many questions and to learn many answers and perceive many things; such is the horror you inspire in me!
>
> (vv. 1297–306, trans. H. Lloyd-Jones)

Thus, the chorus cannot look this spectacle of suffering in the face (*eisideîn*, 1303), so great is their terror (*phriké*, 1306). The *páthos* of Oedipus rebounds onto the *choreutaí*, spectators of the hero's suffering; their emotion is so strong that, like Oedipus, they can neither see nor hear (1312).[21]

3.1. The Mask as a Means of Facing Passions

The pathos of the dramatic action thus provokes corresponding feelings in those who are watching; and the emotions felt by the *koryphaîos* and the *choreutaí*—pity and fear—evoke, in their turn, the feelings that, for Aristotle, make up the essence of the tragedy's purpose. We may even ask whether the philosopher of poetics has not chosen the example of the story of Oedipus precisely to illustrate the process of "purging" the emotions supposedly provoked by its dramatization in tragedy.

This line of argument needs nuancing, of course. In one of the passages from the *Poetics* cited earlier, concerning the role of vision in tragedy, Aristotle imagines an affective reaction on the part of the audience, not the chorus. Furthermore, he hopes that their emotions will be provoked simply by hearing the text of *Oedipus Tyrannus*. But is it a mere coincidence that, in this single passage of the *Poetics,* Aristotle uses not the usual *phóbos* to designate the sensation of fear but rather *phríttein,* the very term used by Sophocles?[22] The coincidence between the emotions felt by Sophocles' *choreutaí* (who are often taken as representative of the spectators assembled at the Theater of Dionysus) and the feelings attributed by Aristotle to the audience of a successful tragedy is, at the very least, striking.[23] The same is true of the philosopher's effort to demonstrate that merely hearing a text should awaken those emotions commonly provoked by spectacle.

From the point of view of visual communication, the story of Oedipus as conceived by Sophocles has a very particular impact. We must not forget that tragic drama in fifth-century Athens formed part of the cult practices dedicated to Dionysus Eleuthereus and performed by different groups in the community. Furthermore, the ritual acts performed for the Great Dionysia involved, in particular, the wearing of masks. Aristotle himself is fully conscious of this fact when he banishes everything having to do with spectacle from his art of poetry, placing it in the domain of the *skeuopoiós*. Pollux's lexicon tells us that assistants to the director, known in ancient Greece as "costume designers," prepared not only the clothing but also, what is more important, the masks of the actors.[24]

As I show in chapter 7 and in another essay, the mask has a function that is central to tragic representation as a cultic act.[25] Enunciative disguise through the wearing of masks is a crucial element in the celebration of the god of cross-dressing and of transitions from interior to exterior (and vice versa). It is the sine qua non for the theatrical dramatization of a narrative belonging to the legendary tradition or the recent past of a civic community assembled in the sanctuary of Dionysus Eleuthereus in the *hic et nunc* of the spectacle. Dramatization, as I have noted, is presented directly to the public without any mediation, whereas a narrative action is usually kept at a distance through the linguistic means of narration: such techniques as phraseology evoking times long gone, adverbs constructing an imaginary space quite different from that in which the listeners find themselves, or the persistent use of the pronominal form *he* in place of the *I* or *you* of direct discursive interaction. Here, however, only the mask can recreate the narrative distance abolished by the mimetic dramatization, or, more exactly, only the mask allows face-to-face interaction while, at the same time, dissimulating. This double function can be traced to the etymology of the Greek term for mask: *prósopon* can be understood both as "that which is close to the eyes" and "that which faces the eyes" (of someone else). Given the terms of which it is composed, the word for mask appears to imply the ideas both of appearance and of confronting with the gaze.[26]

If we undertake to analyze the actual use of these tragic and comic masks during dramatic representations for the Great Dionysia, we find that the primary function of the classical Athenian mask is to dissimulate; only secondarily does it serve to identify. Thus, the individual and social identity of the real face of the actor is hidden, while, at the same time, the identity of the character is not precisely represented on stage. Far from creating an effect of contiguity or alienation, or even reincarnation—functions commonly, though incorrectly, attributed to masks in general—the tragic mask of the classical period serves to distance a voice and a gaze that one might otherwise take to belong directly to the hero of legend represented as "alive" on stage through dramatic *mímesis*. It serves to "shift out" a voice and a gaze, for the mouth and eyes are the two organs corresponding to the holes in the mask's surface; they allow the voice and gaze of the actor to appear to the spectators, beyond the hero he is miming. The mask creates a face-to-face encounter between the participants in the dramatic action and the public, but it also mediates this encounter between the heroes of the story played on stage and the audience, rendering ambiguous the authoritative voice of both the actor and the *choreutaí*.

3.2. Self-destruction and the Limits of Dramatic Illusion

The significance of Oedipus' self-inflicted blindness thus extends beyond the story as reworked and dramatized by Sophocles. It is a gesture that calls into question the very foundations of tragic "discourse," the conventions of masked representation as performed at the cult of Dionysus Eleuthereus. What is more, in appearing on stage with a mask but deprived of sight, Oedipus negates the possibility of visual (though mediated) communication between actor and spectator; likewise, his desire to become deaf works as a rejection of the ambiguous effects of speech. Of course, Tiresias too appears on stage in a mask without eyes. But his blindness, imposed by a goddess, is a given, a fact handed down by tradition. In contrast to this, Oedipus' self-blinding is an act integrated into the plot as Sophocles has reformulated it. In blinding himself, Oedipus tries to destroy not only his own identity as an actor in the drama, but also that of the wearer of the mask. Oedipus cannot, therefore, take on the role of *pharmakós* or scapegoat, which some have wished to attribute to him: what would we make of an expiatory victim who actively wishes to be driven from the city (1289–90, 1380–81, 1436–67, and 1450–51) but ultimately finds himself invited to return to his palace (1515)?[27]

Rather, it is in blinding himself that Oedipus comes closest to the figure of Tiresias even as he distances himself from him. In the traditional story, the soothsayer is blinded by a deity for having seen a divine body; his blindness confers on him, in return, powers of divination giving him access to the realm of the gods. From this story, Sophocles' tragedy borrows only the fact of Tiresias' powers of divination (300–301). In mutilating himself by his own hand (*autókheir*, 1331), despite the presence of Apollo behind this act (1329; cf. 1258), Oedipus sanctions knowledge whose scope seems to be limited to his own identity (1138–35), but broadens to include knowledge of his *daímon,* of the *moîra* imposed on him by the gods (1311 and 1458), which is recognized as such by the chorus (1300–1302).[28] Even if the *moîra* comes to pass by the will of the divinity, the tragic hero takes responsibility for its consequences, an example of what is called double motivation.[29]

> It was Apollo, Apollo, my friends, who accomplished these cruel, cruel sufferings of mine! And no other hand struck my eyes, but my own miserable hand! For why did I have to see, when there was nothing I could see with pleasure?
>
> (vv. 1329–35, trans. H. Lloyd-Jones)

To know oneself is also to know the foundations of the human condition; it is Delphic knowledge, placed under Apollo's control.[30] What remains, then, beyond this knowledge concerning human destiny, beyond the disastrous consequences of the lot given by the god and revealed by the patron of Delphi, is *páthos.*

The revelation of the truth guaranteed by the god means the end of the dramatic illusion. If the self-blinding takes Oedipus to the limits of human knowledge through self-knowledge,[31] the same gesture brings him to the limits of tragic staging. It has been mentioned that, at the end of the play, the hero disappears into the palace instead of going to Cithaeron, as he wishes. As for his own daughters, Oedipus thinks that they will no longer be able to attend any festivities in the city without shedding bitter tears (1489–91). If Oedipus keeps speaking for a moment, if there are nevertheless to be further public festivities, it will only be amidst tears. It looks as if Oedipus' drama as staged in *Oedipus Tyrannus* spells out the ultimate implications of a theological truth: there is no longer any need for words, or vision, or even masks. Again, what remains is pathos, incarnated in the weeping of Oedipus' daughters.

3.3. The Emotional Effects of Dramatic Speech

Even outside the tragic phenomenon of purging passions to which Aristotle's art of poetry points, a contemporary of Sophocles, the sophist Gorgias, set forth reflections on the power of *lógos* that are reminiscent of those illustrated by the tragedian in the dramatization of *Oedipus Tyrannus*. Although there is no room here to enter into the details of his complex theory, we may note that, in his *Defense of Palamedes* (that epic hero who was fooled by the trickery of Odysseus), Gorgias draws a clear distinction between exact knowledge and apparent knowledge (*eidòs akribôs è doxázon*). The former is based on sight (*idón*) and on direct participation or on the testimony of a participant; the rest is *dóxa*. What, then, is the power of *lógos* if not that of arousing the emotions, such as "calming fear, relieving affliction, provoking joy, heightening pity," as Gorgias states in his *Encomium of Helen?* It is poetry in particular that can cause in its listeners shivers of fear (*phríke períphobos*), tears of pity (*éleos polúdakrus*), and the sorrow of regret (*póthos philopenthés*). Is this to say that only speech can provoke these emotions? This is not what the conclusion to the *Encomium of Helen* suggests. In fact, Gorgias affirms, the beautiful Lacedaemonian woman was not necessarily moved by the appearance (*dóxa*) of words addressed to a listener; rather, she was touched by the active visual flux that Greeks included in the physiology of Eros.[32]

We may, therefore, posit an analogy between the feelings evoked by Gorgias and those aroused in the actors and *choreutaí* by Oedipus' act of self-negation; we may also take these emotions to be those that—by proxy, by delegation—the tragedy's listeners and spectators feel. Note, however, that the *Oedipus Tyrannus* goes further than the *Encomium of Helen*. While, for Gorgias, emotions belong to the domain of linguistic or even visual appearance, for Sophocles they are the result of the negation of this same appearance. They are aroused not only by calling into question the power of speech but also, even more, by negating the possibility of the kind of distanced communication offered by the mask. Even if he questions the very foundations of tragic spectacle, however, Sophocles is no sophist: beyond the illusions of *dóxa,* language and sight make apparent the power of Apollo and the *daímon*. It is the dramatic and pernicious revelation of this divine reality through the voices of the actors that ultimately causes the emotions described by Gorgias, a revelation that only a being of divine inspiration such as Tiresias (410), with his blind-man mask, can resist. As far as *Oedipus Tyrannus* is concerned, then, it is to the soothsayer that we must leave the last word, at the moment when he declares to Oedipus:

> I will leave when I have said what I have come to say, nor do I fear your face (*prósopon*), for there is no way for you to destroy me.

(vv. 447–48)

Vision and its negation are so profoundly present in Sophocles' text that, like Aristotle, we might be tempted to overlook the effects of the spectacle itself in the transformation of the *diégesis* into a mimetic drama. In so doing, however, we would indeed lose sight of the self-critical and properly Dionysiac dimensions of the tragedy *Oedipus Tyrannus*, along with the ritual intermediary that the mask provides for Sophocles' authorship.

Through the questioning of speech, vision, and theatrical illusion, *Oedipus Tyrannus* brings us to the general lesson of fifth-century Athenian drama: the "learning through suffering" of something fundamental about the relationship between the human condition and the gods. This is the *páthei máthos* that Zeus concedes to mortals, according to Aeschylus' *Agamemnon* (177).

To summarize what is "tragic" about this learning, we would have to make distinctions between the more local and the more general concerns of classical Greek tragedy as performance. First, masks and costumes—with their functions in mimetic dramatization and face-to-face enunciation through song, as well as dance and music—represent the ritual elements that are constitutive of Attic tragedy as dedicated to Dionysus in local cultic festivals. Second, through plots generally drawn from the Greek heroic tradition, Attic tragedy discusses and questions—in the discursive polyphony resulting from a split, dialogical "instance of enunciation"—problems of civic concern, such as the relationship between *pólis* and *oíkos;* this is the Dionysiac, civic, and, in part, Panhellenic aspect of classical tragedy. Finally, on a more universal but still Dionysiac level, Greek tragedy confronts us, through the dramatic expression of suffering, with the limits of the human condition and with its metaphysical foundations. Because of the diffraction of the voice of poetic authorship among different actors and the *choreutaí*, the listener, then the reader, is invited to take the place of those who mimetically give utterance to the action.[33] Thus, the chorus members sing:

O grief terrible for men to see!

(v. 1297, trans. H. Lloyd-Jones)

VII

UNMASKED BY THE MASK

Enunciative and Pragmatic Effects in Aristophanes

1. The Mask: An Anthropological Category

Even more so than tragedy, Athenian Old Comedy is a show of masks; it constantly plays with costumes and masquerades. It starts from the very beginning of the *Acharnians*, the first comedy by Aristophanes to have come down to us. Making the case for a truce with the Spartan enemy in the thick of the Peloponnesian War requires not only deploying extraordinary oratorical talent but also appealing to noble emotions. When it is a matter of employing the means that rhetoric has to offer to inspire pity, one naturally turns to tragedy, especially to that master of pathos, Euripides. Better than the costumes of poor Oeneus or blind Phoenix, better than those of the beggar Philoctetes or the cripple Bellerophon, it is Telephus' rags that make it possible, when accompanied by his manner of speech, to stir the audience to pity. Dicaeopolis has to employ all his cunning to get Euripides to give him not only the costume of the king in disguise but also his accessories. "After all," says Justcity, as he parodies the verses pronounced by the Euripidean character, "I must seem to be a beggar today—to be just who I am, but without appearing so."[1]

1.1. Incarnations of the "Other"

Thus, *l'habit fait le moine* (to turn the French proverb on its head)[a]: dressed up in these rags, Dicaeopolis has become Telephus, the king who craftily disguises himself as a waif. Do we need anything more to provide clear confirmation of the general conclusions repeated in anthropological research concerning disguises and masks? Is not the mask a universal phenomenon, found in ancient Greece as in so many other places? Does it not reach back to the dawn of time, appearing in antiquity as well as in more recent eras? Does not the mask have a representational function, in particular for the spirits of the dead, among whom we could count the heroized king, Telephus? Does it not, in that case, serve to efface the person wearing it, that person's self dissolving into the dead being's spirit or the reincarnated ancestor: "to be just who I am"?[2] Reversing this formula in the title of an exquisite collection of studies on the African mask, *I Am Not Myself,* an American anthropologist has demonstrated the vitality of this conception of the mask and play with costumes. In the Occident, of course, we find it difficult to endorse phenomena verging on incarnation, but (according to most scholars) that should not hinder the wearer of the mask, "dominated by the spirit," from believing in his new state, his "altered" state. If possessed by the spirit, he would lose his human personality: "he is no longer himself." He would have entirely identified himself with the being that the mask is supposed to represent.[3]

After decades of wavering between positivism and idealism, the modern view of religious manifestations in ancient Greece has once more adopted an anthropological orientation. This comparative opening has resulted in the widespread transmission of what are now the traditional and normative conceptions of the mask and mask-wearing ritual (it is to these conceptions that I was referring). From this point of view, the mask worn during theatrical representations in the classical period would make it possible for the actor to "change" his identity, to be transformed into "another person" by submitting to the power of Dionysus. For, on this view, wearing the mask of the god in the accomplishment of the Dionysiac ritual would mean "entering into direct contact" with the divine power; it would mean accessing, through possession and identification with the god, "radical otherness." An analogous transformation would take place through the donning of the mask of the Gorgon: this doubling of the face with a terrifying mask that confronts you face to face would entail "alienation from oneself." In the rites of "primitives," as on the Athenian stage, the mask would, in this case, make it possible to subordinate the mask wearer's personality to that of the actor.[4] It would be a progression, then, through contiguity, identification,

a. Translator's note: the author's play on the French proverb, *l'habit ne fait pas le moine* ("wearing a habit does not make one a monk," i.e., appearances can be deceptive), consists in deleting the negative.

possession, and alienation that leads, by means of and in the mask, from the "Same" or the "Self" to the "Other." This replication of the ethnological vulgate in anthropological approaches to Greek antiquity will appear less surprising if we recall that a philologist is one of the forefathers who inspired such views: it is to Karl Meuli that we owe the psychologizing theory that masquerade rituals serve to achieve expiatory liberation from the guilt inspired by the dead and their tormented spirits.[5]

From the standpoint of discursive analysis, however, an utterance has meaning only in relation to its context. Let us look, then, at Dicaeopolis' whole declaration in the *Acharnians:*

> O Zeus who sees everywhere, through and under! Euripides, since you've been so kind to me, please give me what goes along with the rags: that little Mysian beanie for my head. For the beggar must I seem today: to be who I am, yet seem not so. The audience must know me for who I am, but the chorus must stand there like simpletons, so that with my pointed phrases I can give them the finger.

> (435–44, trans. J. Henderson)

No sooner has Dicaeopolis expressed his desire to assume not just the mere appearance of a beggar but the mendicant's very being than he realizes that the audience can no longer be fooled. No matter; the spectators before whom he disguises himself will know who he really is. The role of the rhetoric borrowed from Euripides is simply to deceive the Acharnian chorus members, those ignorant rustics. Whence the ironic play on words from verses most likely taken from the *Telephus:* the king as depicted by Euripides no doubt expressed the desire to preserve his identity, but without allowing it to be seen; it would be for this reason that he disguised himself as a beggar. In the case of Dicaeopolis, however, given that he has put on his costume in front of the spectators, he will remain "who he is" despite the rags he has donned. When it is inserted as a part of the story represented and mimetically acted on stage before the public, the disguise conceived by Aristophanes itself participates in the illusion, and everybody is aware of it.

But what is the role of the mask, that mask which the actors and chorus members wear in tragic and comic performances but which is precisely *not* mentioned here? What are we to make of that mask which anthropological research has constituted into an autonomous object and a conceptual category, as it has done in the case of myth, rite, manna, and taboo? Within this perspective, the mask has become a veritable object of museography that is often detached from the other accessories forming a whole of which it is only one element. It is in this case purposely abstracted from the context of its use, its functions, and its ritual and enunciative effects; it is amputated in the process of an abstract and reductionist delimiting of its polymorphism. Things such as makeup, face paint, tattoos, and partial face-coverings are there to remind us of the abstract and artificial character of the anthropological category of the mask.

1.2. Masked Enunciations

When applied to classical tragedy, the vulgate anthropological conception of the mask is dubious. Though used in a Dionysiac context, the mask hardly fulfills the functions of representation and identification that are usually attributed to it. Rather than forming a piece in accord with the costume of the protagonist, whose ethos (even according to Aristotle's theory) is only progressively constituted over the course of the action, the tragic mask serves, above all, to hide, to veil the face of its wearer. It is not actually the scenic identity of the protagonist that takes the place of the civic identity of the mask's wearer: the tragic mask of the Greeks is not an instrument for making a transition into absolute otherness, but the materialization of the simulacrum that the complex "instance of enunciation" embodied by an actor or chorus member represents. If we look at it from the perspective of the enunciation and in the way indicated at the conclusion of the previous chapter (devoted to the scenic implications of Oedipus' act of self-blinding), the use of the mask in classical Athenian tragedy can be seen as a very partial operation of "shifting in"; to be more precise, from the enunciative perspective, there is (partial) "shifting out" relative to the discourse of the one (both the author and the actor) who utters the tragic text and, correspondingly, (partial) "shifting in" relative to the story, the narrative put on stage. Indeed, since there is a "putting into discourse" (*mise en discours*), there is a "putting into drama" (*mise en drame*). As I noted concerning the mask worn by Sophocles' Oedipus, the dramatization before an Athenian audience of the great myths from the tradition entails that, from the perspective of space and time, the narrative action that is usually told in the past tense and situated in an "elsewhere" is actually carried out in the *hic et nunc* of the onstage enunciation.

Furthermore, in addition to the narrative manifestation (the *diégesis,* in Plato's terminology), which is almost exclusively of a linguistic order, there is also the mimetic dramatization (the *mímesis*), which is to be seen; it is this visual effect that Aristotle (as I mentioned concerning the *Oedipus Tyrannus*) excludes from the art of poetry in the strict sense. From a semio-narrative standpoint, then, the *I* of the speaker (or narrator) is superimposed on the *he* of the character involved in the narrated and dramatized action; the speaker's (and enunciator's) mask only partially effaces his identity in replacing it with that of the character who is speaking. Why is a nonfigurative mask used to maintain this perpetual fuzziness between the protagonists of the narrated action on the tragic stage and the masked speaker-narrators? This is because, through the theatrical means I have indicated, the action of the major epic stories suddenly came to be mimed before the audience for whom it was conceived. It is the mask itself that made it possible, in the context of the cult of Dionysus, to turn the narrative around and set it face to face with the civic community assembled in the theater. This is because the Dionysiac mask is the instrument par excellence for undergoing a face-to-face encounter with what is different, historically and spatially speaking; but it is also because the mask, like a veil, effects partial "shifting out/shifting in" and thereby reintroduces the narrative distance that epic poetry creates through use of the aorist (in reference to the heroic past), the "there" (Thebes or Troy), and the third person.[6] The Dionysiac ritual, the masks, and the costumes provide the spectator and receiver of the story with the distance necessary for enduring the spectacle of the countless torments and dismal fate suffered by the heroes of the community's legendary tradition; these elements enable the audience to bear the visual dramatization of mythic narratives that had become terribly realistic, because put into discourse as psychologically oriented dialogue among the various characters involved in the narrative action.

1.3. Comic Masks in Portraits

Do not the dramas of Old Comedy, however, undermine such an explanation, given that they were represented at the same Great Dionysia and Lenaea festivals? Does not the mask worn by the actors involved in Aristophanes' theatrical entertainment point to the character represented on stage, altogether erasing (rather than simply veiling) the identity of its wearer? It will suffice to recount here the ancient biographers' anecdotes about the great Athenian comic playwright. In Old Comedy, personal attacks and, consequently, the designating of individual contemporaries were, it seems, so direct that some could claim Aristophanes' depiction of Socrates in the *Clouds* was what caused the philosopher to be put on trial. What is more, even despite the costumers' efforts in making the costumes realistic, Socrates supposedly stood up in the middle of a comic performance so that those from outside Athens might also recognize him.[7] Aristophanes himself caustically attests to the fact that the masks worn by the actors in his comedies resemble the real-life personalities whose faces they depict. There is a sole exception to this rule: Cleon. No costumer dared fashion a getup resembling his appearance, but the audience, it turns out, was perceptive enough to recognize him easily:

> But there are the Knights, fine gentlemen a thousand strong, who detest
> him and will rally to your side, and all fine and upstanding citizens, and

every smart spectator and myself along with them, and the god will lend a hand too. And never fear, he's not portrayed to the life: none of the mask makers had the guts to make a portrait mask. He'll be recognized all the same, because the audience is smart.

(Knights 225–34, trans. J. Henderson)

This famous passage in the *Knights* has usually been interpreted in a restrictive way, as alluding to the mask alone. Yet what is emphasized in these verses spoken by the servant is the general recognition of the parodied individual; this recognition is made possible by the costumer's contribution to the creation of an overall likeness (*exeikasménos, eikásai*). Only the ancient commentators go the extra step of affirming that the costumers' refusal concerns the mask that is supposed to fashion (*pláttein*) and take the form of (*skhematízein*) the visual appearance (*ópsis*) of Cleon. It appears that comic masks did actually resemble the individuals depicted on stage. Ancient scholars add that no actor dared play the famous Athenian demagogue and that Aristophanes himself took the role, but only after covering his face with red pigment or wine lees to conceal his civic identity and give his voice a dramatized authority. This practice corresponds exactly to the dissimulation of the actor's (or author's) face in the first tragic representations.[8]

The masks worn by Aristophanes' actors, then, seem to serve to identify. The ancient treatises on comedy are also there to affirm and reaffirm: what distinguishes Old Comedy from New Comedy is the resemblance of the comic masks (*prósopa*) used in the former to the faces (*prosópois*) of the individuals depicted on stage, even though this resemblance is downplayed by features serving to provoke laughter; apparently the effect was such that a law is said to have been promulgated, at Cleon's instigation, outlawing personal attacks (*onomastí*) in comedy.[9] However reliable this information from a much later period may be, it is emblematic of one of the fundamental characteristics of New Comedy, which no longer depicts specific Athenian citizens in their individuality, turning instead to the portraiture and parody of type-characters. Nevertheless, Aristophanes' very use of the verb *eikázein*, "portray a likeness of," with reference to the costumer's work, shows that no one is duped by the illusion. The actor does not incarnate Cleon but parodies him, and for Aristophanes, parodying means denouncing—it means demasking. The enunciative instance is thus twice doubled and distanced, both by the voice of the actor and by the mask that he wears.

2. Superposed Disguises

We can be sure of at least one thing at this point: the mask of Old Comedy cannot be dissociated from the costume and accessories that go along with it. Since the texts maintain a certain degree of fuzziness concerning the function of the mask itself, it might be worthwhile to turn to iconography before coming back to the literature with a broader perspective.

2.1. Images of the Comic Mask

Although the documents dating to the fifth century and possibly referring to Old Comedy are rare, paintings on pottery and clay statuettes coincide in offering a strikingly uniform portrait of the comic actor: he has a protruding belly, which is just barely covered by a short tunic and padded buttocks stuffed into some sort of body stocking, fake genitals openly on display, and a face characterized by a protuberant forehead, a flat nose, pronounced features, a gaping mouth open too wide and generally a beard.[10] These traits are numerous and distinctive enough to signal—when they appear together, as they regularly do— that someone wearing such a mask is a comic actor assuming a ritual identity linked to the cult of Dionysus. But the famous *oinochóe* found at Cyrene and dating from the late fifth century, which depicts *two* comic actors in a chariot drawn by four Centaurs, shows that, beyond this configuration of "generic" traits, the scenography of comedy could also represent individuals, whose specific identity might be indicated through various accessories. The club, bow, and lion skin worn by one of the actors in the chariot signals that he plays Heracles, while the wings and clothing of the other, combined with the fact that he is beardless, mark that figure as Nike.[11]

If we may judge from the iconography, the comic mask and costume are the object of a double "shifting out," a double "disengagement" relative to the social and civic identity of the actor who wears them. On the one hand, the actor's generic dressing up makes of him an agent in the Dionysiac ritual into which the comic representation is inserted. As further proof of this, we may note the affinities that the features of the mask and the mock phallus share with satyrs. On the other, the complementary accessories that confer individuality on each actor in the rite transform the person wearing them into a protagonist—that is, into an actor, in the semio-narrative sense of the term[b]—within the story dramatized and played on stage in the theater. The iconography, too, seems to indicate that the (civic) individual disappears behind two levels of disguise, one ritual, the other dramatic.

Furthermore, when the scene adorning the vase is a paratragic one, as is the case on an Apulian *kráter* from the early fourth century, there are even *three* levels of disguise. In the representation of a comic scene parodying Sophocles'

---

b. Translator's note: on "actor" as a semio-narrative term, see Calame 2000a, 18–23 (= 1995, 4–8).

Antigone that appears on that *kratér,* the central figure wears the usual comic costume, with genitals on display and a mask covering his head. But he is also wearing (over his comic paraphernalia) a transparent garment from tragedy, which ties in with the mask that he holds in his hand. This upside-down mask is none other than that of Antigone, and the comic actor is probably about to put on this tragic mask as a substitute for the comic one he is wearing.[12] On top of the ritual dressing up and the costume imposed by the comic action, then, we find superposed in this parody the disguise engaging the actors in the tragic scene.

2.2. Overdetermined Dramatic Identities

Beyond paratragic scenes, scrutiny of the text of Aristophanes' plays confirms the superposing of two types of disguise imposed by the conventions of Old Comedy. To the first "shifting out," we may naturally chalk up the countless phallic references made by the protagonists in his comedies. These allusions, which are often marked by a deictic form, undoubtedly point to a reality on stage. They punctuate the action of the *Lysistrata,* of course, wherein Cinesias repeatedly draws attention to his tumid *péos.* Furthermore, after boasting in the much-discussed parabasis of the *Clouds* of having forgone use of "a pendent piece of leather that is red at the tip and thick, so as to make the kiddies laugh" (539–40), Aristophanes has Socrates catch his new disciple, Strepsiades, with penis in hand (733–34). Similarly, Strepsiades points to another character's protruding paunch to comic effect.[13]

The bulging belly and the phallus can, however, be left out of the picture. In the *Plutus,* Poverty brags of giving people a slender figure, while, in the *Thesmophoriazousae,* the fact that Agathon's costume lacks a *péos* provides a further reason for mockery. Thus, the lack of any one of the distinctive components of the comic costume can serve to distinguish a particular individual; on top of the first "shifting out/shifting in" that introduces us into the Dionysiac ritual, comic costuming superposes another, which tends to give a recognizable identity to abstract figures, like Poverty, or to contemporary personalities, such as the homosexual tragic author Agathon. It ought to be noted that the latter is distinguished by more than just his costume, since Euripides can qualify Agathon—by contrast with his own appearance—as being "pretty in the face, fair of skin, clean-shaven, feminine of voice, delicate, fine to look upon" (*Thesmophoriazousae* 191–92). Halfway between the ritual costume and the "individualizing" costume stands the crossing of masculine roles and feminine ones; the latter are marked not only by a type of clothing but also by fake breasts and a lighter-colored mask.[14]

Through this second "shifting out/shifting in," wherein individual traits are superimposed on or substituted for the ritual phallic costume, we move from the carrying out of the ritual to the performance of the story itself. The individualizing function of this operation is not, however, without ambiguity. Indeed, we may note that the procedure for identifying a character by means of a mask and accessories is not necessarily distinctive enough to take on the role of "rigid designator" that some attribute to the proper name. When a famous protagonist (such as a god or one of the foremost tragic playwrights) appears on stage, he or she is usually designated linguistically, precisely by name. Thus, Euripides is explicitly announced as such at the beginning of the *Thesmophoriazousae*. The same is true in the case of the entrance of Euripides and Aeschylus in the *Frogs,* as well as that of the ferryman Charon, whose appearance on stage is marked not only by the uttering of his name but also by the use of an explicit deictic form. Aristophanes does pass up the opportunity to make facetious use of the ambiguity of certain individual costumes. The effeminate Agathon, who is given a famous courtesan's name, lacks mock breasts but is also without male attributes: he is dressed in a saffron-colored frock instead of a masculine tunic, and he has an oil flask but also a breast band. After having his face shaved by Euripides, Mnesilochus gets the impression that he is seeing Cleisthenes (the famous homosexual known to the entire Athenian public of that era) when he looks in a mirror. Moreover, when we witness Dionysus/Heracles descend to the underworld in the *Frogs,* we see a real disguise superimposed on an individualizing costume. Thus, the god designates himself by giving his full civic identification: Dionysus, son of Stamnios. A few lines later, however, Heracles cannot stifle his laughter at seeing the god equipped with—in addition to the feminized Dionysiac costume—his own heroic paraphernalia: the club and lion skin. This double identity is perfectly marked in the double name that the god's slave assumes when he dons the distinctive costume of the hero: Xanthias becomes Heracleoxanthias after Dionysus bids him, "You be me (*sù mèn génou 'gó*): take this club and this lion skin—if, that is, you've got fearless guts" (495–96).[15]

In this scene in the *Frogs,* but also elsewhere, this type of play on dressing up in disguise unfolds before the spectators' eyes. Aristophanes achieves the greatest comic effects in the dressing up of Mnesilochus (in the *Thesmophoriazousae*), who gets a shave—on his mask—after being told to take off his cloak; then, successively, Euripides singes off the hair on his rear while duly torturing his genitalia, dresses him in a saffron-colored frock girt with a breast band, adorns his head with a hairnet and a head wrap, covers his shoulders with a short, feminine mantle, and puts Agathon's slippers on his feet. Nonetheless, the disguise is not complete, since Mnesilochus' subterfuge is recognized because of the fake penis that he continues to wear under his women's clothing. This brings us back to the two scenes cited at the outset of these reflections on the masquerade in Aristophanes: Dicaeopolis, in the *Acharnians*, explicitly counts on the complicity of the audience to ensure the success of his disguise as a beggar. The audience is likewise called upon in the *Knights* to use their acuity to identify Cleon. The comic illusion is never perfect, since (to paraphrase a felicitous formulation by Suzanne Saïd), "not contented with simply separating the costume from the actor, comedy highlights its limits and demonstrates its unsuitability and ineffectiveness." The human protagonists of the *Birds* mock one another's animal costumes; one resembles a goose that has been painted to be sold off at a low price, another looks like a blackbird with a bowl-cut, a double reference to the *mímesis* on ceramics. And the satire can be directed not only at the individual's costume but also at the generic one, that of the comic actor in general: in the *Frogs*, Xanthias complains that he is not allowed to play the roles that correspond to his comic paraphernalia (*skeúe en komoidíai*).[16]

3. The Illusions of Comic Fiction

Through the successive operations of "shifting out/shifting in" for which they are the instrument from an enunciative standpoint, the comic mask and costume can superpose no fewer than three distinct fictions. These fictions are also at work in comic parodying of tragedy, the analysis of which would require a separate study; they come into play in the costumes of the chorus members, too, who are often half-human and half-animal—or even half-thing, as in the case of the chorus members who are clouds in the comedy of that name.[17]

3.1. Caricaturing Deformations

None of these fictions, however, which are called into question one after the other, maintains an unbroken illusion: neither ritual dressing up, nor the representation of contemporary personalities, nor the disguising of these figures themselves. The ambiguity is so well preserved that it allows Aristophanes to stage the double meaning of the term *prósopon*, which designates both mask and face. At the end of the *Plutus*, the wrinkles on the "face" of the old woman teased by Chremylus would, if the white lead makeup were washed away, turn out to correspond to the "rags" constituting the texture of the mask that she wears. The play on the two levels of the comic fiction is realized through the use of the term *tà rháke*, which refers both to the timeworn features of an old person and to the pieces of cloth of which the mask is made.[18]

*Old Woman:*You bastard, you must be unhinged, to soak me with abuse in front of all these men.
Young Man: A good soaking would do you good.
Chremylus: No it wouldn't; she's got herself ready for sale. If that rouge were washed off, you'd see the tattered remnants of her face.

(Plutus 1060–65, trans. J. Henderson)

All in all, the mask in Aristophanes' comedies belongs to the same symbolic order as the utopia constructed on stage. Whether the Aristophanic utopia is conceived as a return to youth and the Golden Age or as thrusting its protagonists into the catastrophic confusion of the end of the Iron Age, the excursion on which it takes us always culminates in the restoring of reality;[19] we can believe in it only for the duration of the comic reversal and entertainment, under the patronage of Dionysus. Again, the mask serves to unmask a reality from which we cannot escape.

As we saw in the chapter devoted to Sophocles' *Oedipus Tyrannus,* a foray into Aristotle's *Poetics* is never made in vain. At the outset of his treatise, as is well known, Aristotle presents the various musical poetic genres as different modes belonging to the same process: that of *mímesis* or "representation." These differences arise from the means used, the content of the imitation, or the manner in which it is presented. On this view, Sophocles and Homer—who use practically the same means of communication, the same "media" (language and rhythm)— are similar to each other in that the two authors imitate "worthy" (*spoudaîoi*) people; but the tragic poet is also similar to Aristophanes, inasmuch as the two playwrights represent through *mímesis* individuals who act, who "do" (*práttontes, drôntes*). According to Aristotle's theory of poetry, Old Comedy represents on stage, by means of language, rhythm, and music, "mediocre" (*phaûloi*) individuals, who are, at the same time, depicted "in action" (*energoûntes*).

We learn a little later on in the treatise that the sole aim of the imitation of *phaulóteroi* in comedy is to provoke laughter (*tò geloîon*); that which is comic is neither painful nor destructive, as tragedy is. One of the essential means of provoking laughter is precisely the comic mask, the ugliness and deformity of which do not convey pain. According to the Aristotelian conception of theater, the comic mask, rather than designating individuals, is the very instrument of the transformation and entertainment specific to comedy. It is never a matter of incarnating real individuals; rather the point is to represent them in action, of course, but as lower than they are in reality.[20] Comedy, then, is caricature aimed at provoking laughter; the mask serves neither to identify a figure completely nor—on the other side of a binary opposition that is attractive but false and deceptive—to cause "radical" alienation.

3.2. Enunciative Disengagements

Thus, comic dramatization depends deeply on the mask, even more so than tragedy; it has need of the mask not for the purposes of identification but to mark off what is depicted on stage as different, to create distance, even despite the face-to-face confrontation with the spectators. It is, after all, the mask itself that makes it possible to present frontally to an Athenian audience actions that are drawn from the audience members' own political experience, from their own civic present, without the heroic distance that we find in tragedy and the narrative distance that we see in epic. The individuals facing the audience from the Attic stage would be Cleon, Socrates, and Pericles themselves if the mask were not also there to transform reality, both by indicating the Dionysiac cult context of the action represented and by distorting the features of the protagonists to the point of caricature. These different enunciative "disengagements" relative to the story told and dramatized, though also present in tragedy, are even more necessary in Old Comedy, which represents situations not from the heroic age but from the present day.

The blurred distinction that the mask and costume maintain between the wearer of the mask uttering the story dramatized in the comedy (that is, the actor) and the character involved in the staged action allows the (intradiscursive) speaker-narrator and, consequently, the (extradiscursive) enunciator—Aristophanes—to intervene much more distinctly than in tragedy. In the *Acharnians,* for example, the author-enunciator does not hesitate to take up the *I* of Dicaeopolis, or even of the *koryphaîos,* in order to enter into a veritable dialogue with his audience-enunciatee.[21] The enunciative addressing of the audience that is carried out by the (extradiscursive) author through the voice of a protagonist involved in the (intradiscursive) mimetic action is, thus, not restricted to that central choral segment specific to Old Comedy known as the *parábasis.* It is nonetheless true, however, that the parabasis remains the primary occasion for the chorus members or the *koryphaîos* to interrupt the dramatic action (most likely without removing their masks) in order to speak directly to the audience and explain the biographical author's intentions; in speech referring to the play's producer in the third person and generally alluding to the fictional action under way, the chorus members take authority for their remarks, expressing themselves in the first person.[22]

More generally, Aristophanic comedy delights, much more than classical tragedy, in playing with different forms of self-reference.[23] Such reflection about theater would not be possible without the disjunctures created by the mask and by parody. Through his use of costumes, masks, and playful staging, and, above all, his extraordinary parodic language, Aristophanes, as author, undertakes with his audience a veritable contract of truthfulness—or rather of *untruthfulness,* since it is known from the outset that all the Dionysiac play is aimed at *geloióteron.* So it is that, much as one comes back down from the sweet inebriation caused by the *phármakon,* the ambiguous wine of Dionysus, so also the comic masquerade invites us to return to reality. Although we do not know what happened in this domain at the Lenaea festival, it is certain that this return is institutionally marked by the *ekklesía,* the official public assembly that signified the conclusion of the Great Dionysia.[24] The critical scrutiny applied to the way the ritual was carried out during this popular assembly session indicates in a particularly clear way the practical impact that the act of cultic devotion to Dionysus Eleuthereus had on Athenian civic life.[25]

Whether it is historical or not, the case brought against Aristophanes after his presentation of the *Babylonians* in 426 no doubt indicates that the distance created by comic masks and costumes between dramatization and reality—between intra- and extradiscursive—was not always sufficient. Was not the comic author accused of slandering in the presence of foreigners not only Cleon but also the magistrates elected by lot? This is probably a biographical detail that was drawn from the defense that Aristophanes uttered on stage through the mouths of the Acharnians.[26] The law promulgated by Cleon, which (as already noted) aimed at prohibiting personal attacks in comedy, probably represents the same kind of anecdote fabricated after the fact. However that may be, literary critics have hastened to see in this insufficient mediating of comic attacks the reason that explains the shift from the caricaturing and parodying of contemporary individuals in Old Comedy to the satirizing of character types in Middle Comedy.

Perhaps more so than in tragedy, the comic mask and costume insert the playing out of the action on stage into the ritual ceremony for Dionysus; they make the comic representation into a cultic service. While the mask and costume invite, via the caricature of which they are the instruments, critiquing of the contemporary social and political reality, the religious function of the masquerade extends beyond the limits assigned to laughter and influences that reality in return. The comic enunciation, then, does not shift us into the "radically different." Like tragic dramatization, the staging of comedy produces a sort of exemplary image, but this image is transposed by the Dionysiac rite and the wearing of costumes and masks. Both the tragic and comic masks, in underpinning the simulacrum role assumed by a polymorphous "instance of enunciation," and in making possible the face-to-face encounter in a context of reciprocally directed gazes, simply reflect back to the Athenian spectator a (mimetic and, thus, distorted) image of himself or herself. This image is one that arouses fear and pity or laughter and mockery, one that is aimed at provoking a veritable *Verfremdung* (estrangement) effect through ritualized voices of authority deriving from the critical powers of Dionysus.

PART 3

GREEK POETIC AUTHORITIES

VIII

UTTERING HUMAN NATURE BY
CONSTRUCTING THE INHABITED WORLD

The Well-Tempered Racism of Hippocrates

It is only quite recently that scholars have begun to inquire into the rhetorical qualities necessary to the transmission of the first Greek spheres of knowledge that appear "scientific" to us. Among these first *tékhnai*—fields of practical knowledge about the nature of the world and the nature of humankind which are more cosmological and anthropological than philosophical—the art of the physician occupies a central place. In this essentially technical discourse, wherein speculation is put to the service of practical explanation, the enunciative positions of the speaker-narrator are much more numerous than we might suppose in the mode of distant objectivity traditionally attributed to the speech used for "pure" sciences. Indeed, the *I* of the speaker repeatedly intervenes through various enunciative means, instead of remaining in the mode of the simple assertion, which (for us) characterizes discourse of a scientific sort. As a result, the "instance of enunciation" acquires an authority and a profile that orient the image of humankind and the world underlying the explanatory discourse.

In these first treatises in applied art, the point is, yet again, to build an argument and persuade. Consequently, the point is to seduce by means that are also those of speech, in a context where speech still stands close to the voices of the oral tradition and where, among certain "Pre-Socratic" thinkers concerned with the nature of the cosmos, speech still adopts the forms of the most traditional epic poetry. The masks and simulacra of textual authority constituted by the enunciative positions within these frequently polemical treatises assume a wide variety of different profiles; they bring life to a kind of discourse that is far from the even tone and neutrality that are associated with technical and scientific exposés in our own day. The utterance and diction of Greek technical arts often manifest the rhetorical procedures and forms that Aristotle attributes to the epideictic genre: throughout the discourse of *tékhnai* runs a specific rhetoric attributing to that discourse simultaneously the forms of demonstration and the forms of praise. It is in the application of these oratorical approaches that this discourse achieves its pragmatic dimension.[1]

The Hippocratic treatise *De arte*—about which some commentators have wondered whether the author might not be a sophist rather than a physician— begins as follows:

> There are those who have made an art of insulting arts, such that those who do this think of themselves not as doing what I say, but rather as making a display of their own knowledge.

> (Hippocrates, *On the Art of Medicine* 1.1)

This short medical treatise, then, is presented as a *tékhne* which itself implements a certain discursive technique. Although he does not affix his *sphragís*—his "seal"—as Herodotus or Thucydides, for example, would have done at the beginning of their historiographical treatises, the speaker-narrator nonetheless marks the beginning of his discourse with a prominent enunciative intervention (*egò légo*), much as Hesiod does in the *Works and Days*. This intervention allows him to inscribe his treatise within the sphere of the "demonstration of a personal inquiry." While steering clear of a signature, this claim to authorship corresponds exactly to that of Herodotus in the preamble to his work (*histories apódexis*).[2] Carrying out both an inquiry and a display addressed to a relatively broad audience entails making use of a rhetoric capable of creating the same persuasive effects as didactic poetry.

The famous Hippocratic *Oath* situates itself within the same perspective through one of its central assertions, the formulation of which draws on the very rhetorical procedures employed at about the same time by Gorgias and the Sophists:

> With purity and sanctity will I preserve my way of life and my art.

> (Hippocrates, *Oath* 10–11)

Purity, which is not only ritual but also moral, and intellectual sanctity are the qualities required for the development of a medical technique that is associated with a mode of life and essentially conceived as a practice.[3] In an oath that is placed under the authority of the gods—essentially Asclepius and his father, Apollo—the powers of speech are employed in the service of an art involving an intellectual, ethical, and religious commitment on the part of its practitioner. Accordingly, we should not be surprised to find interspersed throughout the Hippocratic treatises enunciative interventions that tend to orient and evaluate the technical exposé.

Insofar as they situate the technical discussion within a particular perspective, the interventions on the part of the speaker-*I* are especially interesting when the medical treatise is based on a veritable conception of the inhabited world. In other words, the point of view orienting it through various enunciative means emerges with more precision when this image of the earth and the populations inhabiting it is based on a theory concerning the influence of the environment on the physiology and character of human beings: the strength of winds, the quality of water, the orientation of locations. Since what is ultimately at issue is the constitution of humankind and the nature of human communities in interaction with their environment and climate, the speaker-narrator inevitably finds himself implicated, as a human being, in the system that he constructs even as he follows the rules of art. Furthermore, since this image of the various communities populating the earth is organized according to a criterion based on differences that are supposedly inherent in the nature of human beings as they relate to their environment, and since this classification involves several value judgments, the point of view orienting such a representation of the diversity of humankind amounts to what we would call a *racist* position; there is, in the Hippocratic treatise *On Airs, Waters, and Places*, both a naturalization of the differences observed in human morphology from one place to another and a hierarchical ordering of these differences.

But, before we look once again at Hippocrates' enunciative rhetoric and the point of view that emerges from it, it would be worthwhile to make a very brief foray into the history of modern racial theories in order to identify the traits characterizing what we may call tempered racism, even if it presents itself as scientific or even medical.

1. A Short History of Ordinary Racism

In this brief glance at the past of our own tradition, I propose to begin with two quotations chosen to provoke historical reflection about the modern concept of racism and the use of putatively scientific criteria to justify it:

From the Tropic of Cancer to the Tropic of Capricorn, Africa has only black inhabitants. It is not only their color that distinguishes them, for they also differ from all other men by the facial features, with wide, flat noses, big lips, [etc.]. If we move away from the equator in the direction of the Antarctic pole, the shade of black becomes lighter, but the ugliness remains: we find that homely people inhabiting the southern tip of Africa.

Only a blind person could doubt that Whites, Albinos, Negroes, Hottentots, Laplanders, Chinese, Americans are entirely different races. . . . Their round eyes [i.e., those of Negroes], their wide nose, their lips, which are always big . . . , and even the measure of their intelligence establish enormous differences between them and the various other human *species.* That this difference is not due to their climate is proven by the fact that Negro men and women, even when they are transported into the coldest countries, always produce animals of their own *species.*

We may well find it difficult to face the facts, but, be that as it may, the first definition of negritude quoted here is the work of the compilers of the *Encyclopédie,* while the second flowed from the barbed pen of Voltaire![4] If we take as our point of reference the combat waged against authoritarian ignorance and in support of tolerance by the authors of these assertions, these statements constitute quite a surprising paradox, to say the least. Nonetheless, they are part and parcel of the thinking of which they are the product, that of the Enlightenment. As paradoxical as it may seem, the scholarly artisans of the fecund intellectual stirrings of the eighteenth century are the source of the modern concept of racism.[5]

There is a another paradox: before the systematic attempts of the enlightened intellectuals of the eighteenth century to provide this strain of thought with a foundation deemed scientific and to turn it into actual racism, pre-racist reflection was stimulated in the sixteenth century by the renewed contact with other peoples that resulted from the "Great Discoveries": the discovery of the New World, the discovery of populations who lived naked while having fabulous wealth at their disposal, the discovery of human beings whose nature was to become the object of fierce debates. Are such peoples human or subhuman? Are they men or beasts? Instead of a process of self-questioning, along the lines of what might have become a form of relativism, what was at issue for such thinkers was to determine whether Native Americans or Africans were worthy of sharing with European Christians common descent from Adam. In his vibrant indictment of the massacres perpetrated by his own countrymen in Central America, the Dominican priest Bartolomé de Las Casas settles the question without hesitation:

As concerns all of these countless universal peoples of all kinds, God made them extremely simple, lacking viciousness and duplicity, very obedient and very faithful to their natural lords and to the Christians whom they serve ...; they are also with a conformation that is delicate, slight and frag-ile. .... It is among these tender lambs thus endowed by their creator with so many qualities that the Spanish, as soon as they encountered them, came on like very cruel wolves, tigers, and lions that have been without food for several days.[6]

The terms of the debate, we can see, are based on the theological dispute; nei-ther the physical constitution nor the character of the American Indians was, at this time, attributed to a physiological or biological difference rooted in the material nature of humankind. Like the Europeans, the Indians are creatures of God; they issue from the same origin.

Let us return to the eighteenth century and examine the principle that was supposed, in the words of Voltaire, "to differentiate men as it differentiates plants." First, there is the element of skin color, a distinctive trait that Buffon ele-vated to the status of a scientific criterion in connection with a theory of the "degenerations" caused by differences of climate. This criterion, which evokes the Hippocratic theory that we shall be examining, was taken up by Carl von Linné in his attempt to classify and hierarchically rank the different races that the human race is supposed to comprise:

> *Europeus albus:* levis, argutus, inventor;
> *Americanus rufus:* pertinax, contentus, liber;
> *Asiaticus luridus:* severus, fastuosus, avarus;
> *Afer niger:* vafer, segnis, negligens.[7]

Even if it is not presented as such, the foundations for ordinary racism have thus been laid. All that is needed is a criterion for distinction based on physio-logical characteristics and accompanied by (herein lies the essence) a value judgment. A seemingly scientific moral hierarchy has henceforth been estab-lished. From this point on, the criteria for differentiating races vary according to will: the facial angle, which becomes the occipital angle when the supporter of this view takes his own face as the perfect gauge of the normative measure; the volume of the brain in its greater or lesser proximity to that of monkeys; the intelligence quotient that is so dear to North American military recruiters (who, it turns out, took the idea from a Frenchman); the biochemical blood index inspired by the Nazis; the collective genetic inheritance as conceived by the neo-Darwinists; the random genetic combinations proposed by "post–neo–Darwinists."[8]

The mechanism remains ever the same: the first step is to provide a criterion for measuring racial distinctions; then, through the value judgment that almost inevitably accompanies every quantified measure, the objects of the distinction are ordered on a hierarchical scale. The most respectable position is granted to the class defined by the greatest quantity; the lowest position is assigned to the category with the smallest quantity.[9] Thanks to the evolutionist perspective that Darwinist theories have disseminated, the system can be refined even further: the elaborated hierarchy is rendered "dynamic" by being made to coincide with a teleological vision of historical development. The hierarchy thus fits into the overall orientation of history—European history, naturally. In following the course of the development of life forms as posited on this evolutionary view, it necessarily proceeds from the simple to the complex, from the primitive to the civilized; it gradually rises from the first stage of dark-skinned "brachycephalic" beings to the refined status of "dolichocephalic" beings to which the white Aryan belongs.

2. Racism and Ethnocentrism

Racism no doubt feeds on motivations that stand outside the quantified physiological justifications that are applied in the attempt to root it in science. Understood more broadly, beyond its link to pseudoscientific foundations, racism belongs to the larger group of disparaging attitudes consisting in the rejection of one human group by contrast with another. The criterion that makes it possible to perceive and express the difference distinguishing one from the other is very often of a social order: over the past few decades, many have tried with great difficulty to combat racism against young people and, especially, racism against immigrants and refugees. More so than differences in social status, however, it is cultural differences that concentrate and consolidate racist attitudes (taken in the broad sense). One rejects his or her neighbor less because of the strangeness of the neighbor's physical characteristics than because of the supposed specificity of that person's customs. Thus, the various forms that racism can take ultimately derive from this more general phenomenon, the scholarly term for which is ethnocentrism.

While seeing in ethnocentrism the affirmation of the identity of a group that defines itself in terms of its own culture and, in so doing, degrades the habits and behaviors of its neighbors, some have claimed that ethnocentrism is universal and is inscribed in the very heart of every human community.[10] It is true that the New Testament, despite the fact that it recognizes a common origin for all humankind, simply affirms that the Hebrews are the chosen people. As for the Gospels, the authors of these texts never question the absolute superiority of the Christian revelation. The Iatmul people of Papua New Guinea, however, provide a counterexample. In their creation myth, the Iatmul present an older and younger brother side by side, both born from the sea foam. The elder brother is the ancestor of the Papuans, the younger of the white people. Does this mean that an inferior position is attributed to the other, to the White man? Not at all, since, after the elder brother's abduction of their sister (who appeared at the same time as the two brothers) and a period of conflict, the younger brother ends up winning the woman, whereupon he has at his disposal countless possessions.[11]

Thus, it seems that the claim to the universality of an attitude of ethnocentrism could benefit from considerable nuancing. Particularly at the dawn of the twenty-first century, the culpability attached—primarily in the academic world—to the processes of acculturation and immigration provoked by colonialism, neocolonialist imperialism, then globalization has brought with it a new sensitivity to difference. While it can lead to a form of relativism that is often without any point of reference and ends up playing into the hand of individualism and neoconservative thought, the recognition of cultural differences nonetheless has the benefit both of denouncing the frequent tendency to hold up occidental values as universal and of allowing the critique of these very values through comparison. The taking into account of cultural differences leads, in particular, to the observation that cultural egotism toward others does not appear to be necessarily inscribed either in human nature or in the constitution of every kind of social group. Even so, a specialist on the issue of racism has affirmed that occidental racism has its roots in the thought of classical antiquity, especially via the mythological figures through which the Greeks assigned a specific status and nature not only to barbarians but also to women and slaves.[12]

This assertion concerning the existence of a specifically Hellenic racism and its foundation in "myth" would be largely justified if the Greeks had elaborated their definition of non-Greeks solely by means of categories deriving from what we think of as mythology, but they, too, actually used a classification of climates and different types of environment in their definition of others. In the context of the Hippocratic art of medicine, criteria based on physical geography and meteorology are applied in an attempt to develop a nomenclature for the populations surrounding Greece. This taxonomy of the inhabited world according to geographic and ecological criteria amounts to a diverse image of the nature of human beings as grasped in their local specificities.

3. Figures of the Other in Ancient Greece

Addressing classical Greek culture, which had seen seven or eight centuries of relatively autonomous existence and development, necessarily entails being situated within a historical perspective. When expressions of it were first set down in writing, notably in the Homeric texts, the Greek attitude toward foreigners was part of a more general framework defining the bases of civilization. Nevertheless, it ought to be noted that the first manifestation of awareness about the existence of "barbarians" is altogether independent from this pondering of the limits separating the civilized person from the savage. Indeed, the very concept of "barbarian," which is expressed through an onomatapoeic term, derives from the perception of the language of others. To be more precise, it arises from the perception of the phonic, auditory effect produced by languages other than Greek, or by Greek imperfectly pronounced by populations whose native language is different.[13] In the *Iliad*, however, when these peoples with stuttering speech fight alongside or against Greeks, their gestures and reactions are the same as those of the Homeric heroes.

By contrast, when Odysseus, carried off to the distant ends of the Mediterranean through Poseidon's malevolence, faces a whole series of foreign communities, it is according to the standard of the Greek definition of civilization that the groups he meets are judged: recognition of the rules of justice and hospitality, piety toward the gods, linguistic communication, political and economic activity concentrated in the agora.[14] But the peoples visited by Odysseus—the Laestrygonians, who are compared to Giants, the Cyclopes, who are man-eating herdsmen, and the Phaeacians, who devote themselves exclusively to seafaring—are but projections of the utopia fable: as soon as they become too different from known men—that is, from Greek men—the story projects them outside the category of human and into the otherness of a fictional world situated between animals and gods, between bestiality and the Golden Age.[15] For the Homeric hero there is, in fact, only one human kind; to it are admitted all those to whom the imagination does not attribute monstrous features. Thus, the Homeric definition of civilization is broad enough to accommodate the numerous *xénoi* of the known world.[16] Granted, this definition has an ethnocentric character, but it constitutes a "Hellenocentrism" that is both generous and accommodating. It should be mentioned that the Greeks of the "archaic" period, given that they were divided into countless autonomous city-states, had nothing like a veritable national consciousness.

In ancient Greece, no consciousness that may be deemed "national" actually appears until the beginning of the fifth century.[17] So it is that we have to wait until the great shock provoked by the second Persian War to see delegates from the various Greek cities finally meet to put an end to their infighting and form a common front of resistance to the Persian onslaught. It is when the Persian threat becomes most menacing, on the eve of the battle of Plataea, that the Greeks end up becoming aware of the existence of a *Hellenikón*, an aggregate of shared characteristics qualifying them as Greeks. The parameters that, according to Herodotus, delimit Greekness all derive from a definition of culture: Greeks are supposed to recognize one another through their common language, their performing of identical sacrifices in shared sanctuaries, their similar customs, and their analogous ways of life, but they also include in their Hellenic identity the sharing of the same blood (*homoaimón*).[18]

When Herodotus (the author of this definition of *Hellenikón*) turns to peoples from outside Greece, he uses more or less the same criteria in his attempts to define the human groups he has met: religious customs centered on the practice of sacrifice, funerary customs, diet and table manners, sexual mores, as well as habitat, local climate, and physical appearance. So, to take the example of the ethnic groups on the eastern fringes of the "inhabited world," the Indians depicted by Herodotus live on the edge of a desert and lead a nomadic life; they do not worry about death, but, in lieu of sacrifice, they kill their sick and eat them raw; when they become sedentary, they live on raw fish or on a vegetarian diet of herbs and grains (probably rice); and they all copulate publicly like animals and have dark skin like the Ethiopians.[19]

Nomadism, human sacrifice, cannibalism, eating raw meat, bestial sexuality, darkness of skin: these distinctive traits of the Indians at the *eskhatiaí*, inhabiting the remotest regions of the *oikouméne*, seem to be the exact opposite of what constitutes the essence of civilization for a Greek. But we should be wary: when applied to Greek thought, the model suggested to us by the binary logic that is so dear to structuralist-inspired methods proves once again to be deceptive, this time in two respects.

If the Indians as described by Herodotus seem to act like perfect savages, they nonetheless have inestimable sources of wealth: the gold produced by giant ants and the "wool" produced by cotton plants. The same is true of all the other communities that carry out their profoundly strange customs in these furthermost reaches of the inhabited world; in compensation for their fundamental savagery, the land of hostile climate that they inhabit provides them with the most beautiful and rare products. We ought to keep in mind that, in the Greek representation of the origins of culture, which is projected onto the outlying regions, the state of being uncivilized always tends partially to conceal the ideal world of the Golden Age. This composite image is based on the principle of *díke*, of justice. Not only does this principle of compensation and balance apply to the representation of each isolated culture, but also it governs relations among different peoples. In other words, it organizes the global image that Herodotus offers of the inhabited world. Accordingly, the absence in Greece—or, more precisely, in Ionia—of the most beautiful and precious objects is compensated for by the benefits of moderate climate, a point to which I shall return later in this discussion.[20]

Not all of the groups about which Herodotus collected information over the course of his *Histories* dwell at the outermost ends of the inhabited world. Of course, the immediate neighbors of the Greeks, the menacing Persians, are the object of a geographical demarcation through the territorial division and opposition between Europe and Asia. As has frequently been observed, however, not only does Herodotus have these oriental populations speak just like Hellenes, but also, more important, he advances extremely nuanced judgments concerning their customs. Even if we pass over the Egyptians, who are deeply idealized by all the Greeks, the Babylonians, for example, are the object of diametrically opposed judgments on the part of the ethnographer from Halicarnassus. On the one hand, after admiring the boats that can be disassembed (forerunner of the inflatable dinghy) used by the boatmen navigating the Euphrates, Herodotus describes the Babylonian system of auctioning off future wives as the wisest custom (sophótatos nómos) of which he knows. On the other, he does not hesitate to qualify as utterly shameful (aískhistos) the Babylonian custom of forcing wives to prostitute themselves at least once in their lifetime in the temple of Aphrodite.[21] What we find is not *the* barbarian but various barbarians, understood in their multiplicity and in the relativism of their respective customs. It was only through the ideological effect of the Persian Wars that a polarization came to be established, especially in oratory, between Greeks, generally represented by the Athenians, and barbarians, identified with the Persians alone.

Thus, in the thick of the fifth century, Herodotus' representation of the humanity and diversity of the cultures of his era cannot be reduced to a simple dichotomy between Greeks and barbarians. Furthermore, despite a few remarks concerning the physical traits of the peoples described, the historian-anthropologist also made no systematic attempt to base cultural differences on *phúsis*, on the nature of humankind; had he done so, those cultural differences would have amounted to "racial" distinctions, but such is not the case.[22]

4. The Racial Stances of Greek Science

4.1. The Rejection of Theology as a Point of Reference

The essential contribution made by the Greek sciences and technical advances coming out of "Pre-Socratic" thought, as is well known, boils down to the idea of basing the explanation of natural phenomena on material, determinist causes rather than on supernatural forces. Whatever its origin, this principle began to develop rapidly within the debate instituted by the civic life of the democratic *pólis* and by the constant critical confrontation of opposing views. It will suffice to mention the explanation of the origin of earthquakes that was attributed to Thales: they are not the effect of Poseidon's anger, it was claimed, but rather the result of tempests agitating the waters on which the disk of the earth floats.[23]

It is the same type of determinist explanation that is taken up in the fifth century in the earliest writings of Hippocratic physicians. The "sacred" disease (epilepsy) is, for the author of the treatise on this topic, no more divine than any other disease; this affliction, too, has a cause (*próphasis*) deriving from *phúsis*, from nature. The purifications and charms applied to this ailment are thus merely a hypocritical screen covering up the embarrassed ignorance (*amekhaníe*) of charlatans; the divinity has no role—and thus no responsibility (*aítios*)—either in the disease or in its cure. The only effective treatment is one based on an appropriate regimen aimed at reestablishing balance within the human organism, according to the climate it inhabits, between opposing qualities: the dry and the wet, the hot and the cold.[24]

With this reference to climate, the physical determinism that the Hippocratic doctors take over from Pre-Socratic thought brings us back to the problem posed at the beginning of this chapter. Indeed, the reference to climate entails variations not only according to the season but also according to region. A theory of climatic variations elaborated within a medical perspective takes us into geography understood in the broad sense, that is, physical and human geography; it leads us to apply to the human organism the differences observed in its environment, in its material surroundings. Does this not constitute a way of reaching—through a particular use of discourse—a distinction between different human groups and of basing this distinction on a physical explanation?

4.2. The Explanation of Illness in Terms of Environment

This medical thought—the secularism of which is only an illusion, since it is formulated by practitioners who are often attached to one of the major sanctuaries of Asclepius, son of Apollo—began to develop rapidly around the time when the work of Herodotus was published. So it is that, from within the medical school on Cos, a little book appeared, which was probably intended for itinerant physicians. It is well known that Greek doctors of the classical period enjoyed fame that was as great as that of the sanctuaries within which they practiced their art; it is for this reason that we find some of them as far away as the court of the Persian king, in the very heart of "barbarian" country. In this context, a manual specifically addressed to the traveling doctor is no doubt a good indicator of the attitude that a Greek practitioner of the science might have had when he found himself directly confronted with the reality of different cultures and customs.[25]

It is of little consequence whether this "pocket" medical treatise was written by Hippocrates or one of his students. Its title—*On Airs, Waters, and Places*—announces what the beginning of the work specifies. Toward the goal of correct research concerning the art of medicine, the manual takes into consideration several parameters influencing the configuration of human physiology: the seasons (especially the effects provoked by seasonal change), the quality of the winds (whether great winds or, by contrast, local ones), the effects of waters (according to their density and degree of hardness), the orientation of cities, and the nature of the soil (according to its degree of humidity and fertility as well as its exposure). But, on top of these external factors capable of influencing the state of a person's health, the author of the treatise adds the way of life of the concerned population, specifically their eating habits and athletic pursuits. These too are among the external causes contributing to the internal state of the human organism.[26]

The whole first part of the treatise is devoted to establishing the causal links according to which the organism, understood as a group of cavities, depends on the different variables mentioned. Within this organic and physical perspective, a state of good health results from the mixing of the two (or four) humors constituting the animate being's physiology and from the regular elimination of potential excesses of these humors: thus, it is the balanced mixing of yellow bile and phlegm—in addition to which blood and black bile can also come into play—and the regular discharging of these humors that define, from an internal, organic standpoint, the character of the human constitution, that is, its nature (*phúsis*). We ought to bear in mind that Alcmaeon of Croton had already posed health as being based on a balanced (*súmmetron*) mixture (*krâsis*) of opposing qualities: the wet and the dry, the cold and the warm, the bitter and the sweet, and so on. According to such a representation, which often resorts to political metaphors, disease is cast as proceeding from the "monarchy" of one of these elements, while health results from an equitable distribution (*isonomía*) among these opposing qualities.[27]

The objection could be made, however, that a link is missing to explain the effect that the enumerated external factors might have on the humors constituting the internal physiology. The Hippocratic physicians located that link in the qualities that people share: in cities facing south and, consequently, exposed to warm winds (which are associated here with the wet), the inhabitants will have phlegmatic diseases, since phlegm is wet of nature and these winds cause it to flow abundantly. Conversely, in cities exposed to the cold north winds (associated with the dry), the inhabitants will suffer from an excess of bile, a humor having to do with dryness. Starting from this first opposition, the binary schema develops into a quaternary schema, but one based on the alternation of qualities rather than on the predominance of one quality over the others. Thus, the inhabitants of cities exposed on the east enjoy the best health because their climate stands in equilibrium between the warm and the cold (as well as between the wet and the dry); but those living in cities oriented toward the west, which are exposed to both north and south winds, suffer from all of the diseases provoked by an excessively fluctuating climate. What is found to be ultimately underlying disease in general are sudden meteorological changes and the strong contrasts between contrary qualities that they cause.[28]

Thus, the Hippocratic reflection on the variations that the human constitution undergoes in relation to its climatic environment cannot be reduced to simple mechanical and structural play with opposing qualities. While it escapes from the schematic tendencies that can result from structuralist play, this theory of health and disease, as the result of the complex combination of qualities constituting antithetical pairs, evokes the medical conceptions of numerous traditional cultures.[29]

We can observe two shifts occurring over the course of the Hippocratic argument concerning the cause of disease and its effects: the shift from one pair of opposed qualities to another (from warm wind to wet phlegm, even though phlegm is elsewhere characterized as constituting a cold humor) and the transition from the criterion of predominance to that of alternation. Of course, if we were to apply exclusively the first distinguishing criterion adopted, both cities exposed on the east and those facing west should enjoy a balanced climate.

For our purposes, what is most important to note, within this complex determinist theory that draws on a plurality of explanatory factors, is the implicit recognition of the existence of a form of human nature. This nature of humankind is fundamentally the same in all regions of the known world; it reacts uniformly to the climatic changes fomented by the particular orientation of certain cities. These changes are not identified in terms of geographical location or, above all, ethnic affiliation. Everywhere, it would seem, the human organism can, through the effect of sudden meteorological changes, become drier or wetter; everywhere, there are phlegmatic people and, on the contrary, bilious people. The same postulate makes it possible for the Hippocratic speaker and author of *Prognostics* to affirm:

> One must have deep knowledge of the signs and other symptoms and not fail to recognize that, in every year and every season, bad signs presage ill and favorable signs presage good, since the aforementioned symptoms are manifestly true in Libya, on Delos, and in Scythia.

> (*Prognostics* 25)

If we take what is at stake in this environmental alchemy of the human body and translate it into the terms of a contemporary debate, we could say that the theory of the influence of climate on the human organism makes it possible to base a relativist view of human cultures on a universal principle.[30]

4.3. The Ethnocentric Reversal

To return to Scythia, the transition from the first to the second portion of the treatise *On Airs, Waters, and Places* contains a considerable surprise. The speaker has just enumerated the multiplicity of ecological factors capable of influencing a fundamentally unified human nature; to the other determinant climatic factors are added the nature of the waters and of the soils. After this detailed and nuanced discussion, the author of the little book turns all of his efforts toward showing "how Asia and Europe differ from each other, particularly concerning the morphology (*morphê*) of the inhabitants of these two continents" (*Airs* 12.1).[31] The focus of the author's interest suddenly shifts from diseases and their causes to ethnic characteristics. Indeed, he claims, Asia contrasts with Europe in the nature (*phúsis*) of everything; what Asiatic lands produce is different, and so are the people themselves.

This utterly surprising assertion is nevertheless accompanied by two important nuances concerning the ethnocentric attitude that the new center of interest of the speaker-narrator seems to entail. First, it is not in Europe but in Asia that, according to the author, the best-cultivated land and the men with the mildest and most well balanced habits (*éthea*) are to be found; this is due (we are told) to the "equally divided" (*isomoríe*) climate there. This term, with its political overtones, recalls the *isonomía* between opposing qualities that Alcmaeon of Croton presents as characterizing a state of good health. Second, this equilibrium belongs solely to Asia Minor; the other regions constituting the vast zone of Asia do not benefit from this privileged situation halfway between warm and cold and between dry and wet. But, before attempting to identify the major traits of the representation of the world that underlie this bipartite division of the inhabited earth, I want to outline briefly the different steps involved in this very explicit line of reasoning. The reasoning elaborated here is a racial one, since it both aims at rooting the observed external differences in the human organism and tends to present physiological distinctions as depending on factors of a physical, if not cosmic, order.

Near the end of the treatise, when it is time to provide a summary in conclusion, the speaker once more draws a connection between the great differences in stature and morphology among the various Europeans and the sudden climatic changes that they undergo. The alternations between warm and cold and between wet and dry in very changeable seasons have a direct effect on the consistency of their semen, which is modified in correspondence to these climatic variations. Whence (*dióti*) the pronounced differences that may be observed in the morphology (*eîdos*) of Europeans according to the city that they inhabit; and whence also—in such an environment, such a nature (*phúsis*)—dispositions (*éthea*) that are characterized in terms of savagery, resistance, ardor, and, finally, courage (*andreía*, the opposite of cowardliness). Moreover, not only are the qualities of the soul (*psukhê*) the reflection of those of the body (*sôma*), but also customs and laws (*nómoi*) confirm and reinforce individual, "natural" dispositions.[32]

In the reasoning of the speaker within the treatise *On Airs, Waters, and Places,* two facts attract the attention of an anthropologist looking to uncover the foundations of the characterization of others in Greek culture. First, there is the role played in it by analogy: to a fluctuating climate corresponds an animated and quick-tempered disposition. It is this projection, by analogy, of the climate onto the temperament and characterization of individuals that is evoked at the conclusion of the treatise. Where there is soft soil and considerable rainfall, where the waters are warm in the summer and cold in the winter, where the seasons are balanced, people are corpulent, lacking in vigor, and wet; their indolence, their lack of technical skills and ingenuity, and their dearth of intellectual curiosity follow from these physical traits. Thus, we shift imperceptibly from the physical qualities of the environment to the people's physiological characteristics, then to their moral qualities, which are the object of an implicit value judgment.[33] It is worth noting, moreover, that technical competence is placed on the same side of the bipartite division as sudden climatic changes and the savage (*ágrios*) temperament resulting from them, a fact that follows from the analogy but constitutes a surprising reversal of what we might otherwise expect. Thus, we end up with a striking assimilation of "savagery" with one of the qualities that, traditionally, is constitutive of the image of civilization in classical Greece.[34]

But this reasoning by analogy about the causes underlying the differences between groups of human beings leads to a second point that is likely to surprise those of us who think in terms of the logic of noncontradiction. Indeed, following a long argument about the climatic and physical causes of the differences in constitution and temperament among various people, another type of influence is mentioned: the impact of *nómoi,* of customs. The conclusion to be drawn is that mores are as important to the ardor and courage characterizing Europeans as nature is.[35] Thus, right alongside the material, physical causes that are put forth to explain the differences among peoples is set the influence of *nómoi,* the relative character of which (as we have seen) is very much present in the minds of fifth-century Greeks. The power attributed to the customs of a given people can even be so great that their customs end up affecting their *phúsis,* their nature, through the impact these customs ultimately have on their semen. So, for example, all Macrocephali have oblong heads because they originally shaped the still malleable skulls of their infants by binding them with bandages. "At first, it was custom that operated . . . , but, with the passing of time, it turned into nature," says the indigenous speaker (14); translated into our (post)modern language, this becomes, "the acquired characteristic ultimately passed into the genetic heritage of the population." This was a widespread idea in the fifth century, when there seems to have been a desire to overcome the binary opposition that the Sophists were attempting to establish between the genetic and the acquired.[36]

4.4. A Representation of the Inhabited World

The role played by customs is not the only thing serving to nuance the seemingly sharp ethnocentric opposition drawn between Europeans and Asiatics. The climatic and, consequently, ethnographic image that the author of the treatise on the environment has of the known world extends well beyond this bipartite division.[37] Europeans are, of course, presented as diametrically opposed to Asiatics, since the ardor of the former results from a fluctuating climate, while the calm indolence of the latter is a consequence of a balanced mixture (*krêsis,* just as in Alcmaeon of Croton) of seasons.[38] But the division of the earth along a north–south axis does not suffice to account for the Hippocratic representation of the world and of the peoples inhabiting it. If we were to draw this dividing line onto a modern map of the Mediterranean world, it would be oriented along a northeast-southwest diagonal. This line is integrated into a system of cartographic organization wherein the cardinal points, which are defined by the direction of each of the four principal winds, are combined with the four quadrants, which are determined by the respective zones where the sun rises and sets in the summer and winter (see the diagram).[39]

To the north of the occidental, European part of the *oikouméne* delimited by the line separating Europe from Asia, we find the Scythians. This ethnic group lives on a combination of grasslands and swamplands with a climate that remains constantly cold and wet all year long. Consequently (we are told), the cavities forming the internal constitution of the human body are, for Scythians, also wet; this internal wetness is reflected externally in their morphology, which is fleshy and soft, so that the men look similar to the women. The eradication of physiological traits distinguishing one sex from the other is sometimes so complete that it can produce men who are utterly feminine, who in that case become eunuchs. It is in this way that the "feminine disease" affecting the Enarees is explained without recourse to divinity.[40] At the same time, however, the blurring of differences between the sexes takes the inverse form in the northeast of Scythia, where the women are very masculine; thus, the existence of the Amazon women of the Sauromatae, in a territory bordering Asia near the Sea of Azov, is attributed to the same cause (*aitíe*).[41]

In the opposite part of the world from the land of the Scythians, in the south of the eastern, Asiatic half of the *oikouméne,* are located the Egyptians and the Libyans. Although a lacuna in the text of the treatise deprives us of the bulk of the Hippocratic doctor's description of these two peoples, we are able to discern that the Egyptians represent the exact opposite of the Scythians because they are subjected to constant warmth (and dryness). The continual conjunction of warmth and dryness, but also the internal contradiction entailed in this very conjunction, seem to have effects that are simultaneously similar to and the opposite of those of the combination of cold and wet affecting Scythian physiology: a relative lack of morphological differences among individuals (because of the regularity of the climate), but probably a general tendency toward masculinity resulting from the co-presence of warmth and dryness (by contrast with the conjunction of coldness and wetness).[42] While the Egyptians of the Hippocratic treatise do not seem to have neighbors to the south (breaking the symmetry with the Scythians and their neighbors to the north, the Sauromatae),[43] the speaker and author of the treatise does situate two very particular populations in the east and the north of the Asiatic sector. First, near the Caucasus, there are the people living on the banks of the Phasis, in a climate that is constantly both warm and wet; the perpetual wetness in this extremely remote region causes them to be fleshy and soft and to be indolent of character, thereby making them like the Scythians. Farther to the north, near the Sea of Azov, are found peoples who are differentiated from one another by numerous traits as a consequence of the frequent climatic changes.[44] These peoples, in turn, are characterized as the opposite of those found on the European side of the very same sea.

The overall picture, as we can now see, turns out to be quite complex. On the one hand, we have the major division between Europeans and Asiatics, which follows a northeast-southwest line of partition; to this division corresponds the opposition between a changeable climate and one that remains constant. On the other, we have an antithesis along an east-west axis, wherein Scythians and Egyptians occupy opposite poles. On each side of this antithesis, pairs of terms are conjoined to form a double opposition: on one side is the cold and the wet, on the other the hot and the dry.[45] This representation of the inhabited world corresponds roughly to the account in the first part of the treatise, wherein the different types of climates are organized according to the same distribution among the four quadrants defined by the winter and summer sunrises and sunsets and by exposure to the corresponding winds: there are cities exposed to cold north winds and, inversely, cities exposed to warm south winds; cities in the east benefit from a temperate climate, while cities in the west suffer from an excessively fluctuating climate. Thus, we come back to that double criterion of distinction mentioned previously (the predominance of a single quality or of a conjunction of qualities and invariability or, conversely, fluctuation), except that, now, warmth is associated with wetness for cities exposed to south winds and dryness with cold in the case of cities exposed to north winds, while the Egyptians and Scythians have opposite combinations of warm and dry (for the former) and cold and wet (for the latter). Furthermore, in the "ethnographic" description, wetness (and wetness alone) seems to have the same effect whether it is accompanied by cold or by warmth: that of a physiological and morphological softening that makes the affected people feminine, like the Scythians, on the European side, and the inhabitants of the region along the Phasis, on the Asiatic side. Finally, in opposition to the antithesis between fluctuating climates and unchanging ones, the climatic uniformity and constancy that characterize mostly the regions on the outermost confines of the *oikouméne* cause a certain homogeneity in the morphology of individuals.

The accompanying diagram presents a possible depiction—as projected on our image of the world—of the Hippocratic physician's representation of the *oikouméne,* with the climates distinguishing the different parts of it and the peoples residing there:

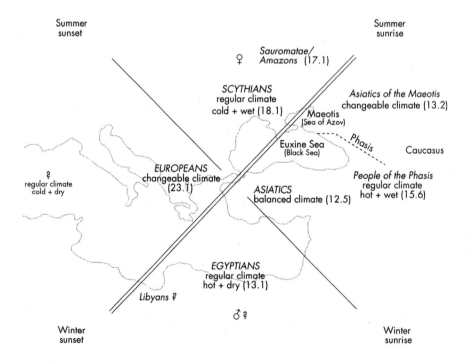

Ethnographic and climatic image of the inhabited world according to the author of *On Airs, Waters, and Places* (text citations in parentheses).

4.5. The Speaker-Narrator's Point of View

Where do the Greeks fall within this complex representation of the inhabited world? Before accusing the author of the treatise *On Airs, Waters, and Places* of ethnocentrism or racism, we ought to ask where he situates himself within his own discursive construction; we should seek to identify the position from which he—as speaker and narrator—addresses his narratee. Paradoxically, once again, but also significantly within a treatise consisting of technical discourse, the author's enunciative interventions, as speaker-narrator, are largely confined to marking the points of transition in the development of his discourse: "So, as concerns the Macrocephali, that is how it seems to me; now, as for those living in Phasis . . ." (Airs 14–15). In addition to these transitional phrases, we also find instructions addressed to the abstract or implied reader of the treatise concerning how he should proceed in his own reflections about the causes of disease: "It is from these things that one must proceed in his reflection about the rest" (2). Sometimes, in place of these indirect recommendations to the implicit reader, we find direct appeals to a narratee evoked through general second-person singular forms to draw on his personal experience: "You could ascertain this in the following manner: . . . after measuring the water, you will find it greatly reduced in quantity" (8). Finally, owing to its epideictic character, the treatise is studded with enunciative assertions such as "I will show this even more clearly" (24.1).[46] The speaker-narrator's voice holds authority, but he does not explicitly put his discourse in perspective relative to his geographical position or ethnic affiliation. Consequently, there is no well-defined "point of view."

It is true that the Hippocratic doctor who assumes the position of the "instance of enunciation," and thus of the speaker-narrator, within the treatise on the environment seems to adopt the same bipartite representation of the world, divided between Europe and Asia, as Herodotus.[47] It is also true that, on top of what is essentially a territorial distinction in the inquiry of the historian from Halicarnassus, he adds value judgments concerning the nature and, especially, the character of the people inhabiting the two continents thus identified. But, to shift from the level of discourse to the underlying social and political realities, that is, from the intradiscursive to the extradiscursive, we ought to bear in mind that the Greeks occupied not only the European but also the Asiatic coast of the Aegean. As Ionians, both Herodotus and the Hippocratic physicians belong—according to the territorial division that they themselves draw—to Asia.

It is probably as a result of this ambiguous territorial and social position—that of a Greek from Asia—that Herodotus adopts constant enunciative stances concerning the political status to be attributed to Ionians and the legitimacy of Persian claims to this Asiatic part of Greece.[48] As in Herodotus' *Histories*, the contradiction entailed in the existence of a Greek territory in Asia seems to be attenuated in the Hippocratic treatise through the principle of balance and the compensatory weighting of differences relative to territorial division. Moreover, this contradiction is what causes the treatise on the environment to avoid a perspective defined in terms of a single center. While, on the one hand, everything in Asia (Minor) is much larger and more beautiful, the fruits of the soil better, the youths numerous and fine-looking, and while Asia (at least in its most temperate region) enjoys an endless springtime thanks to the mildness (*metriótes*) of its climate, on the other hand, "neither courage, nor physical endurance, nor perseverance, nor fervor could arise in such a state of nature" (12). Even if Herodotus, for his part, affirms that Ionia has the best climate in the world (*en tôi kallístoi*), being harbored from the wet cold and from the dry heat, he nevertheless claims that it is at the remotest ends of the inhabited earth that the most beautiful products (*tà kállista*) are enjoyed.[49] After celebrating the mildness of Ionia's climate, Herodotus even concludes his work with the affirmation that "soft countries beget soft men, for it is not the property of any one soil to bear both marvelous fruits and men who are valorous in war" (9.122.3–4).[50]

At the very moment when the Hippocratic author is tempted to give the inhabitants of Asia a racial identity by recognizing the existence of a *génos asienón*, an Asiatic "breed," he turns to nuancing his assertion. Certainly, the Asiatic race is, under the influence of the balanced climate, characterized by its lack of steadfastness and courage; certainly, as a consequence, it manifests utter submission to an omnipotent ruler. Custom, then, reinforces nature. But this thesis is immediately followed by a counterexample: nature can also prevail, independent of climate; it suffices to call to mind the Greeks and barbarians who, in Asia itself, preserve their autonomy and combativeness. The conclusion to be drawn is that only on the Asiatic side of the divide can servile submission and fierce independence very well coexist.[51] The affirmation of this *méga tekmérion* is, moreover, accompanied by a double enunciative intervention that also involves the addressee-narratee: "You will find that Asiatics, too, differ from one another, some being better, others worse. The changes of the seasons are the cause of these differences, as I stated earlier" (16).

Thus, both the fact that the treatise is not focused on a geographical center and the very Greek idea that balance results from the proper mixture of contraries lead us to a position of racial and cultural relativism that is quite remarkable.[52] It is in the conjunction of these two fundamental elements that the unity of the treatise resides. The lack of an enunciative point of reference expressed in geographical and ethnocentric terms in the first part of the treatise is a result of the very aim of the work, which is addressed to itinerant physicians. *On Airs, Waters, and Places* addresses doctors who, by definition, do not adopt a viewpoint focused on a single spatial location, but must rather remain sensitive in each place to the relative proportions of the four opposing qualities (warm and cold, dry and wet), among which the balance or disproportion of some qualities in relation to others can have positive or negative effects on all people. The second part of the treatise does comprise an enunciative perspective marked by ethnocentrism, but this enunciative attitude remains relative, owing to the truly ambiguous position of the anthropologist physician, who performed his discourse in Ionia, a part of Greece that is situated in Asia. The relativism entailed in this position is, furthermore, reinforced by the consistency with which the role played by contraries is represented as a determinist one, wherein climate is the cause of differences in the nature of various peoples. Because of both the doubleness of the extradiscursive spatial reference and the basing of the intradiscursive representation on universal principles, the "instance of enunciation" in the treatise is invested with ambiguous enunciative authority.

Ultimately, the theory of the Greek physician of the classical period, rather than founding a form of racist thought, contributes to nuancing such a position. First, it does so inasmuch as this materialist theory is based on a plurality of oppositions, which makes it possible to go beyond the over-simplicity of thought that is binary and, consequently, prone to black-and-white value judgments. Furthermore, it does so because the physical theory is combined with moral thought based on the principle of the proper distribution of qualities and the compensatory balancing out of disparities through advantages and disadvantages. While, in the second part of *On Airs, Waters, and Places*, an attempt is indeed made to find a physical and organic basis for supposed differences among human groups, the operative distinctions are not treated hierarchically. Whence the absence of a unilaterally racist point of view in the discursive elaboration and orientation of the treatise; whence the measured ethnocentrism of Hippocrates.

5. Beyond the Racial Perspective

It is of no use to claim to find in classical Greek thought, and more particularly in that of the Coan physicians, an absolute model. The knowledge acquired over more than two millennia should permit us to do better. What is scandalous about a racist attitude in our day is that it represents a regression relative to certain forms of thought dating to the fifth century B.C. What is scandalous is the naturalistic basis that neoconservative thought attempts to give to social and cultural discrimination, which, in industrialized countries, is most often directed at groups of foreigners: asylum-seeking immigrants and refugees. In Switzerland today, the social conflation of asylum seekers and economic refugees with illegal immigrants and drug dealers tends to be justified in the name of cultural differences having a putatively natural basis. Certainly, from the standpoint of social status, the position of a slave in fifth-century Athens was not in the least enviable, especially when that slave was a non-Greek. Alongside this social position, however, there was also that of the metic, which granted to certain others, certain foreigners, at least a place within the *pólis*.[53]

Instead of reverting to the sinister model of the 1930s and 1940s, why not take inspiration from a much more ancient example of tolerant moderation in order to try to take it even further? Our scientific knowledge and the technical capabilities that have come out of it give us the obvious means; it is sad to see them used in an inept attempt to justify—through a form of biological neodeterminism fueled by genetic research—differences that are actually of a cultural order. Though a layman, I venture to put forth a hypothesis in lieu of a conclusion: the genetic pool, owing to the infinite number of possible combinations of which it is both the result and the source, ultimately produces only individual men and women. Thus, the sole result of the innate is the singular, the differentiated. It is to the work carried out by culture and social life that we owe, through the procedures of "anthropopoiesis," the grouping together of individuals who are fundamentally different from one another. It is cultural constructions and life in societies that establish social groups within which the individuals (each of whom is unique) can feel a part of a common tribal, community-based ethnic or national identity. The fundamentally relative character of this work carried out through culture should push us not to assimilate or reject others, but to tolerate them and allow them to live alongside us, with their individual and social differences, while remaining attentive to what they can tell us.[54] We ought to do so according to a universal principle of tolerance and negotiation capable of controlling unrestrained relativism, which can lead to racist turns of differentialist thought built on a foundation of economic neoconservatism.

Even if, one day, we were to end up finding a credible biological basis for cultural differences, racism would still be only the result of the kind of hierarchical value judgment that some like to attach—through masks of discursive authority—to these differences, despite their utterly relative character.

IX

ORPHIC VOICES AND INITIATORY FUNCTIONS

The Derveni Theogony and Its Commentary

The papyrus roll found among the votive objects buried with the remains of an affluent citizen in a tomb located in Derveni, a few miles from Thessalonica, is interesting on three levels. This mutilated text from the late fourth century, which was rediscovered in 1962, contains excerpts from the oldest version of the Orphic cosmo-theogony known to us and, above all, a prose commentary on that poem. The commentary on this poem composed in Homeric diction seems to situate it within the ritual circumstances in which it was performed. Of course, the lacunae in the columns of text and commentary from the half-burnt Derveni papyrus oblige the modern reader to undertake the tricky business of conjecture and confront the various philological problems involved in establishing a coherent text.[1] Beyond these technical difficulties, however, such a reader will be sensitive to how the poetic voice of this cosmogonic-theogonic narrative is echoed, in a certain way, by the erudite voice of a commentator who is no doubt attentive to the ritual and performative dimension of the Orphic poem, if not of his own commentary.

1. A Poem Standing between Enigma and Allegory

In what follows I shall leave aside several issues concerning the Derveni papyrus: the problems involved in the very hypothetical reconstruction of the cosmogonic poem commented on in the papyrus;[2] the exact identity of the commentator, who draws the greatest part of his interpretive resources from "Pre-Socratic" physics;[3] and the precise philosophical references of what is a rather composite (when not outright awkward) commentary. I focus instead on how the poetic text and commentary are put into relationship with each other, and on the enunciative position of the commentator, both of which issues deserve more attention than they have hitherto received. In the absence of external indications, the profile of the authority endorsed by the commentator himself—through various enunciative means—in order to ensure the credibility of his interpretation can lead us to wonder what the function of this strange text is.

The text of the Derveni papyrus offers us the sole developed example of a critical procedure already in use at the end of the "archaic" period for the interpretation of narrative poems in Homeric diction. Linked to the name of Theagenes of Rhegium, a linguist before the term was coined, this method of explanation seems to have been essentially based on the very sort of etymological play in which the Homeric bards themselves engaged and of which Plato provides a survey in the *Cratylus*. Even in the *Iliad,* during the violent battle scene in which Achilles, in a rage, attacks the Trojans as they attempt to flee into the eddying waters of the Scamander, the thick fog (*eéra*) spread about by Hera to hamper the escape of the terrified warriors is associated with the name of the goddess.[4] The etymological play on Hera's name emphasizes the role played in the combat by the cosmic elements—water, fire, earth, and "air"—as a part of an explanation that, far from reducing the action of the anthropomorphic agents to the reciprocal influence of physical elements, actually tends toward linking the two. The etymologizing procedure thus confers a cosmological dimension on the narrative action and its human protagonists.

While, on the one hand, the Derveni interpreter does not render explicit his hermeneutic procedures—that is, while he does not name them—he does, on the other hand, repeatedly qualify the poetic text attributed to Orpheus as "enigmatic" (*ainigmatôdes*). This striking characterization of the *póesis* of which Orpheus is supposedly the author first appears at the moment when the commentator leaves off from the description of sacrificial rites (which may have constituted the cultic context for the cosmo-theogonic poem's performance) in order to discuss the text itself.[5] Attention is to be focused on the nature (*phú]sin*) or the explanation (*lú]sin*) of the words (*onómata*) composing a "hymn" whose content is sanctioned by divine law (*them[i]tá*). What is to be undertaken, then, is a lexical semantics, the aim of which is explicit: to provide the meaning of the terms in a poem composed for initiates. This is the best way to interpret the allusion, at the end of column 7 (the first column devoted to commentary on the poem), to the "doors placed upon the ears (of the profane)." Despite the lacunae, the formula naturally evokes the famous hexameter to which Plato refers in his *Symposium*. Modern scholars have even gone so far as to reconstruct this line and insert it at the opening of the cosmo-theogonic poem from Derveni: "I will sing for those who understand (*aeíso xunetoîsi*). Let the uninitiated close the doors of their ears!"[6]

It does not belong to Orphic poetry alone to *ainíttesthai*, since Pindar, for example, repeatedly proclaims his intention to praise his honorand with an *aînos* and so address "those who understand" (*sunetoí*).[7] The Derveni exegete considers that the poet of the theogony on which he is commenting "signifies" (*semaínei*), just as the Delphic oracle "indicates," according to Heraclitus.[8] In fact, the Derveni commentator frequently refers to the knowledge of those who "understand"; that is, he claims to draw on the esoteric knowledge of initiates, who—unlike "those who do not know"—hold the keys to this "enigmatic" epic diction.[9] But what is the actual goal of this exegesis? After all, in the context of Orphic initiation, knowledge of the poem commented on must have been restricted to the initiates who, as such, certainly did not need explanations in order to understand it. Is the Derveni commentary, then, using its written form so as to divulge the secrets of the followers of Orpheus in an attempt at anti-Orphic propaganda? Might it, on the contrary, be pursuing a pedagogical objective, trying both to bring up-to-date for a group of initiates of the fourth century B.C. a more ancient poem, which had become obscure for them, and to restore authority to it through a philosophical reading? Or might the poem itself, in its very conception, require exegetical readings? Might not this exegesis be a part of the initiation process itself? Before sketching out an answer to these questions, I shall try to elucidate the commentator's exegetic procedures for one of the isotopies traversing the poem.

To the modern reader's eye, it seems first of all that the commentator's interpretive proposals are often more clear-cut than the rather ambiguous formulations of the lemmata he quotes. This explanatory procedure, which tends to reduce polysemy, is particularly noticeable in the sexual interpretation that the commentator gives for several passages outlining genealogical relationships. Such an exegesis is all the more tempting as every genealogical narrative is founded on the genital image: narratives deploying genealogies exploit the metaphorical resources offered by the biological process of sexual reproduction. Now, on the basis of what we can decipher concerning the development of the Derveni poem, this metaphorical language makes it possible to present clearly differentiated figures following generation upon generation; the way in which these figures succeed one another seems to indicate the movement and orientation of the whole cosmo-theogony. Linked to one another through genealogical relationships, the "enigmatic" terms and the figures corresponding to them are thus engaged in a narrative intrigue: enigma becomes allegory. The commentary follows this movement while bringing out the physical logic of the cosmo-theogonic narrative. In this play with metaphor and enunciation lies the specificity of an Orphic poetic representation of the creation of the world and the (Orphic) authority of its later commentary. It is these issues that guide the reading proposed here, which focuses on a particular isotopy, that of sexuality.

2. The Reign of the Primordial Entities and Their Separation

As its commentator presents it, the poem begins by describing the establishment of the power of Zeus: obeying oracles probably pronounced by Night, the god receives force and the glorious "demon" from his father. From column 8 to column 12, the commentator's whole effort bears on the exegesis of this act of taking power: symbols of power received from the father, didactic oracles formulated by Night, "who proclaims omens" (with the complicity of the god of light), residence on snowy Olympus (which the commentator likens to *khrónos*, "time," in its height).[10] The quotation given at the beginning of column 8 of the verse that probably began the genealogical narrative brings us to the content of the oracle at the origin of Zeus' enthronement. According to the commentator, the poem gives the content of this oracle only indirectly, through the action resulting from it: Zeus swallows the "venerable" one (*aidoîon*), who first sprang up in (or from?) the ether. The word-for-word reading, which presents itself explicitly as a deciphering of a poem that expresses itself through allusion (*ainízetai*), provides a twofold interpretation for the term *aidoîon*. First, its use is connected with the metaphorical meaning of the term in its plural form: in all of Greek literature, the *aidoîa* designate the masculine or feminine pudenda, the "shameful parts." The commentator justifies this first meaning by referring next to the principle of generation, which the *aidoîa* incarnate in the eyes of men. Then, passing from the plural to the singular and reading a comparison in the poem, the commentator refers *aidoîon* to the sun; the comparison is justified, in turn, by the sun's power to generate beings. Accordingly, what Zeus ingests is the Sun with its generative power, or rather—if one follows the habitual meaning of *aidoîon* as a substantive in the singular—its penis, which incarnates this same procreative faculty par excellence.[11]

Three arguments can support this second reading, which implies that the poet was already playing on the double sense of the adjective *aidoîos* ("the venerable [god?]" = "the penis"). First, at the beginning of column 14, the commentator makes an element "separated from itself" the subject of the springing forth in the ether.[12] Moreover, if we compare the lemma commented on with the fragments of other Orphic cosmo-theogonies, we can assign to Helios and his penis a status analogous to that of the primordial egg from which Eros of the sparkling wings, the Shining One, the First-Born, arises. Finally, the poet seems to adopt a typically Orphic vein of polemic against traditional theology; that is, he seems to have transformed and reversed the succession narrative of the Hesiodic theogony, in which Cronos, after having castrated his father, Ouranos, is forced to swallow a stone in place of his son Zeus. This time, it would seem that it is the grandson who ingests the solar penis of his grandfather, who has been dethroned by his son.[13]

The Derveni poem and commentary provide some elements of this subverted succession story: Cronos is presented as the predecessor of Zeus in a lemma drawn from the poem (col. 15.6). Furthermore, the commentator says that Cronos was born from the Sun with the collaboration of Earth (col. 14.2–3). Finally, the poem itself treated Ouranos, the son of Night, as the first god to possess royal power (col. 14.6), which—the commentator adds—Cronos hastens to take away from him (col. 14.8–13). Given the fact that, in the longest quotation from the poem that the commentary provides for us, royalty, primeval birth, and "venerability" are associated together in a single being, from which gods, rivers, fountains, and everything that existed "then" were born (col. 16.3–6), the reader is led to identify this venerable king with Ouranos.

Of the first-born king, the venerable one. It is upon him that all the immortals came into being, the blessed gods and goddesses, the rivers and lovely springs—all that had been born at that time; thus, he alone came into being on his own.

The interpretation proposed by the commentator for the *aidoîon* and its function as creator of all things leads us to assimilate this Ouranos to the penis detached from the Sun—another reversal with regard to Hesiodic theology—through wordplay on the double meaning of *aidoîon* ("venerable" and "genitalia"), which may have already been present in the Orphic poem.[14] Hence, the genealogical tree subtending the poem, combined with the scheme of the royal succession, would take the following form:

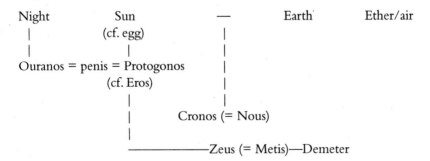

The reconstruction of the vertical genealogical relations is hampered by the horizontal assimilations by which Orphic thought habitually proceeds. In any case, the Derveni commentator sees the establishment of the reign of Zeus as the outcome of a first phase of creation (*génesis*). Having posed this reign as foundational but not first, the poem had to explain its genesis through a genealogical narrative. This was based on the oracles that had marked the first act of genesis and, hence, goes back to the primordial entities that had preceded the power of Zeus. Independently of any sexual union, these anthropomorphic entities seem to come about according to a creative principle to which the commentator, at least, appears to attribute the figure of the penis.

3. The Reign of Zeus and of Eros

Beginning in column 15, the commentator—whose discussion here most probably reflects a ring structure in the poem—returns to the reign of Zeus the wise, the successor of Cronos. As befits his epithet (*metíeta*, col. 15.6), Zeus shares the royal honors with Metis, the incarnation of craft intelligence: "Zeus the head, Zeus the center, Zeus by whom all things were fabricated" (col. 17.12), "Zeus the first" (? col. 18.12), "Zeus the king, Zeus with the bright lightning, principle of all beings" (col. 19.10). Now, an essential generative activity occurs in support of the reign of this omnipotent king, the creator and animator of all things: copulation (col. 21.1). The commentator, most certainly following the poet in the Orphic style of accumulating qualifications, glosses this founding act by a series of names of divinities and of verbs referring to sexual activity: Aphrodite Ourania, who by her *epiclesis* recalls Ouranos, the First-Born; Zeus, who is invested with the powers of the goddess of love through the fact that he appears in this list; Peitho, because—the commentator himself explains (col. 21.10–11)—seduction induces beings to yield to one another; Harmonia (Cadmus' exemplary wife, the daughter of Ares and Aphrodite) because—as befits the etymology of her name—she manages to adapt (*hérmose*, col. 21.12) to each being its complement. But the reign of Zeus-Aphrodite also means yielding to the pleasures of love (*aphrodisiázein*), that is, union between man and woman (col. 21.6–9), hence *thórnusthai* ("copulate" or "impregnate"). According to the commentator, this activity is pursued until each of the beings in movement in the air has found its complement.[15]

At this point Zeus himself must find a sexual partner in the person of a wife. The commentator names her in accordance with the Orphic procedure of juxtaposition, which was probably also used in the poem itself. Zeus' wife is Earth, who is also Mother, Rhea, and Hera; Ge by tradition, Meter because all things are born from her, she is also Demeter because her name combines the names of the first two (col. 22.7–11). The quotation of a verse drawn from the *Orphic Hymns* not only confirms this sequence of names for the commentator but also enables him to add Hestia and Deio to the list; he explains the presence of this avatar of Demeter etymologically by asserting that the goddess was injured (*edeióthe,* col. 22.12–13) in her union with Zeus.[16] Earth-Mother is well suited to be the sovereign god's partner in the generalized coupling and copulation characterizing the advent of Zeus' reign.

The last column of the papyrus (in the form in which it has reached us) presents a final excursion into the domain of sexuality, but this time the interpreter's comments serve to correct a misunderstanding. After listing a series of elements created or recreated by Zeus—such as Ocean (which the commentator assimilates to air), the river Acheloos, the moon that shines for mortals, or the sun (cols. 23–25)—the poem returns to the erotic union of god and mother, and the commentator explains that what is involved is not Zeus' biological mother, despite the ambiguity of her appellation, *heâs.* In his opinion, *heâs* (col. 26.2) must be understood as the feminine genetive form of *eús* ("noble," "generous"), and not as a form of the possessive adjective *heós.* So the commentator does not hesitate to do violence to morphology and syntax in order to avoid incest. His sleight of hand is all the more astonishing for the fact that he makes this maternal figure the equivalent of Nous in the same explanation; and, in the course of his commentary, he has presented Nous as an avatar of Cronos, Zeus' father (col. 4.7).[17] For us, the Orphic poem ends here, in a Homeric formula, with the god's desire to be united in reciprocal love (*em philóteti mikhthênai,* 26.10) with Meter. Zeus' whole taking of command is marked by the power of Aphrodite, who leads to an erotic and fertile union.

4. From Distinction to Union

After the separation into distinct entities comes the union between copulating partners. From the genital standpoint, this is the essential development and marks the advent of the world, which is divided into two formative phases: before and after the beginning of Zeus' reign. The narrative figure of this divine king consuming the Sun's penis provides the link between these two stages of development; this figure explains the genital capacity appropriated by Zeus to engender or confirm all the elements that came about during the reign of his two predecessors. Now, in his effort to decipher and explain abstractly, the commentator superimposes on this narrative differentiation, effected by the act of Zeus, a whole series of more abstract distinctive elements; these supply the narrative sequence of sexual figures and metaphors with a philosophical translation whose initiatory significance will be explained shortly.

To begin with, a temporal difference between "once" (*prósthen*) and "now" (*nûn*) is marked within the poem itself: together with the springing forth of the first-born king-penis arise the primordial entities—gods and goddesses, rivers and springs—that were already present "at that time," as emphasized by the use of the aorist and the pluperfect tenses and the temporal adverb *tóte* (col. 16.3–6, *proséphun, ên gegaôta*). The distinction between this past and the present is emphasized by the commentator, who contrasts the beings that have always existed (*hupêrkhen aeí*) with the entities existing "now" (*nûn*), born from the former (*gínetai,* col. 16.7–8). Thus, there is, on the one hand, a sort of spontaneous existence and, on the other, a generation produced through birth, which led up to the current situation.

Moreover, the first phase is marked by separation. Starting with the penis detached from the Sun (*khoristhén,* col. 16.2), beings experience a state of distinction, separated and distant from one another (col. 15.2). But while the first stage of the cosmogony is dominated by *dia-* forms, the second belongs to *sun-* forms: whereas beings once (*prósthen,* col. 17.2 and 9) floated in the eternal air, now (*nûn,* col. 17.2 and 8) they are related to one another and gathered together. This change of status takes place under the reign of Zeus "by whom all things have been fabricated" (col. 17.12). And it is not by chance that the commentator differentiates once again between the time before and now, between *dia-* and *sun-,* in explaining the generalized copulation that Zeus' power sanctions. In an Atomist flight of fancy, the beings of the first stage are presented as animated particles in the air of the copulative movement, which attaches them to one another until each of them has found its complement (col. 21.5). Such is the philosophical explanation of the sexual and erotic action of Aphrodite, Harmonia, and Peitho.[18]

Finally, both of these phases of cosmic and theogonic creation are dominated by an intellectual power. The first is Nous (Reflection), whom the poet seems to have assimilated to Cronos, since he strikes beings against one another (col. 14.7–8).[19] According to the commentator, it is while the universe is apparently becoming set in motion that Ouranos' royal power is taken away (col. 14.8–14) and beings are distinguished as they are dispersed at a distance from one another (col. 15.1–2); it is then that the sun receives its fixed place in the center, delimiting the high from the low. The transition from this first state of separation and antagonism to the state of organized reunion is connected with the advent of Zeus, who shares the kingship with Metis. Provided with the clever intelligence of craft (col. 15.6 and 13; cf. 23.4) that is incarnated by Metis, Zeus is capable of arranging and constructing the cosmos as we now know it. Zeus' assimilation of the qualities of wise prudence belonging to Metis obviously recalls the new king's absorption of Phanes-Metis to recreate the world in the Orphic theogony of the twenty-four *Rhapsodies.*[20] This organizational work is likewise animated, according to the commentator, by the breath circulating in the air; this is the representative of Moira, herself the incarnation of Zeus' reason (*phrónesis,* cols. 18.1–10 and 19.2–7). Thus, with Moira added to Metis, Zeus, the sovereign principle of all things, is the master not only of the organization of the cosmos but also of time. It is no doubt in this double capacity that he intends (at the conclusion, col. 26.9–10) to be united in love with his own mother, reunifying within himself the third intelligent principle, Nous, and definitively annulling the distinction between the two phases of the creation of the world.[21]

5. Initiatory and Mystic Transition

Having practically reached the end of his explanation, the commentator returns to the role of the Sun as it is defined at the beginning of the narrative (col. 25.10–12). The reader, too, can participate in the ring structure by returning to the beginning of the commentator's proposed interpretation. In fact, at column 9 the passing of power from father to son was interpreted as a transition from a state in which the father (?) prevents beings from reuniting to one in which, thanks to Zeus' mastery, they can assemble and be united with one another.[22] At this point, the role played by Night's oracular voice in this essential change can be understood: referring to the sexual process, she showed how to pass from separation to union by consuming the "venerable" (penis?).[23] Thus, in the genealogical narrative, she plays the role of the "mystic" voice enabling the initiate to leave the world of disjunction in order to rediscover the primordial and ordered unity desired by Zeus.[24] And, as is the case with Diotima in Plato's *Symposium,* this voice uses figures of sexuality in order to reveal the meaning of the initiatory path it proposes.

By means of the genital image, the development of the Orphic cosmotheogony commented on in the papyrus is sketched out in its essential outlines. While the oracular voice that announces this development allows us to divine its initiatory, mystic project and function, the voice of the commentator is, paradoxically, much more impenetrable—all the more so because he displays a relatively broad philosophical culture. Each of his references to a materialistic explanatory system, each of his attempts at etymological interpretation has given rise to a hypothesis regarding his intellectual filiation. Are we dealing with a pupil of Anaxagoras, a disciple of Diognenes of Apollonia, a follower of Heraclitus, or perhaps even Stesimbrotus of Thasos himself or Epigenes, the disciple of Socrates, or Diagoras of Melos, the sophist? Or rather, considering his use of linguistics, might he not be a philosopher like Euthyphro, who gave philosophical explanations of the gods' names, or an exegete closely related to Cratylus, who is familiar to us from Plato?[25] It is clear that posing the question of the commentary's status in terms of the extradiscursive identity of its author leads to aporia.

6. The Voice of the Commentary

Consequently, it is better to start by looking into the modalities of this exeget-
ical voice and the movement of the text as a whole that is uttered by it. From
this point of view, three observations suggest themselves.

6.1. Enunciative Modalities

First of all, the reading of the first columns of the papyrus proposed by the
scholar preparing a new official edition of the document (K. Tsantsanoglou)
provides precious indications concerning the considerations that undoubtedly
introduced the exegesis of the cosmogonic and theogonic poem. A description
of different rites performed by the *mýstai* could already be read in these prelim-
inaries. Among these gestures, the libations of water and milk are certainly close
to what we know about Orphic ritual practices (col. 6.6).[26] Moreover, the allu-
sions to the Erinyes, then to the Eumenides (which are assimilated to souls),
show that these rites concern the relationship between the terrestrial life of ini-
tiates and the world below (cols. 1.7, 2.3–4, 4.9, 6.5–6).[27] The new text now
allows us to affirm that the *mýstai* are led in their ritual gestures by *mágoi* (col.
6.5 and 9) and that all these gestures are addressed "to the gods below" (*daímones
hoi káto[then,* col. 3.6), whom they are supposed to placate (col. 6.1) after vari-
ous crimes have been committed.[28] Accordingly, we may wonder whether this
description does not refer to official mysteries such as the Eleusinian rites. If
such is the case, the commentator would then be adopting a critical position
concerning the ineffectuality of those rites. However that may be, with regard
to the Orphic isotopy traversing the text of the Derveni papyrus, these new
readings reinforce the semantic coherence that inscribes the exegesis of the
poem within the sequence of the description of the rites.

Furthermore, from the standpoint of its modalities, the voice that speaks
these commentaries manifests an undeniable unity on the enunciative level. In
both the description of the rites and the interpretation of the poem, this voice
adopts the objectivizing forms of the present tense and third person: "the *mýs-
tai* perform libations" and "they sacrifice to the Eumenides" (col. 6.6 and 8);
Orpheus "says," "indicates," "makes clear," and "reveals" (passim); for the initi-
ates, the evidence is compelling (col. 23.2–3); the non-initiates "believe" (cols.
9.2–3, 23.6–7, and 26.8). The text as it has been transmitted to us includes only
a single statement in the first person; when the speaker speaks in his own name,
it is only so as to excuse the understandable ignorance of those who have been
initiated "in the cities" (col. 20.1–3). This purely assertive and descriptive mode
corresponds to that used by Crates of Athens in his treatise on Athenian sacri-
fices, by Philochorus in his monograph on sacrifices, and by Melanthius in his

treatise on the Eleusinian mysteries. Whether what is involved is the procession and sacrifice dedicated to Apollo Cynneios, the offering of boiled meats to the Hours, or the consecration of the initiates' clothes to the goddesses of Eleusis, all these gestures are described in the present tense and are attributed to a third-person plural subject.[29] This distanced voice of the scholar who collects and describes his city's cultic customs is much like the Derveni exegete's voice. Easily recognizable in the part devoted to interpreting the poem, it is also found in the part describing the ritual. For example, inasmuch as it recognizes the souls of the dead under the theological figure of the Eumenides (col. 6.9–10) and refers to Heraclitus' thought (col. 4), the text is based on the same exegetical procedures in both parts.

Finally, the same strong opposition between "those who know" and "those who do not know"—that is, between initiates and non-initiates—is found in both parts of the Derveni text. In the part devoted to commenting on the poem, this opposition is particularly pronounced in the interpretation of the nature of Ocean in column 23. While, in this regard, the uninitiated must content themselves with opinions concerning a world of appearances (*dokoûsi*, l. 6), the initiates have the benefit of manifest proof (*eúdelon*, l. 3; cf. l. 2). For non-initiates, Ocean is merely a river, while for initiates, who have correct knowledge (*orthôs*, l. 2), Ocean is the air and, thus (according to the procedure of theological assimilation that is so characteristic of Orphic thought), Zeus. Likewise, when Zeus gathers in his hands his own father's power, the ignorant give a literal interpretation of the text, thinking (*dokoûsi*, col. 9.2–3) that Zeus inherits his father's divine power, whereas the one who knows (col. 9.5) discerns that this power corresponds to the capacity of mixing the elements. In both cases, the knowledge attributed to initiates corresponds to the theological or philosophical interpretation proposed by the commentator. While, in the part devoted to discussing the poem, the initiates' knowledge is of an intellectual or theoretical order, in the part describing ritual practices, this knowledge is rather a moral attitude. In the restored version of column 5, we see the disbelief felt by the non-initiates with regard to the marvels of Hades, a disbelief that prevents them from learning and knowing, dominated as they are by error and pleasure.

6.2. The Didactic Function and Its Authority

Thus, not only does correct knowledge correspond to the knowledge dispensed by the commentator in his exegesis of the rites and the poem, but also it is an object of apprenticeship. Indeed, teaching and learning seem to constitute one of the Derveni commentator's major preoccupations. First of all, they provide one of the keys for interpreting the poem. Thus, in column 10, Night's prophetic voice is interpreted as a voice with a didactic function, since to say is to utter, and uttering has the same power as teaching. Accordingly, *panompheúousa* actually means "who teaches [all things]."[30] Furthermore, to shift from the text's internal references to the description of ritual practice, the development of column 5 relates ignorant people's defiance and incredulity to the consultation of oracles. It seems that their inability to learn makes them impermeable to oracular responses. Finally, the commentary of column 20 establishes a relationship between ritual gestures and the text, thereby providing the latter with an external reference. Indeed, the commentator's professed lack of surprise concerning the ignorance of the uninitiated, in what is his sole personal statement in the commentary, bears as much on seeing as on hearing those "who have performed the rites in the cities." By contrast, if those who are initiated by a man of skill (*tékhne*) do not know after having seen (with a pun on the two meanings of *eidénai*), then they are all the more incapable of learning when they hear the words spoken.[31] Even if the standpoint here is a negative one, since the statement concerns those initiates who continue to feed on appearances (*dokoúntes*, 20.5), it is now clear that teaching concerns as much the ritual practices as it does the understanding of the poem.

From this, a striking homology between the oracular voice of Night and that of the poet called Orpheus emerges. Just as the speech of the former is taken as instruction (col. 10.9–10), so also the latter indicates and explains in order to dispense teaching that goes beyond appearances. Since they both have an oracular quality, they both require deciphering, as the sequence of thought in column 13 clearly indicates. This deciphering, with regard to both the initiatory rites and what is said in the poem, is plainly carried out by the commentator's authoritative voice. At this point, identifying a second homology, we could suppose that the sequence of the commentator's statements follows the movement of the poem itself: just as the development of the theology commented on follows an initiatory design, so too the commentator's voice would be aiming at an initiation. Would it not be appropriate, then, to assimilate the function of the commentator's text to the initiatory statements preserved in the gold leaves of Thurii and Hipponium or the tablets of Pelinna?

From the enunciative standpoint, either these texts constitute direct addresses to the initiand and praise the initiatory process he or she is undergoing, or they are placed in the initiand's own mouth and allow him or her to express directly his or her hope for salvation through the initiatory itinerary.[32] Given the performative force that the speaking of these texts in the first or second person confers on them, they diverge greatly from the Derveni commentary, which is characterized by the distance of interpretations that are expressed in the third person. Accordingly, we might wonder whether the commentary—far from constituting an invitation to Orphic initiation, as has often been supposed—

might not rather be designed to denounce the secrets surrounding that mystic sect by giving a materialistic and rationalizing interpretation for the rites and, especially, the theogony.[33] By itself, the text of column 7, in which the transition from discussion of the ritual to exegesis of the poem is made, seems to preclude such a reading. Indeed, in the course of this transition, probably in order to justify the interpretive procedures he adopts, the commentator explicitly links the "enigmatic" character of the poet's speech and the exclusion of the uninitiated.[34] If the commentator undertakes the work of interpretation, then, it is not to reveal, denounce, and demystify Orphic practices and doctrines but to address this work to a public of initiates or initiands.

But why choose a form of prose whose enunciative modes and content are clearly designed for reading instead of the verses known from the lamellae, which were apparently composed to be sung and heard? We should recall here that Orpheus—the model of the divinely inspired and possessed poet—is also said to have given men the letters for writing. Thus, a speech attributed to the orator Alcidamas (an adversary of Isocrates) cites an epigram to show that it was Orpheus, and not Palamedes, who brought *grámmata* to men after having been taught by the Muses. Supposedly inscribed on Orpheus' tomb by the Thracians, the text of this epigram presents the poet as the *prôtos heuretés* of the signs for writing. This tradition was well enough known in the fourth century for Androtion the Atthidographer to have refuted it by citing the poet's Thracian origin and the renowned illiteracy of this savage people.[35] The iconography of the century in which the Derveni text was written shows us the inspiring Muse holding out a papyrus roll for Orpheus, represented as a Thracian singer with lyre in hand.[36] Is this a roll to which the poet may entrust his song, or is it perhaps a roll on which is written the commentary automatically required by an enigmatic poem? Whatever the case may be, the existence of the half-burnt roll on which the commentary is inscribed, found among the votive objects of the Derveni tomb, requires explanation. Consigned to the fire to protect its secret, the partially destroyed text was no doubt consecrated to the enlightened citizen buried there. The commentary most likely served earlier in this intellectual's initiation—an initiation that was not so much ritual as it was scholarly, a typically Orphic initiation.

X

A CIVILIZATION OF POETS

Liminal Spaces and Discursive Voices in Theocritus' Idyll I

The approaches that arose out of the development of the social sciences over the course of the twentieth century have been widely applied to poetry. Social criticism and criticism inspired by Marxism link the evocative effects of poetry to the social circumstances or economic conditions within which it was produced. In what is ultimately a complementary approach, psychological and psychoanalytic critics have sought within poetry reflections of an individual's feelings and, subsequently, traces of the mechanisms of the unconscious and the repressed. In reaction to such approaches, the formalist and structuralist approach closed the text upon itself while reorganizing its meaning into a hierarchical system of binary oppositions. Beyond these analytic procedures, which are (as the rules for introducing yet another hermeneutic approach dictate) simplified here to the point of caricature, neither "poststructuralists" nor "deconstructionists" have succeeded, through their constantly creative play with transtextual readings and echoes, in diluting the core of meaning that every form of (oral or written) discourse has. Both the enunciative approach, focused on the instance of discourse, and the interpretation oriented toward textual reception (by listeners or readers) have made it possible to open literary works back up to what stands outside of them, but they do so on the basis of the indications that the works themselves present.[1] Far from pinning onto the text preconceived notions about the social or psychological conditions of its production, the approach proposed here attempts (as I have already said) to proceed from the text, from what its materiality provides to help us understand its semantic depth and its discursive form. Starting from the text, I attempt to make my way prudently toward the sociohistorical circumstances underlying it, but also toward the audience for which it was originally intended. Such is the aim of analysis focused on discourse, which opens the decoding of discursive structure onto history while seeking to avoid anachronistic projections, even if they are inevitable.

Beyond the numerous discussions about "literality" over the years, one certainty remains, especially in the social sciences of symbolic practices as they are conceived, in particular, at Lausanne. Whatever its generic limits (which cannot be rigorously drawn), a literary work is one of the results of the human capacity for symbolic production. A manifestation of human culture, it is not only a "representative substitute" or a mimetic image but above all a construction through language of a discrete universe. If the work carried out on language— in all of its effects, from the phonetic to the semantic—confers a certain degree of autonomy on this "fictional" universe, that universe is always based on social and psychological experiences situated in real time and space. It is to this extent that the literary work is also a "representation," a linguistic "interpretation" via symbolic "delegation"; it is to this extent that it is fictional, and not fictive, in character. It is within this semiotics, created from experience that is already the object of representations, that the polysemy of the literary text and the multiplicity of readings it authorizes are to be sought.[2]

With regard to Greek poetry, the contemporary debate about the specificity of the literary work has been activated by the issue of the shift from oral to written literature. The controversy, which has become a *vexata quaestio* since we have access to Greek literature only in the form of texts written down at some point in time, has partially crystallized around the question of whether or not that literature is fictional.[3] This debate is relatively sterile, however, since every sort of literary production involves work through and upon language, even when the communication of a poem is subordinated to a very precise ritual or social occasion. The fact that Sappho and Alcaeus composed their poems to have an educational or political effect on a limited, socially well-defined audience, does not keep these poets from using language in their own specific ways, drawing their audiences into their own universes and creating meanings (through the mediation of the symbolic process) that are based on a historical, social, and cultural but also a personal reality. Accordingly, poetic fiction should be understood (on the basis of the primary meaning of *fingere,* "shape," "fashion") in terms of its etymological meaning, "fabrication." Because of its pragmatic dimension and its reference, the poetic, when understood as the "poietic," leads to the fictional, not the fictive.[4]

But what is the situation in the Hellenistic period, when literature becomes literature in the etymological and modern sense of the term: a written text put forth to be read by a circle of initiated intellectuals? In this concluding chapter of the book, I want to pose this question concerning the poem that opens the corpus of pieces attributed to Theocritus. Indeed, if any Alexandrian poem lends itself—and has lent itself over the last several decades—to structural analysis, it is *Idyll I*. Nevertheless, as we shall see through an analysis that remains sensitive to the various enunciative shifts presented in these verses, the binary oppositions to which those structures can be reduced are constantly transformed, with regard to both the forms of expression that they take and the thematic and semantic levels at which their content is situated. I will show that the relationships heretofore conceived as static actually confer a unique sort of forward momentum on the composition. This "dynamization" of the poem, in its discursive and semantic structures, has two effects: (1) through the confrontation among the various universes constructed within the poem, it leads to the affirming of one of these universes over the others; and (2) through the embedding of several levels of enunciation, it organizes a type of play with simulacra of poetic authority that says a great deal about the literary circumstances of production conditioning such a poem or, at the very least, about the poetics underlying it. In both cases, the reader is oriented toward a space of borders. The utterly peculiar traits of this liminal world shed new light on Greek representations of the marginal, of what stands in the in-between.

1. Enunciative Levels and the Articulation of Meaning

From the standpoint of its enunciative construction, Theocritus' *Idyll I* constitutes a dramatized poem. As such, it presents six different poetic voices:

(a) a *dialogue voice,* which conveys the exchange between the two protagonists of the dramatic poem, Thyrsis and the goatherd, and sketches out the spatial framework of this dialogue (this voice is characterized by the use of vocative forms, the first- and second-person singular of future and present indicative forms and the imperative);

(b) a *poetic voice,* that of Thyrsis addressed to the Muses, then to the Nymphs; while framing and punctuating verses that appear as a poem within the poem, this voice introduces the story of the woes of Daphnis (it is characterized by use of the vocative and the second-person plural, the present indicative, and the imperative);

(c) a *descriptive voice,* that of the goatherd, who devotes thirty verses to describing the object decorated with various scenes that he plans to give to Thyrsis and who thereby defines a new spatial framework (this voice is characterized by use of the third person and the present indicative);

(d) a *narrative voice,* that of Thyrsis singing the erotic misadventures of Daphnis in a spatial context that is set apart from the rest (it is characterized by use of the third person, the imperfect, and the aorist indicative);

(e) an *interrogative voice,* taken up successively by the protagonists of Thyrsis' narrative, who enter the space of Daphnis and pose questions to the hero without receiving a response (this voice is characterized by the vocative, interrogative forms, the second-person singular and the present indicative);

(f) a *monologue voice,* corresponding to that of Daphnis, who—after dismissing Aphrodite and invoking Pan—establishes an upside-down world within a wish; his words (extending over a little more than thirty verses) constitute a poem inserted into Thyrsis' poem, which is itself a part of the *Idyll* (this voice is characterized by use of the vocative and the first, second, and third person in the imperative, indicative, and optative).[5]

The hierarchical intertwining of these different poetic voices leads us to recognize the following structure in Theocritus' composition:

(a) 1–11: exchange of musical and pastoral compliments between Thyrsis and the goatherd

  12–18: goatherd's refusal to play the syrinx tune proposed by Thyrsis

  19–26: goatherd's proposal that Thyrsis sing Daphnis

    (c) 27–56: description of the "ivy" cup (complementary gift)

      27–31: the outside of the cup

      32–38: scene A: the woman and her suitors

      39–44: scene B: the fisherman

      45–54: scene C: the child and the two foxes

      55–56: the outside of the cup

  56–63: linking of the cup to the situation of musical and pastoral exchange

(b) 64–69: proem of Thyrsis' poem with "*sphragís*"

    70: refrain 1 (*árkhete*)

      (d) 71–72: narration of the woes of Daphnis

    73: refrain 1

        74–75: narration continued

    76: refrain 1

          (e) 77–78: Hermes' speech (direct discourse)

    79: refrain 1

            80–81: herdsmen's speech (indirect discourse)

            81–83: Priapus' speech (direct discourse)

    84: refrain 1

              85–88: Priapus' speech continued

    89: refrain 1

                90–91: end of Priapus' speech

92–93: sad fate of Daphnis
94: refrain 2 (*pálin árkhete*)
        95–98: Aphrodite's speech (direct discourse)
99: refrain 2
                (f) 100–103: Daphnis' response to Aphrodite
104: refrain 2
                105–107: Aphrodite and Anchises
108: refrain 2
                109–110: Aphrodite and Adonis
111: refrain 2
                112–113: Aphrodite and Diomedes
114: refrain 2
                115–118: Daphnis' farewell
119: refrain 2
                120–121: Daphnis' "*sphragís*"
122: refrain 2
                123–126: invocation to Pan
127: refrain 3 (*légete*)
                128–130: consecration of the syrinx before death
131: refrain 3
                132–136: wish for an upside-down world
137: refrain 3
                138–141: narration of Daphnis' death
142: refrain 3
143–152: conclusion of the exchange between Thyrsis and the goatherd

1.1. The Double Violation of Bucolic Rules

If we focus on the simple fact of the number of verses attributed, respectively, to the goatherd (61) and to Thyrsis (91), the structure of *Idyll I* corresponds to a poetic exchange between two herdsmen, such as we find in *Idyll 6*, where Damoetas answers back to Daphnis in a bucolic confrontation that ends in a draw and with the exchange of gifts, and in *Idyll 9* (attributed to Theocritus), wherein the bucolic poet is metamorphosed into an artist and rewards the two protagonists of the contest with a gift. This kind of competition was, perhaps, originally a form of entertainment popular among humble herdsmen. The rules governing it, as later transformed into a literary game by the Alexandrian poets, are expressed in *Idyll 8* (another poem attributed to Theocritus): after drawing lots for position and inviting a goatherd to serve as judge of the contest, Menalcas begins to sing, while Daphnis responds by alternating with him in singing the bucolic song (*amoibaía aoidà boukoliká*).[6]

At the beginning of *Idyll I*, the bucolic rules are shifted twice. It is true that the exchange begins in absolute conformity to bucolic conventions, with the goatherd taking up in parallel terms the poetic framework set up by Thyrsis. The goatherd takes up Thyrsis' words *cum variatione;* the variation is so subtle that the pine singing as sweetly as the goatherd pipes is echoed by the song of the shepherd, which is even sweeter than the water spilling down from the rock (vv. 1–3 and 7–8). This chiasmatic equivalence between man and nature defines the semantic isotopy that extends across the whole poem, that of music (in the Greek sense of the term).[7] But the goatherd and shepherd do not decide to measure themselves against each other; rather, each chooses for the other an external partner for an imagined musical competition: Pan for the goatherd (v. 3), the Muses for Thyrsis (v. 9). The evocation of the choosing of prizes after the two contests shows that both the goatherd (explicitly) and the shepherd (implicitly) are imagined as taking second place in their respective competitions. Expressed hypothetically (through the use of the mode of eventuality— in the subjunctive with *ka*—and the potential future), these fictional contests are imagined solely for the purpose of praising the musical skills of the two protagonists: the goatherd can rival Pan in playing the syrinx, while the shepherd sings almost as well as the Muses. The bucolic rules are thus modified a first time in being reoriented toward fiction.

Furthermore, it has often been noted that the expected contest between Thyrsis and the goatherd is undertaken—or at least proposed—by the former, only to be sidestepped by the latter (vv. 12–18). The only song that appears after this, then, is that of Thyrsis. The goatherd requests it by addressing the shepherd as one addresses a god in a prayer: the wish is based on the *hypómnesis* of Thyrsis' musical abilities and his victory over Chromis, then is accompanied by the promise of a gift.[8] At the end of the poetic scene put into dialogue and carried by the first poetic voice of the *Idyll,* Thyrsis—specialist of the "bucolic Muse" (v. 20), shepherd inspired by the Muses (64)—requests the promised gifts himself (143). In this way, Thyrsis dominates the confrontation with his poetic mastery. Formally, the exchange turns into a monologue.

Thus, with respect to its overall discursive structure, *Idyll I* significantly diverges from the poetic rules that were probably set by Theocritus himself. As we shall see, this literary undertaking situates itself at the edges of a norm on more than just this formal level.

1.2. In-between Spaces

From the kind of purely arithmetical standpoint evoked earlier, it is admittedly difficult to deny that the description of the "ivy" vessel offered to Thyrsis by the goatherd constitutes an anticipatory counterpart to the song executed by the shepherd. An enunciative analysis allows us to add two further arguments to those already advanced by other interpreters of this poem in support of seeing the exchange between the two protagonists as a de facto confrontation between the goatherd's poetic facility for description and the shepherd's narrative abilities.[9] Through the twisting of the bucolic rules, which affects the dramatic action conveyed through the dialogue voice, the gifts offered to Thyrsis in recompense for singing Daphnis are partially engaged within the poetic exchange itself. If Thyrsis makes an offering of his poem about Daphnis to the goatherd, the latter will give in recompense a she-goat with her two kids (a gift in accordance with the rules of the game) and also the ivy cup. The impression caused by the dividing up of the verses between the goatherd and Thyrsis is hereby confirmed: both from the point of view of the bucolic rules and from the enunciative standpoint, the "ivy" cup, through the goatherd's long description of it, does indeed occupy a position that is equivalent to that occupied by Thyrsis' song about Daphnis. Furthermore, while the cup is initially presented as a simple addition to the promised gift of a she-goat (v. 27: *kaí*), by the end of the description of this "spectacle for goatherds," it is the sole object proposed as an enticement to Thyrsis (52–62); the she-goat becomes that which the goatherd gave in exchange for the cup at the moment when it came into his possession. More important, by the end of the bucolic scene, the fragrant beauty of the cup is explicitly given in exchange for Thyrsis' honey-sweet voice (146–50).[10] The she-goat, which is merely mentioned in passing here, takes the name of the cup: the *kissúbion* has rubbed off onto *Kissaítha,* the she-goat, which is also etymologically dedicated to ivy.

The enunciative perspective allows us to confirm the relationship of equivalence between the goatherd's description of the cup and Thyrsis' narrative of the woes of Daphnis. It shows that the formal violation of the bucolic rules leads to their de facto reaffirmation. From this foundation, it is possible to strengthen even further the affirmed relationship of homology between the description and the narrative. Whatever the material out of which the *kissúbion* (a pastoral vessel by definition) was fashioned, whatever the historical and archaeological referent for this strange cup, whatever the formal organization of the scenes carved into it, the goatherd's presentation of it makes a careful distinction between the "outside" and the "inside" of the cup (32 and 55). Aside from the problem of how precisely the cup is to be envisioned (a problem tailor-made for feeding philological disputes), the "outside" includes the description of the vessel's complex vegetal decoration, while the "inside" contains the action scenes. However they may be situated in relation to each other on the "real" object, from a discursive standpoint, the description of the vegetal decoration (29–31 and 55) frames the genre scenes

(32–54).[11] If it is true that the ivy cup is indeed the poetic and discursive equivalent of Thyrsis' song, both in its manufacture and in its enunciative insertion into the economy of the *Idyll* as a whole, this means that, from a structural standpoint, the plant decoration corresponds to Thyrsis' narrative. The former frames—perhaps materially (i.e., on the cup itself), but certainly on the discursive level—the genre scenes described by the goatherd, just as the latter (the narrative voice, vv. 71–98 and 138–40) encompasses Daphnis' speech (the monologue voice in vv. 100–136, which itself echoes the interrogative voice in vv. 77–98). Moreover, the description of the cup depends on the goatherd's dialogue voice; and that voice anticipates Thyrsis' poetic voice, which contains Daphnis' speech within it.

The structural studies of *Idyll I* that have been sensitive to the process of the "spatialization" of the discourse have identified three different spaces in the poem: the one within which Thyrsis and the goatherd interact, the one constituted through the three scenes represented on the ivy cup, and the one that Daphnis constructs within his long speech.[12] The homology that I have just drawn, however, brings that number to five; their essential characteristics, which are presented in distinct discursive modes, are the following:

(1) *The bucolic space.* A pine, a tamarisk, a poplar, oaks, springs and flowing water, hills, statues of Priapus, springs of the Nymphs—that is, all the things in the space in which the encounter between Thyrsis and the goatherd takes place—evoke the bucolic setting that is the haunt of Theocritean herdsmen. This typically bucolic landscape is not given a precise geographical location.[13] Nonetheless, this space serving as the setting for the poetic action is twice displaced, as we shall see.

(2) *The décor of the cup.* The vegetal decoration consists of intertwined ivy leaves and flowers along with a band of acanthus leaves. While the ivy and acanthus may well refer to the real decorations on documented Hellenistic vessels in cast metal, they certainly point us to the wild world frequented by Dionysus, but also—through the etymological play on *kissúbion*—to that of herdsmen, such as the Cyclops, who use "ivy" cups.[14]

(3) *The spaces within the scenes depicted on the cup.* Though absent from the scene of amorous rivalry between two men over the Pandora-like woman, the spatial indications in the scene depicting the old fisherman take us to an atypical seaside location, while those in the scene with the child and the two foxes transport us into a vineyard teeming with grapes. These spaces are given no precise geographical location either, and—like the pastoral space—they are situated on the threshold between wilderness and human civilization. Men can enter the spaces of mountain meadows, the seashore, and fields of vines alike in order to extract from them the food products of

civilization while keeping their intervention limited and without recourse to the complex practices of agriculture or sacrifice.[15]

(4a) *The space of Daphnis' narrative.* The formulation of the questions that Thyrsis addresses to the Nymphs at the beginning of his poetic performance distances the space in which Daphnis is situated from the Nymphs' own legendary locale of preference: the valley of Tempe in Thessaly. Meanwhile, the Nymphs' absence from the Anapus stream, which flows into the port of Syracuse, and the Acis, running down from Mount Etna, signals that Daphnis is to be situated somewhere between these two rivers (67–69). What is certain is that the legendary cowherd wastes away in a place where both wild animals and cattle can (without mingling with each other) lament for him (71–72 and 74–75). Thus, the narrative places Daphnis in a geographically indeterminate, liminal space between wild forests and pasture lands. Accordingly, we should not be surprised to see gods and heroes pass through this space out of concern for the disillusioned lover, as do Hermes, a series of herdsmen in the order of their pastoral hierarchy, then Priapus, and, finally, Aphrodite herself.[16]

(4b) *Daphnis' space.* Seen from the perspective of Daphnis himself (once the scene has been set narratively), this same landscape undergoes a series of metamorphoses. The cowherd's mention of wild animals and cattle (forming an almost perfect echo of vv. 71–75) creates a link between this space and that which is defined within Thyrsis' narrative (115–17 and 120–21), one lying between forests and pasturelands watered by streams. But the evocation of the Arethusa spring and the Thybris ditch give it a precise location, on the outer limits of Syracuse: the famous fountain is located along the coast of the island of Ortygia, whereas the ditch dug by Athenian prisoners during the Peloponnesian War ran along the city's fortifications on the inland side. This liminal space is defined by contrast with two other distant places: Mount Ida in the Troad, where oaks and galingale grow amidst the buzzing of bees and where Daphnis tells Cypris to go (105–7), and the steep mountains of Arcadia, which the cowherd asks Pan to leave in order to come to Sicily (123–26).[17] Through this dual movement, both outward and inward, the place in which Daphnis is located is once again situated between a domain open to nomadic civilized activity and a savage universe. The hero's imminent departure down to Hades, however, incites him to wish for this liminal universe to be turned upside down. Inhabited by the love to which the violets, narcissus, and pears are linked, but also by the poetry that the nightingale's song evokes, this landscape is to be transformed into a field full of brambles and haunted by owls upon Daphnis' demise.[18] The wildness brings on death, and the change in the liminal space on the horizontal plane is echoed by the movement of Daphnis along a vertical axis.

1.3. Illusory Acts

In combination with a fashionable approach based on binary oppositions, the recognition of the discursive equivalence between the description of the *kissúbion* and the narrative of Daphnis' death has generally led scholars to contrast the two worlds that the description and narrative respectively delineate. Thus, according to recent interpretations, the distanced, epic *ékphrasis* of three moments of insouciance in day-to-day life stands in opposition to the dramatic and emotional story of Daphnis' combat against love, while both depict futile activity. The artistic description of the three scenes drawn from real life has also been thought to introduce the urban reader to a new universe contrasting with the artificial world fabricated by herdsmen who are poets, highly literate and close to the gods: on this view, the former serves to attenuate the idealized character of the latter. According to yet another line of interpretation, the equivalence established between the scenes on the cup and the story of Daphnis allows us to dispense with the former. The binary contrast can, on this view, reappear: the exuberant vitality of the *locus amoenus* in which Thyrsis and the goatherd interact and which gives rise to poetry is seen as standing in opposition to the bitter pathos into which Daphnis draws us and which evokes the disappearance of a mythic universe.[19]

From a strictly structural standpoint, the space of the *kissúbion* is delimited by that of the vegetal decoration, while the universe of Daphnis is determined by the space that Thyrsis constructs in his narrative. And these two spaces are themselves framed by the space that is in keeping with the *locus amoenus* of the bucolic tradition, within which these two are juxtaposed. We ought now to reexamine the relationships between these two framed spaces while taking into account the narrative actions occurring within them.

Inasmuch as it is strictly circumscribed by the vegetal decoration, which is linked to the world of the savage and the space of transgression that are Dionysus' domain, the space elaborated on the ivy cup can be seen to comprise certain qualities defined by comparison and contrast with the shield of Achilles depicted in the *Iliad* and the shield of Heracles described in the Hesiodic *Aspis.*[20] Far from reflecting any image of the Golden Age, each of the three sculpted scenes on the ivy cup represents a *pónos,* standing outside of time and occupying a marginal space, such as the seaside or a vineyard. But each of these "labors" is characterized, in one way or another, by its vanity. The rhetorical capping of the rival suitors (*amoibadís,* 34) is deployed in vain (*etósia,* 38) and only manages to provoke a smile and back-and-forth glances on the part of the desired woman. For his whole life, the old fisherman has put great effort into a little-valued activity. The child devotes more interest to weaving his beautiful (*kalá,* 52) grasshopper cage than to watching over the grapevines or driving away the two foxes who are after his pouch. All of these figures—the adult men, the old man, and the child—are engaged in the *frustra* that the scholarly readers of *Idyll I* have described. The order of presentation of the three scenes, however, is not without consequence. While the natural sequence of the three canonical periods of life (childhood, adulthood, and old age) are jumbled, the ordering of the scenes here causes the *pónos* to progress toward constructions based on technical skill and cunning. From a rhetorical rivalry over love that produces no results, there is a progression toward productive but marginal work of a similar sort to hunting,[21] then the fruitful weaving of a cage, but for what is hardly a productive activity: capturing grasshoppers. This sequence also constitutes the first trace of the love isotopy that is further developed later in the poem; this isotopy may also be developed through the images of net fishing and the weaving of the cage, in that these images may be metaphors for the snares and ruses of Aphrodite.

The text itself cannot help but establish a homology between the child's weaving (*plékei*, 52; *plégma,* 54) and the intertwined vegetal motifs forming the décor of the ivy cup (29–31 and 55). Serving as a vase for offering libations to the Muses at the end of the poem (143–44), the *kissúbion* is—as a painstakingly crafted object—a metaphor from craft for the bucolic poet's *pónos;* presented in the lopsided bucolic exchange as the equivalent of Thyrsis' poem, the ivy cup is itself a metaphor for the pastoral poem. Much more than the two men competing in vain for the love of a woman, much more than the fisherman straining over his net, the young boy weaving the cage for grasshoppers (which are often characterized in Hellenistic poetry as excellent singers) becomes a metaphor for the adolescent herdsmen who convey the voice of the bucolic poet in Theocritus' *Idylls.* And the cage itself is but a skillfully crafted trap for these pastoral voices. "A spectacle for goatherds" (56), the cup actually constitutes the goatherd's poem, a sophisticated piece of craft devised during the leisure time that guarding flocks allows these idealized herdsmen.[22]

To these intermediary spaces situated between the *pólis* and the uncultivated world—spaces that are used for activities evoking the leisure of bucolic poetry and circumscribed by a frame of wild vegetation—the dualistic structure of *Idyll I* opposes a line of demarcation, a limit, which is defined through the narrative voice of Thyrsis, then through Daphnis' monologue voice, in the manner presented earlier. The wild animals of the forest and the livestock feeding in the pastures never come into direct contact with each other. Through his speech, Daphnis transfers this marginal sector (the geographical position of which in Sicily is kept vague) to the border separating the city of Syracuse from the surrounding sea and land. Through various discursive means, however, this liminal domain is defined through contrast with a series of paradigmatic landscapes traditionally linked to pastoral activity: the vales of Peneius at the foot of the

Pindus mountain range in Thessaly (67), where the Nymph Cyrene fought against lions while grazing her father's flocks and where Apollo fell in love with the beautiful shepherdess-huntress; Mount Ida in the Troad (105), where Aphrodite, accompanied by an escort of subdued wild beasts, came upon the cowherd Anchises while he played the lyre in the pasture; the savage mountains of Arcadia, cherished by the gods (123–26) and rich in flocks of small livestock, where Pan (the goatherd-hunter with a goat's body, child of a Nymph and Hermes) was born; and finally, the banks of the Acis (69), flowing down from Mount Etna, whence Thyrsis claims he originally comes.[23] With the introduction of this last locale, the mountain and stream of Sicily join the list of outlying, mostly uncleared spaces where "archaic" poetry—that of Homer, Pindar, and the *Homeric Hymns*—situated the love trysts between Nymphs and divinities that contributed to the establishment of civilization.

But, while this locale, thanks to the voice of Daphnis, comes strangely close to the most urban city of Sicily, the landscape of pastures cutting into virgin woodlands and inviting love along the banks of the streams watering them is abandoned for another river, whose name is to go unmentioned. It is abandoned for a realm of an entirely different order: that of Hades.[24]

Through the combination of the voices of Thyrsis and Daphnis, the second part of the poem shifts our attention from the well-circumscribed domain in which bucolic activities and their metaphorical extensions take place to the very limits of this domain: the territorial limit between well-watered pastures and the mountainous realm of wild beasts, but also the geographical border between legendary pastoral locales frequented by the gods and the bucolic space of Sicily, which is paradoxically located at the very outer limit of the city. By situating Daphnis at the limits, which he ends up transgressing, and by emphasizing the isotopy of love introduced by the first scene on the *kissúbion,* Thyrsis' narrative renders dynamic what the goatherd's description presented as static. It is only by way of this process of creating movement through the narrative that it is possible to understand the relationship between the space of bucolic exchange itself and the four spaces that are inserted into it by the different poetic voices that weave *Idyll I.*

2. Discursive Functions and Fiction

If we are willing to grant that a literary text not only constructs a possible world but also transforms it,[25] the question arises, concerning the juxtaposition of various interrelated activities, isotopies, and spaces in *Idyll I,* which of these are ultimately held up as predominant over the others. Beyond the structural oppositions that devotees of binary logic have already noted, the dynamic instilled in the text by the narrative and the embedding of various voices within one another points to a precise ethical and spatial conclusion.

2.1. Embedded Voices

The voice that lies farthest in the hierarchy from the line of discourse that carries the text as a whole is undoubtedly that of Daphnis. That voice forcefully lays out the rejection of Aphrodite (100–112), who is presented as the implacable and pernicious power that is decried throughout the tradition of Greek erotic poetry, from the melic to the tragic poets.[26] Daphnis does so not because he resists the amorous desire incarnated by the figure of Eros, but rather because he is consumed by a love that remains unfulfilled and drags him down to Hades. It is practically as if Thyrsis' poetic account served to give narrative form to the link established in the Greek tradition between love and death.[27] Whence the anonymity of the love, which—as in the case of Polyphemus in *Idyll* 6—is in an awkward position in relation to its object and which ends up closing in upon itself. To the oft-discussed smile of Aphrodite in *Idyll I* (95–96) correspond, for example, the coquetries of Galatea in *Idyll* 6 (6–7). An arduous love (*dúseros*) transforms the Cyclops and the cowherd alike into lowly goatherds.[28] The last-minute rescue proposed by an Aphrodite who manifests her usual ambiguity (138–39) is rendered null and void by the cowherd's obstinacy in his desire for love, which has become an irrepressible death "wish" (130); and this impulse toward death is overdetermined through the ineluctable action of the Moirai (139–40).

The interrogative voices, which are situated on the same hierarchical level as Daphnis' voice and also echo it, simply introduce and anticipate the equation (via pain) between erotic desire and death. Who is causing the cowherd's demise (78)? What ill is overwhelming him (81)? Why is he wasting away (82, 88, and 91; cf. 66)? What is the use of attempting to make Eros desist (91)? Daphnis' silence corresponds to the answer that Thyrsis' narrative suggests from the outset: it is the silence of death. From the very beginning of Thyrsis' song, Daphnis' erotic languishing is associated with death (66 and 72); at its end, death is envisaged by Daphnis' own voice (135), then described by that of Thyrsis (139–40). Thus, on top of the love isotopy occurring throughout Thyrsis' narrative, the death theme appears as its double.

Through the two semantic isotopies, love and death, that they intertwine with each other, Thyrsis' narrative voice and Daphnis' monologue voice—along with its complement, the interrogative voices—are inseparable. With the disappearance of the legendary cowherd, departed to Hades, it is the liminal space situated on the fringes of Syracuse that undergoes the impossible metamorphosis into an impossible world.[29] Through this transformation, it is not just the legendary spaces traditionally frequented by the Nymphs, Aphrodite, and Pan, nor only the valley of Tempe, the crest of Ida in the Troad, and the Arcadian mountains that are cast into the *adúnaton;* it is, above all, the Sicilian sites that are the object of this kind of rejection: the Arethusa spring and the streams of the Thybris ditch mentioned by Daphnis, but also the Anapos, the Acis, and Etna, homeland of Thyrsis.

Does this mean that, by opposition to this world of legend and of deathly love, the more "realistic" spaces depicted on the ivy cup are exalted over the others in the poem? Is one *frustrum* with tragic consequences being replaced by *frustra* that are harmless? Several factors could lead us to this conclusion: the fact that the cup is offered as a gift in recompense for Thyrsis' song, that it is substituted in place of the song in the final exchange (143 and 149), that it plays the role of an instrument for making a libation to the Muses in the framing scene at the end of the poem (144).[30] Nonetheless, such a conclusion would mean forgetting that the cup, a fabricated object given to the goatherd by a ferryman, comes from a world outside the pastoral realm. It would mean passing over the fact that the evocation of the cup, in the descriptive voice, is subordinated to the dialogue voice of the lopsided bucolic exchange constituting the *Idyll* as a whole. Furthermore, the scenes decorating the cup are carefully delimited by the bands of vegetal ornamentation, which point to their artificiality.

What remains to be addressed is the space constructed through this exchange itself. In parallel with the double infraction of the normative structure of bucolic exchange in *Idyll I*, a double shift is operated within this space. Inasmuch as it is attached to a hypothetical confrontation between the goatherd and Pan and between Thyrsis and the Muses, the setting involving a symbiosis between nature and music that is put in place at the beginning of the poem can only be an ideal landscape. Linguistically, the use in these verses of deictic forms indicating distance (*ténos*, 1, 6, 8, and 11, underscored by *ti* in v. 1) is carefully distinguished from the use of deictic forms showing what is present at hand, in reference to the setting in which the exchange is "really" going to take place: here (*teîde*, 12), on this knoll covered with tamarisk. In the latter case, we have shifted to a space in which the vegetation remains distinct from the musical activities. Within this second space, another shift takes place, since it is necessary to avoid provoking the wrath of Pan: let us sit here (*deûru*, 21), under the elm, the goatherd proposes, facing the statue of Priapus and the spring of the Nymphs, where there is "that pastoral seat" (*ténos*, 23; once again distance is indicated within the general situation of proximity).

Even as it points to the predominance of the framing space over the described and narrated spaces, the embedding of different discursive voices (in concordance with the modification operated on the rules governing bucolic exchange) creates another shift within this pastoral realm: from the ideal musical space where shepherds and goatherds can compete with the gods to a space that is less fictional and closer to "reality." But where is the *here* designated by Thyrsis and slightly displaced by the goatherd ultimately situated?

2.2. Narrative Transformations

Only the semantic development of the poem can supply the basis for an answer to this question, which raises the issue of the potentially fictional character of the poem. Introduced in the very first verse, the music isotopy is developed throughout the *Idyll*, including through metaphors. The love isotopy, by contrast, is introduced solely through the descriptive and narrative voices, along with those subordinated to the latter. Moreover, this isotopy undergoes a double narrative transformation. First, through the order in which the scenes on the cup are presented (in the descriptive voice), love is depicted as an activity involving futile rivalry (38), only to be abandoned in favor of the craft-type work in which the child is engaged, a metaphor for poetic activity or, perhaps, the traps laid by Aphrodite (52–54). Furthermore, within the story of Daphnis' misadventures (in the narrative voice), death replaces love (through the process discussed earlier). This substitution signals the disappearance of musical activity: drawn down to Hades by Eros, Daphnis makes an offering of his syrinx to Pan (128–30) after refusing to engage in dialogue and, by extension, in bucolic exchange.[31] At the end of the poem, however, when the dialogue voice is again heard, poetry is once more very present and becomes eroticized, in a way, since it is depicted as wholly composed of sweetness and beauty (145–48; cf. v. 61).[32] At the same time, the poetic activity signified by Thyrsis' libation to the Muses and by the comparison of the singer with the honey-sweet mouth to a cicada is inserted into the immediate spatial framework delineated from verse 12 on (*teîde*, 149; *enîde* and *hôde* in its spatial sense, 151). But, just as Daphnis' unhappy love reduces him to the level of a goatherd (86) and condemns him to being nothing but a voyeur to his billy goat's servicing (87–91), so also, at the end of the poem, satisfaction of erotic desire is left to the billy goat, which the she-goats are told to evade (151–52).[33]

Some distinctions need to be made, at this point, concerning the realm of music itself. At the beginning of the poem, the bucolic exchange evokes, on an ideal level, a familiarity between Thyrsis and the Muses, on the one hand, and a rivalry between the goatherd and Pan, on the other. This contrast is partially echoed at the end of the *Idyll*, where Thyrsis addresses a salutation to the Muses, but the goatherd merely tends to his goats. Similarly, after being transformed from a cowherd into a goatherd by the detrimental effects of love, and after being abandoned by the Nymphs themselves (66 and 141, in a ring structure), Daphnis consecrates his syrinx to Pan, the god of pastoral nomadism; it is only his demise that transforms him into a man "beloved of the Muses" (140–41).

This affirmation, over the course of the poem's semantic development, of the predominance of music over love, death, and even the goatherd's activity is underscored by the intertwining of the principal narrative voices at the end of the piece. Thus, just as, at the end of the first part of the *Idyll,* the goatherd's descriptive voice comes to coincide with the dialogue voice through his proposing of the ivy cup as the object of an exchange (the transition occurring at v. 56), so also, at the end of the second part, the mention of the Muses transforms Thyrsis' narrative voice (141) into a poetic voice, such that it is inserted into the bucolic exchange. What is more, through the variation on the concluding formula typical of the *Homeric Hymns* used in this apostrophe to the Muses (144–45),[34] Thyrsis' entire song becomes a votive offering to the Muses (in the poetic voice); that song is also given in exchange for the scenes represented on the ivy cup (in the dialogue voice). It must be added that this farewell addressed by Thyrsis to the Muses echoes the farewell that Daphnis addresses to Arethusa (117); but, while the latter is a definitive farewell, the former is merely a farewell inviting the invoked divinity to rejoice, owing to the echo of the Homeric formula (as seen in chapter 1). Whereas love drives its victim to death, poetry, by contrast, leads to the perpetuation of a situation of exchange with the divinity. It is this same idea that concludes the long speech of the goatherd: "as for your song, you surely will not keep it when you go down to Hades, which causes utter forgetfulness" (61–62). We certainly are a long way from Homeric poetics and ethics.

These enunciative and semantic shifts within the descriptive, narrative, and poetic voices, causing them to merge with the dialogue voice, are further emphasized by the transition (in vv. 144–45) from the description of the libation to the Muses to the invocation of these divinities in the second-person vocative. This invitation to rejoice (*khaírete*) simply echoes the refrain (*árkhete, légete*) punctuating the Daphnis narrative while at the same time constituting the proem (64).[35] Accordingly, not only is the narrative voice as a whole animated by the poetic voice and the inspiration of the (bucolic) Muses (20), but also the dialogue voice of Thyrsis, as participant in the bucolic exchange, is itself marked as depending on those same Muses (whether the Muses' inspiration be fictional or not is another question). We are thus made to return to the ideal situation, the possible world in which there can be a close relationship with these divinities, as described at the beginning of the *Idyll* (7–11).

3. Fictional Spaces and Enunciative Simulacra

The predominance that this convergence of voices confers on the dialogue voice is echoed in the space constructed by the latter. It is a space filled with the sweet taste of song (146–48), a space where the fragrant beauty of the cup washed in the waters of the Hours is at home (149–50),[36] a space where the she-goats are told not to act like Bacchae and to flee the billy goat's attempts to mount them (151–52). The beginning of the poem not only distinguishes this bucolic space from the ideal world in which human beings have a convivial relationship with the gods but also effects a second shift by removing this space from the influence of Pan. This domain of inspired song, the precise location of which remains perfectly vague, is nonetheless provided with what could be an indirect indication of its geographical position. In his *sphragís,* Daphnis not only names himself but also provides a further indication of his identity through his salutation to Arethusa, indicating that he is situated at the foot of the walls of Syracuse (117–21: *Dáphnis egòn hóde*). Since this *sphragís* and that of Thyrsis (*Thúrsis hód,'* 65; cf. *egó,* 145) echo each other, the space of the bucolic exchange in *Idyll I* could possibly be set in Sicily, perhaps on the slopes of Mount Etna.

This is the sole indication creating a possible link—through extradiscursive reference—between the space in which the poem is set and an external geographical location.[37] The deictic forms pointing to things immediately at hand (terms with the suffix *-de*) that are used at the beginning and end of the *Idyll* are solely auto-referential; they refer only to the space constructed by the poem itself (internal referentialization). In melic poetry of the "archaic" period, Alcman and Sappho present a quasi-dramatic depiction of themselves through the simulacra that their poems construct. Theocritus never resorts to this sort of relationship with what lies outside his poem. Through the poem's intertwining of voices, but also through the various ways in which it shifts the rules of the amoebic genre and the spaces embedded within it, *Idyll I* constitutes a mimetic poem par excellence. From this standpoint, the composition is reminiscent of the processes employed by Callimachus, in his *Hymn to Apollo,* for example.[38] From its beginning all the way to its conclusion, Theocritus' poem fabricates its fiction (or, rather, its fictions), and, consequently, the traditional faith in the possibility of life after death through poetry is undermined. Neither the spaces inscribed on the cup, which merely constitute a metaphorical prelude, nor *a fortiori* the space of Daphnis, which is so close to the city and which—through love and death—overturns the values attributed to nature, can represent the implicit "poetic manifesto" of Theocritus.[39] On the contrary, the voices of the poem situate that manifesto within the universe of the bucolic exchange, an exchange that is doubly displaced, such that it stands halfway between the ideal realm where men can sing alongside the gods and a largely idealized image of Sicily itself.

Through these various displacements and the blurring effect created by the intertwining of different discursive voices, the deictic forms indicating proximity reveal themselves to be pure simulacra, erecting a fiction around the fabricated universe introduced by the ivy cup and the legendary and, ultimately, impossible domain in which Daphnis appears. This retreat into the realm constructed through the poetic fiction is likewise indicated by the absence of any reference to a narratee and, thus, to an extradiscursive enunciatee or receiver.[40] What Theocritus proposes to his elusive reader, through the poetic voices and simulacra of authority that he stages and mimes, is to listen—at a distance—to that shepherd's song, which "trickles down more sweetly than the echo of this waterfall tumbling onto the rocks."[41] The function of poetry henceforth becomes that of transferring into an urban milieu the intermediary, fabricated realm of herdsmen musicians.

NOTES

INTRODUCTION

1. Sappho fr. 150 Voigt, quoted by Maximus of Tyre 18. 9.261–69; see A. Lardinois, "Subject and Circumstance in Sappho's Poetry," *Transactions of the American Philological Association* 124 (1994): 51–84.

2. I am echoing here the title of the work in which S. Goldhill studies the poetic consistency of the voice of different Greek authors (Goldhill 1991) and that of the lectures of G. B. Conte, *The Hidden Author: An Interpretation of Petronius' "Satyricon"* (Berkeley, 1996), 1–36, devoted to the "mythomaniac" narrator of Petronius' Latin novel.

3. The concept of "fictional" can replace that of "fiction" to designate the artifact of fiction in its referential relationship to the world; in so doing, we can avoid misunderstandings deriving from confusion about the "fictive" or "fictitious." See Calame 2000b, 42–47.

4. K. Bühler, *Sprachtheorie: Die Darstellungsfunktion der Sprache* (Jena, 1934), 102–48 (= *Theory of Language: The Representational Function of Language* [Amsterdam, 1990], 137–57); with the extensions proposed for Greek literature, particularly by W. Rösler, "Über Deixis und einige Aspekte mündlichen und schriftlichen Stils in antiker Kultur," *Würzburger Jahrbücher für Altertumswissenschaft* 9 (1983): 7–28; and especially J. Danielewicz, "*Deixis* in Greek Choral Lyric," *Quaderni Urbinati di Cultura Classica* 63 (1990): 7–17.

5. Some of the principal procedures for organizing a text in sequences are studied by J.-M. Adam, *Les textes: Types et prototypes: Récit, description, argumentation, explication et dialogue* (Paris, 1992), 19–43; for anaphora, see idem, *Éléments de linguistique textuelle: Théorie et pratique de l'analyse textuelle* (Liège, 1990), 51–61. On the phenomenon of internal deixis in a few Greek texts, see E. J. Bakker, "Homeric *hoûtos* and the Poetics of Deixis," *Classical Philology* 94 (1999): 1–19; and N. Felson, "Vicarious Transport: Fictive Deixis in Pindar's *Pythian* Four," *Harvard Studies in Classical Philology* 99 (1999): 1–31 and the studies in *Arethusa* 37 (2004).

6. Hesiod, *Works* 34–41; chapter 2, §2.2, with the remarks of Nagy 1990b, 255–58.

7. I have stressed the importance of this distinction between the linguistic nature of the "instance of enunciation" enunciatively represented by the speaker-narrator figure and the psychosocial "person" corresponding to the historical author in the introduction to my book, Calame 2000a, 17–40 (= 1995, 3–20), where I refer to the fundamental works that have contributed to my

own reflection. See especially E. Benveniste, *Problèmes de linguistique générale,* vol. 1 (Paris, 1966), 251–66 (= *Problems in General Linguistics* [Coral Gables, Fla., 1971], 217–30).

8. M. Foucault, "Qu'est-ce qu'un auteur?" *Bulletin de la Société française de philosophie* 63 (1969): 73–104, reprinted in *Dits et écrits, 1954–1988,* vol. 1 (Paris, 1994), 789–821 (= "What Is an Author?" in *Textual Strategies: Perspectives in Post-Structuralist Criticism,* ed. J.V. Harari [Ithaca, 1979], 141–60). I make some points about the relationship of reference involved in the discursive construction of a fictional world in Calame 2000b, 38–51. In its etymological meaning, *auctoritas* depends on an *auctor,* considered here as an "instance of enunciation"; see M. Bettini, "Alle soglie dell'autorità," in B. Lincoln, *L'autorità: Costruzione e corrosione* (Turin, 2000), vii–xxxiv (Italian translation of *Authority: Construction and Corrosion* [Chicago, 1994]).

9. A. J. Greimas and J. Courtès, *Sémiotique: Dictionnaire raisonné de la théorie du langage* (Paris, 1979), 79–82, 102–6, and 119–28 (= *Semiotics and Language: An Analytical Dictionary,* trans. L. Crist et al. [Bloomington, 1982]), with the useful additional points made by G. Manetti, *Teoria dell'enunciazione: Le origini del concetto e alcuni più recenti sviluppi* (Siena, 1998), 61–70.

10. See, in particular, G. Genette, *Nouveau discours du récit* (Paris, 1983), 93–107 (= *Narrative Discourse Revisited,* trans. J. E. Lewin [Ithaca, 1988]), with the overview proposed by Manetti [n. 9], 88–95.

11. We should not, however, neglect to make use of the Aristotelian notion of rhetorical *ethos* to glean what we can from the representations of the author and the reader both as proposed in the text itself (by the author) and as reconstructed by those who receive it in the process of performance or of reading. See the contributions published in *Images de soi dans le discours: La construction de l'ethos,* ed. R. Amossy (Lausanne, 1999), as well as J.-M. Adam, *Linguistique textuelle: Des genres de discours au texte* (Paris, 1999), 108–16.

12. See, for example, the references given by A. Ford, "L'inventeur de la poésie lyrique: Archiloque le colon," *Mètis* 8 (1993): 59–73, as well as the study of G. Nagy, "Genre and Occasion," *Mètis* 9/10 (1994/95): 11–25. For a critique of the notion of "lyric," see my study "La poésie lyrique grecque, un genre inexistant?" *Littérature* 111 (1998): 87–110.

13. For Sappho, see (for example) E. Stehle, *Performance and Gender in Ancient Greece: Nondramatic Poetry in Its Setting* (Princeton, 1997), 288–311; for the poetry of Hipponax, see C. Miralles and J. Pòrtulas, *The Poetry of Hipponax* (Rome, 1988), 144–60, who attribute to Boupalos the status of a "ritual paradigm," situating this name between a biographic and a poetic identity. For Hesiod, see chapter 2, §1.2.

14. One may refer to the various studies that I cited in "Eros revisité: La subjectivité discursive dans quelques poèmes grecs," *Uranie* 8 (1998): 95–107, particularly that of B. Gentili, "Die pragmatischen Aspekte der archaischen griechischen Dichtung," *Antike und Abendland* 36 (1990): 1–17, as well as the relevant pages of Nagy 1990b, 373–81.

15. Pindar, *Pythian* 5.72–81 (see chapter 4, n. 14), with the commentary proposed by E. Krummen, *Pyrsos Humnon: Festliche Gegenwart und mythisch-rituelle Tradition bei Pindar* (Berlin, 1990), 108–41. On the question of the nature of the *I* in Pindar, see especially G. B. D'Alessio, "First-Person Problems in Pindar," *Bulletin of the Institute of Classical Studies* 39 (1994): 117–39; and M. R. Lefkowitz, "The First Person in Pindar Reconsidered—Again," *ibid.* 40 (1995): 139–50 (with reference to Lefkowitz 1991, 61–65 and 173–83), who evoke the issues involved in the controversy and the countless argumentative stances to which it has given rise. The scholiast, in his commentary on verse 72 (2: 183 Drachmann), does not hide his own hesitation.

16. On this issue, one should read the reflections of S. Borutti, *Filosofia delle scienze umane: Le categorie dell'antropologia e della sociologia* (Milan, 1999), 87–128.

17. See on this subject the references provided at the end of my study "Performative Aspects of a Choral Voice in Greek Tragedy: Civic Identity in Performance," in *Performance Culture and Athenian Democracy,* ed. S. Goldhill and R. Osborne (Cambridge, 1999), 125–53; see the testimonia gathered by Herington 1985, 24–25, 87–88, and 183–84.

18. See chapter 2, n. 4, and chapter 3, n. 4. For new developments concerning discursive procedures that contribute to maintaining a text's internal coherence, both syntactic and semantic, see the work of J.-M. Adam, *Le texte narratif: Précis d'analyse textuelle,* 2nd ed. (Paris, 1994), 36–55, as well as the work cited in n. 11, 54–61.

19. Remarks concerning this point in Calame 2000a, 34–48 (=1995, 15–24); for the Hesiod of the *Theogony*, see G. Nagy, "Autorité et auteur dans la *Théogonie* hésiodique," in Blaise, Judet de La Combe, and Rousseau 1996, 41–52.

20. J. Kristeva, "Problèmes de la structuration du texte," in *Théorie d'ensemble: Textes collectifs* (Paris, 1968), 297–316 (quote from 311), who furthermore recognizes that the text, as a "meaningful practice," is the object of an exchange between a sender and a receiver; see also idem, "Le mot, le dialogue, le roman," *Critique* 23 (1967): 438–65, reprinted in *Semeiotiké: Recherches pour une sémanalyse* (Paris, 1969), 143–73. On this issue, consult the good historical and conceptual overview by L. Edmunds, *Intertextuality and the Reading of Roman Poetry* (Baltimore, 2001), 8–18; as well as S. Rabau, *L'intertextualité* (Paris, 2002), 15–37, who shows that the use of intertextuality as a tool for analysis is a relatively recent development.

21. According to the taxonomy formulated by G. Genette, *Palimpsestes: La littérature au second degré* (Paris, 1982), 7–14 (= *Palimpsests: Literature in the Second Degree,* trans. C. Newman and C. Doubinsky [Lincoln, 1997]). See on this topic the excellent review by G. D'Ippolito, "Intertextualità in antichistica," *Lexis* 13 (1995): 69–116, and the attempt at critical application of the notion of intertextuality to Latin poetry by Edmunds [n. 20], 133–63.

22. This difference has been noticed without truly being rendered explicit by D. Fowler, "On the Shoulders of Giants: Intertextuality and Classical Studies," *Materiali e discussioni per l'analisi dei testi classici* 39 (1997): 13–34 (with a bibliography on the notion of intertextuality and a list of studies by Hellenists who use it: 28 n. 23), reprinted in *Roman Constructions: Readings in Postmodern Latin* (Oxford, 2000).

23. See R. F. Thomas, "Virgil's *Georgics* and the Art of Reference," *Harvard Studies in Classical Philology* 90 (1986): 171–98 (reprinted in *Reading Virgil and His Texts: Studies in Intertextuality* [Ann Arbor, 1999], 114–41); as well as the remarks addressing the "limits of intertextualism" by S. Hinds, *Allusion and Intertext: Dynamics of Appropriation in Roman Poetry* (Cambridge, 1998), 47–51, who affirms that "the term 'allusion' privileges the interventions in literary discourse of one intention-bearing subject, the alluding poet," thus confronting us with one of the impasses of twentieth-century literary criticism: "the ultimate *unknowability* of the poet's intention." For the idea of filiation reintroduced after a useful overview of the different modes of intertextuality, see T. K. Hubbard, *The Pipes of Pan: Intertextuality and Literary Filiation from Theocritus to Milton* (Ann Arbor, 1998), 1–17.

24. G. B. Conte, *Memoria dei poeti e sistema letterario: Catullo, Virgilio, Ovidio, Lucano,* 2nd ed. (Turin, 1985), 5–14 and 111–22 (= *The Rhetoric of Imitation: Genre and Poetic Memory in Virgil and Other Latin Poets* [Ithaca, 1986], 22–31 and 69–95); see on this topic the synthesis of G. B. Conte and A. Barchiesi, "Imitazione e arte allusive: Modi e funzione dell'intertestualità," in *Lo spazio letterario di Roma antica,* vol. 1, *La produzione del testo,* ed. G. Cavallo, P. Fedeli, and A. Giardina (Rome, 1990), 81–114, and the remarks of Edmunds [n. 20], 9–14. For Greek poetry, see M. G. Bonnano, *L'allusione necessaria: Ricerche intertestuali sulla poesia greca e latina* (Rome, 1990); and, for the Homeric poems, I refer the reader to the thesis defended by P. Pucci, *Odysseus Polutropos: Intertextual Readings in the "Iliad" and the "Odyssey,"* 2nd ed. (Ithaca, 1995), 236–45 and 247–58. For examples of crossing between the epic genre and the iambic genre in the archaic period, see Nagy 1979, 243–64.

25. Sappho fr. 44 Voigt; cf. A. P. Burnett, *Three Archaic Poets: Archilochus, Alcaeus, Sappho* (London, 1983), 219–23 ("a neo-epic song"); see also the commentary of D. Page, *Sappho and Alcaeus: An Introduction to the Study of Ancient Lesbian Poetry,* 2nd ed. (Oxford, 1959), 67–70 ("Sappho occasionally imitates Homeric phraseology, but nowhere else so freely").

26. A. Broger, *Das Epitheton bei Sappho und Alkaios: Eine Sprachwissenschaftliche Untersuchung* (Innsbruck, 1996), 253–77 and 304–9; see also the more nuanced study of F. Ferrari, "Formule saffiche e formule epiche," *Annali della Scuola Normale Superiore di Pisa* 16 (1986): 441–47.

27. See in particular the work of L. Rissman, *Love as War: Homeric Allusion in the Poetry of Sappho* (Königstein, 1983), 119–41 (concerning Sappho's poem 44 Voigt), and J. J. Winkler, *The Constraints of Desire: The Anthropology of Sex and Gender in Ancient Greece* (New York, 1990), 168–78, with the nuanced reply to the dichotomy drawn in Rissman by L. P. Schank, "Sappho Frag. 44 and the 'Iliad,' " *Hermes* 122 (1994): 144–50.

28. Cf. M. Steinrück, "Homer bei Sappho?" *Mnemosyne* 4, no. 52 (1999): 139–54. On the author and date of the *Homeric Hymns*, cf. chapter 1, §1, with the attempt at relative dating of these compositions on the basis of linguistic criteria carried out by Janko [chapter 1, n. 7].

29. See, on this topic, the propositions formulated by Gentili 1995, 69–82 (= 1988, 50–60), and by Nagy 1990, 82–115, concerning the musical aspects of the "lyric" tradition. For the poetic tradition on which Sappho and Alcaeus depend, see J. T. Hooker, *The Language and Text of the Lesbian Poets* (Innsbruck, 1977), 56–83; and A. M. Bowie, *The Poetic Dialect of Sappho and Alcaeus* (New York, 1981), 60–67.

30. On these hypotheses, read the study of P. A. Rosenmeyer, "Her Master's Voice: Sappho's Dialogue with Homer," *Materiali e discussioni per l'analisi dei testi classici* 39 (1997): 123–49, who specifically cites the epigram in the *Anthologia Palatina* 7.15, where "Sappho" presents herself as a feminine Homer. On frr. 16 Voigt by Sappho and 42 and 283 Voigt by Alcaeus, as well as *Iliad* 3.171–80, see chapter 3, §2.1.

31. See, for example, the remarks on this topic formulated by Fowler [n. 22], 13–15; see also Hinds [n. 23].

32. According to the distinction proposed by M. Riffaterre, "L'intertexte inconnu," *Littérature* 41 (1981): 4–7, between references dependent on a particular reader's culture to be perceived and, by contrast, references that impose themselves on the reader through a framework of shared knowledge; see on this issue the contributions in *Intertextualités: La bible en échos,* ed. D. Marguerat and A. Curtis (Geneva, 2000).

33. In a study titled "The *Theognidea:* A Step towards a Collection of Fragments?" in *Collecting Fragments: Fragmente sammeln,* ed. G. W. Most (Göttingen, 1997), 53–66, E. Bowie considers a whole series of possibilities for the quotation, and insertion into a second text, of verses issuing from an oral tradition.

34. *Carm. conv.* fr. 891 Page = Alcaeus fr. 249 Voigt; cf. H. Fabbro, *Carmina convivalia attica* (Rome, 1995), 120–26. We could also mention the shared sympotic authority of the Anacreon poems; see, for example, F. Dupont, *L'invention de la littérature: De l'ivresse grecque au livre latin* (Paris, 1994), 35–81 (= *The Invention of Literature: From Greek Intoxication to the Latin Book,* trans. J. Lloyd [Baltimore, 1999]).

35. Theognis 1003–6, 1020–22, 1253–56; cf. Tyrtaeus fr. 9.13–16 Gentili-Prato, Mimnermus fr. 1.4–6 Gentili-Prato, and Solon fr. 17 Gentili-Prato. See, on this topic, M. Vetta, *Theognis: Elegiarum liber secundus* (Rome, 1980), xxx and 58–62; and G. Colesanti, "Un agone simposiale in Theogn. 1003–1022," *Seminari Romani di Cultura Greca* 1 (1998): 207–29, who lists the various "sympotic chains" that have been identified thus far in the Theognidean corpus (220 n. 52). When Plato (at *Lysis* 212e) cites the distich by Solon that is reused in the corpus of elegiac poems gathered under the name of Theognis, he attributes it simply to "the poet" (*ho poietés*).

36. Anacreon fr. 358 Page associated with the long scene described in Homer, *Odyssey* 6.99–223; see, following a series of interpretations along the same lines, C. Pace, "Anacreonte e la palla di Nausicaa (Anacr. fr. 13 G = 358 *PMG*, 1–4)," *Eikasmos* 7 (1996): 81–6; and I. L. Pfeijffer, "Playing Ball with Homer: An Interpretation of Anacreon 358 *PMG*," *Mnemosyne* 4, no. 53 (2000): 164–84.

37. Pseudo-Plutarch, *On Music* 1134a; Plato, *Ion* 531a and 532a, with Athenaeus 14.620c; cf. Nagy 1990b, 25–27 and 363–65.

38. The notion of "reenactment" is developed in the context of poetic *mímesis* by Nagy 1990b, 41–45 and 373–81. For the notion of (poetic) "performance," see Aloni 1998, 11–38.

39. On the simultaneously discursive and social nature of genres, see the references provided in Calame 2000b, 50–51 (with n. 94). For a critique of the notion of "lyric," see 12. For the question of the historic continuity of particular genres subsumed by this notion, see "Réflexions sur les genres littéraires en Grèce archaïque," *Quaderni Urbinati di Cultura Classica* 17 (1974): 113–28, as well as the excellent overview of the issue by G. F. Gianotti, "La festa: la poesia corale," in *Lo spazio letterario della Grecia antica, vol. 1, La produzione e la circolazione del testo,* ed. G. Cambiano, L. Canfora, and D. Lanza (Rome, 1992), 143–75. The writing of this introductory chapter has greatly benefited from the observations formulated, on the occasion of a preliminary reading, by Lowell Edmunds and Martin Steinrück, both of whom I thank here.

CHAPTER I

1. The manuscripts are described and the relationships among them established by T. W. Allen, W. R. Halliday, and E. E. Sikes, *The Homeric Hymns,* 2nd ed. (Oxford, 1936), xi–lviii; Càssola 1975, lvii–lxvi and 593–622, clarifies the history of the text.

2. See on this issue R. Kannicht, "Thalia: Ueber den Zusammenhang zwischen Fest und Poesie bei den Griechen," in *Poetik und Hermeneutik XIV: Das Fest,* ed. W. Haug and R. Warning (Munich, 1989), 29–52; and Gentili 1990, 1–17.

3. The cited uses of *húmnos* are, in order, from Homer, *Odyssey* 8.429; Hesiod, *Theogony* 33 (cf. *Works and Days,* 662); Alcman, fr. 27 Davies; and Theognis, 993. See Càssola 1975, ix–xii; and H. W. Smyth, *Greek Melic Poets* (London, 1900), xxvii–xxxii.

4. Thucydides 3.104.4–5, citing with several variants the text of *Hymn to Apollo* 146–50 and 165–72 (see also Plato, *Phaedo* 60d): cf. Aloni 1989, 37–47. The scholion on Thucydides glosses the technical term *prooímion* with the term *húmnos,* according to the late usage wherein this word designates a song of praise addressed to gods (see n. 6). We have no evidence for the designation of the *Homeric Hymns* as *húmnoi* any earlier than Diodorus Siculus 1.15.7; see also 1.38.3 and 4.30.4.

5. Pindar's *Pythian* 1.4 seems to point to the form of *kitharoidía* comprising dance and song, *Nemean* 2.1–3 to the work of rhapsodes, and *Pythian* 7.2 perhaps to a choral melic form; see especially Nagy 1990b, 353–60. For the etymology (proposed by Quintillian at *Institutio Oratoria* 4.1.2) and the different uses of the term *prooímion,* see the exhaustive analysis of H. Koller, "Das kitharodische Prooimion: Eine Formgeschichtliche Untersuchung," *Philologus* 100 (1956): 159–206, who argues for limiting the use of this word to preludes introducing citharodic song (see n. 35). By contrast, A. Aloni, "Proemio e funzione proemiale nella poesia greca arcaica," in *Lirica greca e latina: Atti del Convegno di studi polacco-italiano, Posnan 2–5 maggio 1990* (Rome, 1990), 99–130, wants to extend the proem form to include all initial verses where the verb *(ex)árkhesthai* is used. See also the more cautious studies of M. Constantini and J. Lallot, "Le *prooímion* est-il un proème?" in *Études de littérature ancienne* vol. 3, *Le texte et ses représentations* (Paris, 1987), 13–27; O. Kollmann, *Das Prooimion der ersten Pythischen Ode Pindars* (Vienna, 1989), 55–60; and A. Gostoli, "L'inno nella citarodia greca arcaica," in Cassio and Cerri, eds., 1993, 95–105. The history of the substitution of the term *húmnos* in the place of *prooímion* to designate the *Homeric Hymns* is recounted by A. Aloni, "Prooimia, Hymnoi, Elio Aristide e i cugini bastardi," *Quaderni Urbinati di Cultura Classica* 33 (1980): 23–40 (= Aloni 1998, 117–38), who sees these poems as "rhapsodic" compositions; see also Càssola 1975, xii–xvi. As early a scholar as F. A. Wolf, *Prolegomena ad Homerum sive De operum Homericum prisca et genuina forma variisque mutationibus et probabili ratione emendandi* (Halle, 1795), 106–8, considered the *Homeric Hymns* to be proems. See J. Strauss Clay, "The Homeric Hymns," in *A New Companion to Homer* ed. I. Morris and B. Powell (New York, 1997), 489–507.

6. For Aristotle, *Poetics* 4.1448b24–27, praise poetry—as opposed to blame poetry—was originally divided into *húmnoi* and *egkómia;* see Plato, *Republic* 10.607a and *Laws* 700b. The post-Alexandrian rhetoricians specifically designate as *húmnoi* expressions of praise addressed to gods; see Theon of Alexandria, 2: 109, 24–26 Spengel; Hermogenes, 2: 13, 21–24 Spengel; and Menander Rhetor, 3: 331, 18–20 Spengel. Concerning late uses of the term *húmnos,* see also M. Lattke, *Hymnus: Materialen zu einer Geschichte der antiken Hymnologie* (Freiburg, 1991), 13–79.

7. Sappho, fr. 1 Voigt; Pindar, *Hymns* frr. 29–51 Maehler; *Inscriptiones Creticae* 3.2; fr. mel. adesp. 934 Page (= *Paean* 37 Käppel); *PGM* 8.1–60. These cult hymns are compared with one another by R. Wünsch, "Hymnos," in *Realencyclopädie der Altertumswissenschaft,* vol. 9 (Stuttgart, 1916), cols. 140–83 (esp. cols. 156–70); by E. Des Places, "La prière cultuelle dans la Grèce ancienne," *Revue des Sciences religieuses* 1 (1959): 343–59; and by Bremer 1981, 193–215; see the brief complementary information provided in n. 42. For the "magic" hymns, see F. Graf, "Prayer in Magic and Religious Ritual," in *Ancient Greek Magic and Religion,* ed. C. A. Faraone and D. Obbink (New York, 1991), 188–213. In addition, the comparative analysis conducted by R. Janko, *Homer, Hesiod, and the Hymns: Diachronic Development in Epic Diction* (Cambridge, 1982), 99–200, reveals disparities in the very Homeric diction unifying the *Hymns* within a single corpus and generally explains them in terms of different dates of composition; he also claims that "relatively advanced stages in the extant development of the epic *Kunstsprache*" are reflected in the collection of *Hymns.*

8. The difficulty of this division between hymn and prayer is noted, for example, by Des Places [n. 7], 343; it is reflected even in the titles of different studies analyzing the structure of the same addresses to gods: Des Places speaks of "prière cultuelle," whereas Bremer 1981 refers to "Hymns." Analogous wavering between categories has left its mark on the fundamental study of H. Meyer, "Hymnische Stilelemente in der frühgriechischen Dichtung" (Ph.D. diss., Würzburg, 1993), 6–10 and 51–3; prayers in the strict sense (Homer, *Iliad* 1.37–42; Sappho, fr. 1 Voigt) are soon seen to include numerous "kulthymnische Elemente." On this issue, S. Pulleyn, *Prayer in Greek Religion* (Oxford, 1997), 1–15 and 39–55, offers nothing new; see also D. Aubriot, *Prière et conceptions religieuses en Grèce ancienne jusqu'à la fin du Ve siècle av. J.-C.* (Lyon, 1992), 172–93. Käppel 1992, 189–200, has revealed the structural analogies linking the Erythraean *Paean* (fr. mel. adesp. 934 = *Paean* 37 Käppel) with the *Homeric Hymns*.

9. Following the suggestion of Bremer 1981, 196, whose argument is based on the seminal study of C. Ausfeld, "De Graecorum precationibus questiones," *Jahrbuch für classische Philologie, Suppl.*, n.s., 28 (1903): 505–47; see also Meyer [n. 8], 3–5, and, on Homeric prayers, J.V. Morrison, "The Function and Context of Homeric Prayers: A Narrative Perspective," *Hermes* 119 (1991): 145–57. Miller 1986, 1–5, provides a specific form of the "cult hymn" structure ("invocation— hypomnesis—request") for the *Homeric Hymns*: "exordium—mid-section (*descriptio et narratio*)— epilogue"; see also on this issue Koller [n. 5], 175–76, and Càssola 1975, xxi, who calls the final part of the *Hymns* the "*congedo.*" In his outline for a structural analysis of the *Hymns*, R. Janko, "The Structure of the Homeric Hymns: A Study of Genre," *Hermes* 109 (1981): 9–24, settles for the distinctions "introduction," "middle section," and "conclusion."

10. Homer, *Iliad* 2.493; *Odyssey* 1.1; *Iliad* 2.484. The distinction between *"Er"-Stil* and *"Du"- Stil* has been abundantly discussed—without being attributed specifically to the *Hymns*—by E. Norden, *Agnostos Theos: Untersuchungen zur Formgeschichte religiöser Rede* (Leipzig, 1913), 143–66; this distinction has been utilized concerning the *Hymns* by Miller 1986, 2–3. For a comparative analysis of the introductory formulas in epic poetry in general, see my previous study, Calame 2000a, 59–69 (= 1995, 35–44); and see on this issue the brief remarks of Race 1992, 13–38. The terms used in these forms of introduction to designate the song (of the Muse or of the speaker) are generally identical to those used in the preludes of Homeric poetry: *aeídein, (enn)épein*, or even *humneín*; the *Hymn to Apollo* and *Hymn 7* are exceptional for their use of the form *mnésomai*. See n. 28.

11. See on this issue the conclusive study of Norden [n. 10], 168–76, who draws his examples from many forms of prayer. At the close of an investigation devoted to the "Polionimia divina e economicità formulare in Omero," *Quaderni Urbinati di Cultura Classica* 72 (1993): 7–44, L. Sbardella notes the abundance of epithets qualifying the gods in the *Hymns*; this distinctive trait should probably be linked to the cultic function of these compositions.

12. The traditional division of the compositions in the collection into "short" *Hymns* and "long" *Hymns* caused the question of their structure to crystallize within a genetic perspective: it was long debated whether the one group originated from the other or vice versa, and the possibility was also raised that the shortest compositions were no more than excerpts from the more developed ones. The imbroglio of arguments and counterarguments on the issue posed in these terms is summarized by L. H. Lenz, *Der Homerische Aphroditehymnus und die Aristie des Aineias in der Ilias* (Bonn, 1975), 276–86. R. Parker, "The Hymn to Demeter and the Homeric Hymns," *Greece & Rome* 28 (1991): 1–17, aims to show how the account in the *Hymn to Demeter* is constructed from a combination of Panhellenic elements and elements related to the probable place of the poem's performance.

13. Concerning the probable occasion of these two *Hymns*, see Allen, Halliday, and Sikes [n. 1], 417–18 and 427–28, along with Càssola 1975, 395–96 and 425.

14. In this case, this *Hymn* should not be considered incomplete, as supposed by Càssola 1975, 379, on the grounds that it lacks its introductory part and consequently consists only of the prayer part. On the swan's musical qualities and association with Apollo, cf. ibid., 578, with the references provided in C. Calame, *Alcman: Introduction, texte critique, témoignages, traduction et commentaire* (Rome, 1983), 348.

15. See on this topic the useful clarifications provided by Càssola 1975, 297–99; as well as M. L. West, "The Eighth Homeric Hymn and Proclus," *Classical Quarterly* 54 (1970): 300–304; and T.

Gelzer, "Bemerkungen zum Homerischen Ares-Hymnus (Hom. Hy. 8)," *Museum Helveticum* 44 (1987): 150–67.

16. For Koller [n. 5], 176 and 193–94, *agôn* designates the song performed in a contest of citharodes. The allusion to an annual festival in *Hymn* 26 is discussed in Càssola 1975, 407.

17. Concerning the erotic charm attributed to song in archaic Greece, see the references provided in Calame 1999, 36–38, to which add L. Pratt, *Lying and Poetry from Homer to Pindar: Falsehood and Deception in Archaic Greek Poetics* (Ann Arbor, 1993), 37–42; and Pucci 1998, 1–19 and 175–77.

18. The verses constituting the central portion of this *Hymn* are practically identical to verses 94–97 of Hesiod's *Theogony*; we should consider this correspondence to be the result of the shared heritage of an oral tradition rather than seek any kind of genetic explanation; see Càssola 1975, 401–2, who proposes understanding *ándres aoidoí . . . kaì kitharistaí* as meaning "i poeti che si accompagnano con la lira" (Càssola 1975, 580).

19. Käppel 1992, 189–206, shows though a comparative analysis that the Erythrae *Paean* presents both enunciative elements facilitating re-performance of the poem in distinct cult contexts and, in the different versions that have come down to us, variations related to these performance circumstances.

20. Bremer 1981, 196, provides a summary of these different forms of argumentation. In her doctoral dissertation on hymnic compositions, M. Vamvouri-Ruffy emphasizes the argumentative character of the descriptive and narrative part of several types of hymn (Ph.D. diss., Lausanne, 2000).

21. See the detailed commentary of N. J. Richardson, *The Homeric Hymn to Demeter* (Oxford, 1974), 322–24, who notes that *Hymn* 30 may have been influenced by the *Hymn to Demeter* (69).

22. Following other discussions, H. S. Versnel, "Religious Mentality in Ancient Prayer," in *Faith, Hope, and Worship: Aspects of Religious Mentality in the Ancient World,* ed. H. S. Versnel (Leiden, 1981), 1–64 (esp. 43–48), points out that, from the point of view of the speaker, the use of *kháris* entails the idea of praise (of the god), whereas from the god's perspective it points to the notion of pleasure.

23. The concluding verses of *Hymn* 9 combine formulas that may represent doublets; see Càssola 1975, 567 and 303. See also *Hymn* 24, where the request for intervention addressed to Hestia (see discussion in text) is accompanied by a petition concerning the "favor" (*khárin*) granted to the song. The Homeric uses of *khaírein* to refer to the joy (and thus the gratitude) felt on receiving a gift are inventoried by J. Latacz, *Das Wortfeld "Freude" in der Sprache Homers* (Heidelberg, 1966), 76–78. E. Scheid-Tissinier, *Les usages du don chez Homère: Vocabulaire et pratiques* (Nancy, 1993), 57–93, has shown that the use of *khaírein* entails the idea of reciprocal pleasure. See also R. Wachter, "Griechisch *khaîre*: Vorgeschichte eines Grusswortes," *Museum Helveticum* 55 (1998): 65–75.

24. In an article titled *"Do ut des?" Scienze dell'Antichità* 3–4 (1989–90): 45–54, C. Grottanelli has shown that most classical votive inscriptions, through the use of a wide range of terms derived from *khar-,* present themselves as proposed in exchange for what is requested from the god to whom the dedication is made. See also the important study of J. F. García, "Symbolic Action in the Homeric Hymns: The Theme of Recognition," *Classical Antiquity* 21 (2002): 5–39; for *Hymn* 10, see §2.1 of this chapter.

25. Concerning the meaning and etymology of *autár,* see J. D. Denniston, *The Greek Particles,* 2nd ed. (Oxford 1954), 55. These performative and ritual futures retain all of the intentional and votive significance of the Greek future; see W. J. Slater, "Futures in Pindar," *Classical Quarterly* 63 (1969): 86–94; and J. Humbert, *Syntaxe grecque,* 3rd ed. (Paris, 1960), 136 and 151–53. The extradiscursive reference of these future forms is the subject of the discussion offered by I. L. Pfeijffer, *First Person Futures in Pindar* (Stuttgart, 1999), 45–60.

26. The poetic functions of memory and forgetfulness in archaic Greece have been discussed in numerous studies; among the more recent are that of M. Simondon, *La mémoire et l'oubli dans la poésie grecque jusqu'à la fin du Ve siècle av. J.-C.* (Paris, 1982), 103–27; as well as those of J. Rudhardt, "Mnémosyné et les Muses," and D. Bouvier, "L'aède et l'aventure de mémoire: Remarques sur le problème d'une dimension religieuse de la mémoire dans l'*Iliade* et l'*Odyssée*," in *La mémoire des religions,* ed. P. Borgeaud (Geneva, 1988), 37–62 and 63–78.

27. In particular, Koller [n. 5], 176–77, utilized these temporal and aspectual shifts, from the present to the aorist to the future, to establish the proemic character assumed by the *Hymns;* cf. Nagy 1990a, 53–56.

28. It is probably with these texts in mind that one ought to read the two passages in the *Hymns* that seem to allude to the existence of epilogues concluding the epic song, as well as the proem introducing it. The first of these affirmations, which is part of the double concluding formula of the *Hymn to Dionysus* (a *Hymn* that, furthermore, presents several "doublets," in addition to being incomplete; see Càssola 1975, 465–66), assures the god that the group of bards in which the speaker includes himself (*hoi dé s'aoidoì áidomen*) sing him "at the beginning and the end" (*arkhómenoi légontés te*); the second, which is part of the brief central section of *Hymn* 21 to Apollo, affirms that "the bard of the melodious phorminx [. . .] always sings (*aièn aeídei*) you first and last (*prôtón te kaì hústaton*)." The hypothesis that some of the *Hymns* were actually sung as epilogues was formulated by Meyer [n. 8], 19–24. In reviewing the question, Càssola 1975, xxi–xxii, does not exclude the existence of concluding hymns, for which we otherwise have no attestation. West 1966, 166–67, who notes that the two formulations mentioned previously are found at verses 34 and 48 of Hesiod's *Theogony* (see also Theognis 3 and n. 37) and evokes the series of parallels provided by Gow 1950, 327 (in his commentary concerning the beginning of the *Hymn to the Ptolemies,* Theocritus 17.1), remarks that there is now renewed hailing of the Muses at the end of Hesiod's works. The parallel constituted by Nestor's address to Agamemnón in *Iliad* 9.96–113 (*en soì mèn léxo, seo d'árkhomai*), as well as the presence of *aièn* in the second statement just cited, show that these affirmations concern the present intervention; consequently, these affirmations pertain to the *Hymns* themselves, which are consecrated from beginning to end, always, to the praised god.

29. The function and date of *Hymns* 31 and 32 are evoked by Càssola 1975, 439–40.

30. The meaning of *aoidé* as signifying the bard's ability and product is specified in the *Lexikon des frühgriechischen Epos,* vol. 1 (Göttingen, 1979), cols. 976–80; for the meaning of *aoidós,* cf. A. Ford, *Homer: The Poetry of the Past* (Ithaca, 1992), 14–16. The status of the rhapsode follows in the train of that of the bard; see Càssola 1975, xxii–xxix; A. Ford, "Rhapsodia," *Classical Philology* 83 (1988): 300–307; and Nagy [n. 5], 21–28. See also, in relation to the Homeric proems, the study of A. Pagliaro, *Saggi di critica semantica* (Messina, 1953), 3–62.

31. It is worth noting here that, in an edition of the *Iliad* from the first century B.C., the Homeric text was preceded by that of a proem whose first verse evokes the beginning of *Hymn* 25, addressed to the Muses and Apollo; references in Càssola 1975, viii–lx. It will furthermore be noticed that the beginning of the *Argonautica* of Apollonius Rhodius combines a hymnic address to Apollo with an exordium for an epic poem; cf. S. Byre, "The Narrator's Address to the Narratee in Apollonius Rhodius," *Transactions of the American Philological Association* 121 (1991): 215–27; and Goldhill 1991, 286–89.

32. Cf. Lenz [n. 12], 11–13. A comparative (but not contrastive) study of the "themes" belonging, in particular, to the central part of the *Hymns* has recently been presented by C. O. Pavese, "L'inno rapsodico: Analisi tematica degli inni omerici," in Cassio and Cerri 1993, 155–78. For the different modes of "hymnic" predication, see Norden [n. 10], 143–76; and, concerning the forms that the central part of the *Hymns* takes, see Janko [n. 9], 11–15.

33. The possibility has been raised that *Hymn* 21, with its enunciative oddness, corresponds to the final portion—that is, the prayer—of a longer hymn; cf. Càssola 1975, 379.

34. The particulars of the thorny problem posed by the two parts, the "Delian" and "Delphic" portions, of the *Hymn to Apollo* are summarized by Miller 1986, 111–17, who defends the unity of the composition; see also on this issue the good reexamination of Aloni 1989, 17–31, with the unitary thesis presented at pp. 107–31; and the study of J. Strauss Clay, *The Politics of Olympus: Form and Meaning in the Major Homeric Hymns* (Princeton, 1989), 17–94.

35. By comparison with Demodocus' account of the love of Ares and Aphrodite in Homer, *Odyssey* 8.266–366, C. Miralles, *Come leggere Omero* (Milan, 1992), 91–110, has proposed the hypothesis that the *Hymns* were intended for an execution of a citharodic type; see also, for a similar view, Koller [n. 5].

36. On this topic, see Calame 2000a, 66–69 (= 1995, 42–43).

37. In his structural analysis, Meyer [n. 8], 43–47, has well demonstrated that verses 11–14 are closer to the form of cult hymns, whereas verses 1–4 have the structure of Homeric proems. B. A. Van Groningen, *Théognis: Le premier livre* (Amsterdam, 1966), 9–15, reaches the same conclusion; he notes that the expression in the second verse means "always" (see n. 28). See also S. Novo Taragna, "Il linguaggio poetico dei 'proemi' della silloge teognidea (I, 1–38)," *Civiltà Classica e Cristiana* 5 (1984): 213–37. On Simonides fr. 11 West², see Aloni 1998, 200–214.

38. We may also refer to the closing formula of *Hymns* 20, 23, 30, and 31, and of course that of *Hymn* 8 to Ares (see n. 15).

39. Solon fr. 1.1–6 Gentili-Prato. Among the recent spate of German works on this poem, see the study of K. Alt, "Solons Gebet zu den Musen," *Hermes* 107 (1979): 387–406; and the reexamination of H.-G. Nesselrath, "Göttliche Gerechtichkeit und das Schicksal des Menschen in Solons Musenelegie," *Museum Helveticum* 49 (1992): 150–56. The particular function of the prologue of this poem of Solon is defined by A. Loeffler, "Enonciation et argumentation dans le fr. 1 G.-P. de Solon," *Quaderni Urbinati di Cultura Classica* 74 (1993): 23–36.

40. The analogies between the *Theogony* and the *Homeric Hymns* have been noted by P. Friedländer, "Das Proömium von Hesiods Theogonie," *Hermes* 49 (1914): 1–16 (reprinted in *Hesiod*, ed. E. Heitsch [Darmstadt, 1966], 277–94); see also W. M. Minton, "The Proem-Hymn of Hesiod's Theogony," *Transactions of the American Philological Association* 101 (1970): 357–77, and the enunciative analysis of this prelude that I have developed in Calame 2000a, 69–74 and 96–8 (= 1995, 44–48 and 64–66).

41. The resemblances and differences between the structure of the *Homeric Hymns* and the prologue of *Works and Days* have been noted by E. Livrea, "Il proemio degli Erga considerato attraverso i versi 9–10," *Helikon* 6 (1966): 442–75. In the next chapter I attempt to show the impact that these enunciative variations, relative to the *Hymns*, have on the function of the works as a whole.

42. It is worth noting that, independent of the dialectal and rhythmic differences mentioned in the comparative studies cited in n. 7, some epigraphic hymns present in the opening portion (*evocatio*) a mention of the divinity in the third person, as is commonly found in the *Homeric Hymns*; cf. *Inscriptiones Graecae* IV 1², 131 = fr. mel. adesp. 935 Page ("Sing with me, goddesses, the mother of the gods, how she came . . ."), or the hymn of Limenius = 149–59 Powell ("Sing, Pierian Muses, the god of Pytho, who . . ."). In general, however, this indirect address is combined with a direct invocation of the divinity concerned; this is the case, for example, in the Erythraean hymn to Paean/Asclepius (fr. mel. adesp. 934 Page = *Paean* 37 Käppel) cited at the beginning of this chapter (see n. 8), or in the *Paean* of Isyllus (pp. 132–38 Powell = *Paean* 40 Käppel).

CHAPTER II

1. Starting with the study of F. A. Wolf, *Theogonia Hesiodea* (Halle, 1783), 60–73, the prelude to the *Theogony* has frequently given rise to the appearance of new hypotheses: a catalogue of interpretations is provided by West 1966, 151, followed by G. Arrighetti, *Poeti, eruditi e biografi* (Pisa, 1987), 37–52 and 248–50, and C. Grottanelli, "La parola rivelata," in *Lo spazio letterario nella Grecia antica*, vol. 1, *La produzione e la circolazione del testo*, ed. G. Cambiano, L. Canfora, and D. Lanza (Rome, 1992), 219–64. The debate, spurred on by Detienne 1967/1995, 12–28, has more recently been revived in the study by H. Wismann, "Propositions pour une lecture d'Hésiode," in Blaise, Judet de La Combe, and Rousseau 1996, 15–39; see also P. Judet de La Combe, "L'autobiographie comme mode d'universalisation: Hésiode et l'Hélicon," in *La componente autobiografica nella poesia greca e latina fra realtà e artificio letterario*, ed. G. Arrighetti and F. Montanari (Pisa, 1993), 25–39; and M.-C. Leclerc, *La parole chez Hésiode* (Paris, 1993), 170–78.

2. The authenticity of the prelude to the *Works* was questioned by Praxiphanes, a student of Theophrastus, then by Aristarchus, before being athetized by Crates; the references are given in West 1978, 137. See the arguments concerning this issue put forth by P. Mazon, *Hésiode: Les Travaux*

et les Jours (Paris, 1914), 37–41; a review of the question is in A. Lattes, "Sull' autenticità del proemio degli 'Erga' di Esiodo," *Rivista di Studi Classici* 1 (1954): 166–72.

3. On the proem function of the *Homeric Hymns,* see chapter 1; concerning the prelude of the *Iliad,* see G. S. Kirk, *The Iliad: A Commentary,* vol. 1 (Cambridge, 1985), 51–53, and on that of the *Odyssey,* see Pucci 1998, 11–29.

4. For the concepts of "theme" and "isotopy," see Calame 1996b, 59–60.

5. This brief study of structure is based on the comparative reading of the "incipit" and concluding verse of the *Homeric Hymns* to Hermes and to Aphrodite, as well as 9, 14, 17, 19, 20, 30, 32, and 33; concerning the different ways of entering into "hymnic" discourse, I can only refer to my study, 2000a, 59–67 (= 1995, 35–44). On the internal structure of the prelude to the *Works,* cf. R. Muth, "Zu Hesiod, *Op.* 1–10," *Anzeiger für die Altertumswissenschaft* 4 (1951): cols. 185–89, as well as Race 1992, 31–32.

6. Hesiod, *Theogony* 52–62 and 43–52; as West 1966, 147, notes, Pieria in these verses designates the birthplace of the Muses rather than the site of the union of Zeus with Memory. The terms *kléos* and *kleío* refer, in epic poetry, to the function of celebrating and commemorating that this type of poetry has; see G. Nagy, *Comparative Studies in Greek and Indic Meter* (Cambridge, 1974), 246–57.

7. Cf. Hesiod, *Theogony* 11, 47, and 75; these songs charm the king of the gods (vv. 36–37, 51 and 70).

8. Hesiod, *Works* 760–64; cf. West 1978, 344–46, who outlines a veritable history of Pheme as a goddess. In the *Odyssey,* the very name of Phemios, the *polúphemos* bard (22.376), as well as the relationship between *phêmis* and the insolent speech of the Phaeacians (6.270–74) or the hateful poem singing Clytemnestra (24.199–202), reveal the dependence of *phéme* with respect to speech, and particularly poetic speech of praise or blame (cf. n. 23); see also *Odyssey* 14.239; Hesiod fr. 176 Merkelbach-West; and Sappho fr. 44.12 Voigt. For W. J. Verdenius, *A Commentary on Hesiod "Works and Days," vv. 1–382* (Leiden, 1985), 5, *phéme* is the equivalent of Homeric *kléos* even here. It is no doubt in this context that we should also conceive the terms *rhetoí* and *árretoi,* by contrast to the connection with justice that has been devised with some difficulty by M. Mancini, "Semantica di *rhetós* e *árretos* nel prologo agli *Erga* di Esiodo," *Aion* 8 (1986): 175–92.

9. The figures have been noted in general by West 1978, 136; see also W. Nicolai, *Hesiods Erga* (Heidelberg, 1964), 13–14. These figures are not exclusive to the prelude; cf. H. Troxler, *Sprache und Wortschatz Hesiods* (Zürich, 1964), 4–9.

10. Indeed, while the secondary meaning "glorify" is wrongly ascribed to *aéxo* (e.g., Herodotus 3.80.6), in Homeric poetry this term signifies "make prosper," as in the case of an *érgon,* for example: Homer, *Odyssey* 14.65–66 and 15.372; see also Hesiod, *Works* 377 (wealth), and Pindar, *Olympian* 8.88. For use of the verb *minútho* in a context of attributing *kûdos,* see Homer, *Iliad* 15.490–93. Concerning the use of *arízelos,* see *Iliad* 13.242–45 and 18.218–21, as well as the *Lexicon des frühgriechischen Epos,* vol. 1 (Göttingen, 1979), cols. 1273–74. In the *Odyssey,* Odysseus uses this qualifier in reference to his own story. Pindar, *Olympian* 2.58–59, compares opulence (*ploútos*) adorned with acts of merit (*aretaí*) to an *arízelos* star.

11. Hesiod, *Theogony* 444–49, 147–53, 617–20, and 713–21; cf. Chantraine 1968, 196.

12. For the positive meaning "courageous," "brave" or, by contrast, the negative sense "arrogant," "impertinent" that *agénor* can assume, see *Lexicon des frühgriechischen Epos,* vol. 1 [n. 10], cols. 63–65. For the literal meaning of *kárpho* when Athena turns Odysseus into an old man, see Homer, *Odyssey* 13.398 and 430; also Archilochus fr. 188 West.

13. Hesiod, *Works* 190–201 (description of the chaotic situation following the Age of Iron; cf. §4 of this chapter); also Theognis 1147 (the *lógos skoliós* is that of unjust men [*ádikoi*], the injustice being characterized by disdain for the gods and the coveting of others' property). See also *carm. conv.* fr. 892 Page (the man who is "straight" [*euthús*] is one who does not have crooked thoughts [*skolià phroneîn*]); Pindar, *Pythian* 4.152–53 (Aison, the king, "straightens out" the judgments [*euthune díkas*] for his people with his scepter); and perhaps the fragment 14.7–8 Gentili-Prato attributed to Tyrtaeus. Rather than referring to Theognis 535–39, Verdenius [n. 8], 7, rightly explains this "straightening out" through the image of the carpenter's line and square used at Theognis 543–46. For this notion of law in Hesiod, see n. 24.

14. Solon frr. 3.34–39 and 3.15–20 Gentili-Prato; concerning this new conception of law, see M. Gagarin, *Early Greek Law* (Berkeley, 1986), 51–52 and 99–104. For the impact of writing on the process whereby the laws became communal, see M. Detienne, "L'espace de la publicité: Ses opérateurs intellectuels dans la cité," in Detienne 1988, 29–81. In Solon, we are not yet dealing with distributive justice, much less the egalitarian law boasted of by the Theseus of Euripides' *Suppliant Women* 429–34; see G. Cerri, *Legislazione orale e tragedia greca* (Naples, 1979), 86–91. Concerning the notion of justice as balance, see Gentili 1995, 57–62 (= 1988, 44–46).

15. Benveniste 1969, 2: 107–10 and 101–5; concerning the concept of *thémistes*, see also M. Corsano, *Themis: La norma e l'oracolo nella Grecia antica* (Lecce, 1988), 31–44 (with the bibliography provided at 34 n. 6); and J. Rudhardt, *Thémis et les hôrai: Recherches sur les divinités grecques de la justice et de la paix* (Geneva, 1999), 19–43.

16. The resulting disparity between the prelude of the *Works* and the structure of a hymnic proem is well indicated by E. Livrea, "Il proemio degli Erga considerato attraverso i vv. 9–10," *Helikon* 6 (1966): 442–75, and by West 1978, 141, who describes the extension of the scope of *klûthi* through the participles *idòn aión te;* see also L. Bona Quaglia, *Gli "Erga" di Esiodo* (Turin, 1973), 17–28. Taking the example of Chryses' prayer to Apollo (Homer, *Iliad* 1.37–42) and Sappho's "hymn to Aphrodite" (fr. 1 Voigt), Miller 1986, 1–10, draws a convincing contrastive comparison between "rhapsodic" hymns (proems) and "cult" hymns, a distinction that Nicolai [n. 9], 13–18, does not even take into account. See also the study of Bremer 1981, 195–98.

17. Homer, *Iliad* 18.497–508 (the scene depicted on the shield of Achilles), 23.573–85 (the dispute between Menelaus and Antilochus), 16.384–92 (the combat between Patroclus and Hector); see L. Gernet, "Droit et prédroit en Grèce ancienne," *Année sociologique* 3, no. 3 (1948–49): 21–119 (reprinted in *Anthropologie de la Grèce antique* [Paris, 1968], 175–260, esp. 218–23 and 239–42 = *The Anthropology of Ancient Greece,* trans. J. Hamilton and B. Nagy [Baltimore, 1981]).

18. On this substitution in the narratee position, see Calame 2000a, 68–69 and 101–4 (= 1995, 43–44 and 69–71); it has also been recognized by R. Lamberton, *Hesiod* (New Haven, 1988), 106–13, and more recently by P. Pucci, "Auteur et destinataires dans les *Travaux* d'Hésiode," in Blaise, Judet de La Combe, and Rousseau 1996, 191–210; see also Leclerc [n. 1], 204. Ibycus fr. 282.47–48 Davies; Sappho frr. 131 and 49 Voigt (with the parataxis *egò séthen* in a different syntactic structure); Theognis 27–30, 39–40, etc. On the character of the narratee of Theognis' distichs, see Nagy 1990b, 183. Rather than a form of politeness (*pace* West 1978, 142), we should probably take the use of the optative with *án* when the narrator speaks (v. 10) as an attenuated expression (because before Zeus?) of a desire, or even a wish: see R. Kühner and B. Gerth, *Ausführliche Grammatik der griechischen Sprache,* pt. 2, vol. 1 (Hannover, 1898), 233–36, as well as the form *arkhómetha* that punctuates the beginning of the prelude to the *Theogony* (v. 1 and 36). West 1978, 138, and Verdenius [n. 8], 1–2, have well described the transition from the epic mode to the "lyric" and cletic mode represented by the use of *deûte* at verse 12.

19. Even if it is difficult to subscribe to the distinction drawn here by Wismann [n. 1], 17–20, between immediately perceived reality (*etétuma*), fictive linguistic reality (*pseúdea*), and intelligible reality (*alethéa*), it seems that derivatives of *et-* refer to an authentic, empirical reality; see T. Krischer, "*Etymos* und *alethes,*" *Philologus* 109 (1965): 161–74; further references in Verdenius [n. 8], 12–13, and Pucci 1977, 9–10, with n. 9. See also on this same passage J. Rudhardt, "Le préambule de la *Théogonie.* La vocation du poète. Le langage des Muses," in Blaise, Judet de La Combe, and Rousseau 1996, 25–40; the Muses are not likely to transmit *tà eónta.* The *etétuma* should not simply be assimilated with the *alethéa* of the *Theogony,* as has been proposed by M. Puelma, "Der Dichter und die Wahrheit in der griechischen Poetik von Homer bis Aristoteles," *Museum Helveticum* 46 (1989): 65–100 (who cites part of the bibliography concerning the problem); see also M. Detienne, *Crise agraire et attitude religieuse chez Hésiode* (Brussels, 1963), 41–47.

20. The commentary of West 1978, 142–43, provides numerous parallels for this transition from an initial truth to an individual case while analyzing most of the linguistic mechanisms in this passage that come from gnomic literature; on this dialectic between the particular and the general, see also J. U. Schmidt, *Adressat und Paraineseform* (Göttingen, 1986), 29–35.

21. Hesiod, *Theogony* 114–15 and 225–26. There is good reason to suppose that the *Theogony* was composed before the *Works;* see West 1978, 44. The *scholia vetera ad* 11 (11 Pertusi) considered

this passage as a correction of the *Theogony;* see the discussion of this issue in B. Bravo, "Les Travaux et les Jours et la cité," *Annali della Scuola Normale di Pisa* 3, no. 15 (1985): 707–65, which emphasizes the relationship between good Eris and the paraenesis subsequently addressed to Perses. On the possible role of the two Erides in the construction of the poem as a whole, see n. 25. For Livrea [n. 16], 463–67, the *etétuma* announced in verse 10 can only refer to the distinction between the two Erides. On the basis of a keen analysis of verses 11–41, P. Rousseau, "Un héritage disputé," in *La componente autobiografica* [n. 1], 41–72, has shown that the bad Eris probably refers to the morality driving epic warfare. According to this view, Hesiod, for his part, preferred the good Eris of enriching work, and the doubling of the figure of Eris serves the critique and rejection of the Homeric model of the heroic exploit. On the possible relationship between the *Theogony* and the *Works,* see also G. W. Most, "Hesiod and the Textualisation of Personal Temporality," in *La Componente autobiographica* [n. 1], 73–92.

22. In Homer, *Odyssey* 17.382–85, the bard is included in the class of *demioergoí;* metaphors from crafts defining the activity of the poet are enumerated by R. M. Harriot, *Poetry and Criticism before Plato* (London, 1969), 60–65 and 94; and by J. Svenbro, *La parole et le marbre: Aux origines de la poétique grecque* (Lund, 1976), 186–212, who draws the erroneous conclusion that Homeric poetry, because divinely inspired, does not constitute the skill of a craft; for a contrary view, cf. F. Bertolini, "Odisseo aedo, Omero carpentiere: *Odissea* 17.384–85," *Lexis* 2 (1988): 145–64. Divine inspiration is not incompatible with learning a skill; see Homer, *Odyssey* 22.345–49 and Hesiod, *Theogony* 22–34, with the commentary of Maehler 1963, 39–40, and Segal 1994, 119–26. For later poetics, see Gentili 1995, 69–75. On the ways in which phonetic and semantic levels interact, see S. Capello, *Le réseau phonique et le sens* (Bologna, 1990), esp. 132–37 and 151–56.

23. In this respect, blame is not solely being consigned to oblivion, contrary to the claims of Detienne 1994, 59–70, who focuses his analysis on the *Theogony* and is mostly sensitive to the "magico-religious" aspect of the poet's speech. While the polarity between *épainos* and *psógos* was thematized in the praise poetry of Pindar, it is present in Homeric speech and inscribed in the legendary laws of Lycurgus; see Plutarch, *Lycurgus* 8.4 (see also 14.5 and 25.3) with the commentary of Nagy 1979, 22–75, and Gentili 1995, 155–64, as well as the critical remarks of R. M. Rosen, "Hipponax and the Homeric Odysseus," *Eikasmos* 1 (1990): 11–25.

24. The term *díke* in these passages of the *Works* oscillates between the Homeric meaning of "procedure for settling a dispute" or "legal process" and the more comprehensive meaning of "justice," "law." See M. Gagarin, "*Dike* in the *Works and Days*," *Classical Philology* 68 (1973): 81–94, who shows that, despite the control exercised by Zeus over this law pronounced by man, it is a mistake to speak of the "justice of Zeus"; indeed, we may note that Zeus only points the way (*tekmaíretai*) to *díke,* in the sense of "reparation" or "reestablishing law," when *húbris* reigns (*Works* 238–39). Schmidt [n. 20], 24–25 and 125–32, is not consistent when he rejects "trial" as a meaning of *díke* only to assign that of "juridical procedure," then "restoring the balance of justice." See also the analyses of E. A. Havelock, *The Greek Concept of Justice* (Cambridge, Mass., 1978), 135–38 and 214–17, who also emphasizes (as we would expect) the oral character of this law that ultimately exists only in the verdicts that have been pronounced; see as well n. 15. More recently H. Erbse, "Die Funktion des Rechtsgedankens in Hesiods 'Erga,' " *Hermes* 121 (1991): 12–28, has well demonstrated the continuity of the isotopy of justice across the proem and the first part of the poem. For all those commentators who reject the meaning of "procedure for a juridical decision" or "judgment," let us recall the definition given by Aristotle in the *Rhetoric,* 2.1377b20–7: rhetoric concerns decision making (*krísis*), and judgment (*díke*) is *krísis.*

25. By associating the first part of the poem with the bad Eris, and the second with the good one, R. Hamilton, *The Architecture of Hesiodic Poetry* (Baltimore, 1989), 53–58, attempts to show that the first section (up to v. 285) is centered on the straightening out of justice (in the *pólis*), while the second is focused on the production of *bíos* (within the *oíkos*). This division, which is probably justified from an enunciative perspective (see n. 29), simply repeats the analysis of the structure of the *Works* proposed by P. Mazon, *Hésiode* (Paris, 1928), 82–89. W. J. Verdenius, "Aufbau und Absicht der Erga," in *Hésiode et son influence: Entretiens sur l'Antiquité classique* 7 (Geneva, 1962), 111–59, shows that the associative principle underlying the composition of the work leads to a

more complex semantic structure, wherein law and work are put to the service of prosperity and esteem. See also Nicolai [n. 9], 180–86 and 202–8, on the different claims concerning this issue, as well as A. Lardinois, "How the Days Fit the Works in Hesiod's *Works and Days*," *American Journal of Philology* 119 (1998): 319–36.

26. On these notions, see A. Berrendonner, *Éléments de pragmatique linguistique* (Paris, 1981), 35–42.

27. These two processes of reference have been carefully distinguished following A. J. Greimas by D. Bertrand, *L'espace et le sens: "Germinal" d'Émile Zola* (Paris, 1985), 29–32. For the procedures of deixis, see introduction §1 (with note 5). For the spatial meaning of the adverb *aûthi* with a connotation of permanence, see West 1978, 150, and *Lexicon des frühgriechischen Epos*, vol. 1 [n. 10], cols. 1543–47; concerning the polemic over the meaning of *ténde*, see M. Gagarin, "Hesiod's Dispute with Perses," *Transactions of the American Philological Association* 104 (1974): 103–11 (n. 13). Ancient interpreters saw here the designation of a real case; cf. *scholia vetera ad* 37 (21 Pertusi) with the commentary of Bravo [n. 21], 726, who proposes correcting the text.

28. Although H. T. Wade-Gery, "Hesiod," *Phoenix* 3 (1949): 81–93, and B. A. van Groningen, "Hésiode et Persès," *Mededelingen der Koninklijke Nederlandse Akademie van Wetenschappen, Afd. Letterkunde* 20, n. 6 (1957): 153–66, have put forward the hypothesis that the *Works* were pronounced either in order to avoid a trial or to force Perses into a reconciliation, for Nagy 1990a, 64–72, the juridical authority constituted within and by the *Works* is presented as a substitute for kings which expresses a judgment that is ultimately valid for the whole Greek *pólis*. The sensitive reading of these verses by M. Gagarin [n. 24] notes all the signs pointing to a real situation concerning the resolution of a conflict between Hesiod and Perses. That Perses is more than a generic and textual simulacrum has been demonstrated through the arguments developed, following others, by West 1978, 33–40; review of this issue appears in Schmidt [n. 20], 19–24. If Bona Quaglia [n. 16], 26–30, rejects this "performative" interpretation of the *Works*, she rightly discerns the collaboration that these verses create between Zeus and the poet in the (hymnic) reinstatement of justice; cf. also Livrea [n. 16], 455–59. The relationship existing between *díke* and *lógos* in the *Works* has been analyzed with finesse by Pucci 1977, 45–49; see also A. Neschke-Hentschke, *Platonisme politique et théorie du droit naturel*, vol. 1 (Louvain, 1995), 29–44.

29. From the enunciative point of view, the difference between the two developments is marked by the transition from the address to Perses to the appeal to a more generic *you* (Perses is only subsequently named at vv. 286, 397, 633, and 641); cf. West 1978, 36–40, and Hamilton [n. 25], 60–62. Concerning this "broadening" of the narratee, see also Bravo [n. 19], 737–40; A. P. M. H. Lardinois, "The Wrath of Hesiod: Angry Homeric Speeches and the Structure of Hesiod's *Works and Days*," *Arethusa* 36 (2003), 1–20; and especially Schmidt [n. 20], 47–53. Without aspiring to reopen the debate among scholars about the composition of the *Works*, we can recognize with this last scholar that the second development, which is undoubtedly more mixed, is marked by the accumulation of supplementary arguments. On the semantic contrast between the two major sections of the poem, see n. 25. For Pucci [n. 18], this shift from the address to Perses to an appeal to a general *you* signals that the enunciation situation is constructed within the discourse and is thus "fictive"; see also on this matter Rousseau [n. 21], 41–49, who presents as an enunciative fiction the trial that appears to oppose the speaker to his brother; and the study of R. P. Martin, "Hesiod's Metastatic Poetics," *Ramus* 21 (1992): 11–29, who takes "Hesiod" and "Perses" to be mere discursive masks.

30. Hesiod, *Theogony* 80–97, with the commentary of Pucci 1977, 50–59, and of J. M. Duban, "Poets and Kings in the *Theogony* Invocation," *Quaderni Urbinati di Cultura Classica* 33 (1980): 7–20, as well as my note on this issue in Calame 1986/1995, 64–65.

31. The narrator expresses his intention to articulate his *lógos* "with knowledge" (*epistaménos*), not only like the bard to whom Alcinoos compares Odysseus (*Odyssey*, 11.368), but also like the king meting out justice under the inspiration of the Muses (Hesiod, *Theogony* 87).

32. As has rightly been observed by Maehler 1963, 47–48, concerning the fable of the hawk. In its Homeric usage, however, the *aînos* can have the broader meaning of "allusive legend with a particular goal" and thus be the instrument of *paraineîn;* cf. Nagy 1979, 235–42, and 1990b, 146–50 and 314–38; see also Schmidt [n. 20], 118–23 and Ford 2002, 72–80. For the meaning of

mûthos, by contrast with the definition that we moderns attribute to *myth,* see the references I give in *Mythe et histoire dans l'Antiquité grecque* (Lausanne, 1996), 12–35.

33. The appealing narrative analysis carried out by Vernant 1974, 177–94, becomes deceptive when it superposes the two stories; but this reductive aspect is corrected by the new reflections presented in "À la table des hommes: Mythe de fondation du sacrifice chez Hésiode," in Detienne and Vernant 1979, 37–132 (= 1989, 21–86 and 224–37). For the enormous bibliography generated by the story of Pandora, see G. Hoffmann, "Pandora, la jarre et l'espoir," *Quaderni di Storia* 24 (1986): 55–89; and, for a (historicizing) study of the different versions of the legend, A. Casanova, *La famiglia di Pandora* (Florence, 1979). It should not be forgotten that the *Catalogue of Women* attributed to Hesiod provides a third, very different version of the story; see frr. 4 and 5 Merkelbach-West, with the commentary of M. Luginbühl, *Menschenschöpfungsmythen* (Bern, 1992), 213–21. The reorientation of any "mythic" variant to suit its performative or, more generally, pragmatic function has been reaffirmed by P.-Y. Jacopin, "On the Syntactic Structure of Myth, or the Yukuna Invention of Speech," *Cultural Anthropology* 3 (1988): 131–59.

34. As has been noted by P. Judet de La Combe and A. Lernoud, "Sur la Pandore des *Travaux: Esquisses,*" in Blaise, Judet de La Combe, and Rousseau 1996, 301–13, it is difficult to determine whether the *gár* links the attitude of the gods with all of the preceding passage (concerning the necessity to work and stay away from disputes) or only verses 40–41 (which are difficult to interpret).

35. It is for this reason that I call the first narrative of the *Works* the "story of Pandora." This difference of orientation is well described by West 1978, 155–56.

36. The characteristics of the Golden Age mentioned in these verses are evoked by B. Gatz, *Weltalter, goldene Zeit und sinnverwandte Vorstellungen* (Hildesheim, 1967), 35–42. Concerning the threefold orientation of the story of Prometheus in the *Theogony* (commensality, fire, women), see P. Judet de La Combe, "La dernière ruse: 'Pandore' dans la *Théogonie,*" in Blaise, Judet de La Combe, and Rousseau 1996, 236–99.

37. On this subject, read J.-C. Carrière, "Le mythe prométhéen, le mythe des races et l'émergence de la cité-état," in Blaise, Judet de La Combe, and Rousseau 1996, 393–429. Vernant 1974, 189–90, also notes this equivalence between *bíos* and Pandora, but treats it on a metaphoric level as having to do with human reproduction, which is not actualized in the version of the story presented in the *Works.*

38. Homer, *Iliad* 3.50. A detailed analysis of verses 60–82—especially one comparing it to the scenes treating the adorning of Hera at *Iliad* 14.170–86 and Aphrodite in *Homeric Hymn* 6.518— would demonstrate that the description of the carrying out of Zeus' instructions for the creation of Pandora contains fewer inconsistencies than some have claimed it does; see on this issue Pucci 1977, 85–93.

39. Although I would not necessarily go as far as he does in the homologies he proposes, see, on the ambivalence of the figure of Pandora, Vernant 1974, 187–90, and "À la table des hommes" [n. 33], 98–107 (but the Pandora of the *Works* is not a *númphe*). On the charms of Pandora, see D. Saintillan, "Du festin à l'échange: Les grâces de Pandore," in Blaise, Judet de La Combe, and Rousseau 1996, 315–48.

40. West 1966, 310, reminds us that in Homer, *Iliad* 6.142, this epithet is spelled out as "(mortals) who eat the produce of agricultural labor"; see also *Iliad* 21.465, where this manner of feeding oneself is likewise contrasted with the condition of being immortal. Vernant, "À la table des hommes" [n. 33], 68–71, appositely shows that, once it has been hidden by the gods, *bíos* (alimentary resources) must thereafter be drawn from the earth through men's work (thus the *pónos;* see n. 42).

41. Hesiod, *Theogony* 510–14; cf. 585–93. On the etymology of the names of the two brothers, see West 1966, 309–10.

42. Concerning *pónos* as a consequence of *érgon,* see R. Descat, *L'acte et l'effort: Une idéologie du travail en Grèce ancienne* (Besançon, 1986), 59–66; and N. Loraux, *Les expériences de Tirésias: Le féminin et l'homme grec* (Paris, 1989), 63–72 (= *The Experiences of Tiresias: The Feminine and the Greek Man,* trans. P. Wissing [Princeton, 1995]); but also Verdenius [n. 8], 62–63.

43. At verses 117–18, the state experienced by the golden "race" is explicitly associated with the *ároura automáte* that is characteristic of the Golden Age. J. Rudhardt, "Pandora, Hésiode et les femmes," *Museum Helveticum* 43 (1986): 231–46, notes that the afflictions are uncontrollable once they have escaped from the jar; on the meaning of *autómatos* in this context, see also Verdenius [n. 8], 73–74.

44. See, on this subject, H. Neitzel, "Pandôra und das Fass," *Hermes* 104 (1976): 387–419; as well as Judet de La Combe and Lernould [n. 34], 306–13.

45. Cf. the analysis of the version of the story presented in the *Theogony* proposed by Judet de La Combe [n. 36]; see also Zeitlin 1996, 53–86.

46. See, in particular, Theognis 1135–50 (Elpis as the only divinity remaining among men when all the others have left, abandoning them to injustice and impiety), Solon fr. 1.35–38 Gentili-Prato (hopes—which are vain—amidst *noûsoi*), and Semonides fr. 8.6–10 Pellizer-Tedeschi (hopes that nourish men despite the finiteness of their condition; cf. E. Pellizer and G. Tedeschi, *Semonide* [Rome, 1990], 161–64); other parallels and bibliography in West 1978, 169–70. On this topic, see the commentary of Mazon [n. 2], 53–58. For the modern interpretations of Elpis mentioned here, see Hoffmann [n. 33], 73–77, and Vernant, "À la table des hommes" [n. 33], 124–32, whose refined analysis is nonetheless biased by the assimilation of Elpis and Pandora. A useful summary of the interpretive debates concerning the meaning of Elpis may be found in Verdenius [n. 8], 66–69; much is also to be gained from the reexamination of the question by A. M. Komornicka, "L'elpis hésiodique dans la jarre de Pandore," *Eos* 78 (1990): 63–77. Ancient commentators raised the issue of what Elpis' place is among the ills; see *scholia vetera ad* 97 (45 Pertusi) and, from the medieval period, Moschopoulos *ad* 98 (26 Grandolini).

47. Rudhardt [n. 43], 243, rightly notes that the untruthful speeches attributed to Pandora in the story correspond in reality to those of mankind in general; likewise, at verse 305, the idle man becomes the wasp, eater of the bees' produce, which is condemned through the figure of Pandora (*Theogony* 594–98).

48. The benefit to be gained from heeding someone else's advice to anticipate the future is furthermore the object of a gnomic development at verses 293–97; these verses are immediately followed by an appeal to Perses to work and remain mindful (*memneménos*, v. 298) of the narrator's recommendations. On the form that this dictum takes, see West 1978, 50–51 and 230–31; it includes the terms *phrázesthai*, *eipeín*, and *noeín* used in the Epimetheus episode (vv. 83–89). Concerning the progressive broadening of the narratee's profile in the *Works*, see n. 18.

49. The particular position of the "race" of iron in relation to the generations of gold and silver, on the one hand, and of bronze and heroes, on the other (which are presented in a tetradic structure arranged in chiasmus), is described in the studies of M. Crubellier, "Le mythe comme discours: Le récit des cinq races humaines dans *Les Travaux et les Jours*," in Blaise, Judet de La Combe, and Rousseau 1996, 431–63; and of J.-C. Carrière [n. 37], 424–27; it is also worth reading the study of A. B. Neschke, "*Dikè*: La philosophie poétique du droit dans le 'mythe des races' d'Hésiode," ibid., 465–78, which, in proposing a division of the "races" into two triads, rightly points out the shift from the past to the present, then to the future, which traces the development from the generation of heroes to the first generation of iron, then to that of the second age of iron. See also G. W. Most, "Hesiod's Myth of the Five (or Three or Four) Races," *Proceedings of the Cambridge Philological Society* 43 (1997): 104–27.

50. The analysis proposed by A. Bonnafé, "Le rossignol et la justice en pleurs (Hésiode, 'Travaux' 203–13)," *Bulletin de l'Association Guillaume Budé* (1983): 260–64, is along the same lines as that outlined here; for the identification of the protagonists of the fable with kings and the poet, respectively, see Pucci 1977, 61–73, and Lamberton [n. 18], 120–29. I do not, however, find very convincing either the interpretation proposed by S. H. Lonsdale, "Hesiod's Hawk and Nightingale (*Op.* 202–212): Fable or Omen?" *Hermes* 117 (1989): 403–12 (presenting the hawk as a portent addressed to Perses), or that formulated by M.-C. Leclerc, "L'épervier et le rossignol d'Hésiode, une fable à double sens," *Revue des Études Grecques* 105 (1992): 37–42 (taking the hawk as a representative of the gods' vengeance); an overview of the various interpretations of this *aínos* may be found in the latter study.

CHAPTER III

1. Other examples, along with mention of different attempts to classify "priamels" into several categories, are in T. Krischer, "Die logischen Formen der Priamel," *Grazer Beiträge* 2 (1974): 79–91; and S. des Bouvrie Thorsen, "The Interpretation of Sappho's Fragment 16 L.-P.," *Symbolae Osloenses* 53 (1978): 5–23.

2. Herodotus 1.30.2–31.5; other examples are cited by B. Snell, *Dichtung und Gesellschaft: Studien zum Einfluss der Dichter auf das soziale Denken und Verhalten im alten Griechenland* (Hamburg, 1965), 103–4.

3. Frr. 31.2 and 26 Voigt. In the archaic era, the relative pronoun *hóstis*, when not used as an indirect relative pronoun, can only have an indefinite meaning; see E. Schwyzer and A. Debrunner, *Griechische Grammatik,* vol. 2 (Munich, 1950), 643.

4. See on this topic the approach that I proposed in "La formulation de quelques structures sémio-narratives ou comment segmenter un texte," in *Exigences et perspectives de la sémiotique: Recueil d'hommages pour A. J. Greimas,* ed. H. Parret and H. G. Ruprecht (Amsterdam, 1985), 135–47. Hence this first narrative proposition: (1) S: *tò kálliston* = S$_1$: *tis* n P: love n S$_2$: *hóti*. The actantial positions of semio-narrative syntax are indicated in this formulation by capital letters (Subject, Antisubject, Sender) to distinguish them from grammatical functions. For an implicit critique of the semio-narrative approach to fr. 16 Voigt presented here, see P. duBois, *Sappho Is Burning* (Chicago, 1995), 119–25, who does not grasp the double actantial position occupied by Helen in the version of the "myth" imagined by Sappho.

5. The exclusive link that the "Priamel" establishes between the object incarnating beauty and the feeling of love (in the erotic sense) has rightly been noted by H. Saake, *Zur Kunst Sapphos: Motivanalytische und kompositions-technische Interpretationen* (Vienna, 1971), 127–31. Faithful to the German tradition of bibliographical completeness (a concern for exhaustiveness that too often stands in place of originality in the classical philology of the last half century), this study frees me from having to cite the countless attempts to interpret this strophe. A more recent bibliography is provided by D. Meyerhoff, *Traditioneller Stoff und individuelle Gestaltung: Untersuchungen zu Sappho und Alkaios* (Hildesheim, 1984), 55 n. 7.

6. On the Greek conception of love's power, see the references given in Calame 1996a, 23–52 (= 1999, 13–38). Against the numerous attempts to make this strophe a reflection about the relative value of the object of love and, consequently, the object that incarnates beauty, see the arguments put forward by des Bouvrie Thorsen [n. 1], 9–12; in particular, this thesis is defended by Fränkel 1960, 91–96, whose remarks about the structure of Sappho's poem remain nonetheless perfectly valid.

7. Ibycus fr. 282 Davies, with the commentary of Gentili 1995, 178–83 (= 1988, 128–31).

8. Alcaeus frr. 42 and 283 Voigt, with the commentary of A. P. Burnett, *Three Archaic Poets: Archilochus, Alcaeus, Sappho* (London, 1983), 190–98 and 185–90; Meyerhoff [n. 5], 76–103; and C. Segal, *Aglaia: The Poetry of Alcman, Sappho, Pindar, Bacchylides, and Corinna* (Lanham, Md., 1998), 63–83. W. Rösler, *Dichter und Gruppe: Eine Untersuchung zu den Bedingungen und zur historischen Funktion früher griechischer Lyrik am Beispiel Alkaios* (Munich, 1980), 221–32, attempts to link Alcaeus' attack on Helen with the mistrust of women that the group of *hetaîroi* promulgates. See also W. H. Race, "Sappho, Fr. 16 L-P, and Alkaios, Fr. 42 L-P: Romantic and Classical Strains in Lesbian Lyric," *Classical Journal* 85 (1989): 16–33; and, on the issue of the poem's lacunose text, S. Martinelli Tempesta, "Nota a Saffo, fr. 16, 12–13 Voigt (P. Oxy. 1231)," *Quaderni Urbinati di Cultura Classica* 91 (1999): 7–16. Further bibliography and explanations are in A. Bierl, "Charitons Kallirhoe im Lichte von Sapphos Priamelgedicht (fr. 16 Voigt)," *Poetica* 34 (2002): 1–26.

9. Cf. Homer, *Iliad* 2.161–62 and 177–78 with *Odyssey* 17.118–19, to which add *Iliad* 3.171–80, 9.338–39 and 19.325 with *Odyssey* 11.438. See also Hesiod, *Works* 165–66, and Semonides fr. 7.117–8 West. On the version in the *Cypria,* see 39 Bernabé with the remarks of Meyerhoff [n. 5], 58–65; for the *Iliad,* see N. Austin, *Helen of Troy and Her Shameless Phantom* (Ithaca, 1994), 23–68.

10. Pindar fr. 52f.95–98 Snell-Maehler, fr. lyr. adesp. 989 Page, Ibycus fr. 282.5–11 Page; see also Euripides, *Trojan Women* 866, and *Helen* 1117–21, Gorgias fr. 82 B 11 Diels-Kranz; Plato,

Republic 586c, and esp. *Phaedrus* 243a, quoting Stesichorus fr. 192 Davies (cf. also fr. 193); further references in N. Loraux, "Le fantôme de la sexualité," *Nouvelle Revue de Psychanalyse* 29 (1984): 11–31 (reprinted in *Les expériences de Tirésias: Le féminin et l'homme grec* [Paris, 1989], 232–52 = *The Experiences of Tiresias: The Feminine and the Greek Man,* trans. P. Wissing [Princeton, 1995]). See also B. Cassin, *L'effet sophistique* (Paris, 1995), 66–100; and Calame 2000b, 145–67.

11. This viewpoint also lies at the center of the research of Meyerhoff [n. 5]; see on this issue the critical comments formulated by W. Rösler in his review published in *Göttingische Gelehrte Anzeigen* 237 (1985): 149–62. Even the prudent D. L. Page, *Sappho and Alcaeus: An Introduction to the Study of Ancient Lesbian Poetry,* 2nd ed. (Oxford, 1959), 280–81, proposes seeing in Alcaeus fr. 283 Voigt an echo of Stesichorus' earlier attack against Helen. On Alcaeus 283 Voigt, which is supposed to have been written in reaction to Sappho fr. 16 Voigt, see, for example, E. M. Stern, "Sappho fr. 16 L. P. Zur strukturellen Einheit ihrer Lyrik," *Mnemosyne* 4, no. 23 (1970): 321–34. See on this issue, however, the astute remarks of Meyerhoff [n. 5], 87–90 and 111–13; but, in line with the aims of his study, he cannot help seeking a source for Sappho's inspiration, as for that of Alcaeus, and finding this origin in epic poetry.

12. The relationship between the gnomic and mythic parts of fr. 16 Voigt has been noted by H. Saake, *Sapphostudien* (Munich, 1972), 70–74. On the role of Aphrodite in Sappho's poetry, see E. Barilier, "La figure d'Aphrodite dans quelques fragments de Sappho," *Études des Lettres* 3, no. 5 (1972): 20–61.

13. This can be rewritten: (2) S: *tò kálliston* = [S$_1$: *tis* n P: love n] S$_2$: Helen (where the brackets indicate what remains implicit).

14. The development in narrative of the underlying proposition could be expressed in the following manner:

(3) D: Aphrodite ¬ (S$_1$: Helen n P: love u S$_2$: family in Sparta)

(4) S$_1$: Helen ¬ (S$_1$: Helen n P: love n S$_2$ [Paris] in Troy).

(Translator's note: "D" corresponds to the Sender [*Destinateur* in French].)

15. The role of Sender that Aphrodite assumes in the micro-narrative has been omitted by P. duBois, "Sappho and Helen," *Arethusa* 11 (1978): 89–99 (reprinted in *Reading Sappho: Contemporary Approaches,* ed. E. Greene [Berkeley, 1996], 79–88); the author seems to be obsessed with the activist objective of making Helen (and Sappho) into "an autonomous subject." In epic, however, Helen is perfectly aware of the seductive and irresistible role that the goddess plays toward her; see Homer, *Iliad* 3.399–412, with the remarks of Meyerhoff [n. 5], 60–72, who shows that the divine intervention in both the epic version and the Sapphic legend absolves the heroine of any moral responsibility.

Even if he weakens the meaning of the verb *éramai* by making it also apply to the objects dismissed by Sappho's argument, G. A. Privitera, "Su una nuova interpretazione di Saffo fr. 16 L.P.," *Quaderni Urbinati di Cultura Classica* 4 (1967): 182–87, has well noted the role played by Aphrodite in the mythic narrative and in the personal situation described by the narrator. See also the balanced study of M. Williamson, *Sappho's Immortal Daughters* (Cambridge, Mass., 1995), 166–71, as well as "Sappho and the Other Woman," in Greene, *Reading Sappho,* 248–64, which refers to Helen as both "desiring subject" and "desired object." For an attempt to go beyond this opposition between subject and object, which loses its pertinence in the case of Sappho's poem, see my study "Le 'sujet' de désir aux prises avec Eros: Entre Platon et la poésie mélique," *L'Unebévue* 13 (1999): 5–22. See also H. C. Fredricksmeyer, "A Diachronic Reading of Sappho fr. 16 LP," *Transactions of the American Philological Association* 131 (2001), 75–86.

16. On the possible subject of the verbal form *o]némnai* [*s(e)*, see Burnett [n. 8], 288 n. 30. This aorist form, which is temporally situated by *nûn* (now), actualizes the punctual and inchoative aspect of this "tense" (marking a shift to a new state) while playing on the use of the aorist for a present temporal value (despite the past-tense marker that its morphology reflects in the indicative) when the verb in question refers to "a sudden movement of the soul"; see J. Humbert, *Syntaxe grecque,* 3rd ed. (Paris, 1960), 144–45.

17. *Gár* can both present the content of the clause that it introduces as the reason for the state or action previously expressed (presenting an explanation) and link this same clause to an "attitude on the part of the interlocutor" of the order of approval or rejection; in this case, the logical connection between the two concerned clauses is looser, and the phrase introduced by *gár* indicates

the reason for saying what precedes. See Humbert [n. 16], 372 and 388–89, with J. D. Denniston, *The Greek Particles,* 2nd ed. (Oxford, 1954), 61–62.

18. Concerning the philological dispute over this issue, see the viewpoints enumerated by Saake [n. 5], 140–44; we should note that the term *amárukhma* probably refers to the twinkling dart of the concerned person's eyes; see Page [n. 11], 54.

19. The relationship of equivalence put in place at the poem's beginning henceforth takes the following semio-narrative form:

(5) [S: *tò kálliston*] = S_1: *I* n P: love (look) n S_2: Anactoria.

20. See the reflections, following many others, presented in my "Sappho immorale?" *Quaderni Urbinati di Cultura Classica* 28 (1978): 211–14, with the reformulated view of I. L. Pfeijffer, "Shifting Helen: An Interpretation of Sappho, Fragment 16 (Voigt)," *Classical Quarterly,* n. s., 50 (2000): 1–6. On the social function of Sappho's circle, where girls of the Lesbian and Ionian aristocracy received preparation for their future role as married adult women, often through a "homosexual" initiation to love, see R. Merkelbach, "Sappho und ihr Kreis," *Philologus* 101 (1957): 1–29, with the hypotheses that I advanced in Calame 1977, 367–432 (= 1997, 209–52, with reference to numerous recent studies taking up the same thesis with variations). See also the interpretation proposed by F. Lasserre, *Sappho: Une autre lecture* (Padua, 1989), 161–81, which links fr. 16 Voigt to the contest of the *Kallisteía.*

21. On the role of memory in Sappho, see Gentili 1995, 130–31, and Burnett [n. 8], 277–313.

22. (5a) [D: Aphrodite] ¬ (S_1: *I* n P: love n S_2: Anactoria)

(6) [D: Aphrodite/Helen] ¬ (S_1: Anactoria n P: love u S_2: *I,* here)

(7) S_1: Anactoria ¬ (S_1: Anactoria n P: love [n S_2: husband in Lydia]).

23. Concerning the initiatory role of the homophilic relationship in Greece, see Calame 1977, 420–49 (= 1997, 244–63), and 1996a, 101–21 (= 1999, 91–109). The coexistence of the two roles attributed to Anactoria in the poem has even been expunged by Burnett [n. 8], 288–89, who rejects the assimilation of the girl to Helen as the subject of love and takes her only as occupying the function of object of the narrator's love, as the incarnation of beauty.

24. On the complementary relationship among eros, marriage and warfare in Greek tragedy, see S. Durup, "L'espressione tragica del desiderio amoroso," in *L'amore in Grecia,* ed. C. Calame (Rome, 1983), 143–57.

25. Aristotle, *Rhetoric* 2.1393a23–b33. The second example of a parable cited by Aristotle even sets up a relationship, through a "predicate," between a *tis* as (grammatical) subject and a *hóntina* as object (1393b7). A parable, in the Aristotelian sense of the concept, is thus very similar to a comparison, proof of which lies in the definition given by Isocrates 12.227: for him, in affirming that "no one (*oudeís*) could praise the Spartans . . . any more than one could brigands and thieves," one is expressing a "parable."

26. The definition of parable given in *Sémiotique: Dictionnaire raisonné de la théorie du langage,* vol. 2, ed. A. J. Greimas and J. Courtès (Paris, 1986), 161, is as follows: "A relationship of partial resemblance between figurative and thematic isotopies presented as parallel within the same discourse."

27. See ibid. [n. 26].

28. Aristotle, *Rhetoric* 2.1393b3; it seems essential to reiterate that, in conclusion to the discussion devoted to proofs (2.1394a9–16), Aristotle affirms that examples, including the parable, can take the place of syllogisms and serve as a demonstration (*apódeixis*) by virtue of their capacity to carry conviction.

29. See M.-J. Borel, J.-B. Grize, and D. Miéville, *Essai de logique naturelle* (Bern, 1983), 15–28.

30. See, for example, M. Eliade, *Aspects du mythe* (Paris, 1963), 171–96.

CHAPTER IV

1. Sketches of these propositions, concerning the non-existence of an essential nature of Greek myth and the relative nature of the anthropological category of myth, are presented in my

"Évanescence du mythe et réalité des formes narratives," in *Métamorphoses du mythe en Grèce antique,* ed. C. Calame (Geneva, 1988), 7–14; and in *Mythe et histoire dans l'Antiquité grecque: La création symbolique d'une colonie* (Lausanne, 1996), 9–55. Concerning the relationship between traditional stories and individual genres, see Calame 2000b, 1–15 and 38–56. These discussions take up the conclusions of the classic studies of M. Detienne, *L'invention de la mythologie* (Paris, 1981) (= *The Creation of Mythology* [Chicago, 1986]; and P. Veyne, *Les Grecs ont-ils cru à leurs mythes?* (Paris, 1983) (= *Did the Greeks Believe in Their Myths?* [Chicago, 1988]). In addition to the useful remarks of the participants at the first Hellenistic conference of the University of Groningen (devoted to Callimachus; see Harder, Regtuit, and Wakker, 1993), I have greatly benefited from the comments of Peter Bing of Emory University, who has published a convergent study (see n. 12), Albert Henrichs of Harvard University, and Ralph Rosen of the University of Pennsylvania.

2. The texts cited are, in order, Pindar, *Pythian* 9.5–75, 4.4–51, 5.55–95, and Herodotus 4.145–57. We should, of course, also not forget the abridged, epigraphic local version in *SEG* 9, 3.6–11 and 25–51. See the annotated versions, in particular by F. Chamoux, *Cyrène sous la monarchie des Battiades* (Paris, 1952), 69–114, and by me in *Mythe et histoire* [n. 1], 67–156.

3. For interventions of the Delphic oracle in the colonization of Cyrene, see Pindar, *Pythian* 5.62, as well as 4.4–8 and 53–56; Herodotus 4.150.3–4, 151.5, 155.2–4, 156.1–2, 157.1–2, and 159.2–3. By contrast, the local version summarized in the "Oath of the Founders," without entrusting the actual management of the colonial expedition to Apollo, quotes the oracular order given by the god to Battus; *SEG* 9, 3.25–28.

4. If the Cyrenean version of the foundation legend given by Herodotus 4.157.3 actually makes Azilis (or Aziris) an indigenous settlement situated a good night's march from Cyrene, according to Lycophron, *Alexandra* 895, the Asbystae would have constituted the aboriginal population of Cyrene itself; but Herodotus 4.170 situates them south of Cyrene. See the attempts at identification proposed by R. G. Goodchild, *Kyrene und Apollonia* (Zurich, 1971), 17–20, who places the center of the Asbystae at Irasa, between Azilis and Cyrene, and the commentary of Williams 1978, 70 and 77–78. On the movement of the hunt of the Nymph Cyrene from Thessaly to Libya, see n. 8.

5. The institution at Cyrene of the Carneia of Spartan origin constitutes the center of the version of the foundation story presented by Pindar, *Pythian* 5.77–83. On the worship of Apollo in this specifically Dorian festival, see the references given in *Mythe et histoire* [n. 1], 125 n. 105, and esp. I. Malkin, *Myth and Territory in the Spartan Mediterranean* (Cambridge 1994), 52–57, 143–58.

6. In one of the three Pindaric versions of the foundation of Cyrene (*Pythian* 9.64–66), it is the son of Apollo and the eponymous Nymph who, as hunter and shepherd, assumes the *epikléseis* of Agreus and Nomius; see *Mythe et histoire* [n. 1], 101–3. On the cult of Apollo Nomius in rather marginal areas, see Williams 1978, 48. The nomadism attached to pastoral activity is presented as an early stage of human civilization, in particular by Thucydides 1.2.1 and Democritus fr. 68 B 5 Diels-Kranz; see the other passages commented on by Hartog 1992, 216–19; S. Georgoudi, "Quelques problèmes de transhumance dans la Grèce ancienne," *Revue des Études Grecques* 87 (1974): 155–85; and B. Shaw, " 'Eaters of Flesh, Drinkers of Milk,' " *Ancient Society* 13–14 (1982/83): 5–31. The liminal character of space reserved for pastoral activity is well defined by P. Voelke, "Ambivalence, médiation, intégration: À propos de l'espace dans le drame satyrique," *Études de lettres* 2 (1992): 33–58. With regard to the notion of isotopy, see chap. 2n. 4.

7. A floating island with uncultivated soil before Apollo fixes it in place and establishes his own cult there, Delos has a very particular territorial status; see *Homeric Hymn to Apollo* 53–57 and Callimachus, *Hymn to Delos* 11–15 and 30–40, as well as *Mythe et histoire* [n. 1], 85–88, and P. Bing, *The Well-Read Muse: Present and Past in Callimachus and the Hellenistic Poets* (Göttingen, 1988), 100–103. The paradigm of the island inhabited only by goats but ready to receive the civilization of men is offered by Homer, *Odyssey* 9.116–25. On the place of mountains in the Greek image of the savage world, see Buxton 1994, 81–96. On architectural and poetic weaving, see M. Detienne, *Apollon le couteau à la main: Une approche expérimentale du polythéisme grec* (Paris, 1998), 96–100, and n. 28.

8. Pindar, *Pythian* 9.13–17 and 30–34; see Hesiod fr. 215 Merkelbach-West. The displacement of the combat of Cyrene and the lion from Thessaly to Libya, in order to safeguard the flocks not from the girl's father but from the indigenous king Eurypylus (mentioned by Pindar, *Pythian* 4.33;

see *Mythe et histoire* [n. 1], 71–72 with n. 18), is probably the effect of a local version which is reported by the historian Acesandrus (*FGrH* 469 F 4; cf. Apollonius Rhodius 2.509) in his treatise dedicated to the history of Cyrene; it is a parallel version to the one that attributes to Battus himself the power of frightening away lions (Pindar, *Pythian* 5.59), and it is probably taken up again by Callimachus. See Chamoux [n. 2], 77–83; F. Jacoby, *Fragmente der griechischen Historiker* vol. IIIb, *Kommentar* (Leiden, 1955), 366–68, and Williams 1978, 79. On the location of the Asbystae and of Azilis, see n. 4.

9. Callimachus' verses constitute for us the first attestation of the homoerotic nature of the relationship between the god and the young Admetus; see in this regard the hypotheses formulated by B. Sergent, *L'homosexualité dans la mythologie grecque* (Paris, 1984), 124–32 and 182–83. The hypothesis concerning the etymologizing play on the name of Admetus was formulated by M. Depew, "Mimesis and Aetiology in Callimachus' Hymns," in Harder, Regtuit, and Wakker 1993, 55–74, esp. 74.

10. Pindar, *Pythian* 9.59–65; see n. 6.

11. It is well known that, in archaic and classical times, the Greek representation of civilization established, through numerous metaphors, a homology between agricultural production and reproduction of members of the civic community; see in particular the study of M. Detienne, *Les Jardins d'Adonis: La mythologie des aromates en Grèce*, 2nd ed. (Paris, 1989), 187–226 (= *The Gardens of Adonis: Spices in Greek Mythology*, 2nd ed. [Princeton, 1994], 99–122). Note in addition that the very Alexandrian evocation of the Carneia celebration in the midst of flowers and dew, which cause the region to experience an eternal spring, presents this still-pastoral state of civilization as a sort of Golden Age (80–83).

12. On Apollo Boedromius and Clarius, see L. Deubner, *Attische Feste* (Berlin, 1932), 202, and H. W. Parke, *The Oracles of Apollo in Asia Minor* (London, 1985), 112–141, with the complementary remarks of Williams 1978, 66, and A. Henrichs, "Gods in Action: The Poetics of Divine Performance in the *Hymns* of Callimachus," in Harder, Regtuit, and Wakker 1993, 127–47 (128). We should also not forget the scholion to line 69 (Pfeiffer 2:52). On the "hymnic" opening of this narrative section, see P. Bing "Impersonation of Voice in Callimachus' *Hymn to Apollo*," *Transactions of the American Philological Association* 123 (1993): 181–98.

13. Without analyzing the consequences of it, Williams 1978, 67, has not only seen the aim of this new perspective at verse 71 but also noticed that Callimachus' formulation recalls that of Pindar in *Pythian* 5.72–76.

14. In fr. 716 Pfeiffer, the narrator also presents Cyrene as "our homeland." On Callimachus' father and origins, see *Epigrams* 35 and 21, as well as testimonia 6, 8, 16, and 87 Pfeiffer and the scholion to line 65 of Callimachus' hymn (Pfeiffer 2:52). When, in the passage cited at n. 13, Pindar makes the Aegidai who have emigrated to Thera "my fathers" (76), it is all the less sure that the poet refers only to himself for the fact that, in verse 80, the *we* of *sebízomen* certainly refers to the (Cyrenean) chorus performing the poem; see *Mythe et histoire* [n. 1], 126 n. 108, with the references provided in n. 15 of the introduction to this book.

15. Scholion *ad* v. 26 (Pfeiffer 2:50). One can easily imagine that contemporary philologists, like their ancient colleagues, have been vying with one another through arguments to find new individuals to identify with the reference to "my king" (in particular, Ptolemy Philadelphus is often cited as a candidate); see on this issue A. Smotrytsch, "Le allusioni politiche nel II inno di Callimaco e la sua datazione," *Helikon* 1 (1961): 661–67; Williams 1978, 1–2 and 36; and A. Laronde, *Cyrène et la Libye hellénistique: "Libykai historiai" de l'époque républicaine au principat d'Auguste* (Paris, 1987), 362–64. More prudently, E. Cahen, *Les Hymnes de Callimaque: Commentaire explicatif et critique* (Paris, 1930), 46–47 and 69–70, has rightly seen that the legitimacy claimed by the narrator-author places the descendants of Battus (in the past, in Cyrene) and the Ptolemies (in the present, in Alexandria) in the same line; see also H. Herter, "Kallimachos aus Kyrene," *Realenc. Alt.-Wiss.*, *Suppl.* 13 (Munich, 1973), cols. 184–266 (esp. cols. 233–35); and A. Gosling, "Political Apollo: From Callimachus to the Augustans," *Mnemosyne* 4, no. 45 (1992): 501–12.

16. The paean, an ode specifically intended for Apollo, derives its name from the invocation to Paean that punctuates it; see *Homeric Hymn to Apollo* 516–19 (in relation to Delphi), but also Homer, *Iliad* 1.472–74 and Bacchylides 17.124–29; other references in G. Bona, *Pindaro, I peani*

(Cuneo, 1988), vii–xv; and L. Käppel, *Paian: Studien zur Geschichte einer Gattung* (Berlin, 1992), 65–70. On Paean as physician of the gods or god of physicians, see Homer, *Iliad* 5.401 and 899, Pindar, *Pythian* 4.270 (in connection with Cyrene), Aeschylus, *Agamemnon* 146, etc. Jumping ahead, we may observe that the singing of the paean seems to go hand in hand with the act of *euphemeîn;* see Simonides fr. 519.35 Page, with the commentary by I. C. Rutherford, "Paeans by Simonides," *Harvard Studies in Classical Philology* 93 (1990): 169–209 (esp. 173); that would mean that the chorus to which the Callimachean narrator addresses himself is itself singing a paean (vv. 17–18). On the putting to death of the serpent Python, cf. the *Homeric Hymn to Apollo,* 300–304 and 356–61, commented on by C. Sourvinou-Inwood, *"Reading" Greek Culture: Texts and Images, Rituals and Myths* (Oxford, 1991), 227–30.

17. This address to the chorus is prepared for in verse 4 by a rhetorical, general address that recalls those found in archaic poetry (Homer, *Iliad* 15.555, *Odyssey* 17.545, Alcman fr. 1.50 Page-Davies, etc.), then in verse 6 by an invitation addressed in the imperative to the doors moved by Apollo; see Bing [n. 12], 183–85. The presence of the chorus at Delos can be inferred from the qualifying of the palm tree as *Délios* at verse 4, but see Williams 1978, 19.

18. On the use of the "performative" future, see my remarks in "Performative Aspects of the Choral Voice in Greek Tragedy: Civic Identity in Performance," in *Performance Culture and Athenian Democracy,* ed. S. Goldhill and R. Osborne (Cambridge, 1999), 125–53.

19. The mimetic aspect of Callimachus' poem, which describes a cult ceremony without making clear where the poem itself is performed (Cyrene? Alexandria?) has been well noted by Cahen [n. 15], 45–50; see also the confusion expressed by W. Albert, *Das mimetische Gedicht in der Antike: Geschichte und Typologie von des Anfängen bis in die augusteische Zeit* (Frankfurt, 1988), 66–76, and the fine analysis of the polyphony of the poem proposed by Bing [n. 12], 184–89. Less prudently, C. Meillier, *Callimaque et son temps: Recherches sur la carrière et la condition d'un écrivain à l'époque des premiers Lagides* (Lille, 1979), 79–91, sees in Callimachus' poem a cultic paraphrase of a ritual song performed on the occasion of the Carneia. M. R. Falivene, "La mimesi in Callimaco: Inni II, IV,V, e VI," *Quaderni Urbinati di Cultura Classica* 65 (1990): 103–28, who briefly depicts the enunciative games in the poem from the standpoint of the "mobility" of people involved in a choral performance situation, has stressed that the mimetic aspect of the performance described by the narrator could not have referred to an actual choral performance; see also the fine article by M. Depew [n. 9]. For a clarification concerning the secondary (tertiary here) nature of a mimesis for a learned public that imitates through writing a ritual removed in space and time, see A. W. Bulloch, *Callimachus: The Fifth Hymn* (Cambridge, 1985), 3–13. On the confusion in Callimachus' *Hymns* between "diegesis" and "mimesis," see M. A. Harder, "Insubstantial Voices: Some Observations on the Hymns of Callimachus," *Classical Quarterly* 42 (1992): 384–94.

20. This new etymologizing explanation takes up a qualification of Apollo expressed in the *Homeric Hymn* that is dedicated to him (19 and 207); cf. Williams 1978, 38. On the creation of a communication situation that is internal to the text and thus not only fictional, but fictitious, see D. Meyer, "Die Einbeziehung des Lesers in den Epigrammen des Kallimachos," in Harder, Regtuit, and Wakker 1993, 161–75.

21. This early mention of the king actually refers to one of the Ptolemies; see n. 15.

22. This catalogue is well commented on by Williams 1978, 45–48; it is in accordance with the second part of the catalogue provided by Solon fr. 1.51–62 Gentili-Prato. The addition of the archer is explained by the reasons set out in n. 26. See also Pindar, *Pythian* 5.63–72, which falls precisely within a poem recounting the "historical" version of the foundation of Cyrene, and Plato, *Cratylus* 405a.

23. Even if the *Homeric Hymn to Apollo* could have originally been composed from two distinct poems, in the version that has come down to us it presents an organic unity that sets forth the spatial, ritual, and civilizing polarity—divided between Delos and Delphi—of the worship rendered to Apollo in Greece. On the composition and unity of the work, see notably A. M. Miller, *From Delos to Delphi: A Literary Study of the Homeric Hymn to Apollo* (Leiden, 1986), 1–9 and 111–17; and Aloni 1989, 17–31 and 107–31.

24. To the numerous texts showing the affinities linking the swan with Apollo, which are cited by Williams 1978, 20, add all those that make this bird the most perfect of singers; cf. Alcman frr.

1.101 and S 2 Page, Pseudo-Hesiod, *Scutum* 314–19, Bacchylides 15.6, etc., as well as Callimachus, *Hymn to Delos* 4.252. Still other references are in D. L. Page, *Alcman: The Partheneion* (Oxford, 1951), 100; and C. Calame, *Alcman: Introduction, texte critique, témoignages, traduction et commentaire* (Rome, 1983), 348.

25. It is all the more "likely that the Pythoktonia passage serves to introduce this literary discussion" (Williams 1978, 82), because the poetic purity affirmed here stands in opposition to the putrefaction with which the Python is etymologically associated in the *Homeric Hymn to Apollo*, 370–74. This programmatic passage has understandably been seen as paralleling other poems in which Callimachus advocates short, well-wrought pieces as opposed to long, epic-type poems. Cf. *Aetia* 1, fr. 1.1–6 and 17–30; *Iambi* 13, fr. 203; *Epigram* 28; and fr. 398 Pfeiffer. See on this subject G. O. Hutchinson, *Hellenistic Poetry* (Oxford, 1988), 67–68 and 78–84; and A. Cameron, *Callimachus and His Critics* (Princeton, 1995), 405–6; bibliography in Williams 1978, 86–89. Nevertheless, the view that Callimachus is making a precise allusion to Apollonius of Rhodes, if not Homer, would amount to an overly biographical interpretation of this passage; see the detailed discussion of M. R. Lefkowitz, "The Quarrel between Callimachus and Apollonius," *Zeitschrift für Papyrologie und Epigraphik* 40 (1980): 1–19, with the nuances introduced by G. Giangrande, "On Callimachus' Literary Theories," *Corolla Londinensis* 2 (1982): 57–67 (responding to an article by Köhnken [cited in n. 31]).

26. The echoes linking the epilogue with the development of the poem as a whole are obviously more numerous. Against those who affirm the independence of this final part (such as E. L. Bundy, "The Quarrel between Kallimachos and Apollonius," *California Studies in Classical Antiquity* 5 [1972]: 39–94), K. Bassi, "The Poetics of Exclusion in Callimachus' *Hymn to Apollo*," *Transactions of the American Philological Association* 119 (1989): 219–31, has skillfully shown that the strange juxtaposition of the functions of archer and bard proper to Apollo is justified inasmuch as the poetry is also envisaged as a weapon intended to confound the "envious" (see n. 31); see also, in general, L. Bruit-Zaidmann and P. Schmitt-Pantel, *La religion grecque*, 2nd ed. (Paris, 1991), 138–40. In addition, the divine foot that opens the temple doors in verse 3 and pushes away Envy at verse 107 may reflect (through this metaphor for rhythm) the effects of poetry itself. See also on this subject the study by Henrichs [n. 12], 142–45. Cahen [n. 15], while revealing the Cyrenaic orientation of the poem (68–70), also rightly describes this final part as a *sphragís*, as a "signature"—though it is indirect (84).

27. On bees and the putrid, see Aristotle, *History of Animals* 4.535a2–4 and 8.596b14–20; on the production of honey from dew or pure water, see *ibid.* 5.553b29 and Theophrastus fr. 190 Wimmer. It is worth recalling that the dew and the water that seep up drop by drop constitute metaphors for literary production throughout Greek poetics; see passages in D. Boedeker, *Descent from Heaven: Images of Dew in Greek Poetry and Religion* (Chico, Calif., 1984), 80–99. On the bee-priestesses, see Apollodorus of Athens, FGrHist. 244 F 89, according to whom the women celebrating the Thesmophoria are called bees and the appellation is connected with the myth of Persephone's loom and the hospitality offered to Demeter by King Melissus; in an allusion to this legend, the anonymous author of a Hellenistic hymn to Demeter (fr. adesp. pap. 990.1–4 Lloyd-Jones-Parsons) asks the bees to listen to the very song that he is in the midst of "weaving." See also Porphyry, *Cave of the Nymphs* 18; Hesychius, s.v. *mélissai* (M 719 Latte); the scholion to Pindar, *Pythian* 4.106c (= Drachmann vol. 2, p. 113); etc. For the bee-poet, see Simonides fr. 593 Page; Pindar, *Pythian* 10.53–54; Bacchylides 10.10; etc.; See also Plato, *Ion* 534a, which makes explicit the double metaphor bee–poet and honey–song. Cf. J. H. Waszink, *Biene und Honig als Symbol des Dichters und der Dichtung in der griechisch-römisch Antike* (Opladen, 1974), as well as G. Crane, "Bees without Honey, and Callimachean Taste," *American Journal of Philology* 108 (1987): 397–403. Williams 1978, 93–94, provides an up-to-date overview of the question concerning the interpretation of the text of Callimachus.

28. Basing his analysis particularly on the myth of Melissus (see n. 27) and the parallel version that attributes to the Nymph Melissa the discovery of honey and its use for leading men to a civilized diet (see esp. the scholion to Pindar, *Pythian* 4.106a [= Drachmann, 2:112–13]), M. Detienne, "Orphée au miel," in *Faire de l'histoire*, vol. 3, *Nouveaux objets*, ed. J. Le Goff and P. Nora (Paris, 1974), 56–75, has laid out the constellation of conjugal values attached to the figure of the

bee-wife: cultivation, the legitimacy and fidelity of the matrimonial bond, controlled and productive sexuality, domestic virtues under Demeter's authority.
The metaphor of the weaving of a poem was notably developed by Pindar, *Olympian* 6.85–87 (in connection with the drinking of water from a spring), *Nemean* 4.44–45 and 8.14–6, and by Bacchylides 5.9–14; it has been analyzed by J. Scheid and J. Svenbro, *Le métier de Zeus: Mythe du tissage et du tissu dans le monde gréco-romain* (Paris, 1994), 119–38 (= *The Craft of Zeus: Myths of Weaving and Fabric*, trans. C.Volk [Cambridge, Mass., 1996]). For the weaving of the *theimélia*, see n. 7.

29. Apollo's spring, presented here from the perspective of etymology, constitutes the original center of Cyrene since the earliest versions of the foundation legend; see Pindar, *Pythian* 4.294, and Herodotus 4.158.3, as well as Stephanus of Byzantium, s.v. *Kuréne* (396 Meineke). Its archaeological location next to the sanctuary of Apollo is described by Goodchild [n. 4], 109–12; for the texts, see B. K. Braswell, *A Commentary on the Fourth Pythian Ode of Pindar* (Berlin, 1988), 394.

30. The dialectic between praise and blame, which underlies the history of Greek poetics reconstructed by Aristotle (*Poetics* 4.1448b24–27), actually marks all of the poetry of a "shame" culture; see Alcman fr. 1.43–49 Page. Particularly, in the poetry of the end of the archaic period, jealousy (*phthónos*) appears as the force that does violence to just praise (*aineîn*) through reproach (*mômos*); see Bacchylides 13.199–206 (cf. 5.187–90) and Pindar, *Pythian* 1.81–86 (cf. *Olympian* 8.54–59, where the jealousy that could be directed at the poet singing the athlete's glory is compared to the throwing of a stone, and 6.74–78). See on this issue Nagy 1979, 222–42, and Gentili 1995, 155–64.

31. On this poetic program, see the references given in n. 25, with the sensible remarks of Williams 1978, 2–4; for the identification poet–kings–gods, see Henrichs [n. 12], 146–47. M. Poliakoff, "Nectar, Springs, and the Sea: Critical Terminology in Pindar and Callimachus," *Zeitschrift für Papyrologie und Epigraphik* 49 (1980): 41–47, notes that many of the poetic terms and metaphors used in this programmatic passage are of Pindaric inspiration; see also A. Köhnken, "Apollo's Retort to Envy's Criticism," *American Journal of Philology* 102 (1981): 411–22, who—following U. von Wilamowitz-Moellendorff, *Hellenistische Dichtung*, 2nd ed., vol. 2 (Berlin, 1924), 85–87—distinguishes between *mômos* and *phthónos* in order to show that the reproach is the consequence of envy; but Köhnken, in reading *tòn* (*aoidón*) as *tónde* in verse 6, supposes wrongly that Envy's criticism is aimed at the brevity of "this" poem and that this critical part refers only to the *Hymn* itself. In a more pertinent manner, E. R. Schwinge, *Künstlichkeit von Kunst: Zur Geschichtlichkeit der alexandrinischen Poesie* (Munich, 1986), 16–19, notes that Callimachus, in adopting the very form of a hymn and consecrating his poem to Apollo, practically transforms his aesthetic into "religion." We know that, in verse 113, certain manuscripts have the reading *phthóros* instead of *phthónos*, a reading defended by J. Blomqvist, "The Last Line of Callimachus' *Hymn to Apollo*," *Eranos* 82 (1990): 17–24.

32. The *Homeric Hymns* functioned as preludes to what were probably rhapsodic recitations: see Càssola 1975, xii–xxi, and *supra* chapter 1, §1.

33. Concerning the perceptible religious sentiment of Callimachus, see A.W. Bulloch, "The Future of a Hellenistic Illusion: Some Observations on Callimachus and Religion," *Museum Helveticum* 41 (1984): 209–30. On the question of the audience of his poems, see Bing [n. 7], 10–18.

CHAPTER V

1. Plato, *Republic* 601a (cf. *Phaedrus* 275d); Simonides fr. 190 B Bergk; Solon fr. 1.43–59 Gentili-Prato. Gentili 1995, 69–82 and 212–26, has shown both the unifying function of *mímesis* in the Greek conception of different arts and the economic value attached to practices that are conceived of as crafts. See also on this topic S. De Angeli, "Mimesis e Techne," *Quaderni Urbinati di Cultura Classica* 57 (1988): 27–45. I express my gratitude to the experts in iconography, Christiane Bron, Claude Bérard, and François Lissarrague, for the bibliographical suggestions they offered to me.

2. Cf. Herington 1985, passim; Calame 1977, 385–41 (= 1997, 221–38); and Nagy 1990b, 339–81.

3. Homer, *Odyssey* 8.481 and 488; Hesiod, *Theogony* 22 and 31. J.-P.Vernant, *Mythe et pensée chez les Grecs* (Paris, 1967), 51–60, and Detienne 1994, 49–70, have placed special emphasis on the putative "magico-religious" status of the Muses' inspiration for poetic speech and on the gift of prophecy supposedly granted to the poet within a tradition that was still essentially oral. See the nuancing of this position by the contributions of J. Rudhardt, "Mnémosyné et les Muses," and D. Bouvier, "L'aède et l'aventure de mémoire," in *La mémoire des religions*, ed. P. Borgeaud (Geneva, 1988), 37–62 and 63–78, as well as the various references noted in chapter 2, n. 22, concerning the conception of Homeric poets' practice as a craft; further references are provided in S. Grandolini, *Canti e aedi nei poemi omerici* (Pisa, 1996), 139–46 and 159–64.

4. J. Svenbro, *La parole et le marbre: Aux origines de la poétique grecque* (Lund, 1976), 173–86, has rightly emphasized the mercantile aspect involved in exercising *sophía* to show that Pindar's claim to superiority is conditioned by the actual commercial competition that existed between poetry and sculpture, both understood as crafts.

5. Theognis 19–26; black-figure *dînos* fragment, Athens 15499 (*ABV* 39.16). On the enunciative and "memorial" significance of the Theognidean *sphragís*, see A. L. Ford, "The Seal of Theognis: The Politics of Authorship in Archaic Greece," in *Theognis of Megara: Poetry and the Polis*, ed. J. Figueira and G. Nagy (Baltimore, 1985), 82–95; and L. Edmunds, "The Seal of Theognis," in *Poet, Public, and Performance in Ancient Greece*, ed. L. Edmunds and R. W. Wallace (Baltimore, 1997), 29–48. For Hesiod, see C. Calame, "Montagne des Muses et Mouséia: La consécration des *Travaux* et l'héroïsation d'Hésiode," in *La Montagne des Muses*, ed. A. Hurst and A. Schachter (Geneva, 1996), 43–56. G. Siebert, "Signatures d'artistes, d'artisans et de fabricants dans l'Antiquité classique," *Ktema* 3 (1978): 111–31, has studied the signatures of craftsmen as they relate to the social condition of these artists. The first objects to "express themselves" through writing are, of course, tombs; see J. Svenbro, "J'écris, donc je m'efface: L'énonciation dans les premières inscriptions grecques," in Detienne 1988, 459–79 (reprinted in *Phrasikleia: Anthropologie de la lecture en Grèce ancienne* [Paris, 1988], 33–52 = *Phrasikleia: An Anthropology of Reading in Ancient Greece* [Ithaca, 1993], 26–43).

6. These erotic inscriptions are collected from Attic pottery by J. D. Beazley, *Attic Black-Figure Vase-Painters* (Oxford, 1956), 664–78; *Attic Red-Figure Vase-Painters*, 2nd ed. (Oxford, 1963), 1559–1616 and 1698–99; and *Paralipomena*, 2nd ed. (Oxford, 1971), 317–19 and 505–8; see Calame 2000a, 21 and n. 6. [Translator's note: concerning the "enunciatee," see Calame 2000a (1995, 7 and n. 6).]

7. These different types of graphic utterances on archaic and classical Attic pottery manifest much greater variety of form than is apparent in the schematic presentation of them here. They have been studied by F. Lissarrague, who published some of the results of his research in "Paroles d'images: Remarques sur le fonctionnement de l'écriture dans l'imagerie attique," in *Écritures*, vol. 2, ed. A.-M. Christin (Paris, 1985), 71–89. One collection of them may be found in M. Guarducci, *Epigrafia greca*, vol. 3, *Epigrafi di carattere privato* (Rome, 1974), 329–34 and 377–87. More generally, on the first uses of the alphabetic writing system adopted from the Phoenicians, read the reflections of M. Detienne, "L'espace de la publicité: Ses opérateurs intellectuels dans la cité," in Detienne 1988, 29–81.

8. A few of these "sympotic" utterances have been studied by F. Lissarrague, *Un flot d'images: Une esthétique du banquet grec* (Paris, 1987), 119–33 (= *The Aesthetics of the Greek Banquet* [Princeton, 1990], 123–39).

9. The figurative, plastic role of iconographic inscriptions, whether they mean anything or not, has been analyzed by F. Lissarrague, "Graphein: Scrivere e disegnare," *Grafica* 3 (1987): 11–19. Some of the effects of the representation of figures as facing the viewer in archaic and classical images have been studied by F. Frontisi-Ducroux, "Au miroir du masque," in *La cité des images: Religion et société en Grèce ancienne* (Lausanne, 1984), 147–61, and "Face et profil: Les deux masques," in *Images et société en Grèce ancienne: L'iconographie comme méthode d'analyse*, ed. C. Bérard, C. Bron, and A. Pomari (Lausanne, 1987): 89–102. For the role of the gaze in the case of a monument of later date, see C. Bérard, "La Grèce en barbarie: L'apostrophe et le bon usage des mythes," in *Métamorphoses du mythe en Grèce antique*, ed. C. Calame (Geneva, 1988), 187–99. I have

attempted to define some of the kinds of enunciative significance that such play with the orientation of figures' gazes can have in "Quand regarder, c'est énoncer: Le vase de Pronomos et le masque," in *Images et société en Grèce ancienne,* 79–88 (reprinted in Calame 2000a, 165–90 [= 1995, 116–36]).

10. Red-figure cup, Berlin Staatliche Museen F 2285 (*ARV,* 2nd ed., 431.48 and 1653); cf. *CVA* Berlin, 2:29–30, with plates 77 and 78.

11. These different "pedagogical tools" are described and illustrated by F. A. G. Beck, *Album of Greek Education: The Greeks at School and at Play* (Sydney, 1975), 14–21. The fragmentary object hanging in the background of scene B is probably a knuckle-bone sack, which appears in other school scenes.

12. Given the position of the pedagogue (especially in scene B, where his body faces outward while his eyes are turned toward the interior scene), it may well be that this figure serves as a transition between the interior school scenes depicted on the outside of the cup and the exterior gymnasium scene appearing inside, at the center of the same object.

13. Homer, *Odyssey* 1.1; *Little Iliad* fr. 1 Bernabé; *Homeric Hymn to Aphrodite* 1. I have attempted to make an enunciative analysis of these preludes in Calame 2000a, 59–67 (= 1995, 35–54), where yet more examples are cited; see also chapter 1, §2.1.

14. The combination noun + epithet *Skámandros eúroos* is used by Homer, *Iliad* 7.239 (in connection with *amphí,* but in a different context) and 21.130 (*potamós*); *amphí* + accusative to designate a song's subject appears at *Homeric Hymns* 7.1, 19.1, 22.1, and 33.1. See also the (probably mutilated) verse of Terpander fr. 697 Page.

15. Cf. *Homeric Hymn to Demeter* 1 and *Homeric Hymns* 11.1, 13.1, 16.1, etc.

16. *Homeric Hymn* 19.1: *Amphí moi Hermeíao phílon gónon énnepe Moûsa; Homeric Hymn* 22.1: *Amphí Poseidáona theòn mégan árkhom' aeídein.*

17. The phenomenon wherein the nasal is omitted before a consonant has been well described by L. Threatte, *The Grammar of Attic Inscriptions,* vol. 1, *Phonology* (New York, 1980), 485–90.

18. Treatment of the diphthong as disyllabic and reduplication of the consonant to lengthen the preceding vowel are attested in epic poetry; see P. Chantraine, *Grammaire homérique,* vol. 1, *Phonétique et morphologie,* 2nd ed. (Paris, 1973), 51 and 63. In any case, the transcription of a geminate consonant as two letters only gradually became predominant over the course of the fifth century; see R. Meisterhans and E. Schwyzer, *Grammatik der attischen Inschriften,* 3rd ed. (Berlin, 1900), 93–97; on the cup analyzed here, the name of Hippodamas is itself transcribed *hipodamas.*

19. For numerous attestations of the *scriptio plena,* see Threatte [n. 17], 424–27. From a metrical standpoint, the elision is expected; see M. L. West, *Greek Meter* (Oxford, 1982), 10.

20. This phenomenon is attested, in particular, before a dental; see Threatte [n. 17], 488–89.

21. In addition to the elision, this hexameter presents two prosodic features that are expected in dactylic poetry: epic correption, in the shortening of *moi* in hiatus before *amphí,* and the treatment of *sk* in *skámandron* as not making the preceding vowel long by position. See West [n. 19], 11–12 and 17. Upon publication, this verse successively appeared as fr. lyr. adesp. 30 A Bergk, Stesichorus fr. 26 Diehl and fr. mel. adesp. 938 (e) Page.

22. The problem of the poetic use of forms with the ending -*oisa* and infinitives (especially short ones) with the suffix -*en* has been treated by C. O. Pavese, *Tradizione e generi poetici della Grecia arcaica* (Rome, 1972), 43–44 and 103–8. On the contraction of -*oo*- to -*ō*- as an Aeolic-Lesbian dialectal trait, see A. M. Bowie, *The Poetic Dialect of Sappho and Alcaeus* (New York, 1981), 96–97. This exceptional use of *omega* in a fifth-century Attic inscription has elicited comment in P. Kretschmer, *Die griechischen Vaseninschriften ihrer Sprache nach Untersucht* (Gütersloh, 1894), 104–7; and J. D. Beazley, "Hymn to Hermes," *American Journal of Archaeology* 52 (1948): 336–40. It is worth noting that the name Douris in the signature on the vase is written simply with an *o*.

23. The potsherd in question comes from a red-figure cup, Oxford G 138, 3, 5, 11 (*ARV,* 2nd ed., 326.93). The parallel with the Douris cup was made by Beazley [n. 22], 338; see also Lissarrague [n. 8], 129–31 (= 1990, 135–38). From a metrical standpoint, it is possible to identify a paroemiac (the second colon of a dactylic hexameter following a penthemimeral caesura) only if we allow the lengthening of the *iota* in *stesíkhoron.* It is worth noting that the paroemiac is widely used as a metrical unit in melic poetry, in particular by Stesichorus. See West [n. 19], 35 and 53,

along with B. Gentili and P. Giannini, "Preistoria e formazione dell'esametro," *Quaderni Urbinati di Cultura Classica* 26 (1977): 7–51.

24. This has rightly been observed by F. Chamoux, "Un vers épique mal lu," *Revue de Philologie* 44 (1970): 7–10, who, out of desperation, proposes reading *Moîsa moi amphì Skámandron <éph>eur' hôn árkhom' aeídein.* The conjectural insertion of the imperative *<éph>eure* and the relative *hôn* subordinates one of the two incomplete propositions to the other. No poet working in the archaic period, however, ever attributed the technical activity of a troubadour to the Muse; poets of this period either reserve that role for themselves (cf. Alcman fr. 39 Davies, Bacchylides fr. 5 Snell-Maehler, Pindar *Olympian* 3.4–9, etc.) or attribute it to the goddess of craft, Athena (Pindar, *Pythian* 12.7 and 22).

25. On the Ionians' adaptation of the Phoenician alphabet after it was imported to Greece by Cadmus, read Herodotus 5.57–61: the operation is *metarruthmízein* the Phoenician *grámmata* to the Greek (oral) language by adapting them to the *phoné;* see C. Calame, "Rythme, voix et mémoire de l'écriture en Grèce classique," in *Tradizione e innovazione nella cultura greca da Omero all'età ellenistica: Scritti in onore di Bruno Gentili,* vol. 2, ed. R. Pretagostini (Rome, 1993), 785–99. Prometheus, too, as the inventor of writing in classical tragedy, conceives of the alphabet in terms of its syntagmatic possibilities, rather than its paradigmatic dimension, as providing for the *grammáton sunthésis,* the "combining of letters"; Aeschylus, *Prometheus Bound* 460.

26. Horizontal and vertical alignment of letters is inaugurated around the middle of the sixth century by carvers of monumental inscriptions, who were concerned about ensuring legibility. The calligraphic rules they follow have been formulated and illustrated by R. Harder, "Rottenschrift," *Jahrbuch des Deutschen Archäologischen Instituts* 58 (1943): 93–132 (reprinted in *Das Alphabet: Entstehung und Entwicklung der griechischen Schrift,* ed. G. Pfohl [Darmstadt, 1968], 321–80); see the supplementary references and commentary on this topic in Detienne [n. 7], 36–37 and 47. These rules are respected, for example, in the inscription on the papyrus roll that is represented (in the same position as on the Douris cup) on the fragment of the red-figure cup by Acestorides, Greenwich Conn. Walter Bareiss 63 (*ARV,* 2nd ed., 1670, *Paralip.* 417); see H. R. Immerwahr, "More Book Rolls on Attic Vases," *Antike Kunst* 16 (1973): 143–47.

27. The presence of both a trithemimeral and a bucolic caesura without a central caesura in the same dactylic hexameter is contrary to the metrical rule structuring its rhythm; see West [n. 19], 35–36, and Fränkel 1960, 110–15.

28. It is probably not by mere chance that the biographical tradition attributes to Simonides (in addition to mnemonic techniques) the introduction of four new letters into the alphabet; see *Marmor Parium FGrHist.* 239 A 70 and Plutarch, *Quaestiones Convivales* 738f, with the commentary of Detienne 1995, 159–74 (= 1996, 147–59). The myth of Thoth is told by Socrates in Plato, *Phaedrus* 274d–5b; J. Derrida appropriated the episode in "La pharmacie de Platon," *Tel Quel* 32 (1968): 1–48, and *Tel Quel* 33 (1968): 18–59 (= "Plato's Pharmacy," in *Dissemination,* trans. B. Johnson [Chicago, 1981], 61–84). It is true that, in the *Timaeus* (24d–25d), the Egyptians can demonstrate their superiority over Solon because of their broader knowledge of the Athenian past, which they have been able to acquire thanks to writing (as illustrated by the Atlantis myth): refusing to commit one's voice (*phonê*) to writing means condemning a people's tradition to oblivion. Paradoxically, however, when Critias takes up the story of Atlantis in the dialogue bearing his name (*Critias* 108d), writing is no longer the issue; there, indeed, he appeals to Mnemosyne to help him remember what was said (*tà rhethénta*) to Solon by the Egyptian priests. This paradox should qualify the remarks formulated by M. Detienne, "La double écriture de la mythologie entre le *Timée* et le *Critias,*" in *Métamorphoses du mythe en Grèce antique,* ed. C. Calame (Geneva, 1988), 17–33 (reprinted in *L'Écriture d'Orphée* [Paris, 1989], 168–87 = *The Writing of Orpheus: Greek Myth in Cultural Context,* trans. J. Lloyd [Baltimore, 2002]). Aeschylus, after calling writing "the memory of everything" (*mnéme hapánton, Prometheus Bound* 459–61), uses a graphic metaphor to refer to the memorization that Prometheus bids Io to carry out: "inscribe (what I am going to tell you) on the memorial tablets in your heart" (*Prometheus Bound* 789; cf. *Eumenides* 275). As for Euripides, he attributes the invention of *grámmata* to Palamedes, who devised them as "remedies (*phármaka*) for forgetfulness" (fr. 578 Nauck, 2nd ed.).

29. Aeschylus, *Prometheus Bound* 461.

30. D. Bertrand proposes calling these two distinct modes of reference "referentialization" and "referenciation"; see his article "Référentialization," in *Sémiotique: Dictionnaire raisonné de la théorie du langage*, vol. 2, ed. A. J. Greimas and J. Courtès (Paris, 1986), 188–89, and introduction, §1.

31. This relationship between scene A and a sympotic occasion has rightly been noted by Lissarrague [n. 8], 132 (138–39 in the English translation). The rules concerning the proper way to perform *skólia* have been recapitulated for us by M. Vetta, "Poesia simposiale nella Grecia archaica e classica," in *Poesia e simposio nella Grecia antica*, ed. M. Vetta (Rome, 1983), xiii–lx; cf. the red-figure cup Munich Staatliche Antikensammlung 2646 (*ARV,* 2nd ed., 437.128) with the commentary by M. Wegner, *Das Musikleben der Griechen* (Berlin, 1949), 69–78 and 202–3.

32. Following others, I have attempted to show that—in the fifth century, at least—the pedagogical relationship on which the musical and gymnastic education of a young Greek (whether boy or girl) is based always had a homoerotic tinge; Calame 1977, 420–38 (= 1997, 244–63), and 1996a, 103–21 (= 1999, 91–108).

33. On the asymmetry of the homoerotic relationship in Greece, see K. J. Dover, *Greek Homosexuality* (London, 1978), 91–98; and G. Koch-Harnack, *Knabenliebe und Tiergeschenke: Ihre Bedeutung im päderastischen Erziehungssystem Athens* (Berlin, 1983), 34–42, particularly with the couples represented on the *kýlix* by Douris, Paris Louvre G121 (*ARV,* 2nd ed., 434.78).

34. Even when the vase is signed, it is difficult to determine exactly who it is that is "enunciating" the painted scene: the question of whether the signature refers to the painter, the potter, or the head of the workshop is far from resolved; see M. M. Eisman, "A Further note on EPOIESEN Signatures," *Journal of Hellenic Studies* 94 (1974): 172, and Siebert [n. 5], 114–21.

35. U. Eco, *Lector in fabula: La cooperazione interpretativa nei testi narrativi* (Milan, 1979), 67–85 (= *The Role of the Reader: Explorations in the Semiotics of Texts* [Bloomington, 1979]); on the return to the world in the act of reading and on narrative "refiguration," see P. Ricoeur, *Temps et récit,* vol. 1 (Paris, 1983), 109–24 (= *Time and Narrative,* vol. 1, trans. K. McLaughlin and D. Pellauer [Chicago, 1988]).

36. We may ultimately wonder if the verse written on the papyrus might not belong to an unfinished *skólion.* Indeed, we have the text of a series of these (anonymous) songs for banquets: frr. 884–917 Page. Unfortunately, none of their metrical structures (which have been analyzed by West [n. 19], 59–60) corresponds to the prosody of their utterance.

CHAPTER VI

1. Plato, *Republic* 392c–4b, with the commentary of P. Murray, *Plato on Poetry* (Cambridge, 1996), 168–72; and Calame 2000a, 22–23 (= 1995, 6–8). The mimetic aspect of Bacchylides' *Dithyramb* 18 has been highlighted by G. Ieranó, "Osservazioni sul Teseo di Bacchilide (*Dyth.* 18)," *Acme* 40 (1987): 88–103; and by B. Zimmermann, *Dithyrambos: Geschichte einer Gattung* (Göttingen, 1992), 95–105.

2. The aspects involved in the author's delegation of his voice to the various protagonists in classical tragedy have been the object of attention in the contribution of E. Hall, "Actor's Song in Tragedy," and in the essay I presented under the title "Performative Aspects of the Choral Voice in Greek Tragedy: Civic Identity in Performance," in *Performance Culture and Athenian Democracy,* ed. S. Goldhill and R. Osborne (Cambridge, 1999), 96–122 and 125–53, respectively.

3. Aristotle, *Poetics,* 1450a7–b20. The fragmented and unsystematic character of the *Poetics* is summed up well by M. Magnien, *Aristote: Poétique* (Paris, 1990), 19–24; see also S. Halliwell, *Aristotle's Poetics* (London, 1986), 1–41.

4. Aristotle, *Poetics,* 1453b1–14. The interlacing of descriptive, normative, and genetic (essentialist) perspectives in Aristotle's reflections on the poet's art is illuminated by J.-M. Schaeffer, *Qu'est-ce qu'un genre littéraire?* (Paris, 1989), 10–25.

5. Aristotle, *Poetics,* 1447a13–18. This distinction is made again with complete consistency in 1448a24–25. It is applied to tragedy in 1450a7–14 (a difficult passage which it is advisable to read

with the help of the commentary by R. Dupont-Roc and J. Lallot, *Aristote: La Poétique* [Paris, 1980], 199–203).

6. This distinction underlies the point about the perfecting of the form of tragedy at 1449a7–9. The items not treated in the *Poetics* are discussed by D. Lanza, *Aristotele: Poetica* (Milan, 1987), 32–44. On another matter, O. Taplin, *The Stagecraft of Aeschylus: The Dramatic Use of Exits and Entrances in Greek Tragedy* (Oxford, 1977), 477–79, has effectively demonstrated that *ópsis* designates not only straightforward spectacular effects (as described by Plutarch, *Glory of the Athenians* 348e–f) but also the totality of visual elements; see M. S. Silk, "The 'Six Parts of Tragedy' in Aristotle's *Poetics:* Compositional Process and Processive Chronology," *Proceedings of the Cambridge Philological Society* 40 (1994): 108–15.

7. Cf. *Poetics* 1450b16–18, 1449b24–28, 1452b28–30, and 1453b1–7. If one looks closely at the formulation of 1453b8–14, it is clear that not only "spectacle" but also, above all, "actions" must provoke pity and fear in order to induce the pleasure experienced in the performance of tragedy; the expression *en toîs prágmasin empoietéon* may, therefore, refer to the idea of "l'inscription des faits," as proposed by Dupont-Roc and Lallot [n. 5], 186–93. Alongside this admirable exegesis of *kátharsis* by the French commentators, one may profitably consult the restatements of D. W. Lucas, *Aristotle: Poetics* (Oxford, 1968), 273–90, and Halliwell [n. 3], 168–201, while noting that, in two places (1452b38 and 1453b6), fear and pity have as a complement *tò philánthropon:* the idea of order, of justice being done (on which see Dupont-Roc and Lallot [n. 5], 242–43; see also n. 30). Lucas (150) argues that the expression *ho toû Oidípou* at 1453b6 could refer equally well to the plot of the *Oedipus Tyrannus* or to the whole play, but not to the story of Oedipus.

8. Aristotle, *Poetics* 1455a22–33. The peculiar problem posed by a form of theater that has to put before its audience and make "effective" an action that is being performed by other means on stage is well presented by Dupont-Roc and Lallot [n. 5], 278–84. On syntactic grounds, the reading *enargéstata* is nevertheless preferable to the *lectio facilior, enérgestata;* see my arguments on this issue in "Quand dire c'est faire voir: L'évidence dans la rhétorique antique," *Études de lettres* 4 (1991): 3–22. In her article "Les mots qui voient," in *Essais sur l'interprétation des textes,* ed. C. Reichler (Paris, 1988), 157–82, N. Loraux has, perhaps, been excessively influenced by J. Lacan, *Le séminaire VII: L'éthique* (Paris, 1985), 295, when she seems to dismiss this coincidence of visual *léxis* and spectacle.

9. The etymological relationship between *oîda, eîdon,* and *video* is reaffirmed by Chantraine 1968, 779–80. In a figure of grating tragic irony, verse 397 offers (undoubtedly explicit) etymologizing wordplay on the name of Oedipus, linking it with *oîda;* see the comments by P. Pucci, *Oedipus and the Fabrication of the Father: "Oedipus Tyrannus" in Modern Criticism and Philosophy* (Baltimore, 1992), 34, 66–73, and 165–66; see also n. 15.

10. Aeschylus, *Seven against Thebes* 541 and 776 (*omósitos, harpáxandra*); see, earlier, Hesiod, *Theogony* 326 and *Oedipodea Arg.* Bernabé, as well as Pindar fr. 177d Maehler, which mentions the savage jaws of the Sphinx. Additional passages are cited by M. Delcourt, *Oedipe ou la légende du conquérant,* 2nd ed. (Paris, 1981), 104–40; her interpretation of the Sphinx as not only murderous prophetess but also demonic lover does not stand up to a comparison of the texts with the visual representations; see J.-M. Moret, *Oedipe, la Sphinx et les Thébains: Essai de mythologie iconographique,* vol. 1 (Geneva, 1984), 10–29 and 79–91. The ambiguity of the Sphinx's words is considered by C. Segal, *Interpreting Greek Tragedy: Myth, Poetry, Text* (Ithaca, 1986), and the tyrannical nature of its mode of speech is defined by A. Iriarte, "L'ogresse contre Thèbes," *Métis* 2 (1987): 91–105.

11. The course of the visual investigation conducted by Oedipus, which in fact constitutes the plot of the tragedy, has been traced step by step by D. Seale, *Vision and Stagecraft in Sophocles* (Chicago, 1982), 215–60. His careful study removes the need for a detailed analysis here. Although I must agree with Segal [n. 10], that, through the figures of the Sphinx and Apollo, the *Oedipus Tyrannus* constructs an opposition between "unintelligibility" and "intelligible speech," I would not go so far as to affirm that there is "convergence" between the animal's riddles and the god's oracles: to get from one to the other, Oedipus has to be transformed into a seer, a second Tiresias.

12. In two successive studies (one narrative, the other comparative), L. Edmunds has shown that, from the standpoint of plot, the resolution of the Sphinx's riddle is a doublet of the act of parricide, insofar as both constitute a means of gaining the power of kingship. The Sphinx

episode may thus be considered "secondary"; see *The Sphinx in the Oedipus Legend* (Königstein Ts., 1981), 1–39 (reprinted in *Oedipus: A Folklore Casebook*, ed. L. Edmunds and A. Dundes [New York, 1984], 147–73); and "La Sphinx thébaine et Paul Tyaing, l'Oedipe birman," in *Métamorphoses du mythe en Grèce antique*, ed. C. Calame (Geneva, 1988), 213–27. In the expression *pròs posí*, it is hard to see any reference to the content of the enigma, as suggested indirectly by one of the scholiast's interpretations (*ad Oedipum Tyrannum* 130, 170 Papageorgios and 106 Longo) and as argued more recently by C. Chase, "Oedipal Textuality: Reading Freud's Reading of Oedipus," *Diacritics* 9 (1979): 54–68 (reprinted in C. Chase, *Decomposing Figures: Rhetorical Readings in the Romantic Tradition* [Baltimore, 1986], 175–95); cf. R. D. Dawe, *Sophocles, Oedipus Tyrannus* (Cambridge, 1982), 102–3; cf. J. Bollack, *L'Oedipe roi de Sophocle: Le texte et ses interprétations*, 4 vols. (Lille, 1990), 2:72.

13. This transformation is described by Tiresias as a *sumphorá* (454), a reversal of fortune; reversal is a formative element of the tragic plot according to Aristotle (*Poetics* 1452a22–29), who cites the *Oedipus Tyrannus* precisely in connection with this issue; see Dupont-Roc and Lallot [n. 5], 231–32. On the whole scene of confrontation between Oedipus and Tiresias, see L. Edmunds, "The Teiresias Scene in Sophocles' *Oedipus Tyrannus*," *Syllecta Classica* 11 (2000), 34–73.

14. For the analysis of the "reversal" in *Oedipus Tyrannus*, the classic work remains that of J.-P. Vernant, "Ambiguïté et renversement: Sur la structure énigmatique d'Oedipe-Roi,' " in *Échanges et communications: Mélanges offerts à Claude Lévi-Strauss*, vol. 2 (Paris, 1970), 101–31 (reprinted in Vernant and Vidal-Naquet 1972, 101–31 = 1988, 113–40). The relationship between blindness and true vision is correctly stressed by R. Buxton, "Blindness and Limits: Sophocles and the Logic of Myth," *Journal of Hellenic Studies* 100 (1980): 22–37; while M. Coray, *Wissen und Erkennen bei Sophokles* (Basel, 1993), 169–70, insists on the power of *phroneín* as consciousness.

15. At verses 1031–36, the text establishes a probable relationship between Oedipus' name (derived in this case from *oídéo*, "swell") and the piercing of his feet. For another pun on the same name, see n. 9. This is not enough to justify the inclusion of Sophocles' Oedipus among limping tyrants, as has been suggested by, notably, J.-P. Vernant, "Le tyran boiteux: D'Oedipe à Périandre," *Le temps de la réflexion* 2 (1981): 235–55 (reprinted in J.-P. Vernant and P. Vidal-Naquet, *Oedipe et ses mythes* [Paris, 1986], 54–78), as well as M. Bettini and A. Borghini, "Edipo lo zoppo," in *Edipo: Il teatro greco e la cultura europea*, ed. B. Gentili and R. Pretagostini (Rome, 1986), 215–33. See my thoughts on the subject in "Le nom d'Oedipe," in Gentili and Pretagostini, *Edipo*, 395–407. Nevertheless, this new etymologizing wordplay on the name of Oedipus does reinforce the destructive gesture carried out against an identity founded, in a first etymological derivation, on (visual) knowledge (*oída*). For the relationship between the two *parechéseis*, see P. Pucci, "Reading the Riddles of *Oedipus Rex*," in *Language and the Tragic Hero: Essays on Greek Tragedy in Honor of Gordon Kirkwood*, ed. P. Pucci (Atlanta, 1988), 131–54. On the role played by *túkhe* in the destiny of Oedipus, see C. Segal, *Tragedy and Civilization: An Interpretation of Sophocles* (Cambridge, Mass., 1981), 211–4 and 227, as well as Pucci [n. 9], 70–72 and 79–89. See also n. 29.

16. The interpretations cited here are those proposed, respectively, by N. Loraux, "L'empreinte de Jocaste," *L'écrit du temps* 12 (1986): 35–54; Vernant [n. 14], 114–26; and G. Devereux, "The Self-Blinding of Oidipous in Sophokles: *Oidipous Tyrannos*," *Journal of Hellenic Studies* 93 (1973): 36–49 (which should be read from the skeptical perspective suggested by Buxton [n. 14], 33–34); see also L. Edmunds, "Il corpo di Edipo: Struttura psico-mitologica," in *Edipo* [n. 15], 237–53 (more thoughts on this subject in Pucci [n. 9], 76–78 and 153 with nn. 22–27).

17. Di Benedetto, *Sofocle* (Florence, 1983), 127–30, points out that, in contrast to the archaic conception of pollution caused by touching, the tactile gestures take on a strongly emotional quality here. On this issue, see also the remarks of C. Segal, *Oedipus Tyrannus: Tragic Heroism and the Limits of Knowledge* (New York, 1993), 140–42, who shows how Oedipus is transformed from virtual *pharmakós* into a being one can touch.

18. See the metrical analysis put forward by Bollack [n. 12], 314–15 and 327–28. On the meaning of these various cries of lamentation, see M. Alexiou, *The Ritual Lament in Greek Tradition* (Cambridge, 1974), 135–37. J. Gould, "The Language of Oedipus," in *Sophocles*, ed. H. Bloom (New York, 1990), 207–22, speaks of the "total alienation" that separates Oedipus from the chorus members in their capacity as citizens of Thebes.

19. The authenticity of these textually difficult closing lines (1524–30) is widely contested; cf. Dawe [n. 12], 247, and Bollack [n. 12], vol. 4, 1038–54. The "pathemic" dimension of discourse (understood as "all the properties of the sphere of passion that can be manifested") is defined and explored by A. J. Greimas and J. Fontanille, *Sémiotique des passions: Des états de choses aux états d'âme* (Paris, 1991), 83–99 (= *The Semiotics of Passions: From States of Affairs to States of Feeling,* trans. P. Perron and F. Collins [Minneapolis, 1993]). H.-T. Lehmann, *Theater und Mythos: Die Konstitution des Subjekts im Diskurs der antiken Tragödie* (Stuttgart, 1991), 44–50, notes that the tragic voice is often associated less with dialogue than with the expression of emotion.

20. Commentators on this passage are not sure whether the expression refers to the peaceful sleep enjoyed by the chorus before the fatal discovery or, rather, to a reaction of shame or a wish for death provoked by the revelation; cf. Dawe [n. 12], 220–21, and Bollack [n. 12], 3:816–18, who reasonably opts for the second interpretation.

21. Di Benedetto [n. 17], 121–27, has described the sympathetic interaction that arises between Oedipus and the chorus in this essential scene, while Segal [n. 17], 148–53, stresses the complementarity built up between the vision of the blinded Oedipus and the words describing what happened in the palace. W. B. Stanford, *Greek Tragedy and the Emotions* (London, 1983), 76–90, offers some thoughts on the role of the visual in arousing tragic emotions, especially through gestures.

22. Compare Aristotle, *Poetics* 1453b5, with line 1306 of *Oedipus Tyrannus;* see the whole passage of *Poetics* 1453b1–14, with the remarks of Lucas [n. 7], 149–50. On the interpretation of this passage, see the references given in n. 7. C. Segal, "Catharsis, Audience, and Closure in Greek Tragedy," in Silk 1996, 149–72, shows that the whole closing part of the *Oedipus Tyrannus* puts on stage those same emotions that are required of the audience.

23. In the tragedy, the term *oîktos (epoiktísai),* used by the chorus members to express their sense of pity at the sight of the blinded Oedipus (1296; cf. 1462, 1473, and 1508), is equivalent to the term *éleos* used elsewhere, notably in Aristotle; see Stanford [n. 21], 23–26. According to Segal [n. 22], 168, the cathartic effect of the emotions undergone by the leading players in the *Oedipus Tyrannus* is expressed in the tears they shed (1473, 1486). We may recall that it is particularly on the emotional level that the voice of the tragic chorus may coincide with the mood of the audience; see my thoughts on this subject in "From Choral Poetry to Tragic Stasimon: The Enactment of Women's Song," *Arion* 3, no. 3.1 (1994–5): 136–54. On the debated issue concerning the nature of the relationship between the tragic chorus and the public, see Calame [n. 2].

25. Aristotle, *Poetics* 1450b20, and Pollux 4.115; cf. Aristophanes, *Knights* 320–23, which claims that no *skeuopoiós* dared to make a mask representing Cleon (see chapter 7, §1.3). On the ritual and cultic aspects of tragic spectacle, see the contrasting views of R. Friedrich, "Something to Do with Dionysus? Ritualism, the Dionysiac, and the Tragic," and R. Seaford, "Something to Do with Dionysus: Tragedy and the Dionysiac: Response to Friedrich," in Silk 1996, 257–83 and 284–94.

25. See Calame 2000a, 139–63 (= 1995, 97–115), and also chapter 7. The ritual and cultic aspects of the dramatic performances at Athens have been reexamined by S. Goldhill, "The Great Dionysia and Civic Ideology," *Journal of Hellenic Studies* 107 (1987): 58–76 (reprinted in Winkler and Zeitlin 1989, 97–129). See also W. R. Connor, "City Dionysia and Athenian Democracy," in W. R. Connor et al., *Aspects of Athenian Democracy* (Copenhagen, 1990), 7–32; and, regarding the mask, R. Rehm, *Greek Tragic Theatre* (London, 1992), 13–14 and 39–42; as well as A. Henrichs, "'He Has a God in Him': Human and Divine in the Modern Perception of Dionysus," in *Masks of Dionysus,* ed. T. H. Carpenter and C. A. Faraone (Ithaca, 1993), 13–43.

26. See Chantraine 1968, 942, and the complementary observations of F. Frontisi-Ducroux, *Le Dieu-masque: Une figure de Dionysos à Athènes* (Paris, 1991), 9–12. The latter, while she makes much of the relationship between the Greek conception of the face and the gaze, nonetheless does not see that the gaze also animates the theatrical mask; accordingly, it is not possible for the mask to "erase and replace the face that it covers" (11).

27. This by way of reaction to the general interpretations of *Oedipus Tyrannus* cited in n. 16. For a critique of the application of the ritual concept of the *pharmakós* to the tragic figure of Oedipus, see W. Burkert, *Oedipus, Oracles, and Meaning: From Sophocles to Umberto Eco* (Toronto, 1991), 18–21; also Pucci [n. 9], 170–71, and R. D. Griffith, "Oedipus *Pharmakos*? Alleged Scapegoating in Sophocles' *Oedipus the King,*" *Phoenix* 47 (1993): 95–114. This self-referential questioning of the

actual ritual functions that the tragic actors take on is no less common from the lips of the chorus; for the *Oedipus Tyrannus,* see 895–99 with the pertinent discussion by A. Henrichs, " 'Why Should I Dance?': Choral Self-Referentiality in Greek Tragedy," *Arion* 3, no. 3.1 (1994–5): 56–111.

28. In this sense, it is perhaps no accident that Sophocles does not provide an explicit formulation of the Sphinx's riddle; this (deceptive) knowledge of the physical nature of human life, from childhood to old age, would, in that case, stand in opposition to the understanding that Oedipus acquires through the action of the play, which bears on the metaphysical nature of his own destiny and that of humankind in general. Without going this far, Pucci [n. 9], 148–59, has judiciously characterized the visual and cognitive reversal that Oedipus' self-blinding represents; see also S. Goldhill, "Exegesis: Oedipus (R)ex," *Arethusa* 17 (1984): 177–200, who traces on the linguistic plane the stages whereby the search for origins leads to self-blinding. In his comparative study of the different versions of the blinding of Tiresias, L. Brisson, *Le mythe de Tirésias: Essai d'analyse structurale* (Leiden, 1976), 29–45, has successfully shown that the Theban soothsayer has at his disposal a dispensation allowing him to cross the boundary between human and divine; see also L. Edmunds, "The Teiresias Scene in Sophocles' *Oedipus Tyrannus,*" *Syllecta Classica* 11 (2000): 33–73.

29. See on this topic the terms of the problem and the bibliography provided by Vernant and Vidal-Naquet 1972, 43–74.

30. Through his search for himself, Oedipus may be said to reach the limits of the human condition (see Buxton [n. 14], 35–37), but it is not the case that his knowledge takes him beyond them, as claimed by E. A. Bernidaki-Aldous, *Blindness in a Culture of Light: Especially the "Oedipus at Colonus" of Sophocles* (New York, 1990), 35–37 and 66–70, who believes that K. Reinhardt, *Sophokles* (Frankfurt, 1993), 139–44, supports her position; she forgets the incest and parricide, which are a part of Oedipus' fate as decreed by the gods (1175–85, 1360–65, etc.). See Segal [n. 17], 72–95.

31. The connection between self-knowledge and self-blinding in *Oedipus Tyrannus* has been usefully discussed by A. Cameron, *The Identity of Oedipus the King* (New York, 1968), 15–21, and by Seale [n. 11], 247–54. The central role of Apollo in the working out of Oedipus' fate, wherein chance (1080) becomes necessity, has been emphasized by J. Peradotto, "Disauthorizing Prophecy: The Ideological Mapping of *Oedipus Tyrannus,*" *Transactions of the American Philological Association* 122 (1992): 1–15. For F. Ahl, *Sophocles' Oedipus: Evidence and Self-Conviction* (Ithaca, 1991), 259–65, Oedipus' only success in his search for himself is convincing himself of the reality of a fate that is actually a fiction.

32. Gorgias fr. 11a.2–4 with 11.8–10 and 15–19 Diels-Kranz. It is relevant to note that in the treatise *On Non-being* (fr. 3.81–86 Diels-Kranz), sight and hearing take on a special status: in the context of a physiological conception of the senses, sight and hearing are able to present and reveal things, unlike *lógos,* which cannot be identified with reality and being. But Gorgias says nothing about how listening to speech fits into this picture. J. de Romilly, "Gorgias et le pouvoir de la poésie," *Journal of Hellenic Studies* 93 (1973): 155–62, has shed light on the historical antecedents of the Gorgianic conception of speech and poetry. Among others, C. P. Segal, "Gorgias and the Psychology of the *Logos,*" *Harvard Studies in Classical Philology* 66 (1962): 99–155, makes a connection between Gorgias' ideas on the effects of poetic language and the conception of *kátharsis* developed by Aristotle. An analogous theory of the emotions aroused by poetry is developed by Plato in *Ion* 535b–e; see R. Velardi, "Parola poetica e canto magico nella teoria gorgiana del discorso," in *Lirica greca e latina: Atti del Convegno di studi polacco-italiano* (Rome, 1990), 151–65; see also Calame 1996a, 49–52. For an overview of these theories on the emotions stirred by poetry, see the classic discussion by H. Flashar, "Die medizinischen Grundlagen der Lehre von der Wirkung der Dichtung in der griechischen Poetik," *Hermes* 84 (1956): 12–48.

33. On the voice of the chorus, see Calame [n. 2], 141–48.

CHAPTER VII

1. Aristophanes, *Acharnians* 440–41, citing a distorted version of Euripides fr. 698 Nauck, 2nd ed.; cf. the scholiast's comment on this verse (1.1B, 66 Koster) and the brief commentary of A. H.

Sommerstein, *The Comedies of Aristophanes,* vol. 1, *Acharnians* (Warminster, 1980), 178. The transformations that Telephus undergoes in the *Acharnians* have been perspicaciously described by H. P. Foley, "Tragedy and Politics in Aristophanes' *Acharnians,*" *Journal of Hellenic Studies* 108 (1988): 33–37. The character Dicaeopolis is, in and of himself, a mask; see T. K. Hubbard, *The Mask of Comedy* (Ithaca, 1991), 41–53.

2. These questions are but a rhetorical reformulation of the various normative assertions issuing from anthropology that H. Pernet critiques in *Mirages du masque* (Geneva, 1988), 17–30. Collections of studies such as the one published by F. Lupu, ed., *Océanie: Le masque au long cours* (Rennes, 1983), constitute a first step toward the undermining of this norm through the very plurality and variety of uses of masks that they address.

3. H. M. Cole, ed., *I Am Not Myself: The Art of African Masquerade* (Los Angeles, 1985), 19–27.

4. These traditional views concerning the functions of the different uses of masks in Greek culture are drawn (in order) from H. C. Baldry, *The Greek Tragic Theatre* (London, 1971), 79–83; K. J. Reckford, *Aristophanes' Old and New Comedy,* vol. 1 (Chapel Hill, 1987), 197–98; F. Frontisi-Ducroux and J.-P. Vernant, "Figures du masque en Grèce ancienne," *Journal de psychologie normale et pathologique* 80 (1983): 53–69 (reprinted in J.-P. Vernant and P. Vidal-Naquet, *Mythe et tragédie en Grèce ancienne,* vol. 2 [Paris, 1986], 25–43 = *Myth and Tragedy in Ancient Greece,* trans. J. Lloyd [Cambridge, Mass., 1988]), and "Divinités au masque dans la Grèce ancienne," in *Le masque: Du rite au théâtre,* ed. O. Aslan and D. Bablet (Paris, 1985), 19–26; J.-P. Vernant, *La mort dans les yeux: Figures de l'Autre en Grèce ancienne* (Paris, 1985), 80–87; J. M. Walton, *Greek Theatre Practice* (Westport, Conn., 1980), 170–75.

5. K. Meuli, *Gesammelte Schriften,* vol. 1 (Basel, 1985), 71–79.

6. I have developed these considerations in Calame 2000a, 139–63 (= Calame 1995, 97–115); for the narrative distinctions proposed by Plato, see 22–23 (= 6–8), which comment on *Republic* 392c–e.

7. Aelian, *Varia historia* 2.13 (= Aristophanes test. 32.10–25 Kassel-Austin); cf. Plato, *Apology* 19b–c (= Aristophanes test. 27.14–19 Kassel-Austin). On the Aristophanic portrait of Socrates, see K. J. Dover, *Aristophanes: Clouds* (Oxford, 1968), xxxii–xlvii.

8. Aristophanes, *Knights* 225–34; cf. the scholion on verse 230 (1.2, 56 Koster) and Aristophanes test. 1.10–18 Kassel-Austin. The traditional interpretation of this passage is maintained on the basis of inference by K. J. Dover, "Portrait-Masks in Aristophanes," in *KOMOIDOTRAGEMATA: Studia Aristophanea viri Aristophanei W. J. W. Koster in honorem* (Amsterdam, 1967), 16–28 (reprinted in *Aristophanes und die alte Komödie,* ed. H. J. Newiger [Darmstadt, 1975], 155–69). It is true that Cratinus presents hideous eyebrows as the distinctive trait of Cleon (fr. 228 Kassel-Austin); see D. Welsh, "*Knights* 230–3 and Cleon's Eyebrows," *Classical Quarterly,* n.s., 29 (1979): 214–15. Dover adds, on the basis of *Wasps* 1031–35 (where Cleon is presented as a monster with a terrifying look), that the costumer's apprehension of representing the demagogue is motivated less by fear of reprisals than by the ghastly aspect of the mask to be made: this is, in fact, the interpretation proposed by the scholiast. On the custom of masking the face of the actor-author by simply using white lead face paint (a custom that is attributed to the earliest stages of tragic theater), see Calame 2000a, 143–44 with n. 6 (= Calame 1995, 100–102 with n. 6).

9. Pollux 4.143; Platonius, *De differentia comoediarum* 13 (5, 61–67 Kaibel), with the commentary of F. Perusino, *Platonio: La commedia greca* (Urbino, 1989), 61–62; see also *Suda,* s.v. *exeikasménos* (E 1693 Adler), and the scholion on *Clouds* 146 (1.3.1, 43 Koster). Other examples of portrait masks are presented by A. Pickard-Cambridge, *The Dramatic Festivals of Athens,* 2nd ed. (Oxford, 1968), 218–19; and by L. M. Stone, *Costume in Aristophanic Comedy* (New York, 1981), 35–42. The law prohibiting direct attacks in comedy is mentioned by the scholia to Aelius Aristides, *Orations* 3.4 (3:444 Dindorf = Aristophanes test. 26 Kassel-Austin); further references may be found in Foley [n. 1], 33–34.

10. These documents have been catalogued by T. B. L. Webster, *Monuments Illustrating Old and Middle Comedy, Bulletin of the Institute of Classical Studies,* Supplement 29, 2nd ed. (London, 1969): 19–25. A history of the iconographic representation of the comic costume has been outlined by L. Bernabò Brea, *Menandro e il teatro greco nelle teracotte liparesi* (Genova, 1981), 11–20; the comic costume is also briefly described by L. Aylen, *The Greek Theater* (Cranbury, N.J., 1985), 100–104,

and, in more detail, by Stone [n. 9], 60–243. The ritual and self-referential effects of the comic mask and costume have been well analyzed in the study by H. P. Foley, "The Comic Body in Greek Art and Drama," in *Not the Classical Ideal: Athens and the Construction of the Other in Greek Art,* ed. B. Cohen (Leiden, 2000), 275–311.

11. Red-figure *choûs* from Cyrenaica, Paris Louvre, N 3408 (*ARV,* 2nd ed., 1335.34); for other iconographic documents, see the plates in Pickard-Cambridge [n. 9], 210–29, and Stone [n. 9], 456–503; see also J. R. Green, "Dedications of Masks," *Revue d'archéologie* 2 (1982): 237–48, and the corpus astutely commented on by O. Taplin, *Comic Angels and Other Approaches to Greek Drama through Vase-Painting* (Oxford, 1993), 30–47.

12. Apulian *kratér* from S. Agata dating from ca. 370 (*RVAp* 96.4/224), with commentary by Taplin [n. 11], 83–87, who draws a parallel between this "paraiconography" and the paratragedy practiced in comedy itself. Concerning this topic, Dover [n. 7], 168–69, explains that Aristophanes did not leave out the phallic member from the comic costume in the *Clouds,* but the poet refused to use it to the same effect as some of his contemporaries. J. F. Killeen, "The Comic Costume Controversy," *Classical Quarterly,* n.s., 21 (1971): 51–54, and Stone [n. 9], 72–126, have surveyed the debate over the interpretation of this passage of the *Clouds;* in the same chapter Stone provides an exhaustive list of allusions to phalluses in Aristophanes.

13. For the protruding belly, see Aristophanes, *Clouds* 1237–38, *Frogs* 663–64, etc.

14. Aristophanes, *Plutus,* 557–61, *Thesmophoriazousae* 142 and 191–92. The distinctive traits differentiating men from women and the frequent play with cross-dressing that the interchanging of these signs makes possible have been carefully analyzed by S. Saïd, "Travestis et travestissements dans les comédies d'Aristophane," in *Anthropologie et théâtre antique, Cahiers du GITA,* vol. 3, ed. P. Ghiron-Bistagne (Montpellier, 1987), 217–48. As has been noted by A. Ubersfeld, *Lire le théâtre* (Paris, 1977), 128–42, the dramatic protagonist always assumes (from a semiotic standpoint) a plurality of very different roles and references.

15. Aristophanes, *Thesmophoriazousae* 4, *Frogs* 758 and 183–84, *Thesmophoriazousae* 98 (Agathon's costume is described in vv. 136–45) and 233–37, *Frogs* 22, 42–48 and 494–502. The Heraclean paraphernalia donned by Dionysus is explicitly characterized as *mímesis* (vv. 108–9). On the proper name as a "rigid designator," see Calame 2000a, 139–41 (= 1995, 174–75).

16. Aristophanes, *Thesmophoriazousae* 243–68, *Acharnians* 442–43, *Knights* 232–33, *Birds* 801–8, *Frogs* 12–18; see Saïd [n. 14], 223–27. D. Auger, "Le jeu de Dionysos: Déguisements et métamorphoses dans *Les Bacchantes* d'Euripide," *Nouvelle revue d'ethnopsychiatrie* 1 (1983): 57–80, has well indicated the differences distinguishing the dressing up in disguises in comedy from the kind of metamorphosis that can be found in tragedy (72–73).

17. Aristophanes, *Clouds* 340–44. The numerous variations on dressing up in costume found in comic parodies of tragedy have been enumerated by P. Rau, *Paratragodia: Untersuchung einer komischen Form des Aristophanes* (Munich, 1967), 10–27; they have been emphasized by F. Zeitlin, "Travesties of Gender and Genre in Aristophanes' *Thesmophoriazousae,"* in *Reflections of Women in Antiquity,* ed. H. P. Foley (New York, 1981), 169–217 (reprinted in Zeitlin 1996, 375–416). For the different ways in which *choreutaí* dress up, see the figurative and literary documents gathered by A. Pickard-Cambridge, *Dithyramb, Tragedy, and Comedy,* 2nd ed. (Oxford, 1962), 151–62; and by G. M. Sifakis, *Parabasis and Animal Choruses: A Contribution to the History of Attic Comedy* (London, 1971), 73–82.

18. Aristophanes, *Plutus* 1050–65, with the commentary of F. Frontisi-Ducroux, "*Prosopon*: Le masque et le visage," in Ghiron-Bistagne, *Anthropologie et théâtre antique* [n. 14], 83–92. On the double meaning of *rhákos,* see the scholion at Aristophanes, *Frogs* 406 (287b Dübner).

19. On this issue, see the analysis of D. Auger, "Le théâtre d'Aristophane: Le mythe, l'utopie et les femmes," *Cahiers de Fontenay* 17 (1979): 71–101.

20. Aristotle, *Poetics* 1447a13–18, 1448a16–18, 1448a24–28, and 1449a31–35; see R. Dupont-Roc and J. Lallot, *Aristote: La Poétique* (Paris, 1980), 161–62 and 178–79. On the Aristotelian concept of *geloîon* as the essence of comedy, see D. Lanza, "La simmetria impossibile: Commedia e comica nella *Poetica* di Aristotele," in *Filologia e forme letterarie: Studi offerti a Francesco della Corte* (Urbino, 1988), 65–80.

21. Aristophanes, *Acharnians* 497–508, 628–36, 655–58, etc. On this subject, see the sensible remarks of A. Bowie, "The Parabasis in Aristophanes: Prolegomena, *Acharnians,"* *Classical Quarterly,*

n.s., 32 (1982): 27–40; and of F. Perusino, *Dalla Commedia antica alla Commedia di mezzo: Tre studi su Aristofane* (Urbino, 1987), 17–33.

22. The question of the authority to which the voices uttering the parabasis are to be referred in the comedies of Aristophanes has been addressed by Sifakis [n. 17], passim; Reckford [n. 4], 483–91; and Goldhill 1991, 196–205.

23. This play has been highlighted, in comparison with tragedy, by O. Taplin, "Fifth-Century Tragedy and Comedy: A *Synkrisis*," *Journal of Hellenic Studies* 106 (1986): 163–74. See also A. D. Napier, *Masks, Transformation, and Paradox* (Berkeley, 1986), 34–39, who is sensitive to the commentary on the dramatic action itself as made possible by the costume and mask.

24. We know about the way in which this *ekklesía* was conducted from Demosthenes 21.8–10; see Pickard-Cambridge [n. 9], 64–70.

25. Concerning the civic and political character of the Great Dionysia, see the references provided in chapter 4, n. 25.

26. Cf. Aristophanes test. 1.19–31 Kassel-Austin (= *Bab.* T V), which is probably constructed from *Acharnians* 377–84 and 502–8 (= test. 24 Kassel-Austin); see also the scholion at *Acharnians* 378 (1.1B, 59 Koster = *Bab.* T IV). On this putative trial, see Perusino [n. 21], 19–24; T. Gelzer, "Aristophanes 12," in *Realenc. Alt.-Wiss. Suppl.* 12 (Stuttgart, 1970), cols. 1392–1569 (cols. 1398–1401), and M. Heath, *Political Comedy in Aristophanes* (Göttingen, 1987), 16–19 and 27.

CHAPTER VIII

1. The argumentative procedures of the first Greek technical treatises in prose have begun to be studied; see, in particular, G. E. R. Lloyd, *Magic, Reason, and Experience: Studies in the Development of Greek Science* (Cambridge, 1979), 86–97 (on the rhetoric of scientific treatises), as well as J. Althoff, "Formen der Wissensvermittlung in der frühgriechischen Medizin" (on the didactic character and the audience of the Hippocratic treatises), and G. F. Nieddu, "Neue Wissensformen, Kommunikationstechniken und schriftliche Ausdrucksformen in Griechenland im sechsten und fünften Jahrhundert v. Chr." (concerning the use made of several rhetorical figures), in *Vermittlung und Tradierung von Wissen in der griechischen Kultur*, vol. 61 (*ScriptOralia*) ed. W. Kullmann and J. Althoff (Tübingen, 1993), 211–23 and 151–65, respectively. For the techniques of persuasion, see G. E. R. Lloyd, *Adversaries and Authorities: Investigations in Greek and Chinese Science* (Cambridge, 1996), 74–92.

2. Hippocrates, *On the Art of Medicine* 1.1 (6:2, 1–3 Littré); cf. Herodotus' prelude. The terms of the debate concerning the quality of the author of the Hippocratic treatise are provided by J. Jouanna, *Hippocrate*, vol. 1, *Des vents, De l'art* (Paris, 1988), 167–83, who emphasizes the epideictic character of this treatise; see also the study by the same author, *Hippocrate* (Paris, 1992), 344–59. The necessary information concerning the meaning of *historía* and *apódeixis* may be found in my book, Calame 2000a, 115–25 (= 1995, 78–96). For a comparison of the two texts, see R. Thomas, "Performance and Written Publication in Herodotus," in Kullmann and Althoff, *Vermittlung und Tradierung von Wissen* [n. 1], 225–44, who is sensitive to the "proofs" and "testimonies" that the two treatises so often claim to provide; see also on this issue the study of S. Humphreys, "From Riddle to Rigour: Satisfactions of Scientific Prose in Ancient Greece," in *Proof and Persuasion: Essays on Authority, Objectivity, and Evidence*, ed. S. Marchand and E. Lunbeck (Turnhout, 1996), 3–24.

3. Hippocrates, *Oath* (4:630, 10–11 Littré); see on this passage the commentary of H. von Staden, "Character and Competence: Personal and Professional Conduct in Greek Medicine," in *Médecine et morale dans l'Antiquité*, vol. 43 of *Entretiens sur l'Antiquité Classique* (Vandoeuvres, 1997), 157–95.

4. "Nègre," in *Encyclopédie ou Dictionnnaire raisonné des sciences, des arts et des métiers*, vol. 11 (Neuchâtel, 1765), 76b–79a; Voltaire, *Essai sur les moeurs et l'esprit des Nations* (Paris, 1963), 1:6 (original edition: Geneva, 1756 and 1769). Naturally, in contrast to these reflections at the foundations of racism, we may cite the ironical critique that Montesquieu made of them in *De l'esprit des lois*, 4th ed. (Paris, 1757), 15:5.

5. See on this issue L. Poliakov, C. Delacampagne, and P. Girard, *Le racisme* (Paris, 1976), 59–68; and M. Duchet, *Anthropologie et histoire au siècle des Lumières,* 2nd ed. (Paris, 1995) 194–226 (colonialism) and 281–321 (Voltaire).

6. B. de Las Casas, *Très brève relation de la destruction des Indes* (Paris, 1979), 49–50 (first published as *Brevissima relación de la destruycion de las Indias* [Seville, 1552–53]).

7. C. von Linné, *Systema Naturae, per regna tria naturae,* vol. 1, 13th ed. (Vienna, 1767), 28–29 (first publication: Leyden, 1735); G. L. Leclerc de Buffon, *Histoire naturelle: De l'homme* (Paris, 1971), 318–25 (first publication: Paris, 1749; = *Natural History, General and Particular,* trans. W. Smellie [Bristol, 2000], a reprint of the third edition of Smellie's translation, originally published in 1791). On this topic, see L. Poliakov, "Brève histoire des hiérarchies raciales," *Le genre humain* 1 (1981): 70–82.

8. See, on this topic, N. Fresco, "Aux beaux temps de la craniologie," *Le genre humain* 1 (1981): 107–16; and A. Jacquard, "Biologie et théorie des 'élites,'" ibid., 14–54; see also, by Jacquard, *Éloge de la différence* (Paris, 1978), 81–92, as well as the reflections of J. Ruffié, "Le mythe de la race," in *Le racisme: Mythes et sciences,* ed. M. Olender (Brussels, 1981), 357–65. The (late) emergence of the term "racism" and of the corresponding concept have been discussed by P. A. Taguieff, *La force du préjugé: Essai sur le racisme et ses doubles* (Paris, 1987), 49–138; cf. the necessary critical remarks formulated, for example, by M. Wieviorka, *Le racisme: Une introduction* (Paris, 1998), 135–45 (concerning a book that stakes its claim on the universality of individual freedom), and by A. Rivera, *Estranei e nemici: Discriminazione e violenza razzista in Italia* (Rome, 2003), 12–39 (through the concept of discrimination).

9. On this approach of assimilating a numerical scale to a scale of values, see the edifying reflections of A. Jacquard, *Moi et les autres* (Paris, 1983), 62–72.

10. See C. Lévi-Strauss, *Race et histoire* (Paris, 1961), 19–26 (reprinted in *Anthropologie structurale,* vol. 2 [Paris, 1974], 377–422, esp. 382–87 = *Structural Anthropology,* vol. 2, trans. M. Layton [New York, 1976], 232–62).

11. The story has been collected by M. Stanek, *Sozialordnung und Mythik in Palimbei,* vol. 22 of *Basler Beiträge zur Ethnologie* (Basel, 1983), 200–204.

12. C. Delacampagne, *L'invention du racisme: Antiquité et Moyen Âge* (Paris, 1983), 175–87.

13. This is, in any case, the meaning generally assigned to the term *barbaróphonos* used by Homer, *Iliad* 2.267; cf. *Odyssey* 8.294, with the commentary of H. Schwabl, "Das Bild der Fremden Welt bei den frühen Griechen," in *Grecs et Barbares,* vol. 8 of *Entretiens sur l'Antiquité Classique* (Vandoeuvres, 1962), 1–36; and E. Lévy, "Naissance du concept de barbare," *Ktema* 9 (1984): 5–14.

14. See, for example, *Odyssey* 6.119–26 (the encounter with the Phaeacians) or 9.170–92 (discussion of the customs of the Cyclopes). On the utopian aspects of this exploration of the limits of civilization and the forms of life through Odysseus' journey, see P. Vidal-Naquet, "Valeurs religieuses et mythiques de la terre et du sacrifice dans l'*Odyssée,*" *Annales E.S.C.* 25 (1970): 1278–97 (reprinted in Vidal-Naquet 1983, 151–76 = 1986, 15–38); see also F. Hartog, *Mémoire d'Ulysse: Récits sur la frontière en Grèce ancienne* (Paris, 1996), 29–34 (= *Memories of Odysseus: Frontier Tales from Ancient Greece,* trans. J. Lloyd [Chicago, 2001]).

15. On the confrontation with Polyphemus, who is ultimately relegated to the category of savage, see, for example, Homer, *Odyssey* 9. 119, 128, 352, 502, etc. In Homer, the term *génos* generally designates the (human or divine) group as comprising descendants from a common ancestor; see F. Bourriot, *Recherches sur la nature du génos* (Lille, 1976), 240–57.

16. The collective term *ánthropoi,* as used in Homeric poetry, includes all human beings, as opposed to gods and monsters; thus, it corresponds to a notion that is close to that of the "human race"; see H. Seiler, "*Anthropoi,*" *Glotta* 32 (1953): 225–36. Herodotus speaks of a *génos anthrópon* at 2.15.3. On the generally open acceptance of foreigners in Greece during the "archaic" period, see M.-F. Baslez, *L'étranger dans la Grèce antique* (Paris, 1984) (this work was kindly brought to my attention by P. Ducrey); significantly, there was no corresponding legal or political category for the foreigner at that time.

17. Cf. Pindar, *Pythian* 11.51–52 (within the context of the Pythian Games), Aeschylus, *Persians* 334 (facing the Persian naval fleet), Herodotus 1.56.2 (historically, in relation to the Pelagians), 1.60 and 4.108 (concerning barbarians or a foreign people); see also the remarks along these

lines byThucydides 1.3.3.This emergence of national consciousness is illustrated by H. Diller,"Die Hellenen-Barbaren-Antithese im Zeitalter der Perserkriege," in *Grecs et Barbares* [n. 13], 39–82; and by M. I. Finley, "The Ancient Greeks and Their Nation," *British Journal of Sociology* 5 (1954): 253–64, reworked and reprinted in *The Use and Abuse of History*, 2nd ed. (NewYork, 1975), 120–33; on the evidence constituted by Aeschylus' *Persians,* see E. Hall, *Inventing the Barbarian: Greek Self-Definition through Tragedy* (Oxford, 1989), 69–98.

18. Herodotus 8.144.2; also 1.4.4. On the Greek assembly that was provoked by the menace of invasion by Xerxes as pursuing a common aim (*es toutó*) and reflecting the first consciousness in terms of the *Hellenikón,* see 7.145.2; cf. Hartog [n. 14], 89–95. It is true that the term *Panéllenes* had already been used by Hesiod, *Works* 528 and fr. 130 Merkelbach-West, and by Archilochus, fr. 102 West, but to make an essentially ethnic reference; on this question, see the the the commentaries of Diller [n. 17], 45–46, and West, 1978, 292, as well as the study by E. Lévy,"Apparition des notions de Grec et de Grèce," in *Hellenismos,* ed. S. Saïd (Leiden, 1991), 49–69.

19. Herodotus 3.98–101.

20. Herodotus 3.102–5; on the best products of the earth and their location at the *éskhata:* 3.106.1 and 3.116.2; see also 1.142.1 and 1.149.2 with n. 47.The utopian traits attributed to the tribes at the farthest reaches of the earth are discussed by P. Cartledge, *The Greeks: A Portrait of Self and Others* (Oxford, 1993), 76–80.

21. Herodotus 1.194.196 and 199; see F. Heinimann, *Nomos und Physis* (Basel, 1945), 78–85, and Cartledge [n. 20], 36–42 and 59–62. In this regard, the study of Hartog 1992, 225–69 (= 1988), which is otherwise quite suggestive and sensitive to the phenomenon of the assimilation of the "other" to oneself, is too exclusively focused on the binary opposition between the different and the same; the binary image that is given of Herodotus' thought partially results from the point of view adopted in the book, which is essentially focused on the stories of the Halicarnassian "anthropologist" about the Scythians. For another binary, though more nuanced, approach, see the study of J. Redfield, "Herodotus the Tourist," *Classical Philology* 80 (1985): 97–118; see also A. Corcella, *Erodoto e l'analogia* (Palermo, 1984), 84–91.

22. We may also note that often, according to the classical Greek point of view, it is not nature that is the origin of culture but the reverse.

23. Cf. Thales frr. 11 A 14 and 15 Diels-Kranz; also Herodotus 7.129.4. On the concepts at the foundations of Greek science, see (by a Hellenist) G. E. R. Lloyd, *Early Greek Science* (London, 1970), 8–23; and (by a physicist and specialist of epistemology) A. Avramesco, "The Einstein-Bohr Debate I. The Background," in *Microphysical Reality and Quantum Formalism,* ed. A. van der Merwe et al. (Leuwen, 1988), 299–308.

24. Hippocrates, *On the Sacred Disease* 1–2 and 21; see G. E. R. Lloyd, "The Hot and the Cold, the Dry and the Wet in Greek Philosophy," *Journal of Hellenic Studies* 82 (1962): 56–66, and *Magic, Reason, and Experience* [n. 1], 15–27. The author of *On Airs, Waters, and Places* is more ambiguous in his critique of the divine origin of disease in general; see section 22, concerning the sexual impotence of the Anarieis and their feminization (see n. 38). For the treatment of this question in Hippocratic medicine in general, see L. Edelstein, "Greek Medicine in Its Relation to Religion and Magic," *Bulletin of the Institute for the History of Medicine* 5 (1937): 201–46 (reprinted in *Ancient Medicine* [Baltimore, 1967], 205–46), and Jouanna 1988 [n. 2], 259–97.

25. On the profession of physician-artisan and the figure of the traveling doctor in the classical period, see L. Edelstein, *"Perì aéron" und die Sammlung der hippokratischen Schriften* (Berlin, 1931), 89–107 (reprinted in English translation in *Ancient Medicine* [n. 24], 87–110); and H. M. Koelbing, *Artzt und Patient in der antiken Welt* (Zurich, 1977), 132–41.

26. There are countless theses concerning the constitution of the *Hippocratic Corpus* and the composition of various treatises that were integrated into it. On the treatise *On Airs, Waters, and Places,* the question is complicated by the fact that some have wanted to attribute the two consecutive parts of the treatise to two different authors. For an overview of the issue, see J. Jouanna, *Hippocrate,* vol. 2, pt. 2, *Airs, eaux, lieux* (Paris, 1996), 15–21 and 79–82, who supports the unity of the treatise and dates it to around 430; see also G. E. R. Lloyd, *The Revolutions of Wisdom: Studies in the Claims and Practice of Ancient Greek Science* (Berkeley, 1987), 26–30. On the textual

tradition of the treatise, see H. Diller, "Nochmals: Überlieferung und Text der Schrift von der Umwelt," in *Festschrift E. Kapp* (Hamburg, 1958), 31–49; and H. Grensemann, "Das 24. Kapitel von *De aeribus, aquis, locis* und die Einheit der Schrift," *Hermes* 107 (1979): 423–41. For the title of the treatise, consult the critical apparatus of the edition used for the present study, H. Diller, *Hippokrates: Über die Umwelt* (Berlin, 1970), 24. This treatise will henceforth be cited as *Airs*.

27. On the theory of the four humors in general and its role in the Hippocratic school of medicine, see Hippocrates, *On the Nature of Man* 7–8, and *Ancient Medicine* 14; Alcmaeon fr. 24 B 4 Diels-Kranz; see also Plato, *Symposium* 188a. On this topic, see also F. Jürss, ed., *Geschichte der wissenschaftlichen Denkens im Altertum* (Berlin, 1982), 312–21; and L. Ayache, *Hippocrate* (Paris, 1992), 62–65. It should be noted that the author of *On Airs, Waters, and Places* largely confines his discussion to phlegm and yellow bile; the constant shifting back and forth between a binary scheme and a quaternary one in the *Hippocratic Corpus* has been the object of comment by V. Langholf, "Über die Kompatibilität einiger binärer und quaternärer Theorien im *Corpus Hippocraticum*," in *Hippocratica: Actes du Colloque hippocratique de Paris*, ed. M. D. Grmek (Paris, 1980), 333–46. For the designation of the human constitution as a nature (*phúsis*) in the treatise, see n. 30.

28. Cf. *Airs* 3–6 and 10–11; chap. 10.12 shows the necessity of the conjunction of two qualities belonging to distinct oppositional pairs, the warm of the summer and the dry of the north wind, in order to dry out excessively wet, phlegmatic constitutions, but the effect of this conjunction of qualities on bilious constitutions is obviously the exact opposite. The contrast between two very distinct seasons is particularly pernicious (the contrast between a dry winter accompanied by a cold wind and a wet spring with a warm wind: 10.3–4; the contrast between a rainy, mild winter and a dry, cold spring: 10.5–6; cf. 10.10 and 11). An analogous principle is expressed in the treatise *On the Sacred Disease*, e.g., sec. 13.2. On the harmful effect of sudden climatic changes, see Herodotus 2.77.3; within the Hippocratic school itself, see *A Regimen for Health* 1.2, *Aphorisms* 3.1, etc.; see also J. Desautels, *L'image du monde selon Hippocrate* (Quebec, 1982), 29–51.

29. On medical thought in traditional cultures, with what is often a cosmic dimension, see G. R. Cardona, *La foresta di piume: Manuale di etnoscienza* (Rome, 1985), 67–78.

30. On the use of the term *phúsis* in *Airs* in the sense of the "nature of the human organism" or "human nature," see, for example, 9.4, 10.6, 10.12, etc. The idea of the unity of human nature and, consequently, of humankind is common in the fifth century: see Antiphon fr. 87 B 44 Diels-Kranz, Euripides fr. 52 Nauck (2nd ed.), Hippocrates, *Prognostics* 25 (quoted in the text), etc., along with the reflections of H. C. Baldry, "The Idea of the Unity of Mankind," in *Grecs et Barbares* [n. 13], 167–204, and the additional references provided in n. 15.

31. On the influence of the "nature of the country" (*tês khóres he phúsis*) as compounding the impact of the climate, see *Airs* 13.2. It is easy to imagine how this apparent about-face gave rise to an interminable philological debate concerning the identity of the author of the treatise's two parts. The most cogent argument for the unity of the treatise is that of M. Pohlenz, *Hippokrates und die Begründung der wissenschaftlichen Medizin* (Berlin, 1938), 27–41; see also the references provided in n. 26.

32. *Airs* 23.1–8; on the sequence of reasoning going from climates to *phúseis* (understood here as human natures or constitutions) to *eídea* (morphologies) to *éthea* (characters), see 24.7. Another sequence is boiled down to a relationship of cause and effect between climate and character; see 16.1–2.

33. *Airs* 24.8–11. In sec. 13.3–4, analogy is consciously employed in the line of reasoning, and the different human "natures" (*phúseis*) are explicitly compared, on the one hand, to marshy pasturelands and, on the other, to the arid deserts underlying them.

34. On technical intelligence as the foundation on which craft activities are based and, consequently, as one of the cardinal aspects of the Greek representation of both the mastery over wild natural forces and the establishment of civilization, see M. Detienne and J.-P. Vernant, *Les ruses de l'intelligence: La mètis des Grecs* (Paris, 1974), 61–103 and 167–75 (= *Cunning Intelligence among the Greeks* [Atlantic Highlands, N.J., 1978]).

35. *Airs* 23.5–8. It is through the combined effects of nature (a cold and wet climate) and custom (constant horseback riding) that men among the Anareis (see n. 40) and the Scythians become more generally, sexually impotent eunuchs; cf. 22.10–12.

36. See Jouanna [n. 26], 64–67, 224, and 304–5. The idea that certain traits of a *phúsis* are acquired also appears in Democritus, fr. 68 B 33 Diels-Kranz, and Euripides, *Ion* 642–44. On the attempts made in the fifth century to get beyond the antithesis of *nómos* and *phúsis,* see the reflections of Heinimann [n. 21], 27–41 and 163–69.

37. *Airs* 16.7; in Asia, too, there are combative peoples.

38. *Airs* 12.1–3, 16.1, and 23.1; on the notion of *krêsis,* see Jouanna [n. 26], 294–96.

39. The underlying orientation of this image of the inhabited world is made explicit by A. Ballabriga, *Le Soleil et le Tartare* (Paris, 1986), 175–77, with the complementary remarks of Desautels [n. 28], 46–51 and 143–47, and Ayache [n. 27], 38–41. For the geographical component of this representation, see O. A. W. Dilke, *Greek and Roman Maps* (Ithaca, 1985), 27–39.

40. On the Scythians, see *Airs.* 18–22. On the Anarieis, see *Airs* 22, Herodotus 1.105 and 4.67, and Aristotle, *Nicomachean Ethics* 7.7.6 (= 1150b14–22). While Herodotus still attributes this "feminine disease" among the Anarieis to the goddess Aphrodite, Aristotle resists seeing in it either a disease or a trait belonging to the "nature" (*phúsis*) of the Scythian "race" (*génos*); cf. K. Meuli, "Scythica," *Hermes* 70 (1935): 121–76 (reprinted in *Herodot,* ed. E. Marg [Darmstadt, 1965], 455–70); as well as A. Ballabriga, "Les eunuques scythes et leurs femmes," *Mètis* 1 (1986): 121–38; and E. Lieber, "The Hippocratic 'Airs, Waters, Places' on Cross-Dressing Eunuchs: 'Natural' Yet Also 'Divine,' " in *Hippokratische Medizin und antike Philosophie,* ed. R. Wittern and R. Pellegrin (Hildesheim, 1984), 73–85. For the reflections of Hippocratic physicians about the divine origin of disease, see n. 24.

41. The geographical position of the Sauromatae and the much-debated issue of the Amazons are discussed by Hartog 1992, 49–50 and 229–31 (= 1988); J. Carlier-Detienne, "Les Amazones font la guerre et l'amour," *L'Ethnographie* 76 (1980): 11–33; W. B. Tyrrell, *Amazons: A Study in Athenian Mythmaking* (Baltimore, 1984); and K. Dowden, "The Amazons: Development and Functions," *Rheinisches Museum* 140 (1997): 97–128. To *Airs* 17 we must, of course, add Herodotus 4.110–17.

42. For the treatment of Scythians, on the one hand, and Egyptians and Libyans, on the other, as opposites, see *Airs* 12.10, 18.1, 19.1, and 20.3; cf. B. Lincoln, *Death, War, and Sacrifice: Studies in Ideology and Practice* (Chicago, 1991), 198–208. On the problem posed by the lacuna in sec. 12.9, see Jouanna [n. 26], 222 and 298–300. In *A Regimen for Health,* it is the inhabitants of the Pontus region and the Libyans who are treated as opposites, according to the same climatic criteria (2.37); see F. M. Snowden, Jr., *Blacks in Antiquity: Ethiopians in the Greek-Roman Experience* (Cambridge, Mass., 1970), 172–83.

43. It is, perhaps, the Libyans who played this role in the extreme southwest, in relation to the Sauramatae dwelling in the desert in the northeast.

44. *Airs* 15 and 13.1–2. It can be observed that the population of the Phasis region represents, from the standpoint of the attribution of contrary qualities, the eastern term in correspondence with the Scythians, to the north, and the Egyptians, to the south. Thus, to the north are the Scythians (cold–wet), to the south the Egyptians (warm–dry), to the east the inhabitants of Phasis (warm–wet); all that lacks to complete this image is a European population living to the west of Greece and characterized by the pair cold–dry.

45. This image of the inhabited world was systematized by Aristotle; see M. M. Sassi, *La scienza dell' uomo nella Grecia antica* (Turin, 1988), 99–112. It is still present in both Aeschylus' *Persians* and Xenophon's *Cyropaedia;* see on this issue two studies by B. Lincoln, "Death by Water: Strange Events at the Strymon (*Persae* 492–507) and the Categorical Opposition of East and West," *Classical Philology* 95 (2000), 12–20, and "The Center of the World and the Origin of Life," *History of Religions* 51 (2001), 311–326.

46. See *Airs* 15.1, 2.1, 8.10, 24.1, etc. One could cite a multitude of examples. A list of the enunciative interventions appearing throughout the treatise on the environment appears in Jouanna [n. 26], 20–21.

47. On the territorial opposition between Europe and Asia in Herodotus, see the beginning of the work (1.4.4), then in the successive dreams of Astyages (1.106–7), Cyrus (1.209.1), and Xerxes (7.19.1). This bipartite division of the inhabited world furthermore becomes a tripartite one at 2.16 and 4.36–42; see J. L. Myres, *Herodotus: Father of History* (Oxford, 1953), 32–40; G. F. Gianotti, "Ordine e simmetria nella rappresentazione del mondo: Erodoto e il paradosso del Nilo," *Quaderni di Storia* 27 (1988): 51–92; and C. Jacob, *Géographie et ethnographie en Grèce ancienne* (Paris, 1991), 49–63.

48. The Ionians occupy an ambiguous position in this geographical division and, accordingly, Herodotus shows ambivalence in his judgment concerning both their responsibility in the first actions undertaken by the Persians against the Greeks and their collaboration with the enemy in the course of the events that followed, as has been shown by J. Hart, *Herodotus and Greek History* (London, 1982), 84–90, and K. H. Waters, *Herodotos the Historian: His Problems, Method, and Originality* (London, 1985), 125–28. For a comparison between Hippocrates and Herodotus on the issue of the overlap between Europe and Asia, see R. Thomas, *Herodotus in Context: Ethnography, Science, and the Art of Persuasion* (Cambridge, 2000), 86–101.

49. *Airs* 12.3–9. In Herodotus' *Histories*, the system of compensation acts on two levels: on the level of the Greeks' occupation of the eastern coast of the Aegean, the Ionians have the most beautiful of climates, while the Aeolians, farther to the north, have a more productive soil (1.142.1–2 and 1.149.2); on the level of the world, Greece (for which we should read Ionia) enjoys more balanced seasons (*kekreména*), while the outermost regions (*eskhatiaí*) have as their lot the most beautiful products (3.106.1; see n. 20). On the relationships between Herodotus and the Hippocratic treatise with regard to the theory of climates, see G. Lachenaud, *Mythologies, religion et philosophie de l'histoire dans Hérodote* (Lille, 1978), 441–53, and Hartog [n. 14], 99–104.

50. In connection with this, J. Cobet, *Herodots Exkurse und die Frage der Einheit seines Werkes*, vol. 17 of *Historia Einzelschriften* (Wiesbaden, 1971), 171–78, shows that Herodotus concludes his work at the moment when the Persians have won back the Asiatic coast of the Aegean (in other words, they have taken back Ionia), thus, at the moment when the balance is reestablished between Europe and Asia; in connection with this, see also Hart [n. 48] 181–82. Hart rightly links Herodotus' description of the final submission of Ionia with the servile dispositions engendered by the mildness of the climate to which the Halicarnassian historian claims the inhabitants of this region of Asia are subjected; see also D. Boedeker, "Protesilaos and the End of Herodotus' *Histories*," *Classical Antiquity* 7 (1988): 30–48.

51. *Airs* 16.1–8; *pace* M. M. Sassi, "Pensare la diversità umana senza le razze," *I Quaderni del Ramo d'Oro* 3 (2000): 137–62; cf. Jouanna [n. 26], 68–71 and 230. It is to be noted that, while we find in this section the sole occurrence of the term *génos* in the sense of "race" (see n. 15), we also find here the only mention of Greeks contained in the treatise. The term *génos* is used five times (19.1, 20.3, 21.3, and twice in 23.1), but in all but the one passage just mentioned, it is to refer to a subgroup of Scythians as a single people within the larger population.

52. On the concept of a *díke*, a justice based on balance and reciprocity, and on the different metaphorical levels at which this concept can be deployed, see Gentili 1995, 57–62 (= 1998, 61–71).

53. For the status of the slave and that of the metic in classical Athens, see M. Austin and P. Vidal-Naquet, *Économies et sociétés en Grèce ancienne* (Paris, 1972), 115–18, and Baslez [n. 16], 127–35.

54. On this topic, see, for example, F. Remotti, "L'essenzialità dello straniero," in *Lo straniero ovvero l'identità culturale a confronto*, ed. M. Bettini (Rome, 1992), 19–37; and E. Landowski, *Présences de l'autre: Essai de socio-sémiotique*, vol. 2, (Paris, 1997), 15–44. For the theoretical underpinnings of new forms of racism, see A. Rivera, "Néoracisme," and M. Kilani "Parenté (pureté) de sang," in R. Gallissot, M. Kilani, and A. Rivera, *L'imbroglio ethnique: En quatorze mots clés* (Lausanne, 2000), 216–26 and 227–47; and, on the social dangers of genetic manipulation, see M. Augé, "Des individus sans filiation," in *Le clonage humain*, ed. H. Atlan et al. (Paris, 1999), 143–71. Concerning the different symbolic and cultural procedures involved, see F. Remotti, "Thèses pour une perspective anthropopoiétique," in *La fabrication de l'humain dans les cultures et en anthropologie*, ed. C. Calame and M. Kilani (Lausanne, 1999), 15–31; and the collective research by F. Affergan, S. Borutti, C. Calame, U. Fabietti, M. Kilani, and F. Remotti, *Figures de l'humain: Les représentations de l'anthropologie* (Paris, 2003).

CHAPTER IX

1. The editing of the Derveni text has yet to be completed. Accordingly, we will make do with the pirated text published in *Zeitschrift für Papyrologie und Epigraphik* 47 (1982): 1–12, with the improvements offered by R. Janko, "The Derveni Papyrus: An Interim Text," *Zeitschrift für Papyrologie und Epigraphik* 141 (2002): 1–62. A translation based on a revised text has been proposed by Janko and by A. Laks and G. W. Most, "A Provisional Translation of the Derveni Papyrus," in Laks and Most 1997, 9–12; see also the bibliography established by M. S. Funghi in Laks and Most 1997, 175–85. The text now proposed by Janko in "The Derveni Papyrus: An Interim Text" *Zeitschrift für Papyrologie und Epigraphik* 141 (2002), 1–62, is a solid but conjectural reconstruction based on this same transcription, the only one we have; see also the French translation and literal commentary proposed by F. Jourdan, *Le Papyrus de Derveni* (Paris, 2003).

2. The probable place occupied by the Orphic cosmo-theogony narrative "from Derveni" among the various versions that we can reconstruct has been sketched out by L. Brisson, "Les théogonies orphiques et le papyrus de Derveni," *Revue de l'histoire des religions* 202 (1985): 389–420, who rightly warns against the risky reconstructions proposed by M. L. West, *The Orphic Poems* (Oxford, 1983), 68–115; nevertheless, West's proposals concerning the probable dating of the Derveni poem and its commentary (77–82) can be accepted.

3. The allegorical reading proposed by the commentator has, in fact, led to different suggestions regarding his identity; cf. W. Burkert, "Der Autor von Derveni: Stesimbrotos *Perì teletôn?*" *Zeitschrift für Papyrologie und Epigraphik* 62 (1986): 1–5, with the various possibilities enumerated by M. S. Funghi, "The Derveni Papyrus," in Laks and Most 1997, 25–37; and by A. Bernabé, "La théogonie orphique du papyrus de Derveni," *Kernos* 15 (2002): 91–129.

4. Homer, *Iliad* 21.6–7. The interpretive procedures attributed to Theagenes have been analyzed by Svenbro 1976, 108–21; see also A. Ford, "Epic and the Earliest Greek Allegorists," in *Epics and the Contemporary World,* ed. M. Beissinger, J. Tylus, and J. Wofford (Berkeley, 1999), 33–53.

5. *P. Derv.* col. 7.4–8; see also cols. 9.10, 14.6, and 17.13 with the commentary of A. Ford, *The Origins of Criticism: Literary Culture and Poetic Theory in Classical Greece* (Princeton, 2002), 72–89, along with A. Laks, "Between Religion and Philosophy: The Function of Allegory in the Derveni Papyrus," *Phronesis* 42 (1997): 121–42.

6. This anonymous formulation, partially cited by Plutarch, *Table Talk* 636d, concerning a *lógos Orphikós,* has been included by modern editors in the *Orphica,* fr. 334 Kern; cf. frr. 245.1 and 247.1 Kern. It is paraphrased in Plato, *Symposium* 218b (= *Orphica* fr. 13 Kern). M. L. West, "Hocus-Pocus in East and West: Theogony, Ritual, and the Tradition of Esoteric Commentary," in Laks and Most 1997, 81–90, has posited that it is the first verse of the "theogony from Derveni"; see also West [n. 2], 82. Cf. A. Bernabé, "La fórmula órfica 'cerred las puertas, profanos': Del profano religioso al profano en la meteria," *Ilu: Revista de cencias de las religiones* 1 (1996): 13–37, who includes a different form of this verse in his edition, *Poetae epici graeci: Testimonia et fragmenta,* pt. 2/1 (Munich, 2004), as fr. 3F; cf. also K. Tsantsanoglou, "The First Columns of the Derveni Papyrus and Their Religious Significance," in Laks and Most 1997, 93–128, esp. 123–27.

7. Cf. Pindar, *Nemean* 7.61–63, *Olympian* 2.83–85, *Pythian* 5.105–8, etc., but also Theognis 681–82 (with respect to the *sophía* of him who knows), Heraclitus frr. 22 B 1 and 34 Diels-Kranz, or Bacchylides 3.84–86; see on this topic the commentary of Nagy 1990, 146–50, 233–38, and 323–33.

8. *P. Derv.* cols. 23.7 and 25.13 for *semaínein;* cf. Heraclitus fr. 22 B 93 for the oracle at Delphi, as well as Herodotus 5.56.1 for *ainíttesthai.*

9. *Hoi ginóskontes: P. Derv.* cols. 18.5 and 23.2 (cf. 20.2–3 and 8), by opposition with *hoi ou ginóskontes:* cols. 5.6, 9.2, 12.5, 23.5, and 26.8. This is a veritable leitmotiv in the commentary. See also *hoi dokoûntes* (col. 12.3) and *hoi polloí* (cols. 7.10 and 23.1–2).

10. This use of *mén* emphatically (without a corresponding *dé*), typical of Homeric language, is described by J. D. Denniston, *The Greek Particles,* 2nd ed. (Oxford, 1954), 359–61. The relative clause quoted at 8.2 (to which I return in §6.2) is to be linked either to the invocation that must have opened the poem (with a hymnic, predicative formulation, such as: "Sing, Muses, the first entities and those born from Zeus, the all-powerful sovereign") or to the subsequent description

of Zeus' action. The presence of the verb *akoúein* (l. 9) and the expression *thésphata* in the plural (l. 11) in the commentary on these two verses suggests to me that the expression *thésphaton arkhén*, which does not fit into the syntax of the sentence, can be replaced by *thésphat' akoúsas*, provided by the lemma of col. 13.1; but, contrary to the solution proposed by J. S. Rusten, "Interim Notes on the Papyrus of Derveni," *Harvard Studies in Classical Philology* 89 (1985): 121–40 (esp. 125–27), these oracles refer to the speech of Night (cols. 11 and 13) and not Cronos, from whom Zeus simply took over power. Cf. *Orphica* frr. 103 and 164–67 Kern; in fr. 155 Zeus learns from his father Cronos only the "measures" of creation. The very ambiguity in the formulation of these two verses may have caused the substitution of *arkhén* for *akoúsas* in col. 8.4; see also the more complex solution proposed by West [n. 2], 85–86.

11. Used in the singular, *tò aidoîon* usually designates the penis, while in the plural *tà aidoîa* refers to the male or female genitalia in general. This is especially the case in Aristotle's zoological treatises; compare, for example, *GA* 716b28–30 or 718a19 (where *tò aidoîon* is distinguished from the testicles) with 757a5–8 (the hyena or badger has the *aidoîa* of the male and the female; cf. 770b35: the same in the singular). But in *HA* 493b3–5, the female organ, when it is presented as the inverse of the penis, is designated by *aidoîon* in the singular (cf. also 500b6–12, concerning a problem posed by the peculiar morphology of elephants); cf. likewise Herodotus 2.48.2 (in the singular = phallus), 2.51.1 (in the plural, the parts of herms), and 1.108.1 (in the plural, the parts of a young girl), as well as Hippocrates, *Airs* 940–41 and *Nat. Mul.* 4–8. My thanks to P. Ceccarelli for the *TLG* search she performed for me in this regard.

12. It must be recognized that the syntax of the truncated statement with which column 14 begins is not clear; it is hard to see what role is played by the subjunctive *ekhthóre* and the accusative that seems to follow the verb; this masculine accusative certainly designates the sun in its quality of exceptional brilliance (thus, it is not necessary to correct *tòn* into *tò* in col. 14.1, as proposed by Rusten [n. 10], 134). The construction of *ekhthrósko* with the accusative, though rare, is attested in *Anth. Pal.* 9.371.1; thus, the penis would be surging forth *from* the sun, but *in* or *toward* the ether (taking the accusative of the lemma at col. 13.4 as an accusative of direction).

13. For the place of the primordial egg and Eros in the first Orphic cosmogonies, see the parody in Aristophanes, *Birds* 690–702 (= *Orphica* fr. 1 Kern), as well as my commentary in "Éros initiatique et la cosmogonie orphique," in *Orphisme et Orphée: En l'honneur de Jean Rudhardt*, ed. P. Borgeaud (Geneva, 1991), 227–47 (esp. 229–34). For the Hesiodic succession myth and its oriental parallels, see West 1966, 18–31. It should be noted that the verb used by the poet (col. 13.4) to designate Zeus' swallowing of the *aidoîos/-on* corresponds exactly to the one used by the text of Hesiod (*Theogony* 497) to signify Cronos' swallowing of the stone substituted for the newborn Zeus; the theogony of the *Orphic Rhapsodies* also seems to have used this term to designate Zeus' ingestion of Phanes-Protogonos: cf. frr. 129 and 167, as well as 58 Kern. But it will be recalled that, by juxtaposing the lemma of 13.4 with that of 8.5, Rusten [n. 10], 124–26, takes *aidoîon* as qualifying *daímona:* this reading implies the swallowing of the whole Sun; see also West [n. 2], 85.

14. The typically Orphic procedure of accumulating juxtaposed qualifications when designating and invoking a god induces me to take *aidoîon* as a substantivized adjective in the lemma of col. 16.3: the king, the First-Born, the venerable (penis?), is probably Ouranos, if not the Sun itself (according to the proposal of Rusten [n. 10], 135–36, who suggests that Helios and his penis are identified, or that of Bernabé [n. 3], 108–11, who supposes that the Sky's penis is assimilated to the Sun, taking Ouranos' phallus as a metaphor for Helios); the assimilation between Ouranos, Cronos, and Zeus (cf. 14.5–12) should be added to these. The Orphic invocational procedure comprising sequences of appellations in apposition has been analyzed by J. Rudhardt, "Quelques réflexions sur les hymnes orphiques," in Borgeaud, *Orphisme et Orphée* [n. 13], 263–88; cf. *Orphic Hymns* 8, 14, 34, etc., and, in the Derveni poem itself, cols. 17.12 and 19.10. So too in 13.4 the masculine nominative relative requires that we understand *aidoîon* (in the sense of "venerable") as an attribute of the god (?) who "first surged forth in the ether," that is, in fact, Ouranos. On the different phases of the succession story, see Bernabé [n. 3], 103–16, who speaks of a "cosmic pregnancy."

15. The first meaning of *thórnumai* is probably "ejaculate," corresponding to the noun deriving from this verb, *thóros,* "sperm" (Herodotus 2.93.1; Hippocrates, *Morb.* 2.2.51.1; Aristotle, *HA*

510a1); cf. Herodotus 3.109.1. This verb is based on the same root as *éthoron* (*thróisko*), "spring up," "rush forth," used by the poet to describe the springing forth of the primordial venerable (god? penis?) in the ether (col. 13.4); there is probably a sexual connotation in this use of the verb as well. West [n. 2], 91–92, prefers to take *thórnei* as a substantive designating surging forth and ejaculation. In that case, column 21 would be a commentary on the birth of Aphrodite from an ejaculation and, hence, from the sperm of Zeus; see Bernabé [n. 3], 118–19 with n. 132.

16. See in this regard the commentary of West [n. 2], 93–94.

17. Concerning the Orphic marriage of Zeus with Rhea, identified with Demeter and, hence, with his own mother, see West [n. 2], 82 and 93–94.

18. The same distinction between entities suspended at a distance from one another and beings united with one another is taken up again by the commentator with regard to the creation of the sun in column 25. W. Burkert, "Orpheus und die Vorsokratiker: Bemerkungen zum Derveni-Papyrus und zur pythagoreischen Zahlenlehre," *Antike und Abendland* 14 (1968): 93–114, has indicated the interpretive elements connecting the commentary to the physical, and especially Atomist, theories of the Pre-Socratic philosophers.

19. In the poem itself, Nous—assimilated to Cronos—was apparently the only being to come about by birth (col. 16.6 and 9), as though the other beings had always been but depended for their existence on the unique coming into being of Nous-Cronos. This is no doubt why the commentator can treat Nous as the mother figure "of all the others" in column 26.1. The influence of Ionian philosophy, and, in particular, of Anaxagoras, is once again quite noticeable; see West [n. 2], 80–81; W. Burkert, "La genèse des choses et des mots: Le papyrus de Derveni entre Anaxagore et Cratyle," *Études philosophiques* 4 (1970): 443–55; and S. Colabella, "Sul papiro di Derveni," in *Orfeo e l'Orfismo,* ed. A. Masaracchia (Rome, 1993), 67–75.

20. See especially the famous texts *Orphica* frr. 168 and 169 Kern. Besides the now classic work of M. Detienne and J.-P. Vernant, *Les Ruses de l'intelligence: La mètis des Grecs* (Paris, 1974), 125–64 (= *Cunning Intelligence among the Greeks,* trans. Janet Lloyd [Atlantic Highlands, N.J., 1978]), see in this regard the remarks of West [n. 2], 87–88, 101, and 239–43. This cosmological act, summarized by the verbal form *mésato,* is commented on by H. Schwabl, "Zeus (Teil II)," *Realenc. der Alt.-Wiss. Suppl.* 15 (Stuttgart, 1978), cols. 993–1411 (cols. 1326–30); see also L. J. Alderink, *Creation and Salvation in Ancient Orphism* (Chico, Calif., 1981), 25–36, who points out the role that sexuality plays in this act of creation (29).

21. It should be pointed out that, in the Orphic tradition, *noûs* is a quality attributed to Zeus; see *Orphica* frr. 177 and 242 Kern with Colabella [n. 19], 71–73.

22. Cf. col. 9.2–8 with col. 15.10–12; for a text, translation, and commentary of the penultimate column, see the study of W. Burkert, "Star Wars or One Stable World? A Problem of Presocratic Cosmogony (*PDerv.* col. XXV)," in Laks and Most 1997, 167–74. Note the use of *diegeîtai* at col. 25.12 as well as 15.8; see Rusten [n. 10], 138 n. 38.

23. Thus, Cronos and Nyx certainly take on distinct functions in Zeus' taking of power, despite the interpretation suggested by the ambiguous and faulty formulation of the lemma at col. 8.4–5; see n. 10.

24. On the correspondences between the process of cosmic creation and the Orphic initiatory path, see especially M. Detienne, *L'écriture d'Orphée* (Paris, 1989), 116–32 (= *The Writing of Orpheus: Greek Myth in Cultural Context,* trans. J. Lloyd [Baltimore, 2002]), as well as my suggestion in Calame [n. 13], 244–45, further developed in Calame 1996a, 215–25 (= 1999, 192–97).

25. For the sake of bibliographic economy, I refer the reader, concerning the various "authorial" identifications that scholars have proposed, to the survey of Funghi [n. 3]. T. M. S. Baxter, *The "Cratylus": Plato's Critique of Naming* (Leiden, 1992), 130–39, believes that the *Cratylus* engages polemically with the etymologizing explanations of the Derveni commentator; see also C. H. Kahn, "Was Euthyphro the Author of the Derveni Papyrus?" in Laks and Most 1997, 55–63; as well as R. Janko, "The Derveni Papyrus (Diagoras of Melos, *Apopyrgitontes logoi?*): A New Translation," *Classical Philology* 96 (2001): 1–32.

26. On the role played particularly by milk in the initiatory tablets of Thurii and Pelinna, see F. Graf, "Textes orphiques et rituel bacchique: À propos des lamelles de Pelinna," in *Orphisme et Orphée* [n. 13], 87–102, who provides the most important textual and bibliographic references.

27. See A. Henrichs, "The Eumenides and Wineless Libations in the Derveni Papyrus," in *Atti del XVII Congresso Internazionale di Papirologia*, vol. 2 (Naples, 1984), 225–68 (who opts in favor of the Eleusinian *mystai*).

28. The terms cited here from cols. 3.4, 6.5, and 9 are those used in the text and commentary of Tsantsanoglou [n. 6], 105–17.

29. Crates of Athens, *FGrHist*. 262 F 2; Philochorus, *FGrHist*. 328 F 173 = fr. 1 Tresp; Melanthius, *FGrHist*. 326 F 4 = fr. 1 Tresp. Concerning the utterance of the enunciation, the text of col. 5.4 proposed by Tsantsanoglou [n. 28], 94, uses the first-person plural *párimen;* given that this form does not fit well into the syntax of the proposition, however, it is suspect. On the identity of the initiates "in the cities" (col. 20.1–3), see n. 31.

30. On the exegesis proposed for *panompheúousa,* see the brief commentary of Baxter [n. 25], 133–34.

31. The commentator is probably alluding here to the Eleusinian initiates, whom he is contrasting with the Orphic initiands: cf. Rusten [n. 10], 138–40, and Graf [n. 26], 98. We ought to keep in mind that Orpheus was considered the founder of the Greek mysteries in general and that he is said to have introduced the *téckhne* that they involve: *Suda s.v. threskeúei* (*Th* 486 Adler = *Orphica* test. 32 Kern). It should also be pointed out that the new reading of col. 2.8 proposed by Tsantsanoglou allows us to suppose that the performance of the rites was accompanied by "music."

32. See the comparison that I have attempted to establish in "Invocations et commentaires 'orphiques,' " in *Discours religieux dans l'Antiquité*, ed. M.-M. Mactoux and E. Geny (Besançon, 1996), 11–30; concerning the gold leaves, see also the study by C. Riedweg, "Initiation-Tod-Unterwelt. Beobachtungen zur Kommunikationssituation und narrativen Technik der orphisch-bakchischen Goldblättchen," in *Ansichten griechischer Rituale*, ed. F. Graf (Stuttgart, 1998), 359–98.

33. See the hypotheses presented by D. Obbink, "Cosmology as Initiation vs. the Critique of the Orphic Mysteries," in Laks and Most 1997, 39–54; as well as G.W. Most, "The Fire Next Time: Cosmology, Allegoresis, and Salvation in the Derveni Papyrus," *Journal of Hellenic Studies* 117 (1997): 117–35. These obviously stand in contradiction to hypotheses holding that the Derveni commentator is an opponent of Orphism; see Henrichs [n. 27], 255–56; and G. Casadio, "Adversaria orphica et orientalia," *Studi e materiali di storia delle religioni* 52 (1986): 291–322, esp. 299.

34. See n. 6.

35. Pseudo-Alcidamas, *Odysseus* 24 (= *Orphica* test. 123 Kern), with the reply of Androtion, *FGrHist*. 324 F 54; see also Diogenes Laertius 1.5, Plato, *Republic* 364e, and the scholiast's comment on Euripides, *Alcestis*, 968 (2:239 Schwartz = *Orphica* test. 82 Kern), which invokes the authority of Heracleides Ponticus to claim that certain writings of Orpheus had been inscribed on tablets in order to be dedicated on the summit of Mount Haemus in Thrace. See in this regard the commentary of I. M. Linforth, *The Arts of Orpheus* (Berkeley, 1941), 15–26 and 120–23.

36. The iconographic document cited here (*hydría,* Palermo, Fond. I. Mormino 385) is commented on by Detienne [n. 24], 110–12 and 119. On the relationship between Orphism and the written tradition, see W. Burkert, *Griechische Religion der archaischen und klassischen Epoche* (Stuttgart, 1977), 442 (= *Greek Religion of the Archaic and Classical Periods*, trans. J. Raffan [Cambridge, Mass., 1985]); and R. Baumgarten, *Heiliges Wort und Heilige Schrift bei den Griechen* (Tübingen, 1998), 70–80.

CHAPTER X

1. On these trends in contemporary literary criticism, the classical philologist—who often studiously avoids such matters—can consult the highly informative overview of R. Selden, *A Reader's Guide to Contemporary Literary Theory* (Lexington, Ky., 1989).

2. To limit myself to bibliographical references from Lausanne, the notion of "representative substitute" was developed by J. Molino, "Nature et signification de la littérature," *Études de lettres* 4

(1990): 17–64; that of "symbolic delegation" by C. Reichler, "La littérature comme interprétation symbolique," in *Essais sur l'interprétation des textes* (Paris, 1988), 81–113; and that of "symbolic process" by Calame 1996b, 29–54. For an attempt to analyze the processes involved in the linguistic grasping of a referent, see, for example, M.-J. Borel, "Le discours descriptif, le savoir et ses signes," in J.-M. Adam, M.-J. Borel, C. Calame, and M. Kilani, *Le discours anthropologique: Description, narration, savoir,* 2nd ed. (Lausanne, 1995), 21–64. Finally (and, once more, originating in Lausanne), an excellent overview of how the enunciative approach opens onto pragmatics can be found in J.-M. Adam, *Langue et littérature: Analyses pragmatiques et textuelles* (Paris, 1991), 12–32.

3. The debate about the absence of fictional effects that the oral character of "archaic" Greek literature supposedly causes was launched by the study of R. Rösler, "Die Entdeckung der Fiktionalität in der Antike," *Poetica* 12 (1980): 283–319; see also "Ueber Deixis und einige Aspekte mündlichen und schriftlichen Stils in antiker Lyrik," *Würzburger Jahrbücher,* n.s., 9 (1983): 7–28. The debate, which has focused particularly on the poetry of Sappho, is reflected in works by J. Latacz, "Realität und Imagination: Eine neue Lyrik-Theorie und Sapphos *phaínetai moi kênos*—Lied," *Museum Helveticum* 52 (1985): 67–94; and by F. Lasserre, *Sappho: Une autre lecture* (Padua, 1989), 125–26 and 149–50. After being taken up again by W. Rösler, "Realitätsbezug und Imagination in Sapphos Gedicht *phaínetai moi kênos,*" in *Der Uebergang von der Mündlichkeit zur Literatur bei den Griechen,* ed. W. Kullmann and M. Reichel (Tübingen, 1990), 273–87, the debate has been partially resolved by M. Steinrück, *Rede und Kontext: Zum Verhältnis von Person und Erzähler in frühgriechischen Texten* (Bonn, 1992), 278–324, who has shown the distance at which Sappho's poems stand from their performance context.

4. For an overview of the general terms of this debate, I would refer the reader to the references provided in Calame 2000b, 42–52. The interesting cognitive conception of the fictional work carried out by literature which has been developed by J.-M. Schaeffer, *Pourquoi la fiction?* (Paris, 1999), does not offer any original solutions relative to the issue of the pragmatic dimension of fiction.

5. Out of concern for completeness, it ought to be noted that Daphnis' "poem" is, at the outset, actually a response to Aphrodite's words (97–98); nonetheless, it achieves autonomy, insofar as—through the very brief insertion of a seventh voice, making Aphrodite herself speak—Daphnis cleverly throws back at the goddess mention of her own love trysts.

6. Theocritus 8.29–31 and 61; the rules governing bucolic exchange, which were probably of popular origin, have been explicitly formulated by R. Merkelbach, "Boukoliastaí (Der Wettgesang der Hirten)," *Rheinisches Museum* 99 (1956): 97–133 (reprinted in *Theokrit und die griechische Bukolik,* ed. B. Effe [Darmstadt, 1986], 212–38); see also the comparative study of U. Ott, *Die Kunst des Gegensatzes in Theokrits Hirtengedichten* (Hildesheim, 1969), 10–13, who indicates the constant features characterizing the spatial setting where the musical exchange takes place. The status of this space has been well delimited by P. Voelke, "Monde pastoral et monde urbain: Du *Cyclope* d'Euripide aux *Boukoliastes* de Théocrite," *Études de lettres* 1 (1992): 5–22. I take the distinction between "pastoral" and "bucolic" from D. M. Halperin, *Before Pastoral: Theocritus and the Ancient Tradition of Bucolic Poetry* (New Haven, 1983), 8–12 and 75–84. Only bucolic is a literary genre, the creation of which Halperin attributes to Theocritus; on this issue, see the study of J. Van Sickle, "Theocritus and the Development of the Conception of Bucolic Genre," *Ramus* 5 (1976): 18–44; as well as the critical remarks of K. J. Gutzwiller, *Theocritus' Pastoral Analogies: The Formation of a Genre* (Madison, 1991), 3–19, and R. L. Hunter, *Theocritus and the Archaeology of Greek Poetry* (Cambridge, 1996), 14–28. See the overview of Theocritus' use of "bucolic terminology" and the bucolic as a genre in R. L. Hunter *Theocritus: A Selection* (Cambridge, 1999), 5–12.

7. The chiasmus formed by this comparison of man and nature through music has been noted by Ott [n. 6], 87–92, who provides a keen analysis of these verses; see also Hunter [n. 6], 68–71.

8. For the prayer and cult-hymn forms, see Miller 1986, 1–9, who draws on earlier studies. Given the role played by reminding the god/goddess of his/her past interventions in prayer, I would interpret the form *áeides* in verse 19 as an imperfect, coordinated with the aorist *âisas* in 24, unlike Gow 1950, 2:50.

9. See, in particular, C. Segal, " 'Since Daphnis Dies':The Meaning ofTheocritus' First *Idyll*," *Museum Helveticum* 31 (1974): 1–22, esp. 7 (reprinted in *Poetry and Myth in Ancient Pastoral: Essays on Theocritus and Virgil* [Princeton, 1981], 25–46), and Halperin [n. 6], 163–67.

10. If we push the series of correspondences even further, we can see in the cup "washed in the springs of the Hours" (150) an allusion not only to the erotic charm that the Hours possess (to the references provided by Gow 1950, 149, add *Cypria* fr. 4 Bernabé, Hesiod *Works* 15–76, and *Homeric Hymn* 6.11–13: the dressing scenes involving Aphrodite or Pandora) but also to the poetic inspiration that the spring evokes (see vv. 7–8 with the commentary of Gow 1950, 3, and that of G. F. Gianotti, *Per una poetica pindarica* [Turin, 1975], 110–15). In a subtle discussion, F. Cairns, "Theocritus' First Idyll:The Literary Programme," *Wiener Studien* 97 (1984): 89–113, has shown that the cup and its contents are often presented in Greek poetry as metaphorical equivalents for poetic composition.

11. A good overview of the literary qualities of this vessel for rustic use is provided in Halperin [n. 6], 167–73; Ott [n. 6], 93–99 and 137, after listing the various archaeology-based suggestions made in an attempt to provide a material reality to the *kissúbion*, associates the cup in Theocritus' poem with a Megarian bowl with embossed ornament, in which case the depicted scenes would be framed by a double band of vegetal decoration.

12. On this issue see, above all, the study of Segal [n. 9], 3 and 15, but also that of Ott [n. 6], 132–37.

13. See P.-E. Legrand, *Étude sur Théocrite* (Paris, 1898), 196–203; T. Reinhardt, *Die Darstellung der Bereiche Stadt und Land bei Theokrit* (Bonn, 1988), 50–5; and n. 6. Despite what some critics have alleged (see Ott [n. 6], 120 with n. 341), nothing beyond the origin ofThyrsis (v. 65; see §1.3) indicates that the scene takes place in Sicily.

14. On the difficulties involved in trying to identify referents for the description of this decoration, see the commentaries of Gow 1950, 7–8 and 13, and Hunter [n. 6], 76–77. The affinities linking ivy to Dionysus have been noted by E. R. Dodds, *Euripides: Bacchae*, 2nd ed. (Oxford, 1960), 77; see also Cairns [n. 10], 97. If it does not denote the ivy flower (cf. Gow), the helichryse corresponds to a flower to which the Greeks attributed erotic connotations; see C. Calame, *Alcman: Introduction, témoignages, texte critique, traduction et commentaire* (Rome, 1983), 527–28.

15. Greek poetry establishes a relationship between sacrifice practices and the cultivation of grains, which it presents as a metaphor for human civilization; see J.-P.Vernant, "À la table des hommes: Mythe de fondation du sacrifice chez Hésiode," in Detienne andVernant 1979, 37–132.

16. On Hermes and transitions, see L. Kahn, *Hermès passe ou les ambiguïtés de la communication* (Paris, 1978), 86–92; on Priapus as protector of small cultures vis-à-vis the exterior, see M. Olender, "Priape: Le dernier des dieux," in *Dictionnaire des mythologies*, vol. 2, ed.Y. Bonnefoy (Paris, 1981), 311–14. A comparison of the gods and heroes seeking to find out about Prometheus' situation in Aeschylus' *Prometheus Bound* and those visiting Daphnis leads to the following series of equivalences: Haphaestus–Hermes, the *koryphaîos*–the herdsmen, Ocean–Priapus, Io–Cyprus, Hermes–Pan. This homology is no doubt not a pure coincidence; the analysis of it can surely be pushed further than it is by G. Lawall, *Theocritus' Coan Pastorals: A Poetry Book* (Cambridge, Mass., 1967), 20–21.

17. On the Thybris (or Thymbris) mentioned at the same time as the Arethusa spring, see the commentaries of Servius atVirgil, *Aeneid* 3.500 (3:185–86 Stocker-Travis), and Gow 1950, 25–26. The text of the verses concerning Mount Ida is uncertain; Gow 1950, 23–24. The galingale has aphrodisiac connotations (Calame [n. 14], 528), while references to bees' work point to the first stage of civilization within the Greek representation of the development of culture; see C. Sourvinou-Inwood, "The Myth of the First Temples at Delphi," *Classical Quarterly*, n.s., 29 (1979): 231–51 (reprinted in *"Reading" Greek Culture: Texts and Images, Rituals and Myths* [Oxford, 1991], 192–216).

18. On narcissus and violets as flowers connoting amorous desire, see N. J. Richardson, *The Homeric Hymn to Demeter* (Oxford, 1974), 142–44. Among the metaphorical images for the poet and the poet's song, the owl is famous in the archaic period for its dissonant cry (see Calame [n. 14], 343), while the nightingale is singled out for the enchanting melody of its song; H. Maehler,

Die Lieder des Bakchylides, pt. 1 *Die Siegeslieder,* vol. 2, *Mnemosyne,* Supplement 62 (Leiden, 1982), 62–63.

19. The views mentioned here are, in order, those of Ott [n. 6], 132–36, Reinhardt [n. 13], 54–62; and Segal [n. 9], 3–15.

20. Outside of the polemic concerning the function of the three decorative scenes on the *kissúbion,* the comparison with Homer, *Iliad* 18.478–608, and Pseudo-Hesiod, *Shield* 139–324, has led to the consensus observable in Ott [n. 6], 99–110; Halperin [n. 6], 176–86; and Reinhardt [n. 13], 54–58. On the description of the decoration on the ivy cup as "narrative sculpture," see I. Paar, "Champs lexicaux et esthétique littéraire:Théocrite, *Idylle* I, v. 27–56," *Études classiques* 57 (1988): 13–26.

21. Let us not forget that fishing, which is done in the uncultivated world of the sea, is considered in ancient Greece an art involving ruse because of the use of nets; see M. Detienne and J.-P. Vernant, *Les ruses de l'intelligence: La mètis des Grecs* (Paris, 1974), 33–40 (= *Cunning Intelligence among the Greeks,* trans. J. Lloyd [Atlantic Highlands, N.J., 1978]). There is a useful comparison of fishing to hunting in O. Longo, *Le forme della predazione: Cacciatori e pescatori della Grecia antica* (Naples, 1989), 21–40. Interpreters disagree about whether the fishing described in *Idyll* I is successful or not; see Ott [n. 6], 105 n. 290. On the order of the three scenes, see Lawall [n. 16], 28–30.

22. The metaphorical equivalences existing between the *pónoi* of the protagonists in the scenes on the cup, the *pónos* that the vessel represents as a piece of craftwork, and the bucolic poem as a *pónos* have been carefully analyzed by Cairns [n. 10], 95–105; see also Halperin [n. 6], 182–87 and 242–44. The texts praising the voices of grasshoppers trapped in cages are listed in Gow 1950, 12–13 (cf. 110–11 and, of course, Theocritus 7.41, where grasshoppers are compared to the best poets of the day). In Greek poetics, starting with Simonides, comparisons and assimilations between art objects and poetic products are constant; see G. Lanata, *Poetica preplatonica: Testimonianze e frammenti* (Florence, 1963), 68–69 (with bibliography).

23. For commentary on the texts of Pindar presenting the Nymph Cyrene and the space in which she acts as shepherdess and huntress, see my *Mythe et histoire dans l'Antiquité grecque: La création symbolique d'une colonie* (Lausanne, 1996), 99–108. For Anchises as herdsman on Mount Ida, see the *Homeric Hymn to Aphrodite* 53–55; for Paris, see *Cypria argumentum* and fr. 5 Bernabé; Euripides, *Andromache* 274–83, *Hecuba* 644–46, and *Iphigenia in Aulis* 1283–87; Pseudo-Apollodororus, *Epitome* 3.2, etc. The values attached to these legendary mountains are well outlined by Buxton 1994, 81–96; on Mount Ida in the Troad, see W. Elliger, *Die Darstellung der Landschaft in der griechischen Dichtung* (Berlin, 1975), 263–67. The landscape of primordial Arcadia, Pan's haunt, is well described by P. Borgeaud, *Recherches sur le dieu Pan* (Geneva, 1979), 81–105 (= *The Cult of Pan in Ancient Greece* [Chicago, 1988], 47–73).

24. The question of why Daphnis dies is, along with the problem of the nature of the *kissúbion,* another major point of controversy. The reasons for the cowherd's death, allusively evoked by the text, remain ambiguous; see n. 27. C. Segal, "Death by Water: A Narrative Pattern in Theocritus (*Idylls* 1, 13, 22, 23)," *Hermes* 102 (1974): 20–38 (reprinted in *Poetry and Myth in Ancient Pastoral* [n. 9], 47–65) is right to see in Daphnis' disappearance into the whirlpool of the stream a variation on death by water. If this stream is not Acheron, as the scholiast suggests (74 Wendel), it could correspond to the waters (of the Eridan? Ocean? or, perhaps, the Anapos; cf. v. 68) into which the love-crazed throw themselves (whether of their own accord or by the will of a god); the texts are provided by Nagy 1990a, 226–40. At verse 130, Daphnis says of himself that Eros drags him down to Hades. A useful overview of the various interpretations proposed to explain Daphnis' death may be found in Ott [n. 6], 128–29 with n. 371.

25. Such a possible world is, in turn, reconstructed through every (aural or visual) perception of it; see J.-M. Adam, *Éléments de linguistique textuelle: Théorie et pratique de l'analyse textuelle* (Liège, 1990), 11–31.

26. For tragedy, see F. Zeitlin, "The Power of Aphrodite: Eros and the Boundaries of the Self in the *Hippolytus,*" in *Directions in Euripidean Criticism,* ed. P. Burian (Durham, N.C., 1985), 52–111 (reprinted in Zeitlin 1996, 219–84); and Calame 1996a, 159–70 (= 1999, 141–50). For bucolic heroes confronted by dominating women, see J. B. Burton, *Theocritus's Urban Mimes: Mobility, Gender, and Patronage* (Berkeley, 1995), 62–82. Daphnis is not Hippolytus, however; see K.-H. Stanzel,

Liebende Hirten: Theocrits Bukolik und die alexandrinische Poesie (Stuttgart, 1995), 248–68, and Hunter [n. 6], 63–68 and 99–100.

27. If it is undoubtedly a mistake to try to find in Thyrsis' allusive narrative as taken up by Daphnis the legend of the cowherd's double love, as does R. M. Ogilvie, "The Song of Thyrsis," *Journal of Hellenic Studies* 82 (1962): 106–10, the cowherd's death remains the inevitable consequence of an implacable love, willed by Aphrodite and spurred on by Eros (vv. 95–103); a good overview of the issue is provided by E. A. Schmidt, "Die Leiden des verliebten Daphnis," *Hermes* 96 (1968): 539–52. The numerous connections established by the Greeks between Eros and Thanatos have been analyzed by J.-P. Vernant, *L'individu, la mort, l'amour: Soi-même et l'autre en Grèce ancienne* (Paris, 1989), 134–43.

28. As early as Euripides, *Hippolytus* 193–96, *dúseros* designates the state of a person who, because of inexperience (*apeirosúne*) or lack of expedients, does not know how to secure release from an implacable desire—an "obsessive" desire, to borrow the felicitous expression of W. S. Barrett, *Euripides: Hippolytos* (Oxford, 1964), 197. Neither Ogilvie [n. 27], 107–8 ("pathological or unbalanced [*sic* love]"), nor Schmidt [n. 27], 543–44 ("pathologische Liebe"), nor F. Williams, "Theocritus, *Idyll* I, 81–91," *Journal of Hellenic Studies* 89 (1969): 121–23, makes use of the parallel offered by Callimachus' *Epigram* 42: half of the author's soul, which he has lost, is *dúseros* because it has been stolen by Eros or by Hades. On the smile of Aphrodite, see the remarks of Ott [n. 6], 124 n. 358, and Hunter [n. 6], 94–95.

29. On the meaning of this *adúnaton,* see the sensible remarks of Ott [n. 6], 127–28; see also T. G. Rosenmeyer, *The Green Cabinet: Theocritus and the European Pastoral Lyric* (Berkeley, 1969), 264–67.

30. The "realism" of the scenes on the *kissúbion* has been defended by Ott [n. 6], 104–9 and 133–35; see the nuances introduced by Reinhardt [n. 13], 56–58. For Gutzwiller [n. 6], 90–102, the cup presents along a horizontal axis the same world that Daphnis' song constructs along a vertical axis.

31. Emphasized through the play on the assonance of *aoidán/Háidan,* noted by Cairns [n. 10], 112–13, the opposition between death and song is signaled earlier by the goatherd (in the dialogue voice) at verses 62–63, after the description of the *kissúbion.*

32. There is probably a play on words in *adeían* and *áideis* at verse 148; cf. *hádion áiso* in 145. The actual erotic significance of other *Idylls* that tend to create a narrative opposition between poetry and love (see n. 33) has rightly been observed by Goldhill 1991, 249–72. We ought to note, along with Segal [n. 9], 17, that the occurrence of the terms *Moîran* and *Moísas* in the same metrical position in verses 140–41 underscores the contrast between love as leading to death and poetry as incarnated by the Muses.

33. On the opposition between love and music in Alexandrian poetry, wherein poetry is often presented as a remedy for an unsatisfiable desire, see Schmidt [n. 27], 548–50; and W. Deuse, "Dichtung als Heilmittel gegen die Liebe. Zum 11. Idyll Theokrits," in *Beiträge zur hellenistischen Literatur und ihrer Rezeption in Rom,* ed. P. Steinmetz (Stuttgart, 1990), 59–76. The hierarchical relationship that bucolic poetry establishes among cowherds, shepherds, and goatherds is discussed by E. A. Schmidt, "Hirtenhierarchie in der antiken Bukolik," *Philologus* 113 (1969): 183–200.

34. For the meaning and function of concluding formulas in the *Homeric Hymns,* see chapter 1, §2. The convergence of different narrative voices at the end of the poem has been perceived by Goldhill 1991, 245.

35. The two variants of the refrain introduced over the course of its repetition are closely linked to the movement toward Daphnis' death. The first change in the refrain occurs at verse 94, just after the announcement of the end of his destiny decreed by the Fates and immediately before the decisive intervention of Aphrodite. The second change (at v. 127), which is inserted into the invocation to Pan, underscores the fact that the consecration of the syrinx to the god actually means the abandonment of poetic activity and, thus, the imminence of death.

36. Segal [n. 9], 13, has noted that the dipping of the cup in water is simultaneously equivalent and contrary to Daphnis' own descent into water at the moment of his death (v. 140).

37. Peter Burk, the translator of the present book, has suggested to me that there is another element in the *Idyll* that could potentially pose a link between the setting of the poem and an

external geographical location, namely, the reference to the ivy cup as having been given to the goatherd by a "Calymnian ferryman" (v. 57). If this is a passing allusion to a ferry between Cos and Calymnos (see Gow 1950), then another external geographical space at the far end of the Mediterranean from Sicily is casually evoked within the poem.

38. Callimachus' hymn is a mimetic poem at one remove, that is, a written simulation of an oral performance, as we saw in chapter 4, §3.1 (see the references provided in n. 19 of that chapter), and so a mimesis in the same sense as understood by M. R. Falivene, "La mimesi di Callimaco: *Inni* II, IV, V et VI," *Quaderni urbinati di cultura classica* 65 (1990): 103–28; Falivene rightly critiques the way in which this poem is represented by W. Albert, *Das mimetische Gedicht in der Antike* (Frankfurt a. M., 1988), 9–26. Concerning the mimetic qualities of the landscape constructed at the beginning and end of *Idyll I*, see Elliger [n. 23], 324–28, with, more generally, S. Saïd, "Le paysage des idylles bucoliques," in *Les enjeux du paysage,* ed. M. Collot (Brussels, 1998), 13–31.

39. According to the erroneous expression and thesis of Halperin [n. 6], 186–88 and 242–44, who bases his analysis on the works that he cites in n. 104; cf. Reinhardt [n. 13], 60–62, and Gutzwiller [n. 6], 104: "The voices of the goatherd and shepherd tend to coalesce with that of the poet."

40. Starting from the same impression, G. B. Miles, "Characterization and the Ideal of Innocence in Theocritus' Idylls," *Ramus* 6 (1977): 139–64 (reprinted in *Theokrit und die griechische Bukolik* [n. 6], 138–67), speaks instead of "elusiveness." *Idyll I*, accordingly, inscribes itself within Alexandrian poetics, defined as that "die ihr als Kunst ohnehin eigene Künstlichkeit zu ihrem alleinigen Prinzip machte, zu absoluter Künstlichkeit steigerte," in the words of E.-R. Schwinge, *Künstlichkeit von Kunst: Zur Geschichtlichkeit der alexandrinischen Poesie* (Munich, 1986), 47. J. Vara, "The Sources of Theocritean Bucolic Poetry," *Mnemosyne* 4, no. 45 (1992): 333–44, links Theocritus' art with the "bookish erudition" of the Alexandrian *poetae docti.*

41. The reader has no doubt grasped that, aside from a few critical remarks, I have based this reading of *Idyll I* on the work of my immediate predecessors; this deliberate abandonment of polemical debates has, in general, freed me from having to mention texts of Theocritus and other Greek poets that could serve as parallels to support the interpretation proposed here.

SELECTED BIBLIOGRAPHY

Aloni, A. *L'aedo e i tiranni: Ricerche sull'Inno omerico a Apollo.* Rome: Ateneo, 1989.

———. *Cantare glorie di eroi. Comunicazione e performance poetica nella Grecia arcaica.* Torino: Sciptorium, 1998.

Arrighetti, G., ed. *Poeti, eruditi e biografi: Momenti della riflessione dei Greci sulla letteratura.* Pisa: Giardini, 1987.

Benveniste, E. *Le vocabulaire des institutions indo-européennes.* 2 vols. Paris: Minuit, 1969.

Blaise, F., P. Judet de La Combe, and P. Rousseau, eds. *Le métier du mythe: Lectures d'Hésiode.* Lille: Septentrion, 1996.

Bremer, J. M. "Greek Hymns." In H. S. Versnel, ed. *Faith, Hope, and Worship: Aspects of Religious Mentality in the Ancient World,* 193–215. Leiden: Brill, 1981.

Buxton, R. *Imaginary Greece: The Contexts of Mythology.* Cambridge: Cambridge University Press, 1994.

Calame, C. *Les choeurs de jeunes filles en Grèce archaïque.* Vol. 1. *Morphologie, fonction religieuse et sociale.* Rome: Ateneo & Bizzarri, 1977. (= *Choruses of Young Women in Ancient Greece: Their Morphology, Religious Role, and Social Functions.* Translated by D. Collins and J. Orion. Lanham, Md.: Rowman & Littlefield, 1997.)

———. *L'Eros dans la Grèce antique.* Paris: Belin, 1996a. (= *The Poetics of Eros in Ancient Greece.* Translated by J. Lloyd. Princeton: Princeton University Press, 1999.)

———. *Thésée et l'imaginaire athénien: Légende et culte dans l'Athènes classique.* 2nd ed. Lausanne: Payot, 1996b.

———. *Le récit en Grèce ancienne: Énonciations et représentations de poètes.* 2nd ed. Paris: Belin, 2000a (= *The Craft of Poetic Speech in Ancient Greece.* Translated by J. Orion. Ithaca: Cornell University Press, 1995.)

———. *Poétique des mythes dans la Grèce antique.* Paris: Hachette, 2000b.

Cassio, A. C., and G. Cerri, eds. *L'inno tra rituale e letteratura nel mondo antico: Atti di un colloquio, Napoli 21–24 ottobre 1991.* Rome: Gruppo Editoriale Internazionale, 1993.

Càssola, F. *Inni omerici*. Milan: Mondadori, 1975.

Chantraine, P. *Dictionnaire étymologique de la langue grecque: Histoire des mots*. Paris: Klincksieck, 1968.

Detienne, M. *Les maîtres de vérité dans la Grèce archaïque*. 3rd ed. Paris: Pocket, 1995. (Orig. pub. 1967; = *The Masters of Truth in Archaic Greece*. Translated by J. Lloyd. New York: Zone Books, 1996.)

———, ed. *Les savoirs de l'écriture en Grèce ancienne*. Lille: Presses Universitaires de Lille, 1988.

Detienne, M., and J.-P.Vernant. *La cuisine du sacrifice en pays grec*. Paris: Gallimard, 1979. (= *The Cuisine of Sacrifice among the Greeks*. Translated by P. Wissing. Chicago: University of Chicago Press, 1989.)

Ford, A. *The Origins of Criticism: Literary Culture and Poetic Theory in Classical Greece*. Princeton: Princeton University Press, 2002.

Fränkel, H. *Wege und Formen frühgriechischen Denkens*. 2nd ed. Munich: C. H. Beck, 1960.

Gentili, B. *Poesia e pubblico nella Grecia antica: Da Omero al V secolo*. 3rd ed. Rome: Laterza, 1995. (= *Poetry and Its Public in Ancient Greece from Homer to the Fifth Century*. Translated by T. Cole. Baltimore: Johns Hopkins University Press, 1988.)

Goldhill, S. *The Poet's Voice: Essays on Poetics and Greek Literature*. Cambridge: Cambridge University Press, 1991.

Gow, A. S. F. *Theocritus*. Vol 2. *Commentary, Appendix, Indexes, and Plates*. Cambridge: Cambridge University Press, 1950.

Harder, M. A., R. F. Regtuit, and G. C. Wakker, eds. *Callimachus*. Vol. 1 of *Hellenistica Groningana*. Groningen: Forsten, 1993.

Hartog, F. *Le miroir d'Hérodote: Essai sur la représentation de l'autre*. 2nd ed. Paris: Gallimard, 1992. (= *The Mirror of Herodotus: The Representation of the Other in the Writing of History*. Translated by J. Lloyd. Berkeley: University of California Press, 1988.)

Herington, J. *Poetry into Drama: Early Tragedy and the Greek Poetic Tradition*. Berkeley: University of California Press, 1985.

Käppel, L. *Paian: Studien zur Geschichte einer Gattung*. Berlin: de Gruyter, 1992.

Laks, A., and G. W. Most, eds. *Studies on the Derveni Papyrus*. Oxford: Clarendon Press, 1997.

Lefkowitz, M. *First-Person Fictions: Pindar's Poetic I*. Oxford: Clarendon Press, 1991.

Maehler, H. *Die Auffassung des Dichterberufs im frühen Griechentum bis zur Zeit Pindars*. Göttingen: Vandenhoeck & Ruprecht, 1963.

Miller, A. M. *From Delos to Delphi: A Literary Study of the Homeric Hymn to Apollo*. Leiden: Brill, 1986.

Nagy, G. *The Best of the Achaeans: Concepts of the Hero in Archaic Greek Poetry*. Baltimore: Johns Hopkins University Press, 1979.

———. *Greek Mythology and Poetics*. Ithaca: Cornell University Press, 1990a.

———. *Pindar's Homer: The Lyric Possession of an Epic Past*. Baltimore: Johns Hopkins University Press, 1990b.

Pavese, C. O. *Tradizioni e generi poetici della Grecia arcaica*. Rome: Ateneo, 1972.

Pucci, P. *The Songs of the Sirens: Essays on Homer*. Lanham, Md.: Rowman & Littlefield, 1998.

Race, W. H. "How Greek Poems Begin." *Yale Classical Studies* 29 (1992): 13–38.

Scheid, J., and J. Svenbro. *Le métier de Zeus: Mythe du tissage et du tissu dans le monde gréco-romain*. Paris: La Découverte, 1994. (= *The Craft of Zeus: Myths of Weaving and Fabric*. Translated by C. Volk. Cambridge: Harvard University Press, 1996.)

Segal, C. *Singers, Heroes, and Gods in the "Odyssey."* Ithaca: Cornell University Press, 1994.

Silk, M. S., ed. *Tragedy and the Tragic: Greek Theatre and Beyond*. Oxford: Clarendon Press, 1996.

Sourvinou-Inwood, C. *"Reading" Greek Culture: Texts and Images, Rituals and Myths.* Oxford: Clarendon Press, 1991.

Vernant, J.-P. *Mythe et société en Grèce ancienne.* Paris: Maspero, 1974. (= *Myth and Society in Ancient Greece.* Translated by J. Lloyd. New York: Zone Books, 1988.)

Vernant, J.-P., and P. Vidal-Naquet. *Mythe et tragédie en Grèce ancienne.* Paris: Maspero, 1972. (= *Myth and Tragedy in Ancient Greece.* Translated by J. Lloyd. Cambridge: Harvard University Press, 1988.)

Vidal-Naquet, P. *Le chasseur noir: Formes de pensée et formes de société dans le monde grec.* 2nd ed. Paris: La Découverte, 1983. (= *The Black Hunter: Forms of Thought and Forms of Society in the Greek World.* Translated by A. Szegedy-Maszak. Baltimore: Johns Hopkins University Press, 1986.)

West, M. L. *Hesiod: Theogony.* Oxford: Clarendon Press, 1966.

———. *Hesiod: Works and Days.* Oxford: Clarendon Press, 1978.

Williams, F. *Callimachus: Hymn to Apollo, A Commentary.* Oxford: Clarendon Press, 1978.

Winkler, J. J., and F. I. Zeitlin, eds. *Nothing to Do with Dionysos? Athenian Drama in Its Social Context.* Princeton: Princeton University Press, 1989.

Zeitlin, F. I. *Playing the Other: Gender and Society in Classical Greek Literature.* Chicago: University of Chicago Press, 1996.

INDEX

MYTH AND POETICS

A SERIES EDITED BY

GREGORY NAGY

Heroic Poets, Poetic Heroes: The Ethnography of Performance in an Arabic Oral Epic Tradition
BY DWIGHT FLETCHER REYNOLDS

Homer and the Sacred City
BY STEPHEN SCULLY

Singers, Heroes, and Gods in the "Odyssey"
BY CHARLES SEGAL

The Mute Immortals Speak: Pre-Islamic Poetry and the Poetics of Ritual
BY SUZANNE PINCKNEY STETKEVYCH

Phrasikleia: An Anthropology of Reading in Ancient Greece
BY JESPER SVENBRO, TRANSLATED BY JANET E. LLOYD

The Swineherd and the Bow: Representations of Class in the "Odyssey"
BY WILLIAM G. THALMANN

The Jewish Novel in the Ancient World
BY LAWRENCE M. WILLS